THE PSYCHOLOGICAL

FRONTIERS OF SOCIETY

THE PSYCHOLOGICAL FRONTIERS OF SOCIETY

By ABRAM KARDINER

WITH THE COLLABORATION OF
RALPH LINTON, CORA DU BOIS
AND JAMES WEST

GREENWOOD PRESS, PUBLISHERS
WESTPORT, CONNECTICUT

Library of Congress Cataloging in Publication Data

Kardiner, Abram, 1891-
    The psychological frontiers of society.

    Reprint of the 1959 ed. published by Columbia
University Press, New York.
    Includes index.
    1. Social psychology. 2. Ethnopsychology.
I. Linton, Ralph, 1893-1953. II. Du Bois, Cora
Alice, 1903-   . III. Withers, Carl. IV. Title.
HM251.K34 1981   302   80-29605
    ISBN 0-313-22388-2 (lib. bdg.)

Reprinted in 1981 by Greenwood Press
A division of Congressional Information Service, Inc.
88 Post Road West, Westport, Connecticut 06881

Printed in the United States of America

10 9 8 7 6 5 4 3 2 1

FOREWORD

By Ralph Linton

ONE of the most important scientific discoveries of recent years is that science itself is outgrowing the watertight compartments in which its youth was spent. As our store of knowledge accumulates and our techniques of investigation are refined, it becomes increasingly evident that there are a multitude of problems which cannot be solved within the self-imposed limits of single disciplines. Chemistry has reached the point where it has to have the help of physics for its next steps, and physiology the point where it has to have the help of chemistry. In those sciences which deal with man the need for collaboration is even more urgent. Except in the most superficial terms, the workings of society and culture cannot be understood without constant reference to the needs and capacities of the individual. Conversely, particular individuals cannot be understood without constant reference to the cultural and social environments in which they have developed and within which they have to operate. These facts are too obvious to require discussion. The really pressing problem is one of ways and means; how the findings of the various sciences involved can be integrated and applied.

Unfortunately, this problem is by no means simple. Dr. John Dollard once remarked to me that the most effective collaboration was that between two disciplines under one skull, but such collaboration is rarely possible. The application of scientific techniques to the study of human phenomena is a relatively recent development, and the disciplines which have resulted from it are rich in factual content but poor in organization and conceptualization. A thorough knowledge of any one of them still involves familiarity with a multitude of conflicting theories and formulations as well as with the data on which these have been based. To acquire this knowledge is almost a life work in itself. Under the circumstances, the best substitute for two disciplines under one skull becomes two disciplines in two heads which can be brought together over the same problems, and the more closely they can be brought together the better the results.

Dr. Kardiner and I began our collaboration in 1937, thanks to the good offices of a mutual friend, Dr. A. Maslow. Prior to this time we both had been interested in the interrelations of personality and culture but had approached the problem from different directions and with different emphases. Dr. Kardiner's investigations had dealt primarily with the effects of particular projective systems upon the development and perpetuation of particular institutions. He had already published the results of this work in various papers.[1] My own main interest had been in the relation of culture to personality content and in the adaptation of individuals to particular positions within a social system. The result of this work had been published in 1936.[2] Neither of us had as yet arrived at the concept of different basic personality types for different societies; a concept whose far-reaching implications for both psychology and anthropology are only beginning to be explored.

It is an axiom of science that each new advance springs from a certain platform of knowledge and ideas without which it would have been impossible. The concept of basic personality is no exception to this rule. Its ultimate origins can be traced to certain trends in both cultural anthropology and psychology which had been apparent since the early nineteen hundreds. During this period workers in both disciplines had become increasingly aware of the importance of configuration phenomena and of the necessity for studying both cultures and personalities as wholes. Among anthropologists, the great exponent of this approach was the late Dr. Malinowski, but both he and his followers tended to confine their investigations to the structural and operational relations between elements within culture. While Dr. Malinowski in particular was fully aware of the importance of the individual in relation to culture, the necessary techniques for dealing with this relationship were lacking. In psychology during the same period, the rapid advance of psychoanalysis resulted in an increased interest in the integrative aspects of the personality and a realization that personalities had to be dealt with as continuums. The Gestalt school of psychology has, of course, laid even greater stress on configurational phenomena, but since its concepts have not been successfully applied to problems of personality and culture, it need be mentioned only as an example of *Zeitgeist*. Unfortunately, the earlier psychoanalysts carried on their investigations entirely within

[1] "The Role of Economic Security in the Adaptation of the Individual," *The Family* (Sept., 1936); "Security, Cultural Restraints, Intra-social Dependencies and Hostilities," *The Family* (Sept., 1937).
[2] Ralph Linton, *The Study of Man* (1936), Chapter XXVI.

the frame of European culture and largely within that of a single class in European society. Lacking comparative materials, they took many environmental factors for granted and built up an elaborate theory of universal human instincts. The various attempts which were made by Freud and others to apply this instinctual approach to the explanation of cultural phenomena and even to the reconstruction of cultural history struck the average anthropologist as fantastic and led him to minimize the very real contributions which psychoanalytic techniques might make to the solution of many of his own problems.

In spite of these difficulties, the period under discussion witnessed the emergence of a new area of concentration on problems of personality and culture. There was a considerable exchange of ideas and techniques between anthropology and psychology, and a series of new concepts began to emerge. Anyone who reviews the literature must feel that the idea of basic personality type was "in the wind" some time before Dr. Kardiner and I began our collaboration. However, so far as I can discover, the first concrete statement of the concept was that embodied in *The Individual and His Society*, published in 1939. Since that time the concept has been employed by several other writers, with minor variations in content and especially in terminology, but I still prefer the original.

The concept of basic personality types as developed and used by Dr. Kardiner and myself is in itself a configuration involving several different elements. It rests upon the following postulates:

1. That the individual's early experiences exert a lasting affect upon his personality, especially upon the development of his projective systems.

2. That similar experiences will tend to produce similar personality configurations in the individuals who are subjected to them.

3. That the techniques which the members of any society employ in the care and rearing of children are culturally patterned and will tend to be similar, although never identical, for various families within the society.

4. That the culturally patterned techniques for the care and rearing of children differ from one society to another.

If these postulates are correct, and they seem to be supported by a wealth of evidence, it follows:

1. That the members of any given society will have many elements of early experience in common.

2. That as a result of this they will have many elements of personality in common.

3. That since the early experience of individuals differs from one society to another, the personality norms for various societies will also differ.

The *basic personality type* for any society is that personality configuration which is shared by the bulk of the society's members as a result of the early experiences which they have in common. It does not correspond to the total personality of the individual but rather to the projective systems or, in different phraseology, the value-attitude systems which are basic to the individual's personality configuration. Thus the same basic personality type may be reflected in many different forms of behavior and may enter into many different total personality configurations.

Although the delimitation of the basic personality types of different societies has been one important aspect of our investigations, we have been equally concerned with the functioned relations between these types and the cultures of the societies investigated. In other words, we have tried to discover not only what the basic personality types were but also how they were produced and what influence they exerted upon the culture itself. These dynamic features must be regarded as an integral part of the concept as we have developed and employed it. In the course of their therapeutic work, psychoanalysts have discovered that certain configurations of early experience tend to produce certain personality configurations in the adult. Transferring these findings to the investigation of societies as wholes, it becomes possible to make tentative predictions as to what sort of people the child-rearing techniques of a particular society would be likely to produce. The culture of the society can then be investigated to see how far this culture as a whole might prove congenial to individuals of this particular sort. In all the societies which have been investigated so far the compatibility has been of a high order. It seems safe to conclude that in relatively stable cultures, such as those of "primitive" societies, there is a close interrelation between the basic personality type and the culture as a whole. For the individual, this means that the projective systems formed in early childhood will be constantly reinforced by later experience. Conversely, the average individual in such a society will find that most of the culture patterns which he is called on to assume in later life are congenial and can be readily accepted. In other words, in stable societies the basic personality type and the culture configuration tend to reinforce and perpetuate each other. Unfortunately, we have had few opportunities so far to investigate the interrelations of basic personality and culture in changed situations, but there can be little doubt that the basic personality type plays an important part in determining a society's reaction to innovations. Innovations which are congenial to the personality type probably are accepted and incorporated into the society's culture much more readily than those which are uncongenial.

In the formulations just presented no attempt has been made to take into account the many variables which may enter into and modify the relations between culture and personality. To cite only a few of these, a child in any society may derive atypical early experiences from an unusual family situation, the aberrant personality of a parent or elder sibling, or a personal handicap such as lameness. As the number of life histories of "primitive" individuals accumulates, it becomes evident that atypical childhoods are not infrequent even in relatively stable societies and that, just as among ourselves, they result in individual deviations from the society's personality norms. Again, it must be recognized that societies and cultures are continuums and that conclusions which are valid for one point in their histories may not be valid for another. Changing conditions in the life of a society may result in changes in the techniques of child care with a corresponding modification, over time, in the society's basic personality type. Such changing conditions may result either from modifications in the external environment, as when a society is conquered and reduced to servitude, or from the borrowing and incorporation of new elements of culture. The last may seem inconsistent with the earlier statement that societies tend to accept and incorporate only those novelties which are congruous with their basic personality types. However, some new element of culture may have obvious and immediate advantages and be perfectly congruous in itself but at the same time set in train a whole series of unforeseen changes in the accepting culture. The automobile made an immediate appeal to Americans on the basis of their fondness for speed and machinery, but few foresaw what affect it would have on the established patterns of sexual behavior or law enforcement. That the emergence of a new basic personality type as a result of changing techniques of child care will result in further changes in the culture, designed to make it congruous with the new type, can scarcely be doubted, but conclusive evidence on this point is lacking.

Needless to say, the concept of basic personality was not derived from its basic postulates by the simple application of logic. It was developed through the actual analysis of a series of cultures and grew out of the correlations which this revealed. The first cultures investigated were those discussed in our previous volume, *The Individual and His Society*. Until very recently, most anthropological accounts of cultures have adhered to a fairly stereotyped pattern. A friend of mine who had recently returned from a field trip once told me that his material was ready to publish "except for taking the life out of it." The anthropological conventions have required that cultures should be described in terms of norms of behavior without reference to either deviations or individuals. Unfortunately, even the norms for much of the behavior which is of special interest to students of personality have usually been dealt with in summary fashion. The old-style investigator was much more interested in lists of relationship terms and descriptions of religious rituals than in how children were brought up or what were the attitudes between spouses. It was my good fortune to have lived with certain "primitive" groups long enough and intimately enough to be able to supplement the published accounts, including my own, with the data required to make a preliminary analysis possible. Dr. Kardiner, thanks to his many years of clinical experience, was able to grasp the psychoanalytic implications of the material and to reduce it to a form which "made sense" in psychological terms.

These preliminary analyses indicated the existence of a high order of psychological coherence between the various behavior patterns characteristic of each of the cultures studied. The same attitudes and values manifested themselves again and again in different contexts. They also revealed a close agreement between these widely expressed attitudes and the early, culturally determined, experiences of the society's members. Out of this work the concept of basic personality emerged as a working hypothesis. The culture whose study contributed most to this development was probably that of the Marquesas Islands, since it differed most widely from our own with respect to its patterns of family life and child rearing. It provided a situation in which most of the earlier psychoanalytic formulations, especially those with respect to instincts and successive stages of personality development, obviously could not be applied. Even the typical Oedipus complex seemed to be lacking, and sexual frustrations were almost non-existent.

As a working hypothesis, the concept of basic personality brought excellent results when applied to this and to a series of other cultures, but the ultimate proof of its validity was still lacking. This had to wait on the study and comparison of the personalities of groups of individuals within a single society. If our hypothesis was correct, the bulk of the individuals within a given society should have in common those features of personality which had been ascribed to the basic personality type on the basis of the cultural analysis. Unfortunately, the data required for this investigation were not available for any of the societies first studied. The crucial test of our hypothesis came with the study of Alorese culture. In the course of her work on the island of Alor, in the Dutch East Indies, Dr. Cora Du Bois obtained not only unusually complete information on the culture but also an extensive series of detailed life histories, records of projective personality tests, including Rorschachs, and other psychological data. With this material an experiment was set up. The probable configuration of the Alorese basic personality type was deduced from a study of the culture, using the techniques which we had developed previously. At the same time the Rorschachs were interpreted by Dr. Emil Oberholzer, and he was requested to summarize those personality characteristics which appeared in a large majority of the individuals tested. The two studies were carried on quite independently with no exchange of information until the work was completed. The results were then compared and the two pictures of Alorese personality were found to agree on all important points. Dr. Kardiner next undertook the laborious task of analyzing the life histories of a number of the individuals for whom Rorschachs and dream materials were available to see whether these histories might explain their individual deviations from Alorese personality norms. He found that in nearly all cases such deviations could be explained in terms of early experience which was culturally atypical. The experiment as a whole seemed to verify our earlier conclusions with respect to the reality of basic personality types, the mechanisms by which they are produced and their relations to the culture as a whole. Work on two other societies for which similar but less complete material was available produced very similar results. These societies, Sikh and Ojibwa, are not reported on in the present volume. While these three experiments are not enough to provide conclusive proof of the hypothesis of basic personality type, they make it highly plausible and impose on those who do not accept it the burden of finding some better explanation for the observed facts.

Granting the reality of basic personality types, there are a number of problems pertaining to them which are urgently in need of further investigation. One of the most important of these is the question of the range of forms which such types may assume. Even the work done to date has revealed certain combinations of personality characteristics which are exceedingly rare or lacking in our own society. It seems probable that such work may lead to an extension and reorganization of our present personality typologies. Another problem which may prove of considerable practical importance is that of the degree to which personality configurations formed as a result of early experience may be modified by later experiences. As has already been mentioned, in most relatively static cultures the configurations established by a society's patterns of child care tend to be reinforced by a host of later experiences. It remains to be seen what may happen in societies where, for any reason, such reinforcements are lacking. Closely related to this is the problem of whether the personality configuration is especially susceptible to change at particular points in the individual's life cycle. Such investigations will require detailed life history material which is still lacking for any society other than, perhaps, our own. Lastly, it will be important to discover what is the range of individual personality variation in different societies relative to their basic personality types.

Turning to the effects of basic personality on culture, there is urgent need for study of the reactions of particular societies to particular innovations and of the ways in which basic personality type influences the acceptance or rejection of new elements. Closely related to this is the problem of the relation of basic personality types to change in general. It seems as though flexibility and readiness for change may be, in themselves, characteristic of certain basic personalities. At least we know that certain societies appear to be highly adaptable in general, while others are so rigid that they resist change and realistic adjustment to the point of paralysis and ultimate collapse. This brings us at once to the field of acculturation studies, an area in which the concept of basic personality types may prove of paramount importance. It is unquestionably involved in such phenomena as the ability of one society to dominate another in contact situations and in determining the direction of culture change in the societies involved, but we have as yet no adequate data on the basis of which such problems can be attacked.

Still another aspect of the relation of basic personality to culture change is the persistence of certain aspects of basic personality type over long sectors of the social-cultural continuum. Certain generalized projective systems seem to have endured in particular societies for millennia, surviving repeated changes in many aspects of the culture and molding each new institution as it arose. The application of this approach to historic data, as in Dr. Kardiner's final chapter, promises to give new and important results. In short, I feel that the basic personality type concept provides the social sciences with a new research tool whose use cannot fail to have far-reaching results. It is too early to predict what many of these results may be, but it can be predicted that the concept will play an important part in the development of the new science of human behavior which is emerging from a synthesis of the older and more specialized disciplines.

PREFACE

THIS book undertakes to describe a technique for studying the reciprocal relations between culture and personality, and to furnish a reliable critique of cultural forms.

The oldest working hypothesis used for this problem was the "race" concept, which implied that acquired cultural traits were biologically transmitted. The damage wrought by this concept when it is used to describe anything but minor differences in anatomical structure is too well known to need special treatment. It only supplied value judgments, such as "superior" and "inferior," on which no intelligent plan of social action could be based. The *culture* concept was a great improvement over the *race* concept, because it had some usefulness in permitting the analysis of cultural entities into constituent elements, such as mores, practices, and institutions. Moreover, the culture concept opened the door to the psychological explanation of the differences in the practices of different societies.

But the application of psychology to the culture concept was not an unmixed blessing; it led to partial answers and blind alleys. There were three main results of the early attempts along this line. The first was the definition of the *culture pattern,* which was descriptively correct but left the question of the source of the culture pattern unanswered. From the use of the culture pattern two systems were devised which provided a descriptive relationship between culture and personality. The first held that personality was a mirror image of the culture. The second considered that there were certain inherent and persistent tendencies common to all mankind which were modified by culture. It cannot be said of any one of these views that it is incorrect; but they are all partial answers which cannot be reduced to a technique capable of growth and of yielding continuous information.

This book is not just another endeavor of this kind. It espouses none of the culture-personality formulae and aims at no doctrine or theory. It describes and perfects a technique and claims some degree of precision in tracking down the reciprocal relations between culture and personality.

An enterprise with this objective needs make no modifications in the concept of culture, except perhaps to include within it practices heretofore omitted. The more difficult problem is that of choosing from the many psychological techniques in use today the one best suited to the task of coördination. It is precisely at this point that the book begins. It must be granted that all psychological techniques are suited to special assignments in relation to our problem; but this book is based on the assumption that psychoanalytic technique can approach aspects which cannot be touched by any of the others, by any learning theory or topological technique. Moreover, it must not be overlooked that most problems in the study of culture cannot be reproduced in the laboratory.

Once we have settled the place of psychological technique, we proceed to describe the history and vicissitudes of this technique and to use it in connection with three specific cultures, which offer wide contrasts in personality formation.

From the inception of this research I have always regarded the technical problems as paramount. The present book is an attempt to work out the technical problems originally outlined in *The Individual and His Society*. Since the publication of the latter a considerable literature has grown about the technique there outlined, most of it corroborative, some controversial. On the whole, the method has suffered a good deal more from its supporters than from its opponents. This has been due largely to the unfortunate circumstance that most workers attempting this technique are not trained in psychodynamics. With the best of intentions they have succeeded in drawing a red herring over the technical procedure by emphasis on minor points like nomenclature, by treating the conclusions as if they were known all the time, by assuming the correctness of the technique and the assumptions on which it is based, by rushing hurriedly to conclusions, in which attempt some were undoubtedly goaded by the urgency of the social problems to which our time has fallen heir. Still others believe that this technique is not entitled to much credit because it was "in the air," several other attempts along this line being germane to it. This is quite true. It has been "in the air" for several millennia, for its chief operational concept, *basic personality,* is a datum of common sense. The reduction of this common sense conclusion to a technique with some precision is an achievement of Freudian psychodynamics—with a few modifications.

The technique of operation, while demonstrated in each case, is not accompanied by any discussions in psychopathology, except in a few instances where it was unavoidable. The technique is naturally based on Freud's psychodynamics. But there have been modifications in the operational scheme, which is not based on the concept "instinct" but on the *action system*. The advantage that the latter enjoys is that it can be identified by cognitive, coördinative, and executive constituents; whereas the "instinct" had to be identified by qualitative criteria only. The difference between the two operational schemes has been amply set forth in my book, *The Traumatic Neuroses of War* (Hoeber, 1941).The results of the operations in psychodynamics are set down here.

In each instance the derivation of basic personality was an exercise in psychopathology, and as the matter now stands no one without an expert knowledge of psychodynamics can make any contribution to the technique. This reservation holds for the derivation of the origins and interrelations between cultural traits which have no conceivable relation to each other according to common sense. On the other hand, no one but a master of sociological techniques can fully exploit the conclusions reached by the techniques of psychodynamics. Of the latter very little is to be found in this book. However a very auspicious attempt along this line has been made recently by Linton in his book *The Cultural Background of Personality* (Appleton-Century, 1945), which indicates the manner in which the ultimate synthesis is most likely to take place. The simplest of these cultures is Comanche, because of the extreme simplicity of the projective systems. Given the key, one can find one's way around this culture equipped with no more than common sense. The most difficult problem in psychodynamics was Alor, because the constellations found there have no prototypes in Western culture. I feel somewhat ashamed to confess that some of the main points in Alorese personality did not become clear to me until four years after I originally got to know the material.

Basic personality is not a password for a social theory; it is merely the name for a diagnostic summary of the constellations existing in a given society. The sociological implications of this technique have not yet been explored for the simple reason that the technique does not yet describe the social process completely. The most successful attempt thus far has been Alor; but even this is far from complete. In the case of Plainville such elucidation of the social and cultural process was handicapped by the fact that these processes have determinants which are rooted in the past. To overcome this handicap a tentative effort is made in the final chapter to see how the concept of basic personality stands the test of being examined over a long time-trajectory.

In the main, the purpose of the book is to describe the operation of the social process by a technique which takes as its base line the mental and emotional equipment of the constituents of a society. Furthermore, it makes the special point of demonstrating how this equipment came into being. When an ethnographer reports that in a given society divorces are frequent; that the accounts of religious dogmas and rituals are inaccurate and inconsistent; that when people are ill they just lie down and die; that they have little interest in permanent structures; that they have no conscience or tendency to depressive reactions—all these may be unrelated events, or may be deeply interconnected. It makes a great deal of difference, as far as the workings of the society are concerned, which view we adopt. If these traits are interrelated, then they are only peripheral points which indicate how the social process is operating. Certain it is that no relationship can be established between the events mentioned by the standards of common sense; nor would any ethnographer attempt to draw any such connection. These traits would have to be reported as "peculiarities" of this particular group of people.

The contribution that psychodynamics makes is to demonstrate that these traits are related, and, by the very fact that they are so, a special direction is given to the adaptation of the society as a whole, and a special imprint is left on the individual exposed to this particular social process.

This sounds very promising, and it looks at last as if we were really down to fundamentals. This is an over-optimistic view. The moot question is whether the technique takes in enough of the entire social process. My own opinion is that it does not and will not for a long time to come. The reason for this moderation is the knowledge that only a few fundamentals have been conclusively and decisively established, and that these fundamentals are easier to demonstrate on "primitive" societies, where the projective systems have remained in their pristine purity, unmodified by too many layers of rational thought processes, as is the case with the projective systems of modern man. The application of this technique to Western society is a more difficult undertaking because here the social process is governed by higher integrational systems—especially those connected with social goals and value systems and the like—which are more difficult to derive from basic experiences of the growing child.

It must be emphasized that this work rests on no one's personal authority, and its merits do not depend on the concept of basic personality, which is, practically speaking, as old as Herodotus. This work stands or falls by the correctness of the psychiatric technique employed. The question resolves itself to this: Is our conception of the path of integrational processes in man correctly delineated, and is our notational system accurate enough and delicate enough to catch all modalities of adaptation? This question I cannot answer because my most serious handicap in this work has been that, as far as the technical end of the work is concerned, I have had to work completely alone, without benefit of discussion with my fellow psychiatrists. Their avoidance of the problems connected with this work has been due largely to the fact that they regarded it as "sociology," and hence not worthy of attention. My very coöperative anthropological collaborators could not help me; they could only check on the correctness of a conclusion, back it up by new data, or contradict it with opposing evidence. In some instances the conclusions of psychodynamics went against the stated facts, later to be vindicated by further evidence. I am certain that many important conclusions would have come to light had the psychodynamic principles employed been subject to debate.

This book contains a few technical advances over its predecessor. These are: (1) the attempt to specify in greater detail the constituents of basic personality; (2) the attempt to derive the origin of value systems and social goals; (3) the formulation of the concept of differential aggression patterns, a matter which will soon have to become the subject of extensive investigation. For the rest the book is a clinical demonstration of principles previously set forth, with much effort expended for the sake of pedagogic clarity. Considering that the new material under discussion is so many sided and is gathered from the points of view of several psychological disciplines, it is gratifying to note how well the original thesis has stood up against the test.

The particular cultures here discussed were selected because of their striking contrasts in personality configurations. Comanche and Alor are valuable antitheses. Plainville is a living American rural

community, and gives us our first chance to study one not too complicated to be encompassed by a single observer, a virtue possessed
by no urban community.

My role in this research was limited to that of a psychological
commentator on data furnished by ethnographers. In this role I was
responsible for working out a psychological technique and for
selecting the cultures that gave the best opportunity for refining
and perfecting this technique. Needless to add that when a working
scheme like this is debated in class, many suggestions are made, some
adopted and some discarded. The most valuable checks on conclusions drawn are always furnished by the ethnographer whose material is being discussed. The conclusions as presented contain therefore the record of this checking by the ethnographers. In addition
to class work there were many personal contacts with Professor Linton, Dr. Du Bois, and Mr. West. Questions raised by students made
a considerable text for discussion.

In making acknowledgments for assistance in the preparation of
this book, my first and greatest obligation is to Professor Ralph
Linton for innumerable services in connection with it. The chief of
these was the privilege of collaborating with him in the seminar, in
which all the material in this book was originally presented and discussed. I have tried to note and accredit his numerous illuminating
and critical observations. There were many more than I have noted.
Without his foresight and courageous support this whole research
plan would have ceased long ago. In addition, he supplied this research with three valuable texts for social psychology. No one who
has read his *Study of Man* can fail to note how much he has anticipated and influenced subsequent developments in the study of personality and culture. If the research of which this book is a part leads
to any lasting or significant developments, to Dr. Linton belongs the
major credit, for what he has done himself, for what he inspired others
to do, and for pursuing with tireless enthusiasm every opportunity for
research.

To Dr. Cora Du Bois I gratefully acknowledge the privilege of
studying her valuable data in class and am indebted for permission
to use a summary of her data for this book. Grateful acknowledgments are due the University of Minnesota Press for permission to
use some of the data I submitted for the book *The People of Alor*,
by Dr. Du Bois, and for permission to quote freely from the book.

To Mr. James West I am deeply grateful for presenting his excellent material on Plainville at the Seminar, for permitting its use in this book, and for writing the section which bears his name. I am additionally indebted to him for generously lending me the life histories which he took in the field and upon which my chapter on the personalities of Plainville is based. Thanks are due the Columbia University Press for permission to use here some of the data from Mr. West's book *Plainville, U.S.A.*

Not the least among my collaborators were the successive classes at Columbia University whose interest and stimulation were invaluable. Many of them actually did the spade work for the biographical sketches. I am indebted to Dr. Robert K. Merton for reading the manuscript and for many valuable suggestions now included in the text.

A. KARDINER

Department of Psychiatry
Columbia University
January, 1945

CHAPTER I

PSYCHOLOGY AND THE SCIENCE OF SOCIETY

THERE IS today no discipline which can be called a science of society; there is only a group of social sciences, each of which has become isolated and self-contained as regards the subject matter. There has been more agreement in respect to techniques largely through the influence of the natural sciences. The result was that only those data were considered relevant for the social sciences that could be treated by the proofs and quantitative procedures so successful in the natural sciences.

Efforts have recently been made by Lynd, Mannheim, and many others to create a synthesis of the social sciences, and in all these proposals the need for a psychology suitable for such ends was commonly conceded. It was hoped that an authoritative psychology would do away with biased efforts to order the data of the social sciences in conformity with some interest, deliberate or unconscious. The decision to include psychology raised the question of which technique was best adapted to this task and to making available to the social sciences a large segment of human experience previously omitted. Many techniques were proposed and tried, and their success varied. The most unsatisfactory conclusion of these endeavors was that much of this psychological material had to be labeled *irrational*. No technique or set of operational principles can be devised to deal with subject matter of which half is rational and half irrational.

The first task of psychology in a science of society is to wipe out this confusing juxtaposition of rational and irrational elements, for on examining the concept "irrational" we discover that it has the particular connotation of "emotional." This simplifies our task somewhat, for it restates the goal: the precise definition of the role played by the emotional life of man in creating those phenomena—institutions and practices—with which we deal in the social sciences. Psychology must be prepared to analyze those emotional factors which determine the success or failure of certain practices and to specify their vicissitudes. It should furnish a critique of social forms in order to enable us to predict their stability, to locate more precisely the discomforts they create and the compensatory efforts they set in motion.

These tasks require the creation of a unitary system of operational tools; we must be on guard against psychological systems which explain some facets of culture but fail to deal with others; we must likewise guard against systems which restate the obvious.

A psychological enterprise which heeds these precautions can begin in several ways. It can begin with our own society and to that end employ the resources of economics, sociology, and history. Or—in the method chosen for this book—it can use the simpler cultures furnished by anthropology, in order to perfect the technique for later use in our own culture. The chief advantage of the comparative method is that it enables us to free ourselves from those unconscious prejudices which accrue from long contact with a particular set of values and sequences to which we are accustomed. It has the disadvantage of compelling the investigator to engage on a difficult exercise in empathy, to feel himself into value systems other than the ones by which he lives. In both instances we are studying man under varying social conditions and varying degrees of success or failure in basic societal function.

Like its predecessor,[1] this book is still urgently concerned with technique. There are two immediate problems: (1) what contemporary psychological technique is best suited for our task; and (2) how are the resources of this technique to be employed for the ends we seek. But we cannot attack the question of psychological technique before discussing the question of the fixed biological characteristics of man.

Biological Traits of Man

The biologically fixed traits of man are not easy to select, for several characteristics appear to be biological traits (that is, inherited in the germ plasm) which on closer examination seem more likely to be caused by man's social life. Gregariousness, for example, is a case in point; analogies with the same trait as it seems to occur in lower animals are misleading. The social life of the ant is contingent on a division of function predetermined before birth. But in the human being the potentialities for equal participation are not predetermined

[1] *The Individual and His Society;* in association with Ralph Linton (New York, Columbia University Press, 1939).

by the presence or absence of functional appendages—sex is the only differentiation predetermined at birth. It is therefore an error to deal with gregariousness as a biologically determined trait. The same may be said of the long period of post-mature life in man. It is more reasonable to consider post-mature life as a consequence of social life than the reverse.

Upright posture, prehensile hand, the predominant role of vision in adaptation may be considered biologically predetermined, as well as the capacity for speech and the absence of a breeding season. Huxley [2] mentions the following peculiarities of man: capacity for language and conceptual thought; cumulative tradition, constant improvement of tools and machinery; the fact that he is a single species with many variable types; the capacity to make the ways of living uniform; abnormally slow development as compared with other mammals, absence of intrauterine struggle for existence; the variability of fertility, the capacity to bear from one to twenty offspring; the prolongation of post-mature life, leading to the dominance of the post-mature male; the plasticity of mental processes and the capacity to unify them; and finally, gregariousness. Though this is presented as a list of peculiarities of man, not all of them are biologically predetermined traits, and as to man's mental plasticity some question of fact might be raised.

Of these traits the most relevant socially is that man—like all domesticated animals—is a single species with tendency to extreme variability. The second factor most relevant here is the slow growth of man. Huxley relates this fact to the absence of intrauterine competition. Whether this is the case or not, man is born ill equipped for continuation of life *alone*. He must be aided and nurtured longer than other mammals. Behind this situation lies the anatomical retardation of the process of myelination, whereby the voluntary nervous system is placed under central control. On the other hand, those animals who presumably are better equipped *in utero* complete the myelination shortly after birth. This means that in a relatively short time, one-tenth to one-twelfth of the life span, they are able to do what their progenitors can, including reproduction. In the case of these animals one may speak of the dominant control of behavior by inborn patterns. Kuo has demonstrated conclusively that even in this case the so-called instinctual patterns must be cultivated. The only sociologi-

[2] Julian Huxley, *Man Stands Alone* (New York, Harpers, 1941), Chapter I.

cal importance of these considerations is that man is least dominated by inborn behavior patterns, and these patterns must include the drive toward a goal and the manipulations necessary to achieve it. In the long run this slow acquisition of adaptive patterns greatly augments their possibilities. But it also means that the adaptive patterns of man are acquired and that the inborn tendencies can be bent in one direction or another. It means a long period of dependency; a long period of growth. Both these processes are greatly facilitated by social life. Man is therefore not an animal who operates by instincts but by acquired processes, which control these drives.

During the long period of growth the capacities of the child for organized action undergo continuous change. As the capacities of the child alter, the conception that he has of himself and of those around him and of the external world changes correspondingly. Coincident with these adaptive capacities during growth complicated somatic changes take place.

The statement that adaptive processes are "learned" is a manner of describing the results of a process rather than the process itself, and for our purposes the minutiae of the procedure are as important as the result. These processes are not by any means uniform. One process involves the whole sensory-motor apparatus, through which orientation, locomotion, manipulation are "learned." These manipulations are subject to continuous development throughout life and culminate in skills. These sensory-motor processes become automatized, need no revision throughout life and are subject to few vicissitudes—these being due to failure consequent upon illness, old age, or modifications through traumatic inhibition. The other series of learned processes concern relations to the human beings in the environment. These latter processes are the earliest the child encounters, and the "conditioning" of the child begins here.

It matters little in what form these conditionings are described provided we understand what the conditions are to which the child is reacting, what adaptive mechanisms they set in motion, what fixed constellations they give rise to, and how they can be identified. The characteristics of these constellations are that they tend to become fixed and integrative, that is, subsequent reactions are based upon them and compounded. New combinations are made with the old ones as a base. These integrational systems are complicated in nature. They are formed against a background of needs, wishes, drives, frustrations, satisfactions. These "learned" processes are different in nature from learning that two and two are four, or "learning" how to use a bow and arrow. These constellations are important to identify because they form the cognitive basis of motivational behavior. In man it is impossible to understand behavior without its cognitive base because, as we shall see presently, this cognitive basis differs from society to society and even among different individuals in the same society. Since the conditioning of the child differs in different societies, we can designate the whole process of conditioning as the *growth pattern.*

Current Psychological Techniques

Psychology is the science of adaptation, its determinants, its modalities, and motivations, and of the mental and emotional phenomena that accompany the vicissitudes of adaptation. Psychology attempts to describe the minutiae of adaptation and to explain sequences of varying orders which are not apparent to common sense. The scope of psychology is wide, ranging from the way a mouse learns to overcome obstacles in a maze in order to reach food to the derivation of a religious ritual; but the psychology which explains the first will not explain the second. Psychology is not a homogeneous science. There are today many psychological techniques, each suited to special assignments though none can claim universal applicability.

Psychology has a long past but a short history. All current techniques arose either from the physiological laboratory or from hypnosis and psychiatry; the former began with Wundt (1876), the latter with Breuer and Freud (1886). One cannot understand current techniques without studying the failures of the classical psychologies founded by Wundt.

His work began when the physiology of the special senses had been worked out by Helmholtz and the anatomy of the brain had been established as the coördinator of the special senses, internal environment, and motor apparatus. The starting point of the classical psychologies was therefore *perception* as the content of consciousness. The technical problem was whether consciousness could be broken down into constituent elements and what could be done with this new information. The analytic task proved workable. Consciousness was broken down into its constituent sensory elements and therefore consciousness was assumed to have an atomistic structure, the units of which were held together by *association*. The explanations of these sensory processes had to be made by way of coincidental processes taking place in the central nervous system, that is, by a psycho-physical parallelism. Not all the data of consciousness could be treated by this analytic method, and hence in the treatment of emotions, motivations, and drives the classical psychologies failed.

The classical psychologies failed because they approached too small a segment of experience; because they did not reconstruct the human personality; because they made no direct explanations but relayed them through another series of physiological processes (even less known than those observed); they set up a blind alley by creating an artificial mind-body problem; but most of all they failed because only very limited use could be made of their conclusions.

Not the least cause for the decline of the Wundtian psychologies was that they were completely out of line with the most influential doctrine of the nineteenth century, the theory of evolution which studied struggle, function, change, survival, inheritance—in short, adaptation. Biology described adaptation in terms of a long-term trajectory. It examined the particular techniques of survival and among them emphasized a group of activities called instinctive, that is, having the property of being goal-directed but unlearned, and, therefore, inherited. With the explanation of adaptation as a goal, the pursuit of cognition as an operating tool could not suffice as long as it was not known exactly what place perception had in the entire process of adaptation. The functionalists James and Dewey were influenced by the theory of evolution but could not deal with any but the most elementary forms of adaptation. They could not take the social environment into account.

The revolution against the classical psychologies did not take the form of discarding the experimental methods introduced by Wundt. But the method of explaining psychological facts by physiological processes was swept away, carrying with it the whole mind-body problem, in fact denying that there was any mind or consciousness. Instead the new psychology took behavior as its guide. Not the least of the contributions of the theory of evolution was the establishment of the continuity of the adaptive processes of lower animals with those of man, whose isolated position had been maintained largely by theological assumptions. However, the conclusions based on animal psychology had to be limited to those types of adaptation available in animals.

The most important initiator of this method was Pavlov, the Russian physiologist, who studied the salivary reflex in dogs in connection with a series of conditions established and controlled by the experimenter. The method was known as (conditioned) reflexology. Though *behaviorism*—a term conceived by Watson—antedated Pavlov, the union of both techniques became the nucleus of an extensive school of psychological research which is among the most influential today.

Pavlov's great contribution was the establishment of a reliable method for studying a small segment of adaptation apparently quite complete in itself. What remained to be demonstrated was whether this method could establish a sufficient number of principles to account for the total adaptation of the animal. Revolutionary as the technique was, its methods and conclusions were not very different from those of the classical psychologies. We have here another atomistic psychology in which adaptive processes were considered to be made up of units held together by some synthetic principle. The basic unit was the reflex, and the synthetic principle was conditioning, which is only a more precise definition of what the classicists loosely called "association."

Watson employed the basic procedure of Pavlov but did not limit himself to the salivary reflex, and extended the method to more complicated situations than those dealing with the organization of behavior toward hunger-satisfying activities. His procedure was also like that of Pavlov in that he attempted a fine, microscopic examination of these segments of experience in the hope of establishing principles that would apply to all the possibilities in adaptive maneuvers.

But Watson's criticism of the classical psychologies did not prevent him from repeating the same errors in new ways. Watson created a unitary system at the expense of deleting data that could not be dealt with by his technique. Thus he disqualified not only "consciousness," but also all forms of direct experience. By conjuring away direct experience through exclusive attention to behavior, he made an exaggerated claim which was never validated. Unless the behavior of animals is interpreted according to the pragmatic and purposive standards of direct experience of the human observer, all behavior always remains a series of disconnected and meaningless events. In his series of controls, Watson failed to account for the observer, who did not operate with instruments on the pattern of the pressure gauge, rule, or thermometer, but with instruments of judgment, inference, and a host of complicated learned processes which go to make up his common sense. Watson's claim of objectivity was not validated; the unnoted leak in his controls was the human observer.

But the work of this school was exceedingly important and highly instructive. It drew attention away from the fruitless recognition of the formal constituents of awareness, began to handle awareness in organized forms actually used by animal and man, and observed its fluctuations or changes in relation to series of related events which ended in some form of executive maneuver called behavior. It was the executive side of behavior which was explained chiefly; it explained motor behavior, its modifications and modifiability which could be classed under the general head of *learning* of a special kind. Not isolated organs, but total manipulations toward a goal or its avoidance became important.

It can be truly said that all the behaviorists were now studying pure behavior devoid of valuational orientation. The question was what information could be yielded by charting the stimulus-response relationship without knowing the direct experiences which lie in between stimulus and response. This direct experience involves all the coördinative functions, such as discrimination and judgment. The fact is that as one leaves the simple problems of adaptation to mechanical obstacles and hunger drives—that is, the older problems (phylogenetically considered)—behaviorism becomes less sure-footed. Thus the transition to man, in Watson's work at least, was very unconvincing; there arose a series of arbitrary explanations, especially when fear, rage, love, and other emotions were involved. So emotions become visceral habits, just as skills become motor habits and thought processes laryngeal habits. This is a thin program to apply to human subjects. In the form in which Watson left behaviorism it could explore only a limited number of problems of human adaptation. The revolt against classical psychology made therefore the same errors it tried to correct; it remained atomistic. *Instead of using perceptor systems, behaviorism used effector systems.*

Much as the original behaviorist disliked to resort to anything "mental," and worked in the faith that the compounding of reflexes could account for behavior, latter-day followers of this school have been compelled to introduce the Gestalt into the cognitive field as playing a role in the establishment of conditioning; they were also obliged to include judgment and discrimination in setting the conditioned reflex into action, in its extinction or inhibition. Likewise they were reluctantly compelled to admit the drive toward a goal, the satisfaction of appetites, or the avoidance of pain or failure as vital factors in establishing learning processes. Then came the crucial question. Let us suppose that the conditioned reflex has given a much better picture of the processes at work in supplying motors to behavior; the next question, crucial for psychology, is what kind of behavior can it be used to evaluate? Certainly not all behavior, but only limited types of adaptation. Behaviorists are often in the habit of demonstrating the universal applicability of the principles they have established by applying them to a neurotic reaction in a human being. This is a very misleading procedure. It does not demonstrate the efficacy of the operation at all, because the relationships described in a neurotic reaction in the human being were established not by this technique but by psychoanalysis. The demonstration only proves that the relationships described in a neurosis can, with many omissions, be approximately translated into the language of behaviorism. The most serious limitation of behaviorism and learning theory for sociology is that neither has a means of accounting for what we shall later designate as projective systems, which cannot be called "learned" processes.

The criticism of the classical psychologies gave rise to another psychological technique, the "Gestalt" psychologies, whose representatives were Wertheimer, Köhler, Koffka. They insisted that nothing of value could be learned about cognition by trying to reconstruct it out of sensations. To begin with the atomic elements of cognition and to assume that the end results are assembled out of these elements is to begin at the wrong end. Their experiments too began with perception, but emphasized (as the essential) the totality of the perception (which is the point of view of common sense) and not its constituents. The Gestaltists wanted to know what processes and activities perception sets in motion. They moved in the opposite direction from the classicists. They studied certain aspects of the learning process—memory, insight—and studied them as entities and not as the summation of partial activities.

The basic unit used was the Gestalt, which means a totality of form or sequence (as in a melody or dance step). Interest was focused upon the sequences of entities rather than on the constituents of which they are composed. Thus the interest in neurological processes which underlay perception yielded to the disposition of the Gestalt, as for example in *meaning*. We do not perceive bundles of sensation, but *objects,* and meaning is not conferred by mere association or contiguity, but by relations to the object, like utility.

One can thus go along with the Gestaltists all the way they have taken us without objection. Whether they have worked out a consistent scheme whereby larger units of action can be identified and whether the dynamics give us usable insight into the structure of behavior is still *sub judice.* The concepts "Gestalt" and "field" have a much wider applicability than the conditioned reflex; they have access to perception, coördination, and executive functions (behavior). The only dynamic principle identified by them is that of "dynamic interaction," and others within the Gestalt. Since this principle of dynamic interaction is not further qualified, it has little operational value. As a method it has not yet been worked out, although no objections can be raised concerning the workability of its operating tools. One can however raise the question of what promise it holds out for answers to important questions. It can give us information of a kind about certain types of learning processes, and hence is useful in pedagogy. Can it be used to explain human character and can it deal with emotions and motivations? That remains still to be seen. Lewin's topology, an outgrowth of Gestalt psychology, claims to be a precise method of representation of psychological relationships. Its success is not established, and its problems are largely those defined by psychoanalysis. With these problems topology deals in an experimental method and promises to reveal many details which cannot be caught with the psychoanalytic method.

Psychoanalysis

Hard on the heels of the classical psychologies another psychology arose which originated from different traditions, from medical or therapeutic psychologies. Its forerunners were not the metaphysics of the eighteenth century, but hypnosis and psychiatry. This was the psychology of Freud—psychoanalysis—whose beginnings may be dated from 1886. This psychology must be examined for its peculiar aptness for describing certain aspects of human adaptation.

The relations of this psychological technique to the other current and academic psychologies have for a long time been obscured by several factors. Psychoanalysis began as a medical procedure dedicated to the therapy of neuroses. Its constructs were foreign to the traditions of academic psychologies, and the relationships between various factors described by these constructs were totally unexplored by those psychologies. Furthermore the growth of the Pavlovian school and its behavioristic ramifications and the methods it employed were at complete variance with those of psychoanalysis. The latter dealt with *direct experience,* which was tabooed by behaviorists, who maintained that direct experience could not be treated "scientifically." But perhaps the chief reason for the isolation of psychoanalysis was that it was an instinct or *drive* psychology interested in long-term aspects of adaptation. At its inception psychoanalysis exploited the sexual aspects of adaptation and for a time sponsored the idea that sexual energy or *libido* was the common currency into which all drives could be transformed.

The signal and durable achievement of Freud's system was that it was an appraisal of man from the point of view of *biography;* it was a method of evaluating the life history of the individual. He established definite criteria for the study of the *character* of the individual, whether or not he had neurotic symptoms. At the very outset we find that psychoanalysis, in comparison with the other psychologies reviewed, is a psychology which leaves the minutiae of adaptation unsettled while it attempts to follow certain gross maneuvers of the personality over the entire trajectory of a life span. His approach was original. Instead of taking a small segment of experience Freud undertook to follow the fate of certain urges, drives, and appetites which enjoyed continuity over a lifetime. The drive singled out for particular study was the sexual "instinct," and since this drive had a continuity throughout life Freud was able to arrive at the significant conclusion that neurotic symptoms were purposive. The particular character of this purpose is less important; but that it was an unsuccessful attempt at adaptation was of the greatest significance for the study of personality. Later Freud was able to move on to the study of *character* as opposed to symptoms—and this is proving to be his most noteworthy contribution.

As regards Freud's technique, he employed direct experience for the simple reason that his subjects could talk. They could identify their goals. This was not the same as the introspective procedures of the classical psychologists. It was direct experience as the common man understood it from the experiences he had, qualified only by his accuracy in reporting and in the use of language. It was not used to dissect minutely experiences of sensation, but took the entire flow of experience and studied its sequences, emphases, and vicissitudes. In direct experience Freud also included the direct experience during sleep, that is, dreams. From this data Freud discovered that with the aid of the drive principle (instinct) he now had a definite frame of reference. The system of coördinates was direct experience and behavior over a wide arc as related to the gratification or frustration of wishes, needs, or drives. Psychoanalysis has two advantages over behaviorism for social psychology. It reckons with factors which govern the continuity of reaction types; and by its use of direct experience it is able to establish constants which are indicators of the coördinative processes which lie between stimulus and response.

Then came a discovery which was a new departure for all psychology —that frustrations of gratification, if they occurred in childhood, led to permanent modifications in personality. Therefore if we are to study the personality, it must be approached genetically. Furthermore he discovered that the effect of a frustration on the personality was a mobilization of certain defensive attitudes, actions, or avoidances; that the abandoned activity was replaced by substitution or compensation; and finally that all these processes—defensive, substitutive, or compensatory—enjoy a continuity and can be identified by definite constellations in the current life of the individual.

This is the essence of the Freudian psychology. The fact that Freud originally dealt with neuroses in which sexual difficulties were paramount led at first to the exploration of the sexual development of man. This special development of psychoanalysis in the direction of sexual adaptation need not however blind us to those aspects of psychoanalysis which pertain to a general psychology.

All this indicates therefore that Freud was studying complicated interrelationships in a constant state of *change;* in other words, his was a dynamic psychology. To describe these events Freud had to devise a notational system and to bind the events described into a meaningful relationship, that is to say, a theory. It is this aspect of psychoanalysis which has created the greatest difficulty and confusion. Psychology has at its disposal no such notational system as exists in mathematics and can be put to use in physics. There is only common sense, and common language. The difficulties which psychoanalysis had are at any rate no greater than those of any other psychological system. But the fate of a psychology rests, at least in part, on the notational system used, as the vehicle of the data to be considered and the significant relationships into which they enter.

At all events Freud began by following the fate of drives through various vicissitudes. The first thing he learned about the sexual drives was that they could be identified by certain qualitative standards derived from representation of certain erogenous zones: the genital, oral, and anal. He also discovered that they could be used interchangeably. Hence it followed that a general name could be given to the sexual drive irrespective of the particular form in which it was expressed. This he called *libido*, and was able to show what at first flush looked like a regular succession of somatic primacy, in the order oral, anal, and genital. Then he discovered certain vicissitudes of the instinct or drive: it could be repressed, that is, banished from consciousness or awareness, though its effects could unconsciously persist; it could be sublimated (expressed in forms removed from their original goal); or it could be turned into its opposite (sadism can be replaced by masochism, or "peeping" by exhibitionism).

Certain specific dangers attend any drive psychology. Freud was secure in this operational system as long as he was dealing with neurotic symptoms and as long as his task was to discover their meaning as *substitutive* efforts. He had reliable qualitative criteria which could be readily identified in the direct experience of the subject. It became a question whether the same criteria could be applied to instincts other than sexual. One series of phenomena which already raised some questions were those of sadism and masochism, which could only partially be treated as sexual manifestations. This difficulty of assigning to sadism and masochism a proper place in the scheme of instincts proved a forerunner of other serious difficulties. These came when Freud tried to deal with the so-called *ego instincts*. The criteria so useful in studying the sexual instinct were lacking in this case and hence the vicissitudes of these "instincts" could not be followed, nor could their ontogenesis be traced. This gave Freud much trouble, which he tried to circumvent by seeking a more elementary factor common to both instincts. This, he said, was the *repetition compulsion*. From this he attempted to derive two elementary instincts—life instincts and death instincts—the latter compelling the organism to return to the inorganic state. These reflections, interesting as they are, did not simplify the instinct theory, and besides they are clinically useless and can in no way be identified in the material under investigation. Life and death instincts, though they have some descriptive or philosophical value, cannot be employed as operational concepts.

The trouble was not with Freud's observations but with the notational systems used, the organizational principles, and the explanations contingent upon them. The facts and relationships between these facts stand, and can be verified by anyone. The notational system was apparently at fault and blocked the road to important developments. A bit of animism had crept into the system of thinking, as a result of which the tail was wagging the dog. This can be clearly seen in some of the vicissitudes of "instinct" which Freud described. For example, it can be repressed. Here we still see the organism acting. It can be turned into its opposite. In this formulation the turning-about process is an activity of the organism and not an attribute of instinct. But Freud's notational system was not prepared to study the processes taking place within the organism. He did however contrive an exceedingly ingenious device which partially overcame the handicap. This device consisted of identifying these processes by the phenomena they produced. These processes were called repression, regression, displacement, identification, projection, introjection, reaction formation, isolation, undoing, etc. The manner in which these processes operate is not precisely known; but of the fact that they can be clearly identified there is no doubt. It is safe to claim that few psychological discoveries of any time rank with them in importance, for they describe the adaptive maneuvers of man in relation to certain strivings, such as utility, security, etc., or obstacles to their satisfaction. It is these so-called mental mechanisms which made it possible to identify certain stereotyped constellations appearing in dreams, fantasies, myths, etc., and indicated the way to the actual conditions out of which they grew.

The mechanism which Freud singled out for special study was that of repression, on which rests the theory of the unconscious. It was on the basis of this study too that Freud was able to explore, in a measure, the structure of the human personality. This he did in defining three provinces of the personality: the id, the ego, the superego. Incomplete as this personality scheme is, it provides a background for describing the manner in which mores influence the individual, how conscience originates, and what maintains its tonicity.

Since this is not an attempt to give an exposition of psychoanalysis but merely to describe its subject matter, operating tools, and the results that can be anticipated from it, we can now make some comparisons with the other psychological techniques sketched. First psychoanalysis began to answer questions about human adaptation that were of interest to the common man. It concerned itself in a methodical way with emotional life, with motivations. It described certain conspicuous failures in adaptation and described a method for studying them. Beginning as a psychology for therapy, it gradually became a general psychology. The genetic viewpoint in the study of psychology has been followed by all current psychological techniques. The problems defined by psychoanalysis have become the occupation of all current psychologies—though some of them admit this more freely than others.

This survey of current psychological techniques was presented as an introduction to the most pressing problem of this book. If we are to make psychology one of the social sciences, what aid is it ready to give us and which of the techniques of modern psychology can help us in our task at the present moment. Will the hope sustain us that the animal psychologies can formulate principles that we can confidently follow? The classical psychologies made that promise and came to naught. But there are several reasons why this hope is slim. Granted that animal psychology has a definite place and that certain types of learning processes can be accurately studied on lower animals and applied without change to man, this is a very narrow province, and one which plays a very small role in human life. The conditioned reflex established a valuable series of data; but the behaviorists did not make good their claim to devise a scientific psychology without the aid of direct experience. They had to use the direct experience of the experimenter rather than that of the subject. The Gestaltists are undoubtedly on a productive tack, but so far can give to sociology no effective tools because they cannot deal with motivation and emotion as effectively as with perceptual units. Topology has devised a notational and representational system; but the problems on which it operates were defined by psychoanalysis. In short, we have no psychological technique today that satisfies all requirements, either because its techniques or conclusions are not ready for adoption by the social sciences on any large scale or because the relevancy to these problems is dubious. There remains only psychoanalysis, and by this is meant the significant relations into which the phenomena of direct experience and behavior can be ordered. Once these relations are grasped, the events can be described with any number of different notational systems—in the language of Gestalts, topological systems, or stimulus-response sequences. Gestalt psychology lies closest to psychoanalysis in its operating implements and assumptions; but it does not employ the same techniques, nor does it study as wide an arc. The behaviorists and stimulus-response psychologies have excellent techniques for studying the structure of all manipulative behavior: the so-called ego functions of man concerned with orientation, locomotion, manipulation, and mechanical skills. They are however less suited to deal with the emotional life of man and are completely incapable of dealing with the projective phenomena which play so significant a role in human adaptation.

We can draw several important conclusions about the human mind from the history of psychology. Two general types of psychology have been prominent: those which are based on the study of projection phenomena, which may be called dynamic psychologies (for example, the drive and direct experience psychologies); and the mechanistic systems. The dynamic psychologies have access to the so-called subjective phenomena, the emotions, motivations, etc., and the mechanistic psychologies build integrational systems on the pattern of the chain, the lever, and the adding machine. The latter reproaches the former with being unscientific, only to be accused in turn of regarding the organism as a problem in mechanics. Psychology in its attempts to be "scientific" has long been bending backward in emulating the assumptions and operational tools of physics and chemistry of a century ago—tools which were suited to the subject matter of these disciplines alone. Their transplantation to psychology cannot be made without modification. Notwithstanding these handicaps, the experimental psychologies can surely solve the problems of certain orders of integrational systems, those dealing with orientation, locomotion, manipulation, simple forms of dominance and submission. But even these cannot be completely described in mechanistic terms since they are subject in the living organism to such goals as utility, security, or mastery in one form or another. They cannot then be described without a bit of projection, no matter what verbal tricks are employed to disguise this fact. On the other hand the common assumption that one cannot be "scientific" about the direct experience of man, with its vast projective superstructure and its varied uses in human adaptation, is totally unwarranted. To delete this aspect of human psychology is to omit the province in which lie man's greatest problems in personal and social adaptation. In the light of these two orders of psychological phenomena it is futile to look for a unitary operational system that will fit all facts. It is for the present a quest for the philosopher's stone. Psychology has moved closer to its goal by discarding atomistic hypotheses, by employing large units as they occur in nature—the Gestalt, the field, the complex, the action system—and by studying these constellations in motion, which shows up their vicissitudes. We must be satisfied for the time being to map out broad qualitative outlines, and to respect the operational difficulties that accompany each new notational system devised.

Psychoanalysis and the Social Sciences

The principles which psychoanalysis can give to the social sciences are best illustrated by the following case history. It can demonstrate how integrational systems are built, how the executive capabilities can be fostered or crippled to procure satisfaction of needs and drives; it can describe how motivations are contingent upon executive capacities available for ready use; and it can describe the surface manifestations which these integrational systems take in the overt behavior of the individual and how they are justified when in operation. It can describe the character of the individual and the rationalizations he presents to justify it.

A man of thirty complains of having great difficulty with women, of a constant anxiety state in addition to several specific phobias, the chief of which is the fear of making a speech, constant feeling of unworthiness, incapacity to compete, and hence a sense of failure. In relation to women he is unable to formulate any objective apart from sexual relations; he is always profoundly dissatisfied with any woman and has a complete inability to love any. His relations are always tentative and filled with anxiety, and he fears being trapped by an undesirable woman who will exploit him. His panic rises until he deserts her and the performance is renewed with another.

His relations with men are hardly more successful, though he puts up a better façade. He is deeply incapable of any real competition, but has intense longings for leadership. His concealed hatreds result in rendering him more submissive. His speech inhibition is related to these trends. On the surface the idea of making a speech is associated with grandiose feelings; he expects the most astonishing results, "to bowl them over," "knock them cold"—to compel his audience to recognize his supremacy. In this connection it should be noted that he is subject to occasional asthmatic attacks. Failing both with women and in competition with men, he is obsessed with a feeling of hopeless ineffectuality.

The subject was the second son in a family of four, one brother two and a half years older, one brother three years younger, a sister six years younger. He was a healthy child, and for the first twenty months received excellent care. A change in family fortunes altered this condition. His father had to open a small shop, a consequence of which was that the father worked all night and slept during the day while his mother tended the shop. She was therefore unable to give this child the care he had heretofore received. At this point a new adaptation became necessary for the child. The tensions of hunger, the wish to be fondled, and so forth, could no longer be satisfied in the usual way. He cried furiously but his cries were unanswered. His entire control system, heretofore effective, became useless. Eventually he stopped crying. The heretofore friendly mother became an inaccessible object, and making a demand on her became an activity filled with hazards.

When he was three a younger sibling was born. This made his precarious situation worse. He remembers that at three to four he had a recurrent nightmare, repeated during the analysis. He remembers waking up in anxiety after a dream that burglars had entered the house and were about to attack him. A feature of these dreams was his inability to cry out for help. During these night terrors he sought relief by running to his mother's room. More often than not he was sent back to his own bed, which he occupied with his older brother. To the latter he had already developed sufficient rivalry to be unable to use him as a parental surrogate. It is futile to identify the burglar in his dreams; it may have been the younger sibling or the older; the father or even the mother herself. The point is that he was filled with an anxiety created by the inability to have access to the mother, together with intensely hostile feelings to all rivals.

The next definite landmark in his development came a few years later. When the patient was six to eight, while his older brother was able to read, the patient could not. He often heard his older brother reading to his mother and heard her praise his efforts. At this time he formed the conviction that speech, which by now had become inhibited with him, was a powerful weapon of courtship of which he was incapable. He sat enviously in the adjoining room thinking very meanly of himself and utterly incapable of venting his hatred of his brother.

We must pass hastily over his masturbation history; few external threats were introduced in connection with this activity, and his fantasies in connection with it partook of the deep masochistic quality of defeat and hatred. He never, however, abandoned the mother as his object, and did not turn to the father for aid. Many years later, at twenty-seven, while he was in the throes of conflict about a girl to whom he was attentive, he was seized with a panic while making a speech, and to his profound humiliation, he had to break off.

Since our interest in this case is not psychopathology, but integrational systems which govern action, we can profitably track a few of them down. Toward the mother (or any object from whom he has similar expectations) he has deep hatred and mistrust, but he still retains unconscious longings for her. The mistrust is a certainty that he cannot get from her what he wants, but the goal is unconsciously retained. This attitude is fortified by the knowledge that he cannot prevail upon her to yield to his wishes. She still appears (as does every woman) powerful and resourceful; he, weak, helpless, and unable to enforce his will. No experience since infancy has given him a chance to alter this conception of woman; in fact he was not aware that woman had these implicit attributes until it was exposed in analysis. Yet he operated in this important aspect of adaptation, with a conception of woman, based on painful experience, which was bound to defeat his conscious and conventionalized relations to her. The phenomenon of displacement is therefore due to a generalization *projected* onto new situations. These processes are all unconscious.

These early experiences also gave him a special conception of himself and his capacities. He now has a feeling of smallness and insignificance, for which he compensates by fantasies of successes in the future that can never materialize.

The original experiences with his mother laid the basis of an integrational system which qualified all other experiences. When the rivalry situation became acute, he could not take the necessary risks to insure his success, because the object was unattainable anyhow. Each time a normal self-assertive impulse arose, it was magnified to the dimensions of a crime, and its suppression ended by lowering his self-esteem and increasing his fear of retaliation. This particular problem he solved in childhood with a fantasy of having his father put him into bed with his mother. During the analysis he acted as if I forbade him relations with women and even asked me to get one for him. These fantasies are adaptive in that they seek a realization of his goal without the attending risks.

What we have presented here is a projective integrational system which qualifies the meaning which the female has for our subject. Consequently he can enter into no successful relationship with her. Of this projective system the subject is completely unaware. This system cannot be recognized or accounted for by any behaviorist or learning psychology. He describes his relationships to women in conventional terms, and justifies his flight from them by reasons which are also conventionalized. These latter we call *rationalizations*. In terms of what we have just described a rationalization is a conventionalized explanation of behavior motivated by (unconscious) projective systems and brought into consonance either with superego or reality systems, or both.

The subject we have studied is a member of our culture, and most of the vicissitudes crucial in the formation of his character seem not to have been determined by the culture in which he lives, but by the specific characters of his parents and by several accidental factors in their lives. This is not precisely the case. Some factors were accidental, as was the change in family fortunes which interrupted the good care he got from his mother. But good maternal care is a feature of our culture. The organization of the family is an institutionalized feature of it, as are the many disciplines to which he was subjected. The sex mores within which our subject's conflicts move are fixed by the culture. The rational systems with which he operates are determined by cultural conventions.

The crucial psychological question is whether this projective system, in the way in which it is established and in which it operates, can be put to some use in sociology. The answer presents itself readily. If we can establish that similar projective systems operate in all individuals in a given society because the integrational systems are based on similar experiences from contact with institutions or practices followed by all members in the society, then we can not only account for similar dispositions in the individuals, but also for the specific needs of that society. Suppose it was a practice in our society to give all children good care until two years and then withdraw support; then we would expect that the trend in their personality formation would follow along the lines indicated by the subject we just discussed. The only question remaining is whether the reaction types to this particular frustration follow specific or consistent lines. The answer to this is not precise; the reaction types are uniform and consistent within a given range, but they are not all precisely alike. No two individuals exposed to the same frustrations will have precisely the same reaction because there is variation in the succeeding integrations and hence a difference in the resultant character constellation. To the same frustration as the one described another child may react with the following integrational series: Mother is worthless; I can expect nothing from her; I do not need her; I am powerful, great, and omnipotent; etc. The resulting character structure will be paranoid and not hysterical. The specific needs of a paranoid individual will be different from the character we described.

Our operational unit is not a perceptor or executive entity (behavior), we do not employ stimulus-response; we do not use the drive operationally, nor do we use affects or motivations in this way. What we use can be designated as an *action system,* which is a large molar not atomic unit. In the composition of an action system are receptor, effector, and coördinative elements to which are closely related *affects* and *motivations.* Attempts to make psychological systems on the basis of affects or motivations alone have no more success than behaviorism, because affects and motivations are contingent upon available executive capacities.

Conclusion

It is evident from the history of the systematic psychologies that the requirements of a psychology suitable to the needs of sociology are of a specific character. Such a psychology must be holistic, and cannot use the operational tools of one which may be useful in the study of a single facet of adaptation, like perception; it must be able to follow change and motion, it must be dynamic. It must be a genetic psychology in order to follow integrational systems from their inception, and to be able to identify their vicissitudes and modalities under the influence of various stresses. It must be able to account for complex motivations. It must be able to recognize the influence of various drives and the effects of various controls imposed on drives and impulses. It must be able to account for the adaptive role of fantasy and must be able to detect the emotional constituents of rational thinking.

Such a psychology must be able to track down the sources of the affectivity potential of the individual, the capacity for idealization, the patterns of self-esteem and aggression, the psychosomatic patterns, the super-ego formation, and the like. It must be able to analyze such complicated end products as values, ideals, religion, for these are the currency of the social life of man. The only psychology that can approach these problems with any hope of success is psychoanalysis. To render this psychology useful some modification in operational concepts must be made; but the clinical observations which Freud originally described have not been amended.

CHAPTER II

THE TECHNIQUE OF PSYCHODYNAMIC ANALYSIS

PSYCHOLOGY can be of use to the social sciences only if its use can be reduced to a technique which is verifiable, teachable, and can be corrected or changed in the face of new evidence. Systematized opinions in technical language are no more binding in psychology than in any other field. Generalizations which codify the obvious are not techniques capable of yielding new information.

The predecessor of this book was an adventure in technique. This technique was the outgrowth of a few simple observations. After a culture like that of Tanala had been presented in detail, certain correspondences were noted. In Tanala the relation of the individual to the ancestral gods seemed strikingly like the relation of the child to the parent in this culture. There was the same emphasis on obedience. The first conclusion was that obedience to a duty was universal. We found as we studied the same correlation in Marquesas that this was not so, and correspondingly discovered that in Marquesas there was no emphasis on childhood obedience. The folklore in Tanala showed a typical father-son relationship, in which jealousy was repressed and a passive feminine attitude appeared in its place. In Marquesas myths father-hatred was absent, and in lieu of this father hatred there was strong fear, hatred, and distrust of the woman. In other words, according as the experiences varied, so did the products of the *projective systems* in folklore and religion. This gave us our first clue, and the same procedure was used on more and more phenomena.

As we proceeded we found it necessary to have a cultural unit to describe the various practices and customs, and for this purpose the concept *institution* could be used operationally. The institutions were therefore treated as the vehicle through which specific influences were brought to bear on the growing individual. If therefore we again look at the correlation in the previous paragraph, we find that if childhood disciplines constitute one order of institutions then religion and folklore comprise another. We called the former primary and the latter secondary. Also there was something created in the individual by his childhood experiences which formed the basis for the projective systems subsequently used to create folklore and religion. This group of nuclear constellations in the individual was designated the *basic personality structure.* This concept proved to be only a refinement of a concept long since used descriptively by Herodotus and Caesar and known as *national character.* The term *basic personality structure* was chosen to obviate the lack of clarity in the terms group, national, or social character, because a group can no more have a common character than it can have a common soul or pair of lungs. Moreover the constellations identified in basic personality structure were not finished character traits, but a matrix in which these character traits develop. For example, in Alor we find distrust as a permanent feature of basic personality; but this distrust may show itself in any number of different character traits. What was new and important about this concept was not its name, but the technique of its derivation and the introduction of a genetic viewpoint into sociology. The concept of basic personality structure thus became a powerful operational implement, for through it we acquired a precise means of delineating the interrelationship of various social practices through their compatibility or incompatibility with certain constant identifiable human needs and drives.

Whereas this operational scheme was made possible by the ability to identify remote derivations of basic experiences through the use of projections, further experience with new cultures and new material in the form of biographies showed this scheme to be oversimplified and decidedly incomplete.

The first difficulty arose in connection with the use of the concept *institution.* This concept was originally defined to connote "a fixed mode of thought or behavior which can be communicated, which enjoys common acceptance and the infringement of or deviation from which creates some disturbance in the individual or group." This definition did not work in practice. It was found that in some societies (e. g., Alor) some of the most important sources of projective systems were not institutionalized but were related to other practices which were. Poor maternal care in Alor was an accident resulting from the mother's having to work all day in her fields. The basic institution is that the mother works in the fields all day; the neglect of the children is not institutionalized, though almost universal. There are no sanctions against good care of the children. We can therefore amend the concept primary institution to read: *primary institution or related practices, whether institutionalized or not.* To substitute the word *practices* for institutions would not be any more satisfactory than either *institutions* or *mores.* Moreover the latter terms would imply the backing by a specific rationale, which, though often the case, is not universal. Institutions should be defined to mean what people do, think, believe, or feel. Their locus is within the human personality; and they have an accommodative or adaptive function. In connection with primary institutions, the question frequently arose concerning their origin. This question could never be answered. Linton [1] pointed out that this question was not pertinent to the present endeavor. The primary institution is treated as the taking-off point for the individual, not for the culture. The origin of an institution has nothing to do with the effect it creates on the growing individual.

A second technical difficulty arose in connection with the identification of the products of the projective systems, called secondary institutions. Here much confusion arose because many institutions could not be classified as either primary or secondary. This fact alone, that there were institutions outside and independent of the projective system, indicates either that our formulation of the determinants of basic personality structure is incomplete or that institutions exist outside its range. This is very likely to be the case with institutions or practices of purely rational origin.

The important point about this classification into primary and secondary institutions is that it is closely bound to the concept of basic personality structure. It means that institutions cannot be compared with each other or establish relations with each other directly. This relationship is mediated by the personality.

In the earlier work we had no opportunity to check the validity of basic personality against actual biographical material and social changes. The only cultures that have a long recorded history and plenty of biographical material are the oriental cultures and our own. But these could not be confidently approached until certain elementary problems had been solved.

The use of the concept basic personality structure therefore includes the following questions: (1) What are the key integrational sys-

1 In seminar at Columbia University.

tems and their institutional background? (2) Are the effects of normative institutions the only sources of basic personality structure? (3) How can the concept be tested against biographies and how could the inevitable variations of personal character in the same culture be reconciled with it? (4) What are the effects of knowledge empirically derived and verified by criteria outside the range of the "common sense" of the culture upon institutions of projective origin? In other words, what are the relations of scientific knowledge to the basic personality? The last is of course significant for the study of our own society, where science has so evidently altered the social utility of the projective systems employed in religion.

The Key Integrational Systems

Any selection of key situations which influence personality formation is bound to be incomplete. We are prejudiced in our selection by our experience with individuals in our society and particularly by the constellations which predominate in neuroses. This is admittedly a bias. We have already surveyed a sufficient number of cultures to know that constellations important in our society are not universal, and some situations in our society are overlooked because they do not act as impediments to development in our culture but do in others. If we had no opportunity to examine any culture other than our own, we would never surmise that maternal care and nurture are exceedingly important to the cohesiveness of the society and so would never look to maternal care as a key situation. This we can learn only by comparison with other cultures where maternal care is inadequate. By this time we have studied ten cultures intensively and have a sufficient number of contrasts to indicate a workable list.[2]

Maternal care
    Constancy of attention—or abandonment
    Feeding regularity
    Surrogate parents—activities of
    Help in learning processes—walking, talking
    Pre-walking and post-walking care
    Weaning—age, methods
    Sphincter control—when inducted, associated ideas (cleanliness, obedience, etc.)
Induction of affectivity
    Solicitation of response; handling, play, fondling

2 Marquesan, Tanala, Comanche, Pomo, Alor, Navaho, Plainville, Tapirape, Sikh, and Ojibwa.

Maternal attitudes to child—care or neglect, honesty to children or practice of deception
Insistence on obedience and presence or absence of reward systems—superego formation
Early disciplines
Consistency
Punishment—reward systems—when punishment is inflicted, place of choice for inflicting bodily pain, etc.
Sexual disciplines
Masturbation, interdicted or permitted, attitudes of elders—neglect, ridicule, castration threats, tolerance, or used as placebo
Playing with opposite sex—permitted openly or tacitly, attitude of elders
Institutionalized sibling attitudes
Rivalries encouraged or suppressed
Aggression—controls
Induction into work
Age—duties, rewards, degree of participation
Differences between sexes
Attitudes to work—division of economic responsibilities
Puberty
Alteration of participation in society
Premature or deferred
Parental aid in preparation for marital status
Marriage
Mating mores
Difficulties in mating created by parents
Position of woman, freedom of choice
Economic status requirements
Fidelity requirements, freedom of divorce
Character of participation in society
Status differentiation
Function differentiation
Life goals
Factors that keep the society together
Superego formation
Coöperative and antagonistic phases
Permitted and controlled activities—sanctions
Projective systems
Religion
Folklore
Reality systems, derived from empirical or projective sources
Arts, crafts, and techniques
Techniques of production
Differentiation of function
Participation in distributed products—status differentiation, degrees and controls of prestige

The technique of applying these principles can be illustrated by taking a particular combination of conditions. Society A is one in which the mother cares diligently for the infant for two weeks after birth, and thereafter only two hours in the morning and two hours in the evening, the rest of her time being spent in the gardens raising vegetable food. For the major portion of the day the care of the infant is left to older siblings or others. The child probably is given enough food, but many tensions are unsatisfied for long periods. No systematic teaching of talking or walking occurs. The child shifts for itself. It is masturbated to keep it quiet. Add to this, teasing and later deliberate misrepresentation. To this situation someone may say: "What does a child or infant know, and therefore what difference does it make? It gets enough food, doesn't it?" This view overlooks the fact that the infant has no ready-made reactions; that by the conditions described a specific environment is created for the child; that its needs and tensions are constant, and if they are relieved with little effort or discomfort on the part of the child, one integrational system will follow; while if the tensions are unrelieved, the resulting constellation will be different. The child will eventually develop a definite attitude to the parent, to itself, and to the tensions which cause it so much discomfort. These attitudes are adapted to the particular conditions and tend to become habitual, automatic, and compounded. Moreover the constellations formed under these conditions can be predicted with a fair degree of accuracy. The constellations thus created will not all be alike, but the range can be predicted.

A child under these conditions cannot develop an undivided feeling or attitude to the mother. He must feel some hatred, some distrust, some isolation, a sense of having no one whom he can positively count on. Moreover the functions which develop under the influence of good care, confidence in himself, interest in the outer world, enterprise—these will all suffer. Sexuality is stimulated, but it is detached from the image of an affectionate person who stimulates it.

The next question that arises is whether these attitudes need remain permanent. They need not, if other factors are introduced into the child's life which would tend to counteract them. However if they are not counteracted, they tend to continue. If the child as he grows encounters influences which tend to reinforce these reactions, by the time he is an adult they constitute his character. By that time there is formed a definite pattern (for perceiving human relationships and dealing with them) which is totally unconscious, and a definite and specific system of projections is likely to spring from these early experiences. When adult he may invent a story, a pure fabrication, in which we may detect the operation of these constellations formed in childhood. These constellations may be recovered in dreams in distorted forms.

We have had up to this point a series of inferences about the probable effects of certain formative institutions. How can this guess be substantiated or contradicted? If our hypothesis is correct, namely that these conditions in childhood become consolidated and form a basis for subsequent projective use, then we can expect to find some evidence of it in all projective systems—religious, folklore, and perhaps other institutions. In other words, if we know how the basic personality is established, we can make certain predictions about the institutions this personality is likely to invent. If we follow the particular personality created by the above mentioned conditions, we expect to find folk tales dealing with parental hatred, with desertion by parents; we expect to find a religion devoid of any concepts dealing with reward for good deeds or punishment for bad ones. We expect no emphasis on the idea of reinstatement into the good graces of the deity through suffering. We expect no idealization of the deity.

The utility of the concept of basic personality structure does not end here. We find institutions other than folklore and religion derived from that same source. If we could do no more than predict types of religion and folklore, the usefulness of this procedure would be very limited and would be entirely inadequate for our society where the projective systems have been largely deflected from use in religion. Since the personality has in it elements of distrust toward parents, we could not expect this lack of trust to be limited to the parents, but extended to others. When the whole chain of elements entering into this particular integrational system is completed, we would also expect to find bad relations between the sexes, frequency of divorce, and also institutionalized obstacles against divorce.

The more the ethnographer tells us about the traits of these people, the greater the number of institutions that we can place as derivatives of this *basic personality structure*. For example, we hear that the people discussed above have no interest in the arts and their skills rate very low. We also hear that they surrender easily to illness. These traits fall easily into place once we know the basic personality structure; but these particular traits *could not be predicted,* and there are likely to be some that cannot be accounted for even when we know the basic personality.

We cannot therefore maintain that the prediction value of the concept of the basic personality structure is its chief merit; we do not know the possibilities of early conditionings accurately enough to make predictions on a large scale. We may be able to do so when we have comparative studies on about fifty cultures, and even then original and unique details are likely to surprise us.

The chief merit of this concept is that it offers us a basis for examining the structuralizations in society and for relating institutions to each other, not directly but through the medium of the individuals who compose it.

This is as far as our procedure can take us, given only the accurate description of institutions. Conclusions made from this source alone can have but the status of guesses, more or less approximate. There is another way not only to check on our conclusions but to furnish us with a fresh source of information—that is, the biographies of the individuals in the society.

What Additional Factors Enter into Basic Personality Structure?

If we were to stop our consideration of basic personality structure with those systems which, though they originate in actual experience, become the unconscious basis for projective systems, we could be justly accused of omitting several very important sources of "learning," which play a prominent role in the adaptation of the individual. There is a large contingent of data imparted to the child by direct tuition.[3] To this group belong all explanations about the outer world, how to deal with it, and the relations of man to it, and the conventionalized attitudes which govern the relations of people to each other. These systems are consciously inducted, much of their content being subject to demonstrations of a kind, and in some instances are modifiable.

The introduction of this category of "learned" systems brings with it unavoidable difficulty. In the previous section (page 17) we de-

---

[3] A recent effort to account for social dynamics on the basis of direct learning processes has been made by J. W. M. Whiting, *On Becoming a Kwoma* (New Haven, Yale University Press, 1942). This approach would be valid if man did not *integrate experience.* It therefore presents a one-dimensional picture of mental processes on the basis of which no dynamic of social stability or change can be formulated.

scribed an aspect of common sense derived from actual experiences in interpersonal relationships which form the basis of projective systems, some of which are used to explain the outer world. Now we introduce a system taught directly. These two systems cannot possibly be incompatible if they are used to explain the outer world. If they were, one would tend to disappear, and the system eliminated would of necessity be the one most amenable to change, the conscious system. More likely than not a taught system at complete variance with the projective system could not be accepted. This simple idea can be illustrated as follows: Suppose that a missionary attempts to convey to a primitive people the idea of redemption through suffering and atonement. This is presented as a bit of reality, and hence it is "taught" as such. Whether or not this idea has any significance to a primitive man depends on whether it has a certain plausibility according to his own experience. If he has not himself experienced the logical sequence of committing an act interpreted as a misdeed, being punished for it, and then being reinstated, the proposition as stated must remain meaningless. For it is merely a projection, rationalization, and generalization from the basic experience.

What we are saying therefore is that the entire projective system tends to exercise a polarizing influence over all taught reality systems that are presented to the individual; there are bound to be inconsistencies and exceptions.[4] But all aspects of the reality systems do not by any means fall under the influence of the system. One can in fact establish a series in which the projective system has less and less influence. It naturally has the least influence on manipulation of crafts and techniques. But other systems, which are taught also, fall decidedly under the influence of the projective system. Let us take two instances, one in which a drive is involved and another in which no drive is concerned.

[4] To this point we can add a comment of Dr. Robert K. Merton: "It is not, of course, only the projective systems which polarize reality systems. Patterned experiences, differing according to social class, will also make certain beliefs 'meaningless' and 'unacceptable.' A particular type of belief in redemption through suffering and atonement will not spread among the upper social strata of a society, but will have rapid diffusion among the lower strata of the same society. It can also be shown that certain social and economic views or certain scientific systematizations spread rapidly at one time and slowly at another because they are compatible with the generalized personal experience of certain segments of the population. I have found, for example, among 17th century physical scientists, that the Puritan projective system patently exercised a selective influence, such that an undue proportion of these scientists derived from Puritan circles. . . . The English century of genius is not unrelated to Puritanism." (Personal communication.)

The first can be taken from a very common injunction in both primitive and civilized society. It is the proposition: "If you masturbate then you will become insane" (or some other dire consequence). For the moment we are less concerned about the disposition of the somatically determined tensions than we are about the form in which the injunction is implemented. The consequence of insanity is stated as a fact, which is a ready-made rationalization to justify the prohibition. The impulse to masturbate is thus accompanied by an anxiety which is channelized into a specific direction. The danger is made to appear as a real danger, for if it did not arouse terror it would hardly act as a deterrent.

This reality aspect occupies an important place in the conflict which centers about masturbation. If the activity in question is abandoned, it may undergo repression, and the only manifestation of its existence may be the anxiety about insanity. This can be represented graphically thus:

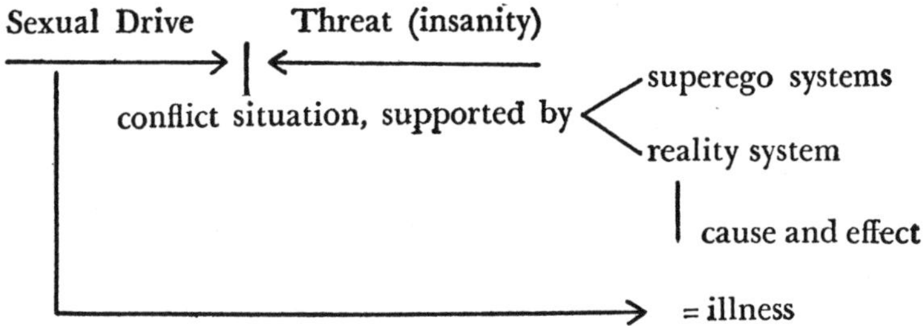

Thus the fear of illness may emerge as the only manifestation of the original impulse to satisfy a somatic sexual tension. The place of the reality aspect (masturbation causes insanity) is therefore shown to be related to the superego (conscience) systems created in a society.

This is an opportune place to discuss how extensively such an idea as the one described above can become systematized. This belief about the pernicious effects of masturbation persisted until about a half century ago. Before the advent of bacteriology almost every illness was attributed to masturbation, and long treatises based on "scientific" empirical observations were written in proof. This is an illustration of scientific rationalization. The unknown factor in this complex rationalization is the unconscious insistence that masturbation should be punished. The scientific data were merely organized to support this assumption.

There are other types of reality systems taught by direct induction which are unrelated to any drive. The Pomo and Navaho are both taught at an early age to bury excreta lest they be used as bait. This is an anxiety which can cling to the individual for a lifetime. But it is natural to assume that an anxiety of this kind would be reinforced by strong interpersonal tensions. In childhood, however, this belief becomes a part of the reality system, and the anxiety is controlled by appropriate defenses and precautions which become institutionalized. Thus the excretory function becomes associated with a special set of ideas laden with anxiety. These ideas are different from those we encountered in Tanala, where the associated idea was neither cleanliness nor fear of poisoning, but obedience. Several tension-release systems depend on which of these ideas becomes associated with the excretory function. The anxiety system just described can be represented thus:

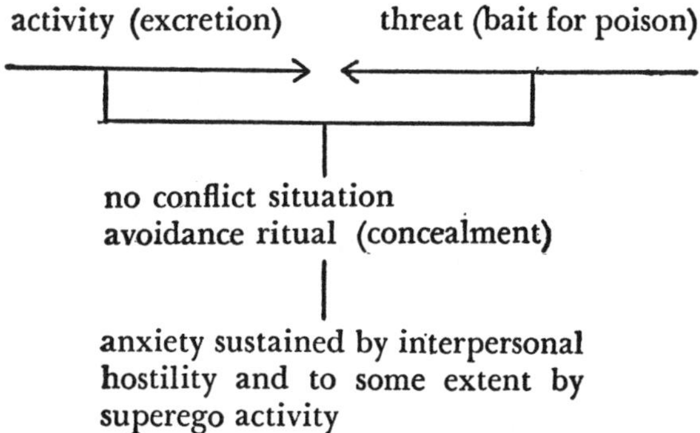

A system like the one described can outlive by centuries the original circumstances that gave it origin, whose meaning can no longer be reconstructed. Among certain tribes of the Navaho the practice of concealing excreta has disappeared owing to the influence of whites. It would be interesting to know whether the disappearance was facilitated by the diminution of interpersonal hostilities and mutual suspicion.

In relation to these systems the question of the place of primitive taboo systems arises. The taboo systems may differ in origin. For the greater part they are taught as a part of the external reality system, in much the same way as we are taught to avoid a live electric wire. The relation of taboo systems to the culture as a whole cannot be precisely defined. We would expect them to be compatible with the basic personality structure. At the same time, as in our culture, many taboos are likely to persist in spite of the fact that no precise relationship to basic personality structure can be established.

In this hierarchy of systems in the basic personality structure there are the purely rational or scientific systems, subject to direct demonstration and discarded when proven wrong. This hierarchy of systems in basic personality structure can be arranged as follows:

1. Projective systems based on experience with the aid of rationalizations, generalizations, systematization and elaboration. To this category belongs the security system of the individual and superego systems, that is, those dealing with conscience and ideals.
2. Learned systems connected with drives.
3. Learned systems in which no drives are involved but ideas associated with activities.
   Groups 2 and 3 lay the basis for specific psychosomatic tension release routes.
4. Taboo systems, all learned as part of reality.[5]
5. Pure empirical reality systems, subject to demonstration.
6. Value systems and ideologies (which cut across all the previous systems).

At this point it is important to decide the position of *value systems.* They cannot be placed in any of the categories above. Some value systems belong to ideals, for example, honesty; some value systems derive from ideas associated with activities and hence directly taught, for example, cleanliness. Others derive from a social complex which precipitates out qualities having a high value at one time and not at another. Such a value is "freedom," which can never be defined in absolute terms but only in relation to the particular conditions which create an issue about it. No Comanche or Alorese would have any conception of freedom in the sense in which it is commonly used today in our society.

The question of ideologies presents the same difficulties as value systems. They are compounds of projective systems, in the interest of which empirical evidence is mobilized, and have therefore the same structure as rationalizations.

These are all constituents of the basic personality structure but they are not homogeneous; they vary in the degree of conscious representability and in the degree to which they are modifiable. Group 1

---

[5] The inclusion of taboo systems was suggested by Dr. Linton.

is completely unconscious and can only be identified through its projective manifestations, from which source it can be traced back to the institutions which gave it origin. This system is least susceptible to modification except by way of the institutions which gave it origin. All the other systems are subject to validation by some kind of empirical demonstration. Group 5 is subject to direct demonstration; the others are held in place by a chain of rationalizations of which the following is typical. A native of Alor tells us that his younger brother falls ill and is given appropriate medicine. The boy does not recover. His father, a seer, divines that he has failed to get well because a pair of carabao horns was stolen from the hearth. The carabao horns are replaced and the boy gets well. This is a closed system of rationalizations that cannot be beaten. If the boy had failed to get well with the replacement of the horns, some other explanation would have been offered. The manner in which these rationalizations are defended by the natives is fantastic in its tenacity. The commonest of all rationalizations used is that "everything was done right, but it was too late." This leaves the system intact. Why are these systems maintained on such "flimsy evidence" concerning their efficacy? Because they cannot be readily replaced and because a bad system has better anxiety-staying powers than no system at all. Systems like this present a never-ending, vicious logical cycle.

The viability and modifiability of these systems (1 to 5) is indicated in the order they are presented. This order is important in attempting to evaluate the extent to which diffusion of culture can take place. The most easily diffused are the manipulative and purely empirically derived reality systems, and manipulative techniques whose utility value is directly discernible. The least modifiable are those systems which are unconscious and those in which only parts are conscious, the rest being maintained by deep-rooted emotional interests.

The Biography as Social Source Material

Constructing a biography is one of the most difficult of psychological enterprises. As in the description of a society, we have here a wide range of things to look for. Dollard [6] has demonstrated several points of view from which the life history can be documented, each varying in emphasis and selection. This much is certain: we cannot leave to

[6] John Dollard, *Criteria for the Life History* (New Haven, Yale University Press, 1935).

chance or to the narrator's discretion or prejudices the selection of material he gives us. Dollard defines this undertaking as "a deliberate attempt to define the growth of a person in a cultural milieu and to make theoretical sense out of it." Taking an adequate biography involves a knowledge of the culture in which the subject lives; the pattern of his personal accommodations to it, created by the specific circumstances of his environment throughout life; and finally some theoretical scheme for arranging the data.

It is important to know the culture in which the individual lives because everything he tells us is attuned to its values and emphases. The subject does not, however, know his own culture as an arbitrary arrangement of institutions. He is a product of it and he has no insight into what made him what he is. He is only aware of those places in his cultural milieu which gave him specific frustrations, gratifications, or other vicissitudes. Much that he tells us he takes for granted. For example, he has a working conception of the outer world which he began to learn about in his earliest perceptions. He has been "taught" certain ready-made interpretations of its nature and how to deal with it. This is what may be called his "reality system," and this he has in common with all other members of his society. Much of what he tells us is in terms of this particular reality system. If we do not understand this, we can never follow what he is trying to impart to us. We must, in other words, understand the particular environment in which he operates and the particular methods he has for dealing with it.

The vicissitudes he describes to us as his life story include much about the human beings in his milieu and the specific relations he has with them. We also note that this individual has a specific *character;* he has specific likes and antipathies, aptitudes, sympathies, avoidances, etc. We may also note that when similar circumstances arise in his life he tends to react to them always in a similar way. Thus Mangma (see p. 172) whenever he encounters a difficult situation runs away from it. He has a specific attitude toward women, not always contingent on the specific attributes of the woman. He has specific interests, such as gardening, and we note this fact because it is an unusual interest for a man in Alorese society. He has certain attitudes toward himself; he is sensitive, and tends to impress us with abilities he does not have. When we describe his character we are describing attitudes toward himself and toward others and behavior patterns which tend to be repetitive; so when we know his character, we know his idiosyncratic traits, what to expect of him, and how to get on with him when we need to.

But we cannot be guided exclusively by what he tells us about himself. We must observe him in the actual process of living from day to day. If we do not, we shall miss some very important data. Moreover we must try not only to follow him in his daily activities, we must know, if it is possible, what he dreams at night. We must assume that our subject will try to put as good a face on his story as possible, and hide all he regards as damaging. If possible, he must be given an incentive to tell about himself honestly. And if an interpreter is present who is a member of the same society as the subject, we are bound to get a highly edited account. However if we observe his day-to-day activity, note his reactions to the ethnographer, and cross-check on his dreams, we can distill from all this a reliable story of his life and a dynamic picture of his personality.

When we have all this data we face the most difficult task of all, the theoretical framework in which it will be encompassed. We cannot use a purely descriptive scheme, for a string of qualifying epithets like "sensitive," "anxious," will not help us much. We must use a dynamic scheme and use it genetically so that we can consistently trace the growth of the individual and so appreciate his motivations. We must know the experiences he had which made him adopt certain modes of behavior and not others. In a large measure we have dealt with this problem in the derivation of the basic personality structure, and there is not much need to repeat it.

For the purpose of substantiating the thesis of this book one biography in a culture will hardly suffice. We must have an adequate sampling of sex, age, and status differentiations, and no arbitrary number can be regarded as adequate. We need a sufficient number to make adequate comparisons, but it is more important to find where the deviations are. As we progress in our study of biographies we note the banal fact that no two in the same culture are alike. But the deviants are as important to us as the norms.

The uses of the biographies are numerous. Here is our first chance to see whether our guess about the kind of personality a given set of institutions will create is at all approximated in reality. We can reverse the procedure and operate from personalities to institutions. It is only in a biography that we can see how the various institutions are functionally articulated.

Next comes the question of comparing the results of the biographies. The comparison with the basic personality structure will establish a sufficient number of points at which aberrations may appear. These aberrations do not vitiate but rather confirm the procedure of deriving basic personality structure. If, for example, we study eight biographies in a comparative way and discover that no two describe the same situation with respect to parental care, then we expect these differences to be registered in the personality structure in a very specific way. If Rilpada has in his character structure a few uncommon traits, such as a delicate conscience, a willingness to get on with his friends, a tendency to forgive and forget, and a tendency to idealize his father, we know that some influence not typical in this culture has been operating. We can locate this in the form of a powerful, solicitous, and intelligent father who devoted much time to his son.

The points at which we note character variations indicate not only differences in personal fate, but also differences in cultural practices. In a culture where maternal neglect is the rule, the exceptional case who gets good maternal care will show distinctive characteristics. This comparative aspect of biographical analysis is likely to be most informative where status differentiations include not only differences in the dominant interests of the individual but also differences in the factors which make for specific character formations. Thus in studying basic personality structure in our culture new differentiations must be made not only for sex and age, but especially for status. Current struggles in the modern world cannot be understood without a study of specific tensions arising out of the anxieties and claims of each status.

Reality Systems and Culture Configurations

In our survey of psychological techniques we found psychoanalysis best suited to our needs because it established certain laws governing mental processes not accounted for by other psychologies. A great deal of stress was laid on the genetic aspects, because if we must study integrational systems we must begin at the beginning. The value of the whole genetic approach lies in its being able to show us how certain integrational systems come into being; and we made it our special concern to track down those systems we designated as projective, in contrast to those of taught or rational origin on the basis of which scientific systems are built. In every society studied we found evidences of these two systems. The empirical reality systems we found in the manipulation and making of tools, the knowledge of planting, and so forth; the projective systems in religion, folklore, and many other systems.

These two types of mental process depend upon different orders of experience. The differentiating feature is not that one has an emotional constituent and the other not. Both have emotional components. Rational thinking is driven by curiosity and has such goals as mastery and utility. The emotional component of projective thinking is made up of all those affects which accompany human relations. In the systems built on a projective basis the conclusions drawn do not depend on any fixity in nature, but on sequences which are contingent on institutionalized practices conveyed by parents or other people in the environment of the growing child. Hence our interest in the genetic aspects. The experiential base of a projective system is generally forgotten; its only remains in the personality are to be found in the conditioned perceptions, meanings, affects, psychosomatic reactions, and behavior. It is a feature of such projective systems that they are capable of extension upon situations which have no actual resemblance to the experiences on which they were based. This may be called *symbolic extension*. Projective systems are established under the influence of the pleasure principle, avoidance of pain, or expediency. The conclusions on which projective systems are based are not inherent but are the record of traumatic experiences. Projective systems are therefore excrescences developed from nuclear traumatic experiences within the growth pattern of the individual. Just as the character structure of the individual has a large component of these projective systems, so the basic personality in any culture contains them. The fewer the anxieties in the growth pattern, the simpler the projective system (Comanche). It is these systems which have given rise to the complaints about the "irrational" factors in society. Their purpose is adaptive, to relieve the mutilating effect of painful tensions. In practice they often miscarry in ways which will be specified.

The interconnections between these two systems are not simple.[7]

---

[7] There is one additional point that must be noted about projective and rational systems: that there is no difference between the actual logical or ratiocinative processes in

In infancy the two are connected at the point of maternal care. Good care which fosters growth leaves the child more enterprising and self-confident, free to exercise curiosity and manipulative capacities. Too great dependency on the mother paralyzes the development of curiosity and manipulative skills. It is not infrequent that one finds very pathological characters with brilliant intellects; yet the intellect is saddled with the task of solving these problems involving the projective systems, without success. But the record of the attempt is written into the symptoms the subject brings. Among primitive peoples it does not follow that where maternal care is good, the child is always enterprising. Other factors are apparently responsible. The two systems can be represented thus:

Schematic Representation of Projective Systems

Nuclear experiences which define apperceptions and emotionally directed
  interests, e.g., punishment for delinquency

Abstraction and generalization
    e. g., "If I am obedient I will suffer no pain."

Projection and systematization
    e. g., "I am ill, therefore I have wronged."

Rationalization = ideology = a system to overcome tensions

"There is a supreme being who observes my behavior. He has the attributes of omnipotence and omniscience, etc. If I do wrong I will be punished. If I suffer I will be reinstated." Once this system is accepted as a reality, any number of rational systems can be devised to "prove" it, to modify it, or to render it workable.

Schematic Representation of Rational Systems

Perception by sense-organ combinations and motor coördinations
  = meaning = utility

Objective = to exploit, avoid, manipulate, destroy

Attitude to object = interest, curiosity, systematization
  = knowledge = science

No projective mechanism used and no repression required for correction; no social obstacles put in its way today (there were in the Middle Ages)

The projective and rational systems each furnish a basis for cultural configurations or institutional patterns. We are much less con-

---

the two systems. The difference between them lies rather in the subject matter on which these mental processes are exercised.

cerned with the morphological aspects of these institutional patterns than we are with the problem of dynamics of social change and of social stability. All societies have institutional patterns based on both projective and rational systems; no culture can be dominated by either one to the exclusion of the other. But it makes a great deal of difference for cultural stability and change whether the institutions are polarized toward either one or the other system.

Furthermore, in the practical thinking of everyone in every society a mental mechanism is used which is compounded of both projective and rational components—that is, rationalization. This term merely means a logical or "reasonable" series of arguments to support an unconscious motive, drive, or interest. The simplest form of rationalization is the "explanation" offered by a person who has just carried out a post-hypnotic suggestion. The most complicated forms of rationalization are to be found in social ideologies. This does not mean that every ideology is a rationalization; it can approximate the scientific only when freed of bias or defense of interest.

If we consider a culture like Tanala, dominated by projective systems, we find that these systems define the nature of the outer world, man's personal fate, and supernatural beings and methods for dealing with them. These were all derived from constellations established in connection with training begun in infancy and consistently followed throughout life. This is the psychological definition of *animism,* a term which has by usage been narrowed to connote the projection of human attributes on inanimate objects. This latter phenomenon is the most naïve expression of this tendency to projection, but by no means its only form.

The importance of this whole system is its derivation from *actual experience.* Why do the Tanala believe that no remedy is effectual unless accompanied by some compulsive ritual? Because their actual experience has led them to the conviction that all good things happen after obedience to some arbitrary command. This constellation is created in the Tanala by experience beginning at six months, when they are expected to have complete sphincter control and are beaten if they fail, and is followed by similar disciplines throughout their normative years. This means in effect that a conclusion of limited application is generalized to encompass the whole of reality and that this reality is evaluated and reacted to on the basis of a pain-avoiding principle, obedience, which not only furnishes no reliable picture of external reality but prevents the formation of any other. The fact is that in this culture obedience actually brings rewards in the form of comfort and security. This nuclear constellation, a logical deduction, creates an unconscious base from which any number of projective systems can arise; hence it becomes a part of their common sense; and to expect that phenomena in the outer world will follow the same pattern is not unreasonable, but it is not rational empiricism. The Tanala also have a firm belief in fate, which can to some extent be altered by magic. This idea, which looks like pure "ideology," is likewise derived from experience. The authority of the father is absolute, and status is so fixed within the family that there is no escape from it. This situation is so universal that anyone who did not hold this belief would be decidedly out of contact with the socially effective realities. But this relationship between the derivatives and the original experience is completely unconscious. Such a belief in fate is not held by the Alorese; their experience conduces to no such idea. In other words the ideologies of primitive peoples are generalizations and abstractions of actual experience and not the product of unbridled imagination. That these ideologies give the impression of being wanton and arbitrary is due to the fact that we do not have the key to understand them.

There is still another important sequel to these considerations among the Tanala. This personality with its peculiar common sense is attuned to a particular set of institutions and adjusted to a particular type of economy accompanied by special techniques suited to the environment—the dry cultivation of rice. When the exhaustion of jungle compelled the abandonment of the dry-rice method for the wet method, a great many unpleasant consequences followed. For the first time there was a scramble for the fertile valleys, the family organization was broken up, and the old communal ownership of land gave way to private ownership. Since the personality was not geared to these new conditions, the consequence was that there was a great increase in anxiety, in mutual rivalry and hostility, in black magic and hysterical illnesses, created by the absence of adaptive techniques in the face of new and insistent realities.

We can draw the conclusion from Tanala that a culture in which external reality is evaluated by projective systems, the adaptability of the society is much impaired. The external reality can be manipulated in a limited number of ways if perceived in accordance with the analogy of an all powerful father and an obedient child. When the father's power gives out, as it did in Tanala, only disorganized aggression and panic could ensue. The individual who deals with the outer world on the basis of obedience can develop no sense of responsibility for his own fate and cannot therefore develop those manipulative powers of which he is capable. The intensity and cruelty of an exacting superego is no surrogate for responsibility for oneself. All the suffering the individual inflicts on himself as a consequence of superego demands have no relevancy to the external world, or to the difficulties within the social order.

Another illustration of the principle found in Tanala occurs in medieval cosmology. Thomism is a conception of the world based upon the same principle as in Tanala—a powerful father whose commands are natural law. But here a new factor is introduced in the system, not present in Tanalan cosmology, a conception of natural law. But it stands under the aegis of divine command. This idea is compounded of two elements: of an empirical reality system—natural law—and a projective system; but this empirical system is drawn under the influence of projective constellations. It may be called a compromise. But if natural law is only another of the many instances of divine will, the attitude of the individual to natural law is not modified. It is no invitation to manipulate natural law to the needs of the individual; nor does it augment his sense of responsibility in dealing with natural law. As long as natural law is only a new manifestation of divine will, then one's security does not depend on manipulating reality, but on submission to divine will. The projective screen may be mistaken for reality and important changes in adaptation will be attempted by way of this projective screen, while the social realities are either ignored or they drift aimlessly.

When natural law was finally freed from its contingency on divine will—and the lives of Galileo, Descartes or Pascal are witness to the fact that this was not an easy task—it is reasonable to expect that it would have altered man's conception of himself, his relations to deity, and to the outer world. Under the impact of these alterations in responsibility for oneself, a new freedom to exercise investigative and exploratory impulses must take place. With it there must be a redefinition of the relations to deity, a new allocation of the superego or conscience mechanisms. In the face of these alterations new social changes were bound to follow. But all this does not necessarily mean that natural law was interpreted to mean that the social order itself came under the domination of scientific thinking. The social order would have to improvise its organization as it went along under the impact of the new interpretation of the outer world and its mastery.

We have noted some high points in the accomplishments of that movement in Western history which began with the Renaissance, through the Reformation, down to the present. The social order was never regarded as coming under the influence of natural law. The abortive attempts to make natural law apply to the social order in the so-called Age of Reason were unconsciously polarized in the direction of justifying the expediencies which accident had provided.

The social order, and its institutions, is the source of all projective systems, and when a conception of external reality is based upon this source it is not to be expected that we can derive from it any implements which can serve us as a critique of the very sources from which it originates. This is like trying to lift oneself by the bootstraps. The only hope lies in subjecting the social order to the same kind of critique that was applied to the outer world with so much success. This and only this would mean a triumph for scientific over projective techniques.

That a society which is dominated by projective techniques lacks adaptability can be amply illustrated by contrasts found in the cultures described in this book. In Comanche we have a culture which is least dominated by projective thinking. Their religion is devoid of complex ideologies, though a superior being is recognized. These thin ideologies are completely devoid of any power to affect the stability of the society. Their mythology is largely a carry-over of the culture from which it originated. Otherwise it consists largely of the exploits of former war chiefs. The poverty of projective systems is due not to their lack of imagination but rather to the accidental fact that in the growth pattern of the individual no serious tension points are created which cause the formation of compensatory systems to overcome the mutilation of expressive impulses, sexual or otherwise. In Alor we see a culture in which projective systems are poor in organization because too many and confusing tension points are created in the growth pattern so that the individual is overwhelmed by them and can never create any effective organization. In our culture, like that of Tanala, we find a very rich excrescence of projective systems which are highly organized and capable of influencing stability because the growth pattern has numerous tension points, though not enough to overwhelm the individual. There are also in our culture, as in Comanche, strong ego fortifying factors.

When a society has a highly elaborate projective system, there is the strong temptation to change adaptation by alterations in the projective screen. This is generally no more effective than for a patient who has a phobia for subways to use the bus instead; doing so does not remove the phobia and leaves all the factors which cause the phobia untouched. Such adaptive maneuvers abound in the history of Western society. In certain areas the adoption of Christianity originally was such a maneuver. It altered the projective system, but left completely alone the social realities which cause this particular system to be formed, just as the cult of Osiris left the sufferings of the agrarian proletariat alone while it offered an illusory deferred compensation in the form of a boon collectable after death. In short the adaptation is crippled by the apparent validity of illusory compensations as compared with real ones. The fantasy or projective screen hides social realities, and one cannot come to grips with them because the fantasy screen itself becomes the chief object of preoccupation and is mistaken for the reality to be dealt with. By the same token gratifications in the projective system can be accepted for real ones—for a while, at any rate.

The question as to which of these mental processes predominate forms a crucial chapter in the history of Western society. Generally it can be said that since the Renaissance the projective systems have been much altered, when compared with early Christianity. Why is this factor so important? The alteration of the life of Western man is not limited to the more accurate knowledge of the outer world. This greater scientific knowledge brought with it great alterations in the basic personality of Western man. It gave rise to a new conception of man in relation to himself, as well as to the outer world. This new conception is not describable in terms of freedom or liberty alone; it augmented the responsibilities of man for his own welfare, and helped to define this welfare in new terms, and so to define new social and personal objectives. This story of the changes is not, however, without its comic and tragic aspects. This change not only redefined relations to the deity; through its promotion of mercantilism and manufacture it indirectly had a hand in setting in motion forces which eventually led to the elimination of feudalism and to promote the predominance of the bourgeoisie with all the accompanying blessings and evils. But these were all indirect results. The most significant consequence was the alteration of the whole superego system. All this was not a planned change, but an unconsciously systematized series of alterations, in connection with which some significant oversights were committed which did not come home to roost for hundreds of years.

The development of scientific reality systems had therefore a powerful influence in altering not only the manipulation of the outer world but the social order as well, which had to accommodate itself to the new goals. These social changes which make Western history of the past four hundred years were not planned but were improvised.

In our work in this book we can put the projective screen to good use as a diagnostic indicator of changes in the social order. Much of recorded history follows the fate of this fantasy screen rather than the social realities of which they are merely the shadow.

What was once true of the projective screen is now true of the history of social ideologies. But in evaluating social ideologies we are no longer working with a pure product of projection, but rather with a rational system polarized in the direction of unconscious motivations. The more free an ideology is of the latter, the more likely its validity and the more closely it can approximate scientific conclusions. These are the operational principles to be used in surveying two primitive cultures and one segment of Western society.

CHAPTER III

THE COMANCHE

Compiled from information supplied by

Ralph Linton

THE COMANCHE INDIANS live at present in the area known as the Texas Panhandle and in southwestern Oklahoma. They came there from the Montana plateaus and were originally closely related both ethnically and linguistically to the Shoshone. In their marauding and nomadic life they came to operate over a large territory extending as far south as Mexico. The exact time of migration of the Comanche cannot be definitely fixed. They arrived in their present location between the time of the Pueblo revolt and the return of the Spaniards, 1680–1690.

The northern Plateau origins of the Comanche and their linguistic relation to the Shoshone are important landmarks in a study of their culture. Evidence points strongly to the fact that many features of their original culture were completely forgotten, and that they tended to accept constant changes in their ways of living. This adaptability they retained even after contact with the whites. When finally defeated, they adapted themselves successfully to the new ways forced upon them.

The Plateau Culture

On the Plateau the life of all the tribes was dominated by hard economic conditions. The high, arid sagebrush territory offered little in food resources. These were mainly wild vegetable foods, roots, and seeds, some deer and antelope and other small game. In connection with the antelope there developed an extensive body of magic and ritual. Though seeds were harvested and stored in season, the food supply was precarious, and as few as ten people could rarely live together in one spot for any length of time.

The pattern of life was migratory, although throughout the winter the Plateau people remained in sheltered valleys where they could find protection from the high winds, and where fuel and open water were available. In summer they moved camp frequently. Each local unit had its own district within which it traveled about. But there was no clear family ownership of domain, and in spite of the exceedingly hard food conditions there was no punishment for trespass. Families could move about freely into each other's territory. The term *family* means these little camping groups.

The material culture of the Plateau period was extremely simple. The people lived in crude, temporary brush shelters. Mortars were used for crushing seeds, and fairly good basketry was made, although it was not comparable with that of California. They used crude wooden bowls and probably pottery. However, the amount of goods any family could accumulate was limited by the transport problem. They moved camp during the summer season at intervals of a week or less, depending on how long it took to exhaust the available foods. In moving, all goods were carried on the women's backs. Dogs were kept only as pets.

Social organization was rudimentary; scarcely any political organization existed. A number of local camp groups, or families, would gather a few times a year, in seasons of plenty, for a dance. The maximum size of such a group was probably 200 or 300 people, and the meetings were of three or four days' duration, commensurate with available food. This was their nearest approach to a band organization. The composition of these groups varied. The family belonging to one group one year might go over to another the next.

The Plateau tribes had no chiefs; the few men who had influence were always medicine men. Later, when the Shoshone tribes came into contact with the whites, a pattern of chieftainship emerged, stimulated partly by the fact that after they got horses groups could stay together; and partly because the whites found it more convenient to deal with one man than with a fluid group.

In their social organization the basic unit seems to have been the family group consisting of a man, or a man and his brothers, with their wife or wives, sons, daughters, their spouses and children. Considerable respect for age, as such, existed, extending to old women as well as to old men and resulting in a passive dominance of the old. The older men knew the territory and could give sound advice to the youngsters.

There was no clan organization of any kind. A simple bilateral incest rule, much like our own, was observed. Social organization was subordinated to the exigencies of the food supply. One married where one could and where the group was of the size which the territory could support. Fraternal wife-lending and even polyandry were practiced, as well as the customary marriage of a deceased wife's sister. There was no bride price and marriages were unstable, the partners separating at will. Within the family there was a relationship of mutual respect between parents-in-law and sons-in-law and also between brother and sister, but this respect did not extend to strict avoidance rules.

Families tended to be matrilocal, though the young couples adapted themselves to whichever group had a surplus of supplies at the time. Courting was initiated by the young people themselves, few marriages being arranged by the elders. Women occupied an inferior position although they did their full share in providing food; but they were rarely mistreated. There was little jealousy or mutilation of wives for faithlessness. Rigid menstrual taboos in an isolated menstrual hut were observed because it was believed contact with women at such times destroyed a man's hunting efficiency.

A technique of birth control deliberately limited the population. Infanticide was probably practiced as well. Yet adoption of children with the consent of the parents was customary. Parents gave away their children quite readily to someone who could take better care of them. This had interesting repercussions later because it became interwoven with the whole pattern of treating captives.

Puberty ceremonies for both sexes were calculated to give skill in later occupations, especially to make boys good hunters.

In contrast with the later Comanche, these tribes were completely without war patterns; they did not fight each other even over trespass. Although they were frequently raided for slaves by fiercer neighbors, they always ran away. They considered themselves humble and harmless people, content to spend their time hunting.

In the Plateau tribes there were numerous medicine men who used their skill for benevolent purposes, and they were usually paid fixed but small fees. The main powers of the medicine men were secured through dreams in which a supernatural being appeared to the individual and gave him certain songs and methods of procedure. Apparently not much transfer of power took place from one individual to another.

The formal religious beliefs of the Plateau people included a vaguely defined Great Spirit, ultimate source of all powers. Rarely did such a being interfere in human affairs. The people also had a lively fear of ghosts, but an extreme vagueness about future life. Believing that ghosts lingered near by at death, they moved camp immediately, burned the shelter in which the person had died, and destroyed all his belongings, including everything that had been in contact with him. Death was polluting, mainly because of the fear of the ghost. No one would go near the house site of a dead man for several months after his death.

Though medicine was elaborate, lack of malevolent magic is noteworthy. However, the medicine man's power could be used for malevolent purposes. Occasionally medicine men were commissioned to kill someone; but deadly magic was used reluctantly, for if the powers were not worked off, the surcharge would be fatal to members of the medicine man's own family. Certain simple prohibitions and taboos were connected with each of the medicines.

Animals provided a source of power. A general force and power lay behind everything. Certain animals had it, as certain men had it; the being with power would appear in dreams and bestow power upon the dreamer.

It was out of some such background that the historic Comanche culture developed. Apparently the Comanche came south following the foothills of the mountains, arriving first in the sand-hill country of Nebraska and then moving on into southern Oklahoma and Texas. The Comanche held a centralized position, a no-man's-land in relation to the whites. On one side was New France, on another New Spain, and to the northeast, the Americans brought pressure. During the colonial period the Comanche raided New Spain for horses and captives, selling them both to the east. They became one of the great distributors of horses in the Plains. Subsequent to the Louisiana Purchase (1803), when they had the United States on one side and Spain on the other, the Comanche raided the United States side and sold their loot to New Spain. In this manner, they grew rich and adroit, becoming racketeers. The Pueblo peoples constantly complained about how the Comanche came ostensibly to trade, but actually to rob them. When the Comanche could no longer sell captives, they stole children whom they held for ransom. They also became great cattle rustlers, moving many cattle from Texas into New Mexico. It was not until the Comanche were finally put on reservations that these practices were stopped.

These people were really raiders more than traders, for they rarely paid for anything. They took what they wanted by force until trading posts were established on the reservations. The only trading they did was when wagon trains came up from Mexico under a truce, bringing things they needed—ammunition, salt, blankets, etc. Although they were constantly raiding the Mexicans, they maintained contact with them, sending messages via sheep herders, who were unarmed neutrals whom it was unsporting to kill.

The country over which they roamed was rich from the point of view of natural resources; it consisted largely of prairie, with many rivers running through it, abundant supply of wood in the valleys, and good grounds for winter camping.

Comanche Plains Culture

The subsistence economy was consistent with the Comanche's nomadic life. Vegetable foods were used mainly for variety. These consisted of berries and roots, gathered chiefly by the women. Meat was the most important article of diet and was obtained by hunting the buffalo, which was abundant at all seasons. This easy accessibility of buffalo rendered the Comanche largely independent of communal hunting. Scarcity of meat rarely lasted more than two or three days.

Antelope was unimportant for food; it was hunted chiefly for its hide, which was used for clothing. But it had a ritual significance—a carry-over from the old Plateau culture, because there was hunting medicine and an elaborate ceremony connected to it. This ritual did not obtain for the buffalo hunt. Deer, black bear, and smaller game were also hunted, but mainly by the young boys. Rabbits and prairie dogs, shot by boys and women for sport, did not figure in the economy. Birds, particularly the eagle, were killed for their feathers, but were usually taboo for food.

Hunting was a man's business, but some women took part for the sport. Far from being a bad influence for hunting, women sometimes were very expert and won reputations as archers. Girls and young women often went along on the buffalo hunts but they went after small game, not the buffalo. The buffalo was hunted both individually and in a communal hunt. In the communal hunt the men lined up on horseback and charged the herd to stampede it. Then, riding up on the animals from the rear, the men drove arrows into them at short range.

Game ownership was proved by marked arrows and was never the subject of quarrels. Some of the meat was dried and stored, but no large accumulation of supplies was necessary. If several men went out together on an individual hunt and made a buffalo kill, they followed a kind of war pattern; each man as he reached the kill grabbed a leg, or some other part of the animal, which entitled him to that portion. This plenitude of food is strikingly verified by the fact that there are no stories of serious food shortage in the mythology, with the one exception of the widespread Plains myth of "letting out the buffalo." People ate whenever they wanted to, four or five times a day, as there was always food around. Any visitor was immediately offered food.

Among domesticated animals, the horse was naturally of the greatest importance. The Comanche raised and traded horses extensively; they ate horse meat with relish. Horses were given as gifts, as fees to medicine men—in fact, they became the principal medium of exchange. The horse was an appliance or instrument rather than a personality. Dogs, on the other hand, were regarded as distinct personalities. Many stories were told of their peculiarities and they were all individually named. Black bears also became pets. These bears were caught as cubs and treated almost like members of the family, being considered almost human.

Material Culture

The material culture of the Comanche was of the ordinary Plains pattern, supplemented from an early period by a tremendous amount of loot—blankets, cloth, guns, iron tools, etc. The chief industry was preparation of hide for clothing and tipis. The men made their own bows and arrows and did a little work in wood and stone, stone pipes, etc. They used iron arrow heads; the bottom of a frying pan often furnishing them with the iron. The women made, owned, and pitched the tipis, tanned the hides, and made the clothing for both sexes when it was not trade goods; a man's best clothes were of buckskin. They made no basketry or pottery. Utensils were mainly of hide. The Comanche obtained and used the iron kettle for cooking so early that they have forgotten their former methods.

The Comanche used scarcely any beadwork. At most a narrow line of beading was put at the bottom of a man's leggings or around the hem of a woman's dress. A peculiar design, like a trident with several points, was painted on the robe worn by a first wife. The number of points symbolized the number of men the husband had killed. Otherwise garments were not painted. Some semi-naturalistic paintings were connected with medicines; these were used principally on shields. In this case the painting was done exclusively by men. Comanche decorative fringing made up for the lack of good beadwork. The Comanche costume was handsome, but more restrained than that of the northern tribes. The men were exceedingly proud of their appearance and their fine clothes and of having their faces properly painted.

Property

Individual ownership of all objects was recognized, but hoarding or accumulating material wealth was not practiced, except for horses. Most of the loot from raids was dispersed by the warriors who had taken it, shortly after their return. Gifts were made to honor a son; that is, any gift presented to a boy was expected to be returned by his father with a much larger gift. A constant turn-over of objects thus took place. There were no cases of fighting over wealth. Men tried to accumulate horses but gave and lent them freely. Generally horses were not given to children. However, if the father were killed and the children went to the mother's father, the father's father would give the children horses to make them more welcome to the mother's people. Women could own horses as well as tipis.

Many of the Comanche establishments were of surprisingly large size. Some polygynous families set up as many as five tipis; the minimum for a respectable family was a dwelling tipi, a sacred tipi—if the owner were a medicine man, to keep his sacred objects free from pollution—and a separate tipi for the adolescent son. Inside, the tipis were comfortable, with lazyback beds against the wall, a fireplace in the center, and various possessions hung on frames at the heads of the beds. The tipis were quite large, each one requiring ten buffalo hides.

On the march the Comanche needed four pack horses as a minimum, in addition to family horses; the buffalo and war horses were driven along with the herd. The packing of the horses for moving camp was done by the women, in a highly efficient and systematic way. A woman on the march knew where every object was. The peace chief picked the place for his tipi and the others selected their camp sites, always with the same neighbors as before on right and left. Groups moved frequently, sometimes because food was exhausted, but often simply because the camp was getting dirty. The marches averaged ten or twelve miles. Although each village moved as a unit and each family took the same position in it, families sometimes went off by themselves and remained apart for two or three years before rejoining the main camp group.

Social and Political Organization

The Comanche tribe was never a political unit. It varied from nine to fourteen bands at different times. Each of these bands, of from 100 to 300 people, occupied a vaguely defined territory, ranging within the natural limits of such an area. Every band had a nickname, Antelope Eaters, Wasps, etc. Each band differed slightly in its habits and dress. Families or individuals could shift from one band to another, but if they did so they were expected to take on the new band's customs. The bands were distinct entities but of somewhat shifting content. Each possessed a favorite dance and a "company" or group of warriors who performed this dance. The "company" did not include all men in the band, but it had no distinctive insignia and there was no development of society ritual.

The band moved together or broke up into separate camping groups according to the size of the unit and the character of the food supply. Sometimes bands split up because of quarrels between leaders, and new bands would be formed in this way. Sometimes one band would be at war with the Spaniards while the other groups were at peace; one band made peace with the Americans while the others were still fighting. The whole tribe did not assemble for the Sun Dance, but bands within easy reach were invited and came. In the 1870 Sun Dance, four bands got together, probably the largest number of Comanche ever assembled.

Each band had its own peace chief. He was always an older man, gentle, wise, and good to the women and children. He had no real authority, either executive or police, but the band respected him, and he used what pressure he could to settle minor disputes. The position was an honorary one, a sort of advisory office: he acted as announcer for camp movements after an informal council with the older men.

These councils of the older men took place in the evening around a fire. Those who had tobacco took turns as host. First the pipe was passed around. The pipe owner smoked first, putting his hands on the ground to call down a blessing. Then passing his hands over his body, he would blow smoke in the various directions before passing the pipe to the next man who would repeat the same ritual. After the smoking a general discussion ensued, which took up all decisions that referred to the group's movements, but no personal disputes. The old men recited their war deeds and boasted about youthful wife stealing and exploits in war, etc. The young men could sit in on these meetings but they rarely did; they regarded the old men rather contemptuously. The young actually played jokes on their elders in these meetings. The latter functioned in an advisory capacity, but had no say in the organization of war parties.

The most influential men in the bands were the war chiefs or leaders of war parties. They were warriors of recognized prominence, entitled to lead war parties by the general consent of the rest of the band. War chiefs kept their position as long as they were successful. A man who failed in several war parties would lose his standing. The highest war leader was chief of the "company" and was entitled to carry the war whip and take charge of the dances. These men exercised no formal civil authority, but they possessed great power through prestige. In reality they managed the tribe. They enlivened camp life with competitions. They always had supernatural powers, but they were rarely medicine men. Their medicines were believed to be specifically for war use and included healing medicines, but no malevolent magic. In spite of strong rivalry between war chiefs, not a single case is known in which one worked magic against another in order to interfere with his success; this would have constituted a foul, and the perpetrator would have lost all status. When war chiefs fought, they fought to kill.

There were no social classes of hereditary origin. However, a basic division differentiated the tribe into captives and full bloods. The Comanche took many captives for sale to other tribes, to augment their own numbers, or for ransom. On raids they carried off all the youngsters they could, taking adult women rarely, and never taking adult males; these were tortured and killed instead. They preferred to take youngsters about ten or twelve, old enough not to require much care and young enough to be acculturated. Girls were kept as house slaves, later becoming wives of their captors. The full-blooded wives were jealous of the captive women and mistreated them; they often made them do all the heavy work and in general made their lives miserable. The boys were set to work herding horses and at other menial jobs. As they grew up and learned Comanche ways, they were allowed to go on war parties. All places in the tribe became open to them on the regular prestige basis.

Some of the greatest war chiefs had been captives, but always a certain reproach attached to the fact, so that in a moment of anger one warrior might say to another, "Well, you are nothing but a captive"— good cause for a fight. These war leaders of captive origin often developed into the cruelest of the Comanche. The full enfranchisement of the captive came not only with war honors but even more with marriage to a Comanche woman. A hard-working young captive was in demand as a son-in-law, because such men, being in an unfavorable position, took better care of their wives and behaved much better to their parents-in-law than the full-blooded Comanche.

Top rank in Comanche society was attained by the fine warrior, still fighting and still able to lead war parties. When he was past the fighting age, his status declined quickly. The prestige of a man was reflected on his immediate family, on his wife and daughters, and to a lesser extent on his sons. However, prestige never became hereditary and constantly needed to be validated. An unsuccessful war party would lower a man, and a successful one would raise him up. The old men ranked below the men of fighting age; they were ranked on personal traits or the possession of medicine powers. An old man who was feared for his magic and not much respected might find himself in trouble. Wealth played no direct part in the ranking of individuals. The war leader had a greater turn-over of wealth from loot, and he was expected to dispense it with a free hand. As a result he would probably not be exceedingly wealthy.

The status of women depended entirely on that of their male relatives. The highest position a woman could obtain, aside from that of the very rare medicine woman, was as head wife of the leading war chief. In spite of the extreme competition between men for war honors, the importance of social ranking, etc., there were no true transvestites, that is, men who assumed the woman's role. Occasionally effeminate men enjoyed women's occupations and did not go on the war path. But Comanche men objected very strongly to homosexuality, an attitude almost as strong as our own.

As for family organization, no traces of clans have been found. The family group was much like our own except for the extensive polygyny of the head of the family. The old men, unless they were medicine men, were pensioners in the household, and the old women had to do most of the work.

Kinship

The basic key to the Comanche kinship system is the custom of intermarriage between two groups or fraternities; the fraternity was made up of members of the same generation level, real and classificatory siblings, that is, all cousins. There was no inter-fraternity exchange marriage, but the sororate and sororal polygyny were practiced, as were also the levirate and fraternal polyandry; the last, however, was rare. Also there was the anticipatory levirate, in which a married brother would allow his younger unmarried brother sexual relations with his wife, in the expectation that when the younger brother married, he would reciprocate the favor. Consequently there was little fraternal jealousy, but a great deal of extrafamilial jealousy. There was naturally no marriage between siblings. The feeling about brother-sister incest was strong.

The father-son relationship is one of respect and affection. The uncle-nephew relationship is one of indulgence and comradeship. The boy looks on his father as having mild authority and on his uncle, his mother's brother, as his comrade with whom he can take liberties. The mother-daughter and aunt-niece relationships are parallel.

As for brothers, their relationship is one of mutual helpfulness and affection. They are expected to stand together. The term "brother" receives most interesting extensions. A man who commits adultery or absconds with another man's wife is called brother by the man whom he has wronged. The offended husband may be standing ready with knife in hand to slit his throat, yet he addresses him as brother. The idea is that men who share a woman ought to be brothers.

Through an institution of formalized friendship, a man gets another brother, or "friend," who actually stands in a closer relationship than a real brother. They enter into each other's kinship systems and use the same terms in addressing each other's relatives. Marriage with the "friend's" sister would be regarded as incest. However, since these two are like brothers, the tendency would be for them to marry sisters; the result was that the term for the wife's sister's husband was "friend." Formal friendship was an important institution, so important that it over-shadowed the true brother relationship, and the term "friend" practically replaced "brother" linguistically.

There was a parallel "friend" relationship between women in which they took over the same kin terms and usually became plural wives of the same man. They treated each other as sisters.

Grandparents were generally great playmates of the children, and were treated kindly.

The brother normally had the power of giving his sister in marriage. Girls feared their brothers. However, an older sister of the classificatory type could act with authority over the small boys; she could scold them and transmit the mother's orders to the boys.

In regard to the in-laws, the basic principle was to classify them as consanguineal relatives whenever possible, in other words, to make them into blood relatives. This was a method of bridging the hostility which was potential in the in-law situation. For example, parents-in-law were made consanguineal relatives by calling them grandparents of one's children. Similarly, a daughter-in-law was called "mother of my son's children."

A joking relationship between brothers-in-law, characterized by teasing and sexual and practical jokes, was an important and enlivening element in the society.

Marriage

There was a strong tendency toward marriage within the band, but no fixed rule. In marriage outside of the band arrangements were usually informal, with no ceremony and no bride price. Marriages were variously contracted, the romantic method being most frequent. There was no seclusion of women and no premium was placed on virginity, but promiscuity was discouraged. The young people met away from camp or got together on berrying expeditions. The girls also visited the boys at night in their separate tipis. The Comanche felt that it was the women, particularly older women, who were aggressive in courting.

Boys often talked under the tipi edge to a favorite girl, then pulled out a tipi stake and crawled in to spend a large part of the night in her bed, getting away before dawn if he did not want to marry her. These contacts ended variously. If the couple suspected the opposition of the parents, or if some man had a previous claim, the couple would elope and return after a short time. Generally the marriage would then be accepted. If no opposition was expected, the boy simply slept late in bed with the girl, and the proper behavior for the father when he found them was to make the boy a brief and friendly speech—that is, that he was glad his daughter had found a husband—and invite him to breakfast.

Frequently marriages were arranged by the parent or the brother. Parents would try to attach some desirable man to the family, or if that could not be arranged, they would get some hard-working captive. The family would also arrange a marriage for the favorite daughter, disregarding in this case the nominal rights of the brother to give away his sister. By the marriage of a favorite daughter to a captive, the family would be able to maintain its control over the situation and not lose the daughter. If not otherwise specified, in the arranged marriage, the girl nominally gave the husband a claim to all of her sisters as wives when they grew up. These claims might be waived, depending on the status and temperament of the husband. A good old man might waive his claims, and he would be approved for doing this. A bad old man, especially a bad medicine man, would extend every claim he had, not because he wanted the girls but to collect damages from the young men who married them. There was a strong feeling that sisters made the best plural wives, but polygyny was not limited to sisters. Captive women were taken as wives, and also women from other families. The greatest hostility existed in these non-sororal households. One man had two wives who were so hostile to each other that each occupied only half a tipi, separately taking care of her own half.

The highest position in the household was that of the head wife, who was the oldest. On her death this office passed to the next younger sister. There was no rule as to the division of sexual favors among the wives.

The break-up of marriages was exceedingly frequent. The wife's family could take back their daughter if the son-in-law's treatment of her or her parents was unsatisfactory. Such separations usually took place early in the marriage. Couples might separate by common consent. If there was no other man involved, the husband's honor was not affected. Children usually accompanied the mother, but when they were old enough they could choose which parent they wished to stay with. The husband could discard a wife, or drive her off, but rarely did so; or a wife could leave her husband by eloping with another man.

Elopement was closely integrated with the prestige system. The wife joined a war party, placing herself under the protection of the head warrior. She did not leave camp with the party, but joined it later by stealth. Another pattern was for the eloping couple to join the war party together. The war party, completely under the war chief's orders, would fight the pursuing husband and his friends. The husband would ride in and demand that his wife be returned. But she never was returned, because this would cause the war chief to lose face. However the lover was supposed to pay damages to the husband before the matter was settled. The object of these damages was not to make money out of the affair, but to hurt the individual by depriving him of a favorite dog, a good buffalo hunting horse, etc.

The main thing involved in these constant conflicts over women was the injured husband's prestige. In some cases the husband would know what was going on and be good-natured about it, but if the adultery were talked about in public, he had to take action.

Institutionalized friendship, mentioned briefly before, was of great importance. Each man of any ability had a comrade-in-arms. The selection of this partner originated when the two went courting together as adolescents. Comrades-in-arms had complete trust and mutual confidence and were considered closer to each other than real brothers. A man turned to his "friend" for help before turning to his relatives. In battle, if one left the other on the battlefield, he would lose all prestige; they were supposed to stick together always. There seem to have been two types of "friend" relationship. In the first the partners were of equal status, and they had not only close friendship but also a joking relationship, with occasionally quite violent practical jokes. In the second form of "friendship," the partners were of unequal status. A man of low position or a captive would become "friend" to a full-blood of high status or a great warrior. He would accompany his "friend" on the war path and do everything for him—cook, take care of his bed, etc. In return, the "friend" would protect him and share his loot with him. Occasionally there was wife lending between "friends," but often, as two or three informants said, when a man offered his wife to his "friend," the latter would refuse to avoid jealousy.

War

War was the main activity of Comanche men, also the mainspring of the culture. The importance of war is shown in the high position of successful warriors, and in the constant narration of war exploits in ceremonies; and it is particularly emphasized in the folklore and biographies. The life story of the average old Comanche is nothing but a long collection of war stories. Other events—marriages, deaths —are mentioned casually as having taken place between such and such raids.

War parties were constantly going out, either for loot or for honor, frequently both. To end a mourning properly, a scalp had to be brought back and danced over. In addition, the young men went out continually on their own, to gain honors. In the old days, any band of the Comanche would have two or three war parties out at the same time.

The war chief always had supernatural power, but he was rarely a medicine man. Usually each party took along one individual with buffalo medicine; this was the primary healing medicine, the user of it acting as surgeon. The day before departure the party paraded through the camp in full regalia. That night there was a big dance, followed by much sexual promiscuity between the warriors and the unmarried women. An orgy on such an occasion is atypical for primitives in general, but here there was no sexual taboo in connection with war.

During the expedition everyone was under the absolute authority of the war chief. The main object of the raids was horses. Only the party whose leader had been paid to end a mourning had to take a scalp. Any serious loss of men reflected on the leader. Some raiding parties went only a short distance, won an initial success against the enemy, and returned, feeling the expedition had been validated. On the other hand there were long plundering raids down into Mexico, where the party would establish a base in enemy territory, make sorties out from it, and send loot back to the main camp. Some of these parties stayed out two or three years.

Before battle, all warriors painted and went through the medicine rituals. Just before the battle, each man gave his powers to all the other warriors; this could be done without loss because these Comanche powers were infinitely extensible. Even the great war chiefs shared their powers with each other, especially the power of invulnerability. There was no thought of payment; the act was a friendly one, and the power reverted to its owner after the battle.

When two opposing war parties met, the combatants came out between the lines riding up and down. A man with bear medicine would come out at this time and ride up and down the enemy line four times to show his invulnerability, while the enemy shot at him. After such preliminaries, the battle would begin in earnest. Charges were made back and forth, with attempts to get to close quarters and strike the enemy.

The system of war honors and coup-counting was simple compared with those of other Plains tribes. Two honors could be counted on each enemy; one went to the man who killed him, the other to the man who first touched him. The important thing, however, was not to get an honor but to kill the enemy. It was a point of honor to carry off one's dead and wounded, the wounded being more important than the dead. A brother-in-arms who left his brother wounded on the field of battle would lose respect completely.

The "Contrary Ones"

Contrary, backward behavior is common among Plains Indian tribes and frequently goes with membership in men's war societies of high rank, usually named Crazy Horse Societies. There was no such society among the Comanche, but there were "contrary" individuals.

These "contrary ones" smeared themselves with ashes or white paint and kept up their backward behavior around camp all the time. When it was cold they complained of the heat and took off their clothes. They were continually playing practical jokes. Once an old woman asked a "contrary one" to get her a buffalo robe. He said, "No, I won't," the equivalent of saying he would. He disappeared for several days and then brought back the skin of a Pawnee which he hung over the fence in front of the old woman's lodge. The skin scared the old woman when she came out in the twilight and saw it. Other people said, "Didn't you have sense enough not to ask a 'contrary one' to do anything for you? They are always joking." They were not particularly well liked, but people put up with them because of their extreme courage in battle. However, if a "contrary one" showed cowardice, when he got back from the expedition the men would bait and irritate him, attack and finally kill him.

This backward pattern of behavior is present in all the tribes to the north. It has perfectly defined formulas of action; if a "contrary one" agrees to something, this is his way of saying he will not do it. Usually "contrary ones" did not marry. They made up love songs and sang them where no one could hear. Women avoided them.

According to some informants, warriors who became sash wearers, thus proclaiming that they took an oath never to retreat from the enemy, had been called "contrary ones" in their youth. As little boys of nine or ten they had acted in a disobedient, contrary fashion, and as they approached manhood they continued to act in a backward, contrary way. Some "contrary ones" were cured of their negativism by a war chief who would take them out on a war party and see to it that they won honors.

Magic and Power

The business of war and war activities was pervaded by Comanche ideas of supernatural power. First of all, they had a concept of power throughout the universe, manifesting itself through natural phenomena, through animals, and through men. This power was impersonal, the equivalent of the "mana" concept.

This power was differentiated, and was directed by its holders, whether animals, men, or natural phenomena. Power could not be created by man, but it could be obtained from natural phenomena and animals and could be transferred from man to man. The greatest powers were the earth, the sky, and the sun, with which the eagle was felt to be associated. These great powers were the ones that punished the breaking of taboos. Sky power was never transferred to men. Earth power could be transferred only to a man who had been wounded and left for dead, who recovered without assistance and came back to camp alive. Certain mountains also had strong powers.

Next to the power of these great natural phenomena was that of the eagle. Other animals gave lesser powers. The bear gave invulnerability. The burrowing owl gave the power of being hard to hit. Beaver and buffalo gave power good for healing. Mountain lion power gave tremendous strength. Snake power gave the curing of snake bite.

Meadow lark power allowed a man to go directly home. No power was obtained from the horse or the dog, or from the coyote. The only love charm was based on minnow power.

In addition to these animals, there were certain powerful beings. Scalped man was the one spoken of most. A group of tiny black dwarfs who shot animals with invisible bows and arrows gave great power in hunting. An ogre, identified with the owl, was important in child training because the child was constantly threatened with this giant black owl with fiery eyes who comes to abduct bad children.

Power was transferable without loss to the donor, and, once acquired, was kept in the tribe by transfers, both temporary and permanent. Warriors transferred power temporarily to their comrades in battle. Permanent transfers were usually an act of friendship, not given for a fee. Older relatives or friends gave power to a boy to help him succeed. There was also the belief that powers could wear out. A strong power might gradually diminish in efficacy as time went on. A strong power might be transferred by the owner to four, eight, or twelve others without any loss to the original owner. Such a group, receiving a power, formed a medicine society. All members of such a society kept the same taboos and painted their shields with the same design. Most Comanche power was directed to war and healing.

Another interesting point in connection with power, probably unique with the Comanche, is that power might be obtained from the ghosts of medicine men. This was obtained through sleeping by the grave of the medicine man, not moving all night, no matter what terrifying thing happened. The ghost would then transfer the power asked for. Sometimes the sleeper would have a vision; in this the ghost did not come in human form but as a great wind and then a giant bird, which conveyed to him the power that he wanted.

If a man who had received power in this way tired of it, after middle age, he would return the power to the ghost. He would revisit the grave, ask the ghost to take back the power, then bathe ceremoniously and throw any medicine objects connected with this particular power into running water. After this ritual, he would be free of associated taboos.

The Medicine Man

Most powers were accompanied by objects of some sort which served as symbols and as focal points when they were transferred. The most important medicine objects were shields. They were painted in accordance with the vision of the man who had first obtained the power and were carefully covered until the actual moment of use, when the warrior went into battle. When not in use the shield was hung up outside the lodge facing the sun, being shifted around so that it would continue to face the sun all day long.

Every power had its taboos, mostly food taboos, although some affected conduct. Contact with grease was injurious to most powers, hence avoidance of grease was a war taboo. There was prohibition against passing behind the medicine man who possessed eagle power. Most bear medicine carried a taboo against eating the heart of any animal. One of the favorite ways of squaring accounts with or injuring a person was to make him break his taboo by feeding him some of his tabooed food without his knowledge. Violation of a taboo injured power and its holder. These taboos were often irksome, which is the reason young men gave for refusing to accept some powers and old men for abandoning their medicines.

All men, with few exceptions, possessed medicine power of some sort. The medicine man had power to an unusual degree; he was usually an old man who dealt in healing and divination and in malevolent magic. Young men might heal, but generally did not practice malevolent magic or divination.

Women, with a few exceptions, had no power before the menopause. After the menopause a woman could acquire power as readily as a man. It was common for a medicine man to have his wife assist him, teaching her everything that was required for curing, except rituals for the actual transfer of power. Immediately after the menopause the husband gave power to her. This was interpreted as a method by which the husband could provide for a wife in case she became widowed. Also, even before this power had been transferred, the wife had important functions in connection with the medicine man; many times she was approached by an emissary of the patient who requested her husband through her to take on the case. After the menopause, the distinction between the sexes, as far as medicine power went, was largely disregarded.

Divination was used to determine where the buffalo were or to find out what was happening to a war party long absent. But healing was the main function of the medicine man. Healing was done by singing over the patient twice a day for two days. Between singings he sucked out the sickness to destroy it. The most important part of the healing apparatus was a fan made from the feathers of different birds, held over the patient so that its shadow fell on the affected area. In cases of sorcery the fan would be held up and in the shadow of it the medicine man could see the face of the sorcerer.

However, the number of illnesses attributed to sorcery was small. Diseases were thought of not as material objects, but as kinds of insects, living things which had gotten into the body and caused the pains. To heal pneumonia, the medicine man moved his fan up and down over the breast of the sick man. As he sang, the disease came to the surface, and he could see it as a black spot on the skin, surrounded by a halo of light. He leaned over and sucked out the pain. The pain went down the medicine man's throat and stuck there. The healer said it felt like a hot coal on his tongue. Then he spat out a small black object and put it on the fire.

For his services, the medicine man usually received gifts. Sometimes he bargained for his fee in advance, but this was not considered good form. The medicine man was paid after recovery. If his efforts failed he would surrender the job to another medicine man. Payment was definitely connected with prestige. A patient paid what he could afford. A medicine man would be despised if he refused to take cases because the patient was poor.

In addition to healing, the medicine men, usually only the older men, held contests designed to show people the extent of their power. These general contests were held chiefly to impress the laity, occasionally to settle personal rivalries.

There are numerous stories of malevolent magic, but in practice it was rare. The test in such cases is the number of people in a community who believe that malevolent magic has actually been worked on them; the number was surprisingly small. Individuals who attributed sickness to supernatural causes were usually those whose medicine had been injured by an infraction of a taboo, or who had had some accident, such as meeting a ghost, which resulted in a stroke. Malevolent magic was never used between rivals of war age. Sometimes younger women used it against men in a rather special form. The men spoke of this with great reluctance, and it was considered the worst type of malevolent magic. The woman would climb up a mountain, cut off a piece of her own flesh, usually from her arm, and offer it to the sun. She would then bury the flesh under a stone with a prayer that as this wasted away, so might her male victim waste away. This had nothing to do with love magic, but was a means of getting even with a man. The motive for it was usually jealousy; it was the equivalent of husband poisoning. The men had likewise a magic against women who refused them; this would drive the woman crazy.

The old medicine men, on the other hand, were thought to use a great deal of malevolent magic, much of it motivated by jealousy. When a handsome young man was admired by the women, he would be in extreme danger from old men even if he let their wives alone. The old men hated good-looking young men and would sorcerize them out of sheer spite. They also used magic to guard their wives.

In this killing and inflicting of disease no bait was required. The method of dealing with sickness caused by malevolent magic was characteristic; the medicine man identified the disease as due to sorcery and indicated who the sorcerer was. The relatives of the sick person then visited the sorcerer, behaving very politely and asking him to cure the sick person. If he displayed any reluctance to do so, they brought pressure to bear. Payment in furs was usually offered as an inducement. If the sorcerer flatly refused to have anything to do with the case, or if he tried to cure the patient and failed, the relatives frequently killed him. The only alternative to this procedure was for the suspected medicine man to swear on the pipe by the earth and the sun that he was innocent of the accusation. If he did this, the relatives would wait for the next spring to see if he spoke the truth, because if he lied, he would be dead by that time. The killing of old medicine men was common with the Comanche and provided an effective check on the development of malevolent magic or blackmail techniques.

Ceremonies

The Comanche held two communal ceremonies: the beaver ceremony, and the Sun Dance. The beaver ceremony, which may have been borrowed from the Pawnee, was held to remove witchcraft and was beneficial to victims of tuberculosis. However, the whole group participated in order to get the benefits. Apparently this ceremony was concerned with contact with the earth medicine, which was purifying. As one informant said, anyone who took part in the ceremony felt that all evil influences and sickness had been washed away. The beaver medicine men had a bull-roarer which symbolized the beaver's tail. They went around outside scattering the ghosts with it.

It was customary for several men with beaver medicine to work simultaneously. Beaver medicine was dangerous; it might be malevolent and the man who had it was likely to be a sorcerer.

The Sun Dance was taken over by the Comanche in very recent times; they used much of the paraphernalia of the Sun Dance in the north, but the ceremony bore a typical Comanche interpretation. The last Sun Dance among the Comanche was held in the 'seventies. The primary purpose of this dance was to test the power of a new self-announced medicine man. The procedure usually was as follows: a medicine man would receive a supernatural sanction to give a Sun Dance through a vision. He would then invite others to coöperate. Young men would go through the rituals and dance, first two of them, then two others, and so on, in couples. They would be watched, and particularly the further war record of these men would be noted to see whether the medicine man's powers were authentic. By taking part in the dance, one received a transfer of power according to the general power transfer pattern. The form of the lodge and the exact ritual in each case was prescribed by the medicine men and differed from time to time. The men danced intermittently and were not supposed to eat or drink throughout the four days of the dance. However, some informants said that they were allowed to eat berries and fruits and drink the sap from the inside of the slippery elm. They were also allowed to go down to the spring and bathe under guard. (One good medicine man said they probably stole a small drink on the way.) The ceremony was a sheer endurance test, although it contained no aspects of self-torture. The men who participated were not in search of visions. They got power from the medicine man.

Folklore

Comanche folklore contains stories of different types. First of all, there are animal stories, mainly about Coyote, who was a trickster but often got the worst of it. There are in addition many stories of war exploits; they are semi-historical, but more or less embroidery is added to the facts. One epic of an actual Comanche chief is expounded almost indefinitely. The story is that the party of Comanche to which this boy belonged was killed and he was left as a baby, lying beside his dead mother. A Comanche war party came along several days later and found him still alive. The child had no clothing, and in order to keep him warm they wrapped him in the cover of a shield. By implication, this poor orphan received medicine in this way. He was brought up and adopted by one of the warriors who had found him. Then a long series of episodes are told of his war parties, most of them probably historical. There are many discrete episodes of war stories, of actual brave deeds, and real coup-counting stories and performances of a particular man at a particular place.

The story of the "magic flight" concerns children who were mistreated and ran away from home. They met an old woman, a child-eating ogress. She invited them to her tipi. The oldest of the three children, a girl, felt responsible for her younger brother and sister and, realizing what was taking place, kept awake all night. In the morning, on the plea of going down to the stream to get water, the children escaped. Then follows an account of the various obstacles they met. At the stream they asked a frog to help them; so every time the old witch called out to ask where they were, the frog called back, which is the explanation of the frog's croaking. But finally the witch realized the deception. The children ran to another stream where there was a crane. The crane lay down and allowed them to use her neck to cross the stream; but when the witch came along, the crane gave her the same privilege. The children next came to a buffalo bull, a buffalo cow, and a little red buffalo calf. They begged for protection, and the buffalo cow charged the old witch, but was killed. Then the bull charged, and the old witch killed him too. The little red calf butted the witch so hard that he sent her up into the moon—where she can still be seen.

The Comanche also have a creation story, which probably shows biblical influence. Then there is the story of the "letting out of the buffalo," which certainly belongs to the period before the horse. The story goes that one man had all the buffalo and kept them penned in a mountain. The people were hard up for food and had bad luck with their hunting. Coyote turned himself into an attractive puppy and played around outside the lodge of the man whom he suspected of withholding all the buffalo. He made friends with the buffalo owner's boy. The holder of the buffalo suspected that something was wrong—this puppy did not look quite right to him. He wanted to kill it, but the boy had taken it as a pet and insisted that it sleep with him. Boy and puppy got into bed together and through the night, from time to time, the father would come over and try to sneak the puppy out and kill it without awakening his son; but Coyote, who was very ingenious, would scratch the boy just before the father got there, and the boy would wake up. Finally, when morning came, the puppy went out and saw the father go over to an opening in the mountain. He drove out one buffalo to kill it. Coyote, in puppy form, leaped into the buffalo lodge and stampeded the buffalo who then scattered all over the plains.

There was one quite extraordinary story of a man whose wife died. He was determined to bring her back from the Land of the Dead, which lay somewhere over to the west. He made many pairs of moccasins and loaded up two horses with dried buffalo meat. He traveled many miles. Finally he had to leave the horses and food behind, but he continued on to the west and crossed the Divide. He arrived in the valley where the dead were camping. Everything there was very much as it is on earth, except that the lodges faced west instead of east. As he came into camp, the youngsters all looked and said: "Oh, there is a raw man," meaning a living man. He found the lodge of his wife. After some discussion his father-in-law allowed the wife to come in and said to him: "We will let you take her back to the Land of the Living, but you must let her follow you; you must never touch her or look or speak to her until you have crossed the Divide. Then when you get into the plains, kill a two-year-old buffalo bull, take out the kidney, and pass it to her behind your back. After she eats this, she will be embodied once more and you can be her husband. But never strike her or she will come back to us." So they started out, the woman walking behind, trying her best to make him turn around; but being a warrior of great determination, he did not. He went on, with his wife following, until they had crossed the Divide. He killed the buffalo bull, took out the kidney and gave it to her in the way he had been told. She ate it, but even then he wouldn't take a chance by turning around. When finally she put her hands on his shoulders, he turned and there was much joy and they came back to the camp together. This was in the spring and they lived together all through the summer. Then in the fall, they were in bed and the nights were beginning to get cold. They had an extra buffalo robe for a cover and both of them sat up at the same time to reach for the robe. The husband's hand slipped and flew back and struck his wife in the face. She screamed out: "Now I must go." He heard her voice as she went back to the Land of the Dead.

A story of incest appears in several different forms. Once a young man had a separate lodge and a woman came to him in the night for several nights. He found her very attractive and was curious as to who she was, so he rubbed his hand in red paint and in the course of the embrace rubbed the paint on the back of her buckskin robe. The next day when the girls were out playing, he recognized his mark and knew that the girl was his sister. He was much horrified and got a dogwood stick, sharpening it at both ends, and waited until the next night. He placed the stick upright between them, and when the girl came they were both pierced and killed. The boy's body was honored, but her body was mutilated and thrown out.

The Life Cycle

A taboo prohibited intercourse during pregnancy, but no extensive taboos affected the behavior of either parent, nor were there indications of food taboos for pregnant women. (Certain foods were better to eat, but there were no strict taboos.) Women in pregnancy wore otter skin belts with little bells attached. The reason for this was probably to make birth easy, since the medicine men called in for cases of extremely difficult birth had otter medicine. They relieved the woman by singing their four songs and then taking an otter skin and drawing it down the woman's body. After doing this, they said the baby would be born immediately.

No contraceptives were used, but abortion was a fairly common practice, especially for unmarried women. It was done by a mechanical process, usually after the foetus was fairly large.

Birth took place in a special tipi with a professional female midwife, who was usually well paid, getting the customary four articles as a fee. The medicine men would be called in only in cases of long-delayed and difficult birth. Men were excluded from the lodge during a birth. A pole was planted beside the bed and the mother went through the birth pangs kneeling and holding on to this pole, or sitting up while the midwife pressed down on the abdomen. As soon as the child was born, it was picked up by the mother and placed on her right. The afterbirth then was expelled and the navel cord cut with no particular ceremony. They squeezed the blood out of the cord, and threaded it through a flat piece of soft buckskin which pressed against the child's abdomen; in a few days it would dry and drop off. A definite indication of the Comanche's indifference to magic was the fact that they did not save the navel cord as is customary in many places in the Plains. The afterbirth was put in a hackberry tree, where it could have been taken by anybody who wanted to work malevolent magic.

The mother spent ten days lying-in. The father was excluded and not allowed to see the child, although he was informed of its sex at birth. During the lying-in period, the mother spent much of her time lying over hot stones covered with grass to stop hemorrhage. She was allowed to eat no meat, and subsisted mainly on warm water and soup, particularly thick soups made with corn, to stimulate lactation. The only taboo during this time was that she could not comb her hair or wash her face, the first to prevent hair from turning gray and the second lest she become wrinkled.

At the end of the ten days, the mother emerged from the lodge, bathed in the creek, and then returned to her husband's lodge, carrying the child, who was put on the cradleboard. A taboo prohibited intercourse for one month after the birth of the child.

At the birth of the first child the father was given gifts by the wife's parents; appropriate gifts were also made to the child. Arrows were given to a boy; if it were a girl, a horse might be offered since women could use them as well as men.

Two types of cradle were used: one for the daytime and one for the night. The day cradle was of the general Plains pattern—a flat board with a buckskin cover lashed down the front with a hood over the top to protect the child's head. Sometimes there was also a curtain over the child's face as added protection. For boys in the day cradle no diapers were used; the child's penis was brought out through the lashing in the back so he could urinate when he wanted. The girl in the day cradle was put on a sort of wooden funnel arrangement which ran down the back of the cradle. The night cradle was a rawhide cylinder in which the child was put and laced up tight. Here diapers were used. They were made of buffalo calfskin with the hair on, and were washed frequently so that they became soft. The child in the cradle was placed between the parents in bed. The child was taken out in the morning and at night when he was changed from one to another type of cradle, and at this time was washed, greased and finally powdered with a powder made from rotten cottonwood rubbed up in the hands until it became soft. After ten months or so the child enjoyed being out of the cradle for a while and would kick and fight when put back on the cradleboard. Children were nursed while on the cradleboards. The Comanche avoided the occipetal flattening of the head by putting a pad under the nape of the neck. The upper arms were tight against the board, but the forearms were left free. In this arrangement, there was little chance for movement. Children of six months when taken off the cradleboards, had arms as stiff as though they had been pinioned. The child remained on the board until he was able to crawl, or sit on the horse in front of his mother. He was put back on the board whenever the band moved camp. This technique provided a way of taking care of the child and keeping him out of mischief. If the mother wanted to gather berries, she hung the cradleboard on the limb of a tree, so that it would bounce up and down. A crow feather was fastened on to the cradle to keep away ghosts, and a porcupine tail was put on it for quick weaning, since the young porcupine grows up quickly and leaves its mother. Weaning, however, varied with the family and the attitude of the parents.

When the child was placed between the parents in bed at night, the father assumed most of its care. He slept on his left side so that his right arm would be free. In the morning, the mother got up and made breakfast while the father lay in bed and played with the baby. Nursing was carried on from birth. In case a mother was unable to nurse the child, a wet nurse would be found. The child was nursed whenever he cried. In weaning, bitter stuff was occasionally applied to the nipple to discourage the child, but usually the child was handed over to the grandmother, who gave him her dry breast. In any case, weaning was not too early and not difficult. The first food fed to the child would be strips of boiled fat, then meat to suck.

As soon as the child could walk, his mother would take him out of the tipi and teach him to urinate outside. When he was able to talk, he was expected to defecate outside the tipi although in winter accidents were forgiven. The Comanche waited until the child could walk before they expected sphincter control.

In training children, parents did not use physical punishment, but threatened them instead. The distinction of treatment between boys and girls began quite early, probably at about three or four years. Up to this time, the boy spent most of his time with his mother, although the father played with him daily, but after this the boys went off in gangs of their own, free of all responsibility. Girls stayed with their mothers, and were put to work at an early age, except in the case of an honored child. The singling out of a particular child for honor and good treatment was a general Plains institution. Among the Comanche every boy was treated as an honored child, but only certain girls were thus favored. The honored girl child was relieved of all duties. Feasts were also given for an honored girl.

Children began to ride nearly as soon as they could walk; but boys had more opportunities to ride than girls. The average boy could saddle up his horse at the age of five, but usually the father would saddle up the horse for him and turn him loose on it. The boy gangs would be away at the creeks all day. Often the girls joined them. They played house together, which included sexual play, that is, playing at being married. The boys also hunted a great deal; they had small bows and arrows from the time they were big enough to walk. They hunted all sorts of game.

A boy's first kill was celebrated by his family; he brought the animal back to camp and the first grown-up to see him would call out to him and take the arrow with the game on it. Then this adult would tell the father, who would give him a gift, the size of the gift depending on the father's wealth—it might even be two horses. As the boys grew older they played extremely rough games; they threw mud balls at each other, held arrow throwing contests, shooting contests, etc. The still older boys played more and more with the horses; they would raid horses out of the herd, mounting them and racing them without the owner's knowledge. In this way they got good preliminary training for horse stealing. They also stole food. In other words, they ran wild, but did little mischief. On rainy days they simply sat around in the tipis and listened to the old men telling stories. Throughout most of every day, however, they were with their own gangs away from the grown-ups, and self reliance was required. The boys were never whipped. Children were scolded sometimes, even by their fathers, but not often. The father's attitude toward the son was in reality one of extreme placation. One Comanche informant explained this by saying that the boy was certain to be killed in war and so the father wanted to do everything for him. Another practical explanation was that if the father did not treat the boy well, the boy in turn would not be good to his father in his father's old age.

Classificatory sisters, who were often older than the boy, disciplined him by threatening to hang him or to use physical violence. The result of this was that the boy felt a thorough hostility toward older female relatives which lasted for life. No disciplining in the real sense came from the father; he spoiled the son, deferring to all his wishes. In the stories there are repeated records of sulking techniques used by the boy to get his own way. If the adolescent boy wanted anything, to go on his first war party, for instance, he would go into the lodge, cover his head up, and just lie there and sulk all day. He would not even eat. His grandmother or mother would go to his father and tell him that the boy had not been eating and he had better find out what was the matter. Apparently the sulking always worked and brought the parents to terms.

Gifts to honor the son, or gifts made to the son, had to be returned by larger gifts from the father. This resembles the honored child pattern elsewhere. There was one case of a boy who had been given a rifle which he brought triumphantly to his father. But his father upbraided him because now he would have to give the donor a horse. In line with this was the right of the boy to dispose of his sister in marriage if there were no other claims on her. Brother and sister did not observe a rigid avoidance except that they could not be in the tipi alone together. There was respect between them and a certain amount of hostility, in accordance with the strong feeling against brother and sister incest. The avoidance was not a lasting one; as soon as the girl married it wore off.

The Comanche did not hold any particular puberty ceremonies; no ceremony at all for boys. A girl of a rich family, usually the favorite daughter, at this time was supposed to get hold of a horse by the tail and run after it, which was to make her spry. The boy after puberty was given a separate tipi in which he slept, entertained his friends, and spent most of his time. The purpose of this seems to have been to isolate him from cooking and the daily life of the family, so he could more readily receive power. It also served a practical purpose in that women visited the boy there at night.

Sexual play between children began at an early age, and was carried on quite freely as long as the two children were not brother and sister. The Comanche paid no attention to virginity; they took these childhood relations more or less for granted. There was a strong feeling that women did most of the courting. The young men, particularly attractive young men, were constantly pursued by women.

The boy's first war party usually took place when he was seventeen or eighteen. Before going out, he stayed in his tipi for some time, his relatives, an older brother or mother's brother, doing everything possible to give him power. He did not fast at this time. He was fortified by power transfer, so he would be able to succeed in war.

Serious courting began about the same time, seventeen or eighteen for men, but with little success unless a man had collected a few war honors. Also at this time a comrade-in-arms was taken; this always began with two "friends" doing their courting together. One of them would watch outside the tipi while the other crawled under. After a while he would crawl out again, and let the other take his place. After the first war party, the boy passed into his period of maximum military and social importance. As a warrior, he competed with other warriors for honors, and if he was lucky, built himself up into war leader status.

Position of Women

Young women, not only from puberty until marriage but during the first few years of marriage, were normally relieved of all heavy work. The girls before puberty and the older women did the work. The young women were supposed to be free to amuse the young men and to have a good time. After a first child had been born, the care of the child would be delegated to the grandmother on either side. Most of the housekeeping was also done by older women so that the wife would be entirely free to take care of her husband and meet his demands of every sort. This behavior is rationalized on the same pattern as the spoiling of the boy: the adult man who was a warrior would soon be killed, so life should be a pleasant thing for him. According to certain informants, women sometimes continued to do most of the heavy work even when they had young children, but there was probably much variation in this. According to the same source, women sometimes became extremely active sexually after the menopause, and went around stealing young men. If true, this was probably made possible by the fact that a woman then could acquire and use love medicine, which younger women could not.

After marriage, men preferred affairs with women younger than themselves or with married women of their own age. Nevertheless, there was a tendency for the young ambitious man to marry a middle-aged widow because she would know how to take care of him better. The middle-aged women could tan hides, make clothes, keep the tipi in order, and the ambitious young man would thus get on better in the world. There was little feeling here about marriage between persons of a wide age difference. It seems to have worked the same way on both sides; a young man would marry an older woman, or an older man would marry a young woman. This usually operated through the levirate, or through gifts by some rich old man to a girl's parents, and frequently led to elopement or other troubles.

The Comanche also mentioned women who went wild. After the death of a child a young woman who had previously been entirely respectable would become exceedingly active sexually and would have a whole series of affairs. This behavior, which sometimes lasted two or three years, was recognized as a sort of psychotic state and did not result in the same sort of difficulty that accompanied elopement or break-up of a marriage. The husband would feel sorry and would wait until she recovered and then resume the regular marriage relationship. Women acquired no particular respect with age but as they became more skillful in the arts, they derived a little honor from their work. In many families the wife would hold a long established position of control. The husband was not exactly henpecked, but he paid much respect to his wife's wishes. It was recognized that she was head of the household and that he would do what she told him.

For the old man there were two roads after he passed the active warrior age. The good old man abandoned his medicines and dropped back into a condition of innocuous dependence upon the younger generation. The attitude of such old men toward their sons who supported them was one of almost pathetic gratitude. It was not felt that the son necessarily owed any obligation to his father, who had cared for him. The focus being on the men of fighting age, when a man passed this age, he was useless and therefore was fed and clothed and cared for out of good will, but with no obligation. A good old man could be appointed peace chief.

The position of old women differed from that of the old men in that they always earned their keep. As long as they were able to work they could remain useful. However the man's activities centered on hunting and war completely. They had no real handicrafts, and when a man grew old, he became a dead weight with nothing to do but tell stories to the children on rainy days. He was therefore kept on out of good will. The good old man gave up all his competitive attitudes and constantly acted as a mediator, using pressure wherever possible to prevent fights between the younger men, smooth everything out, keep everybody happy. In other words, for him there was an implication of complete change in character as soon as he passed warrior age.

The bad old man, on the other hand, instead of abandoning his medicines, did all he could to build them up and, as his actual powers for war and hunting decreased, to increase his supernatural powers. These gave him a certain competence through healing and also gained him, not exactly respect, but consideration through fear of his malevolent magic. In Comanche folklore, the evil magician is always an old man. The man of fighting age never figures as an evil magician in any of these stories. These old medicine men carried on into old age, through this channel of operations with the supernatural, some of the competitive patterns which characterized the warrior. A bad old man also exercised all the claims he could in marriage, so that he could get all his wife's younger sisters, etc. He might have some power, but he attracted much hatred, and often suspicion, as a malevolent sorcerer. He might be killed if he could not heal the person he was supposed to have bewitched.

Death

At death the corpse was bathed, dressed in its best, and buried, usually in a cleft in the rock or on a mountain. Medicine men were frequently buried near the crest of a mountain where other people who wanted their powers could come and appeal for these—a combination of the Plains mountain cult with a ghost cult.

What happened to property was still highly uncertain. This provides a good example of a cultural feature in transition. The Plateau tribes universally destroyed all the property of a dead man, which did not mean much when all their property was carried on the backs of women in moving camp. They also left the camp site for several months. The Comanche, on the other hand, had acquired much property and were uncertain what to do with it. Apparently they started out by following the regular Plateau pattern of destroying property; however, with the arrival of horses, a real problem arose because some individuals owned very large herds. One man, for example, had a herd of 3,000 horses. The killing of this much livestock would not only have been a serious economic loss to the entire band, because horses were loaned for war parties and buffalo hunting, etc., but also was repugnant to the Comanche, who did not like to see such destruction. They had no pattern of ostentatious waste. They solved the problem by killing a man's favorite horse and only a certain number of the others. The owner of 3,000 horses and 300 arrows when faced with death said, "Take these arrows and kill as many horses as you can with them, then divide up the rest of the horses between you." What they actually did, and do now, was to destroy any property which was in direct contact with the dead man—such as his clothes. At a recent Comanche funeral they dug a pit and put all the dead man's clothes, bedding and favorite possessions into it, including a brass French horn. However they had not decided on any definite rule for the inheritance of horses. A man could give away his possessions before dying instead of making a will. He could not make a will that would be valid—the power of the ghost was not enough for this. Relatives usually got together and the relative who was strongest, the man who could count the most coups, took what he wanted; the others quarreled over the remainder. With the increase in property there was also a marked increase in hard feeling between the relatives after a death.

In the case of a medicine man's death, his tipi was usually left standing; the band just moved away. Sometimes the tipi would be taken up and rebuilt on low ground beside a stream where it would be carried away by the flood water. The medicine man's objects were either left in the tipi or thrown into running water, which had a desacralizing effect. The family indulged in violent mourning, particularly the women. The female relatives of the deceased stripped down to loin clothes and gashed their thighs, arms and body until blood flowed. They pounded themselves on the head with a stone "so that they could cry some more." After crying as much as they could, they cut off their hair, blackened their faces, and for a considerable period after the death were not supposed to bathe or dress in good clothes or take part in a dance. The mourning that the men did was less severe and did not include hair cutting as a rule. However a man might cut his hair for an only son and he might gash himself at this time.

One interesting item is that because of the amount of property buried with the dead, grave robbing was not uncommon. This reflects again the Comanche attitude toward the supernatural; they were willing to take a chance.

Ideas of the afterlife were vague. The Comanche believed that ghosts went to a place somewhere to the west beyond the high mountains. In the folklore there is an exceedingly interesting story of a woman who died and then returned; that is, she came out of her trance, not having quite reached the land of the dead, but being close to it.

One cannot categorize in any exact terms the difference in attitude toward the death of a wife, of a woman in childbirth, the death of favorite daughters and sons, or of girls in general. One might expect to find special rites for a woman dying in childbirth, but there were none. They believed in no differentiation in the next world for those dying of old age or in battle or for any other cause. Mourning for a wife or for a favorite son, would depend entirely on the feeling toward them. A mother was expected to mourn violently for a child, but not for an infant. Infant mortality being high, they recognized that infants often died in the first few days and did not go into mourning for them. On the other hand, the death of a child that had grown up would cause great grief; the greatest grief of all being for a son just beginning manhood. A man might mourn long and violently for a wife or son, or a wife for a husband. The technique for ending mourning by asking the leader of a war party has been mentioned.[1]

[1] Dr. E. A. Hoebel furnished additional information on kinship. Miss J. Mirsky is credited for added information on the role of women among the Comanche.

CHAPTER IV

ANALYSIS OF COMANCHE CULTURE

THE CULTURE of Comanche affords us an opportunity to study a type of very strong, adequate personality structure in a society which was extremely labile and destined, through the operation of historic forces, to rapid extinction. The opportunistic character of this society makes itself felt everywhere, be it in the adaptability, the readiness for change, the contempt for death, or the tenuous character of its religion. Comanche resembles a transitory culture like that of a gangster or guerilla band. Whatever its origins from the plateaus to the north, the effective period in which Comanche functioned was approximately a century; afterwards they were surrounded by the rapidly expanding United States, corralled into a territory, and retired by force. When the frontier civilization became stabilized under the central government, the brigandage of the Comanche could serve no useful purpose; it became a nuisance and had to be stopped. But this meant the end of Comanche culture.

This historical aspect can best be appreciated with the aid of a map. The Comanche operated in a territory corresponding roughly to southern Oklahoma and the Texas Panhandle. To the east were the French colonies, which ceased after the Louisiana Purchase. To the north and east were the English, and to the west and south, the Spanish settlements. The Comanche acted as middle-men racketeers, plundering all the surrounding territory for loot to sell to the British, the French planters, and the Spanish settlers. The French needed slave labor and horses. These the Comanche supplied by raiding south into Mexico. The Spanish settlers wanted cattle, and in return the Comanche got guns with which they obliterated all competition with warlike neighbors such as the Apache. When the game of brigandage was up, the Comanche ceased to have a function.

In connection with this historical situation, certain questions arise. Why did the Comanche become the most successful of these predatory tribes, and how is it that some of their neighbors, notably the Kiowa, did not take to this form of life but remained stationary in a rather stable culture? Was there something about Kiowa culture which made this type of existence undesirable? The Kiowa are known to have had a rigid social system with high emphasis on prestige fixed by heredity and with permanent vested interests which impeded mobility. There are undoubtedly many more features. If we are therefore to discover why the Comanche became what they did, we must look to the old Plateau culture for guidance and consider which of the old institutions remained, which were changed, and what new ones were added. With a good deal of justice, it can be pointed out that this is an inconclusive program to work on, that brigand cultures can sprout from any antecedent cultural background, provided the external reality pressures become sufficiently acute and the opportunity for success sufficiently promising. We can concede that this may be true for transient cultures, which the Comanche's can hardly be called any more than can any other nomadic predatory culture, such as that of the Arabs. Comanche showed every indication of a distinct *culture* and was not a transient organization like a guerilla band, which disintegrates after an acute emergency.

We cannot trace the progress from the old Plateau exhaustively because that culture is none too clearly delineated. Nevertheless there is enough to suggest that the traits of Comanche were only extensions of the older culture and not a fresh start. The Plateau culture was nomadic. This meant that locale and the appurtenances of fixed abode had acquired no meaning. This was true of Comanche. Property that was not portable could thus acquire no value. The food situation was much better in Comanche than in the Plateau, since buffalo were present all year round, and the rituals associated with hunting thus ceased to be of any significance and sloughed off. The hunting medicine for antelope nevertheless persisted.

The Plateau culture had no political organization and no clan organization. These were unchanged in Comanche. The bands of varying composition were likewise unchanged. The powerful and most influential figure in the society did however change from the medicine man in the old culture to the war chief in the new. This shift is an important point of orientation, as we shall presently see. Of no less significance was the change in the attitude toward the aged. These occupy a position of high prestige and respect in a society where the aged have transmissible wealth or hereditary vested interests, where they have something of importance to teach the young, and where their experience is such that it can be transmitted and hence of value to the young. In the Plateau the old had more of value to give the young than was the case in the Plains. The attitude to children was also different in the two cultures; in the Plateau, where subsistence was meager, infanticide was common—though the practice of giving children away for adoption to those who could better care for them was a buffer against the social damage of this practice. In the new Plains culture not only did infanticide cease, but the practice of adoption continued (not only within the Comanche, but from among those captured), and in addition the position of the child became more important in the group. This point about the freedom of adoption and the diminishing importance of the biological blood tie must be closely related to the absence of permanent vested interests and the heightened importance of the performance of the individual to establish and validate his status.

The incest taboos, fraternal wife lending, and the sororate marriage were unchanged from the Plateau culture. In-law avoidance was perhaps stronger in the Plains culture than in its predecessor. The taboos concerning the menstruating woman persisted but took on perhaps a slightly different meaning. Linton says they were relaxed because they were related to hunting medicine, which had become unimportant. Also in the Plateau there was no patrilocal residence, which might lead to overcrowding.

There were no aggressive war patterns in the older culture and little intratribal fighting. Though there was a little fighting with warlike neighbors, there were no special honor aspects to war. The admiration was rather for ingenuity, the trickster Coyote being much of a culture hero.

There was some change in relation to the supernatural. Ghosts were feared in the old culture but not in the new. This anxiety in the form of destruction of the property of the deceased degenerated into a token performance in the Plains culture. The Plateau culture had a religion which was not rich in philosophical ideas; nor was that of the Plains. The concept of the transmission of power, essentially a religious concept, underwent a profound change. In the old culture it existed in the form of a property inherent in all animals and things. But it was acquired through dreams and not transmitted. Power ran in families. In the Plains culture it is transmitted from man to man with a few notable exceptions, such as the derivation of power from the earth and from ghosts. Moreover it is pooled by the entire group.

From this survey of the differences between the old culture and the new, we can detect a decided drift. The dwindling importance of the aged; the disappearance of infanticide; the increase of adoption, especially of captured children; the disappearance of hunting medicine; the disappearance of fear of ghosts; the concept of power transmission —all these changes point to a new direction in the development of the personality. Their consistency with the altered goals of the culture is remarkable. The new culture stressed the high development of the individual for certain limited objectives—prowess, daring, enterprise, strength, and skill. It destroyed the value of the aged; and augmented the pleasure of self-enhancement, all outside the culture. The new culture created new life goals, new personal ideals; but it created new types of anxiety; and it is in relation to these anxieties that we can expect malevolent magic and violence to appear. This is what we find, and it is connected with old age. War skills are not, however, anything which have a lasting value, and nothing on which one can base a lasting security or even a durable prestige.

The absence of internal exploitation, the absence of status differentiation, and the absence of skills, except war and hunting, are other noteworthy features of the culture.

Though this was not a scarcity culture, its abundance could find no lasting expression, and could only be maintained by constant enterprise. In such a culture every resource in cunning and skill had to be given complete freedom to develop. The objectives of this culture required the absence of restrictive disciplines and the discouragement of all submissive and dependent attitudes. In the absence of status differentiation, excepting degrees of daring and skill, no emotional attitude could come to rest or be organized around any recognized form of passivity—such as homosexuality, which is exceedingly rare and in great disrepute. Personal development could go in only one direction, a situation which must have created an enormous burden on the growing boy, because differences of temperament and biological inequalities must have existed here as elsewhere. And the only evidence we have of these aberrant individuals who could not pursue the goals defined by the culture is to be found in the institution of the "contrary ones." These strange fellows merely emphasize the fact that in a society where there is no differentiation of function and where there is only one ineluctable course to pursue, the protest of the individual can only take a form of contrariness. But even in this instance the contrariness does not show itself in the repudiation of the social ideal, for many "contrary ones" distinguished themselves as good soldiers and even became war chiefs, but in other contrary activities not injurious to the common good.

Personal Development

In order to understand these cultural changes, we might find it advantageous to examine the development of the individual, to point up the successive influences to which he is subjected. This survey can answer the questions as to what active constellations are formed in the personality. Since there was no hereditary status differentiation, no emphasis on primogeniture, and hence no special privileges or immunities, the development could vary only with respect to congenital endowment, sex, and the variations in character of the individual parents.

The parental role in this society, especially in the case of the males, was limited in scope. Parental responsibility ended after the first hunt. Up to this time, the parental role was to foster the growth of strength and enterprise.

In the prenatal period there was a conspicuous absence of taboos upon the parents. There was an absence of anxiety concerning the fate of the child through the hostile activity of others, as is shown by the fact that they did not save the navel cord or bury the afterbirth to protect the child from harm. There was a vestigial couvade for the father, and the ideal of devoted parenthood is shown by the fact that desertion of the child by the mother was considered disgraceful. In other words, the child was welcome, it was wanted, there was no anxiety about what would happen to it. There are no evidences of suppressed hostility to it. Both boys and girls were needed and wanted.

Maternal care was good, in the sense that it was constructive, consistent, devoid of contradictory elements. The child got the care of both parents. The cradleboard, though it hampered movement in the early months of life, insured proximity of the mother and hence persistent care. This care provided that the tensions in the child were not permitted to accumulate to such extent as to cause undue anxiety, hostile attitudes to the parents, and eventual mistrust in one's self.

As regards basic disciplines, the specific implement of the socialization process, here again, as we previously noted in Marquesas,[1] we find

[1] See A. Kardiner, *The Individual and His Society;* the section on the Marquesas.

that these conduce to a strong, self-confident personality structure. Food is plentiful from birth on, weaning is effected by means of the dry breast. Sphincter control is not associated with severe punishments or disapproving attitudes and is begun only after the child has learned to walk. The child is not crowded with premature responsibilities, and those it is obliged to assume are cotemporal with its capacities. The contrast with Tanala [2] is striking.

This point is worth stressing as a factor in socialization. The case of premature induction of strict sphincter control by brutal methods of enforcement creates for the child a special kind of image of the parent and of the activity. There is no possibility for the child to imitate the cruel activity of the Tanala parent, and the activity in question becomes distorted in its meaning from a physiological activity to one of incurring anger and disapproval or of abjectly winning freedom from these torments.

The punishment-reward systems in Comanche are clear and consistent. No punishment is employed. Instead, threats are used, which are not very effective if not carried out. The threats of the bogy man really mean abandonment of the child to the horrors of the unknown, without parental protection. On the other hand, there is in Comanche a strong factor of encouragement to do as the parent does, and a tendency to elaborate praise of achievement. This cannot fail to create a strong incentive to continue the praised activity and to derive a high degree of satisfaction from it.

The gang life of the boys is in every way a replica of the activities of the adult without the risks or responsibilities and is moreover a direct apprenticeship for the later adult role. This is a bit of economy, in that attitudes toward childhood sports are readily transferred to adult activities without alteration.

As regards the role of the father to son, there are some unique features. The father serves as ideal, without greatly magnifying his stature, either by the great deeds he does, which involve a complicated apprenticeship, or by virtue of severe restrictions he is able to impose. The father never becomes the object of hatred. Such disciplines as there are, for the greater part, are delegated to the older or classificatory sister. The father remains the playmate of the little boy and even has a tendency to "spoil" him, a situation that the mother or sister has to deal with when it arises. The child sleeps between the two

2 *Ibid.*, p. 251.

parents and undoubtedly has much opportunity to see parental intercourse. However, since the child's sexual activities are in no way restricted later on, the untoward effects that such scenes have in our society must be much diminished.

We see therefore that in Comanche the necessities for repression of strong drives in early childhood are rather scant. This means in effect that development can proceed on the constructive side unimpeded by the necessity to channel out compensatory activities or by placing undue stress on the fantasy life of the child. Comanche are not given to dreaming and visions. The result is emphasis on the achievement aspect of activity and not on the anxieties with which it may be associated. This can be readily verified in the matter-of-fact way in which they view death in battle. In other words, we have here a seeming paradox: a society in which death of the young is constant, but in which anxiety about death is minimal; a high degree of security, notwithstanding the constant threat of annihilation. The emphasis on direct action also renders the individual less interested in receiving bounties and protection from the deity and renders unattractive the concept of achieving illicit ends by the employment of magic. Accomplishment and not obedience and conformity becomes the technique of winning social approval.

We see therefore little opportunity for the development of neurotic anxiety, a fact that is highly supported by the relative absence of malevolent magic, either to defend oneself against or to use upon others. The only time in life when this is likely to play a role is with the waning of physical powers in advancing age.

The security system of the individual in Comanche is therefore constructed on rather simple lines. It consists of perfecting one's resources for dealing with the outer world, and since the tasks that confront the ego are of a limited nature and can be achieved, there is a minimum of appeal to deity, except what is contained in their concept of medicine or power. What we see on the other hand is an extreme reliance on coöperative functioning, using the pooled resources of the total manpower of the community. There is no society which we have heretofore studied in which this most valuable aid to survival —social coöperation—is so expertly used, and where the coöperation is used in such a way as to preclude the possibility of being disrupted by intrasocial or interpersonal hostilities. The entire religion is molded to coincide with this objective, and is implemented by the most ingenious concept of *power,* which can be borrowed, lent, pooled, and freely dispersed among the entire group. Their concept of power does not create this situation; it is rather an indicator of the communal plan on which all activity is based.

This leads us to try to discover how it is possible for such strong coöperation to exist in this society without being disrupted by the strong competitive element that exists there. First, every man in the community profits by the exploits of the entire group. The spoils are not divided equally, favor being shown to those most responsible for its success. But the advantages and disadvantages are not so far apart. Even more important, there is no permanent vested interest that is cumulative and self-perpetuating (like land produce or interest on capital), nor could it be made hereditary. There is one notable exception to this—evidently an institution of late introduction—the accumulation of horses, which could be used as currency. The chief reward was a heightening of prestige; but since this depended on a perishable commodity bound to disappear with advancing age, and since prestige had to be constantly validated, a powerful check was here introduced on any egocentric tendencies. The alignment of forces was therefore such that the main interests of the individual were preserved by coöperative solidarity, and the disrupting influences thus minimized.

There were such disrupting influences but they were channelized chiefly in the struggle for women. But here again the centralizing influence of the necessity for solidarity prevented the competition for women from disrupting the society. The tendency was not to injure the man but to punish the woman, and to accept damages in lieu of a fight.

In this connection we must note the absence of homosexuality and transvestitism. This is no surprise. Passive attitudes of any kind on the part of the male would have destroyed the society, as long as the economy depended on enterprise and prowess. Homosexuality was not only absent but was despised. On the other hand, the institution of "friend" was exalted to a very high status. This did service to the ideal of coöperation, but it excluded the exchange of wives—a practice that could endanger solidarity. One might look upon this institution as homosexuality in a sublimated form, but without much profit. More in conformity with the concept of homosexuality are the "contrary ones," most of whom did not marry and whose chief form of resistance was defiance and contrariness. Yet the "contrary ones" could not mold their ideals to anything except the common one of warrior.

The unusual feature of Comanche culture is the uniformity of the demands made on the male, and the absence of any margin of choice in social function. This means in effect that the burden that the ego had to carry was a very onerous one indeed, from which there was no escape, and which had of necessity to terminate in the decay of power and prestige. If the individual survived by virtue of his prowess in youth, he had to pay for it by increasing insecurity in old age. At this time he had to take on roles of progressively diminishing importance and depend for his support on his younger colleagues. This may be one of the reasons why the culture is polarized toward the young male and why the father refrains from imposing restricting conditions on him that would spoil his attitude to the older man later in life. It is therefore quite consistent that the fate preferred by the Comanche is to die in battle.

On the other hand, there is a good deal of tension between the young men and the old. The latter do not surrender their prerogatives, especially with women, without a fight and they supplement their waning powers, physical and sexual, with a good deal of magic, thus frequently inviting either humiliation or death. There is no other time in the life cycle when the man needs supernatural powers. But even under the protection of magic powers, the old man wages a hopeless fight, and the safest adaptation possible for the aged male is to accept the crumbs of prestige offered in the office of peace chief, in which he makes the relatively unimportant decisions about where the next camp shall be or sits on a court that is devoid of real power. Some do accept it with gratitude.

Security System of the Woman

The security system of the woman in Comanche is built on lines somewhat different from those of the male. She has a decidedly subordinate position, she rarely stands on her own merits, she cannot compete with the male except in medicine after menopause, and is constantly a pawn in the prestige struggles of the men.

The female child, though she is not most often the honored child, is not discriminated against. She has the same sexual freedom as the male, but occupies an unfavorable position as regards her brothers;

strict brother taboos and the fact that the classificatory sister is the disciplinarian, makes her the target of the brothers' dislike. She has no value to him, and the brother is generally relieved to have her married off. Her labors carry no claims to prestige, and she is relieved of them only to render her better able to gratify the sexual and adventurous needs of the men.

In spite of these social disadvantages in early life and in marriage, she has some freedom of mobility. She can leave one husband for another, and let the men settle the score between themselves. She can moreover contract a marriage with a younger man where her experience has some value. Furthermore, in the more stable marriages she has an acknowledged influence on the husband. As she grows older her security becomes greater. She can after menopause actually become a medicine practitioner and be treated on a par with men. In comparison with the male, therefore, the woman starts with initial disadvantage, but she has greater mobility as she gets older.

The Lines of Tension in Comanche

In the development of the Comanche child there is little evidence of deep repressions for which, from our previous researches, we would expect new institutions to arise to afford expression. We shall presently look to Comanche religion and folklore for evidence; but we have a bit of evidence in what happened to some of the survivals from the old Plateau culture. Here we must do something which is the reverse of the procedure used in comparing the Tanala and Betsileo.[3] There we found that the personality formed under the institutions of Tanala was subjected to a great increase in pressure, with consequent great increase of anxiety in Betsileo. In Comanche the reverse seems to have happened. There was an evident diminution of anxiety and mutual hostility in the move from Plateau to Plains. The couvade, as it is practiced among the Comanche, seems like a vestigial hangover devoid of any significance. If it was originally the expression of hostility to the child, then there is much reason to believe that it has lost its force with the Comanche, for there was every reason why the child should be wanted. The food supply was good; the newcomer could be an aid to his parents. The other restricting rituals about birth also indicate a great diminution of anxiety. There are no anxieties built up either about eating or defecation, as we saw in Marquesas and

[3] Kardiner, *op. cit.*, p. 291.

Pomo respectively, hence the individual grows up without any great drive toward accumulation, or anxiety about parting with anything pertaining to himself.

The family complex, which most commonly has the configuration of the Oedipus story, is not present as such in these folktales that have come to our attention; but it exists in the form in which we observed it in Trobriand. The emphasis falls on the sister taboo, and in the stories the sister is the seductress and the boy an innocent victim. Discounting the customary distortion, we can take this to be the prototype of the Oedipus complex; but it is devoid of the hostility to the father and devoid of the guilt derived from that source. The sexual tensions in both boy and girl are permitted adequate discharge throughout life and are subject only to the restrictions caused by the conflict of the older and younger generations of men. A strong bit of evidence for this is the absence of the almost universal taboo against sexual relations before battle. This merely indicates that the constellation "sexual pleasure provokes punishment" is absent.

Question arises about the frustration in the child of the need for support. The situation here is not comparable to that in Marquesas.[4] The only source from which such an anxiety can arise in Comanche is in the frequent break-up of the family through separation or divorce. The option of the child to choose the parent with which it is to remain is some compensation for this trauma. There is, however. a more serious threat to the dependency needs of the growing child in the form of an inescapable ideal of bravery and accomplishment. All children cannot be equally capable of assuming these attitudes, and there are in this society children who cling to the mother instead of seeking the harder course of emulating the father. For these children there is no escape; no institutionalized forms of passivity are recognized, and in all probability these children are the "contrary ones." In the absence of biographical studies this cannot be stated with certainty; but the likelihood is very strong.

There is one line of tension that is quite clear—that between the sexes. The frequency of divorce and separation and the fact that magical retaliatory measures may be instituted by the woman both point to a good deal of mutual antagonism. In this case I believe the process to be like the one we found in the Marquesas. Male solidarity is an economic necessity; all institutions, "friend," transfer of power, etc.,

4 Kardiner, *op. cit.*, p. 197.

permit the consolidation of men for a concerted effort. The conflicts of the men for the women usually, though not always, result in the woman's being punished, as if this were the line of least resistance. Perhaps the most startling bit of evidence in connection with this is the institution of wife-sharing between brothers. No hostility is permitted to arise between them, and the man who has relations with one's wife automatically becomes one's brother. The sister avoidance is probably the earliest institution which makes this channeling possible; for the disciplinarian, being a classificatory sister, and also sexually taboo, becomes the natural target of hatred.

The fact that intrasocial hostilities are at a low level is clearly brought out by the notable absence of fear of the dead and of ghosts, manifest in the freedom with which they appropriate property from the dead and permit the old custom of destroying property of the dead to be observed only in token.

Religion and Folklore

The practical religion consists of a series of rules for the transmission of supernatural power. In reviewing these practices we ought to see under what conditions this power is transmitted and maintained. In view of the fact that in early relations to the father obedience plays such a small role and punishment is not used as a means of implementing discipline, we would not expect suffering or conformity to discipline to be a means of soliciting this power. The technique of solicitation is merely to express the wish to have it and to render oneself worthy of possessing it by a demonstration of strength, endurance, or determination. Not helplessness but resourcefulness is a claim for power. This power, after it is achieved, is used *by the recipient, and not by the donor or deity*. And since power and skill are perishable commodities in this society, supernatural power also wears out. This is a replica of what they actually observe in real life, that old men lose their daring, agility, and skill. In its projected form this fact reads: *power* wears out.

The meaning of the food taboos in connection with power is not clear, only that it entails some renunciation but not privation and impedes complete freedom of action. This is mentioned as the chief reason why some men do not wish to have it. The real impediment imposed by power is the inability to be afraid and run away from certain dangers.

The rules about getting power from the brother or maternal uncle are merely another illustration of the lines of solidarity in this culture; it is between the same age groups, not across generations. The fact that powers are cast off at the time of diminishing military effectiveness is another support to the idea that *power* is merely a euphemism for courage and skill.

Their rituals are likewise devoid of suffering. The Sun Dance as it was appropriated by the Comanche was usually associated with masochistic and self-destructive rituals. These could not possibly have any meaning to the Comanche and were accordingly deleted, so that the Sun Dance consisted of merely a demonstration of feats of strength.

Their folklore is a mixture of old and new. The Coyote stories are undoubtedly old. But they have one unique feature: Coyote is not subjected to innumerable deaths from which he is always revived. The war hero stories are undoubtedly new. The story of the faithless wife who sides with the Ute against her husband and is punished by him is another evidence of the underlying distrust of women, undoubtedly a projection of their own anxiety about loss of power for war and sex alike.

The story of the magic flight of children is a Comanche Haensel and Gretel story. It has the interesting feature that whereas the children are helped by the various animals to escape from the cannibalistic ogress, it is the little calf who butts the witch into the moon. This is the only clue we have in the folklore of strongly frustrated dependency cravings. It belittles the importance of parental care, and in sour-grapes fashion indicates that they don't need the parents anyway, they can look after themselves. This seems very like a protest against the unusual burdens placed on the child to emulate the parents and to become prematurely independent.

The story of letting out the buffalo is a strong indication of deeply suppressed insecurity that could be surmounted by hoarding of buffalo, and is probably a survival of the Plateau when food was scarce.

Basic Personality Structure and Social Goals

The survey of Comanche culture up to this point is a repetition of the procedure followed in the preceding volume. We have a sufficient amount of material to draw up a chart of the basic personality structure and to demonstrate its derivation from certain institutions. We can further demonstrate that the personality formed under these influences has a limited capacity to follow the patterns of the Plateau culture, owing to a complete shift in the locus of anxiety and tension in the new culture. To be sure, there are some innocuous survivals; but the main lines of the culture altered the direction of development, and with it came a complete change in the reality perceptions of the personality, and hence new directions for activity were defined. But Comanche material is not included in this book for this purpose, for it has nothing new to teach us in this direction. It is included largely because it furnishes a striking contrast to the personality and institutional configurations found in Alor.

From the point of view of the social configurations and goals of Comanche, there are some important inferences to draw. We can confidently state that, as compared with the Plateau culture, there is considerable lessening of intrasocial tension; the institutions of which these tensions were the expression sloughed off, the aggression was turned outward toward other groups and activities. This change was facilitated by two material factors: the horse and the gun. They both increased the mobility of the entire group a thousandfold and introduced a novel element of action at a distance. But these material factors would not have been very effectively used if it were not for an internal preparedness for their use. How is such a preparedness built up?

In Comanche we can detect at least two factors which are closely interwoven. The first factor is the absence of restrictive disciplines and the presence of consistent praise or reward systems. This lays a general groundwork for daring, freedom from inhibition, for a high self-esteem. The second factor is the emphasis on activity itself in the specific forms of riding, shooting, running, muscular development, dexterity, etc. This requires a specific integrational system, subject to very specific vicissitudes. We can schematically represent several of these vicissitudes thus:

I. Action + satisfaction = ego enhancement = meaning = utility or mastery = increased interest = *skill* = approval = increased self-esteem and social approval.

II. Action + failure = ego impoverishment → meaning = failure of mastery = diminished interest = *avoidance* = lower self-esteem and lower social approval.

Let us suppose that the action concerned in Cases I and II is essentially for survival; then avoidance is impossible, and the activity must continue, but at a cost of great anxiety which can be eased by supernatural aid. Skill under these conditions is impossible. The relation of a general self-confidence, created by absence of restrictive disciplines, to the development of specific activity skills is a general one, because inhibitions are contagious and tend to extend themselves. The damaging effects of avoidance can be mitigated if there is a substitute for the avoided activity, where there is an element of choice. This is possible in many instances. Skills once acquired can be lost by the intervention of failure created by the organic factor of advancing age. The activity can then be avoided if there is that option or if there are reinforcing factors introduced to buttress the effect of anxiety—for example, magic—and on the basis of this new adjunct the action system is established.

Once these action systems are developed, the specific configurations of the society will depend on where they are exercised. In Comanche this is extremely simple; they are not exercised within the group but outside of it. This means that the anxiety-provoking situations within the society must be controlled to insure greater coöperation. We therefore find that all situations creating intrasocial friction in the Plateau tend to disappear. The only friction points left are (1) the tension between the young and the old and (2) the sexual competition between the men. We must note the absence of fixed class or status lines, a democratic mobility of status even associated with diminishing importance of blood ties, freedom of adoption, etc. These are dealt with in such a way as to diminish their disrupting influence, at the expense of the woman. And even she is put on a basis of parity with men when her sexual value has disappeared and she can no longer be the source of internecine strife.

The fact that the assertive action patterns are exercised exclusively outside the society severely limits the development potentials of the society as a whole. The society could exist only as long as there were slaves to steal and cattle to rustle. In other words, this fine ego structure of the Comanche was bought at the expense of criminality perpetuated on others and at the cost of complete collapse of the society once this criminality was incapable of being exercised. No internal growth or expansion of the society was possible. The results of acculturation of Comanche bears this out. When they were retired under government protection, the culture continued to exist largely in the memories of the old men. Children became less important, no feasts were given in their honor. Personal freedom was much curtailed, the sexual development was permitted free range. The aged again became important, because the young could perform no exploits to compare with them. The status of the old was further enhanced by the creation of vested interests. Education is western, with the development of contempt for Indian ceremonies, except for social dances. Lover and wife cannot get away, and collection of damages for wife stealing is gone.

In Comanche we have therefore a prototype of a society which has developed a high degree of freedom for the individual who is strong and uninhibited but devoted to "criminal" ends. It can serve us as a contrast to those societies which are internally anarchic and externally highly moral. There is no exploitation of one individual by another within this group. The only instance of it is in slavery, where the compulsory obedience has a high scarcity value. In this connection one observation is of greatest importance, namely, that the slave, who is the only member of the society whose security depends on obedience, not only can become a great war leader, but that he may become most cruel to the people of his origin. This is very like the case of a baptized Jew who becomes a most violent anti-Semite.

The reason for this difference between the native and adopted Comanche can be conjectured. There is a difference in the process of superego formation in each case. The Comanche only adopted children in the formative years. Hence there was opportunity for the new influences to mold their character structure. A superego created on a basis of obedience is different from one based on the acceptance of an ideal. The latter is based on the idea: "I wish to be like you"; the former on the idea: "If I do not obey I shall be punished or deprived"; this necessitates the suppression of hostility, which in turn is a source of masochistic fantasies and accompanying inhibitions. The tensions built up around these masochistic fantasies are released when the individual finds himself in the position of his original persecutor, that is, in a position of leadership. The adopted Comanche under the obligation to maintain status with his fellows must still repress his hostilities, but this is not the case with the people from which he originated, for they are just replicas of his old self for which he now has profound contempt. This additional cruelty is therefore a new form of the residual masochism in reverse. The Comanche evidently value this rare trait of obedience in their captives, for it makes the latter extremely dependable, a trait not to be found in the native Comanche except for the hunt or any other communal undertaking.

Conclusion

The culture of Comanche was used as an introduction to this volume partly to review the procedure already fully described in an earlier work; partly to demonstrate several cultural configurations not found in cultures previously undertaken; and partly to furnish contrasts to two other cultures to be examined.

The data of Comanche permitted us to go no further in technique than we did in the previous volume. It supports the validity of the concept of basic personality structure as an operational tool. In this culture—aided in part by the bit of history at our disposal—we could demonstrate the consistent relationship between what we called "primary institutions" and those we called "secondary." The strong ego formation permitted by the primary institutions is very clearly reflected in the religious concepts of the Comanche and in the practical working out of these concepts. The absence of ingratiating procedures with the parent is reflected in its absence in their practical religion. The complete absence of the concept that misfortune is due to disobedience (sin) informs us also that this constellation had no opportunity to be formed in their development. It was this original correlation which was the basis for the entire series of concepts, primary institutions, basic personality structure, secondary institutions. However, since the publication of the first volume, much confusion has arisen about what seemed to be an arbitrary distinction between primary and secondary institutions. In the case of some institutions it was difficult to allocate them to either group. There is undoubtedly a flaw in this classification—undoubtedly an oversimplification. We have yet to see whether this operating scheme will have to be changed if we are confronted with the direct experience of the individual as we shall be in the next culture to be studied.

On the other hand, Comanche gave us an opportunity to observe a striking contrast with Tanala culture. In this latter society we observed a great increase in anxiety when a change in subsistence technique (dry to wet rice cultivation) placed increased burdens on a personality in which obedience and ingratiation were the chief adaptive attitudes. In Comanche we observe a great diminution of anxiety, as compared with Plateau culture, associated with the disappearance of certain primary institutions and the alteration of others to conform to a new objective. Comanche moreover taught us some important facts about how relative the definition of *danger situation* is. The commonest danger situation which confronts the Comanche warrior is death. Yet there is no evidence of any neurotic anxiety about the idea of personal destruction; nor are there any desperate attempts to elaborate fanciful conceptions of post-mortem existence. The inference is therefore justified that an ego structure devoid of hypochondriacal elements created by the suppression of essential drives, does not necessarily conceive of death as an anxiety-provoking prospect. We do not see this anxiety about death, but we do see neurotic configurations about the loss of powers associated with old age, and the consequent degradation of the personal ideal. At this point the neurotic embellishments take on the guise of magical reinforcements.

Comanche culture taught us another valuable point about the survival of certain institutions which tend to persist notwithstanding their incompatibility with the culture as a whole. This is true of the menstrual taboos and of the rudimentary couvade. How is it that these institutions can survive? The menstrual taboos are survivals which indicate conceptions of danger associated with the female, not supported by any experience of the Comanche themselves; and the couvade, rudimentary though it is, is evidence that the child must be protected from the father. This surely has no relevancy here. Its functional use is gone. The child is wanted and needed. The form can persist because it is unattached to any reality system, and must therefore be attached to any anxiety-provoking factors. Such a survival we observed in Pomo and Navaho, where the child is inducted into anal training with the idea that unless the feces are safely concealed, they can be used as bait for poison. Such an anxious conception can in itself become a focus for anxiety, even if the hostility within the society is not very great. Naturally it would tend to become aggravated when these hostilities are stronger. The persistence of such institutions in Comanche indicates that not all institutions are functionally meaningful and cannot therefore be classified as either primary or secondary but remain adventitious.

But the most important psycho-sociological lesson in Comanche lies in the phenomenon of *polarization*. This means in effect that when a dominant interest is defined in a society, the institutions tend to arrange themselves in relation to this interest. This phenomenon is naturally created not by the institutions themselves, but by the adjustments of the individual in the direction of conserving his major interests. Comanche is a society which could not survive strong tensions within the society. The individual male must be strong and enterprising; but these qualities can be of use to the group as a whole only if there are no internal blocks to action but at the same time no passivity of one male to the other. This does not mean that there is no competition. There is a great deal of it, but it does not interfere with security or with the common goal of the society. The conditions under which competition undermines the common goal is when it is reinforced by strong unconscious passivity, which we shall presently discuss. In Tanala we saw a group solidarity built about obedience and passivity. A society like the latter, however, can exist only where there are fixed statuses, vested interests, and where the protection given by the strong to the weak can be implemented with concrete boons. In Comanche there were no vested interests, although in this constantly changing culture one could begin to see consolidation taking place along lines of wealth. There is little doubt that if the society had continued much longer, a definite cleavage along this line would have taken place. But as the culture is described in its present form, the phenomenon of polarization stands out with great clearness. This can be seen from the accompanying chart. The consistency with which these institutions are arranged is quite remarkable. It is not unlikely that if the main objective of coöperative action by the young men of the society were to fall away, the tonicity which holds the other institutions in line with it would tend to drift in the direction of a new polarizing force. One of the strongest supports for this conception of the institutions is the fact that where the common goal is weakened, hostilities break out. The older men, who are no longer warriors, fall out of line of the common goal; they are obliged to play a subsidiary role and frantic efforts to retain vestiges of their erstwhile power undoubtedly unleash much hostility to the young, and vice versa. Here the hostility is unbridled, unless the old men are content with their subordinate roles. Such conflicts cannot have any disrupting influence because they tend to remain localized and at the periphery of the culture. The fact is that the old men do attempt to create

		Absence of passive attitudes
Absence of vested interests (capital and interest)		Religion—transmission of power
		Interpersonal rivalries toned down
Equable distribution of spoils	Solidarity of young males	Wife sharing
		Institution of "friend"
		Woman chief sufferer in infidelity
Limited implementation of prestige and its limited duration		No cause for father hatred
		Derogation of old age—no hesitation about use of magic by old men or of young men to kill the old men

a vested interest by force. They cannot succeed as long as the productive economy depends on prowess and enterprise. This is solely within the control of the young men.

It is easy to see from this chart that if circumstances compelled some alteration of any of the institutions on the left side of the chart, those on the right would not hold together. The creation of vested interests, the unequal distribution of spoils, or the indefinite prolongation of attained prestige would not give equal opportunities to other males, and would inevitably compel the formation of passive attitudes of the weak to those in power. This is one of the nodal problems in sociology, —the relation of vested interests, durable and inherited status, or prestige and passive attitudes. The arrangement in Comanche is one that prevents the accumulation of hostilities between males, and this in turn permits the father to have an attitude toward the boy of permitting him to grow into something like himself. Personal power over others does not have to take the disguised form of disciplines which throttle development. This seems very desirable, but one can with complete justification ask, of what value is this personal freedom of development in a culture which is devoted to criminal ends.

This points up a problem in sociology, whether there is an essential connection between vested interests, passivity, and consequent hostilities. There are plenty of hostilities in Comanche, but they are not likely to be of the repressed kind which necessitates characterological defenses, needing channelization in fantasies or new institutional expression. There is no evidence that this is the case.

With this culture we make a new departure in procedure, namely to coördinate the comparison of different orders of institutions with the direct evidence of personality studies. For this purpose the Alorese present an unusual opportunity.

CHAPTER V

THE ALORESE

Compiled by the author from seminar notes and from the book
THE PEOPLE OF ALOR
By Cora Du Bois

THE ensuing account of Alor is in some ways a duplication of the more lengthy
one published by Dr. Du Bois, *The People of Alor*. The first section, the description of the culture, is a condensation of seminar notes, supplemented by some direct quotations (with the kind permission of the University of Minnesota Press)
from Dr. Du Bois's book. Had Dr. Du Bois written the account of Alor here included it would no doubt have been better presented. If there are any residual
errors, they are my sole responsibility. This account follows the order of presentation given in seminar, where neither the ethnographer nor I had any idea as to how
the psychological analysis would shape up.

The analysis of Alor as here presented is the record of an experiment. It was
known in advance that the various types of psychological data—the most complete ever to come to my attention—would require the collaboration of several
specialists. Dr. Du Bois had therefore to arrange for the study of her data in such
a way as to preclude the possibility that the various specialists might influence
each other's conclusions. The failure of this precaution would have prejudiced
the success and disinterestedness of the whole enterprise.

The order of the study was first an account of the culture, the main points of
which are included in Chapter V. This material was studied for what light it could
cast on the personality formation in Alor. The essence of this analysis, included
in Chapter VI, was presented in seminar. Some few points are new. It was the discussion of this aspect which led to a reëxamination and elaboration of points presented by the ethnographer. Then followed the study of the biographical sketches
—only five of which were studied in class. In this part of the work we were assisted
by Mr. and Mrs. Horowitz, Mrs. Esther Wittfogel, Dr. Ruth Bunzel, and Dr. Du
Bois, all of whom digested and rearranged the data to render them accessible for
study. These preliminary studies were all subsequently checked more carefully.
However, even in our preliminary studies, the conclusions of the projective
analysis seemed to be corroborated. Such discrepancies as did exist were not
understood until the biographical material had been gone over several times. In
these personal analyses I received invaluable help from Dr. Du Bois, because
alone I found the material too great a tax on my powers of empathy, and I did
not know the reality systems of the Alorese.

Following these studies, Dr. Emil Oberholzer presented the conclusions of his
preliminary studies of the Rorschach tests. He knew nothing of my conclusions,
nor I of his. The Rorschachs were studied "blind," that is, without knowing much
about either the culture or the individuals concerned. Dr. Oberholzer's conclusions were truly startling as regards their correspondence to the conclusions

reached by the projective analysis. Though the agreement was not complete, it was close enough to indicate that we were on the right track.

The biographical sketches here published differ in detail from those I submitted for Dr. Du Bois's book. I had in the interval restudied all of them and pointed the descriptions to the specific needs of this volume.

The justification for publishing a separate account of Alor, involving some duplication, is that I considered the material too valuable from the point of view of technique to let it pass in the form in which the material was handled in Dr. Du Bois's book. The latter is invaluable for source material; the conclusions of the analysis are adequately enough presented there, but the technique of operation is completely obscured by the manner of presentation. Her book is written from the life cycle outward, and in the description are included many inferences and conclusions drawn from the projective analysis. This procedure may have its merits; but it is not a record of the technique. Moreover, some confusing impressions are created. Can one really predict personality formation as one ascends progressively up the life cycle? The answer is no. The indicators of what are the permanent effects of traumatic experiences in childhood are found in religion, folklore, and a host of other facts gathered from the description of the institutional set-up. The constellations found in the latter tell us what to look for in the life cycle.

Chapters VIII and IX are entirely new. The array of material was too vast to encompass on the run. I could not forego the opportunity of coordinating and evaluating the various types of psychological source material, and of making a start, at least, in the study of value systems. The relation between basic personality, individual character, and value systems is still very obscure. What inferences I have here recorded must be considered highly tentative. Neither could I ignore the opportunity of studying the correspondences and discrepancies between the Rorschach experiment and the analysis of projective systems.

Dr. Du Bois's material on Alor is a landmark in the technique of cultural psychodynamic analysis—not likely to be superseded for a long time. For any effort I have made in launching and consummating this research, I have been more than amply rewarded in the striking results achieved. Grateful acknowledgments are due both to Dr. Du Bois and the University of Minnesota Press for innumerable courtesies.   A. K.

ALOR is a small island in the Netherlands East Indies, about 600 miles east of Java, 700 miles due west of northern New Guinea, approximately 700 miles north from the nearest point of Western Australia, and about eight degrees south of the equator. The culture of this area is generally Indonesian, but the people considered here are predominantly Papuans.

The climate is determined largely by the Australian land mass, subject to southeast and northwest prevailing winds. There is a wet and a dry season. The wet season begins toward the end of October and is at its height in January and February; the dry season starts in May and reaches its peak sometime in August. This seasonal rhythm accounts for many special problems in water supply and agriculture.

The island is approximately fifty miles long and thirty miles wide and supports a population of about 70,000, of which 10,000 are Mohammedan. On the extreme west of the island there is a port, Kalabahi, where there are a few stores at which the natives trade.

The mountain group which concerns us is oceanic negroid in type and short in stature, the males averaging five feet, 1 inch and the females about 4 feet, 10 inches. Skin color varies from light bronze to dark black, and hair form ranges from straight to kinky. The population is fairly constant, for although the average number of children per woman is four, the mortality of children under ten is high.

These people bear the load of much disease. Yaws, malaria, and dysentery are endemic. Various tropical skin ulcers are common. There is much upper respiratory infection, especially toward the end of the dry season, also some leprosy and benign goiter. Smallpox and blackwater fever have been eliminated during the past ten years, but medical care is still very inadequate.

Contacts of the mountain people with the Dutch government are slight. Each village has a steward. Above him is an officer (*tumukum*) in control of several villages. This officer in turn is responsible to a *kapitan*. There are three or four kapitans to each *rajahship* or district, of which there are four on the island. The government is concerned with major offenses and with the settlement of disputes and litigation and maintains a small military garrison. But the chief tie between the natives and the government is the collection of taxes. The tax is about $1.25 yearly per head of family, a sum which represents two months' labor. In addition each man is required to do a month of state labor to maintain the horse trails. The money for paying the tax is generally procured by the sale of produce in Kalabahi where the natives also purchase cloth and a few other articles.

The village described here—Atimelang—is close to a volcanic crater 2,500 feet high and is surrounded by a ridge of about 400 feet which has a narrow outlet to the east. The climate is pleasantly cool, with temperatures from 59 to 86 degrees. The lowest temperatures, toward the end of the dry, cold season, cause much discomfort to these unclad people. The humidity is high—100 percent in the morning, less by noon, but high again in the evening.

The valley has a relatively dense population. Within a radius of a mile there are five hundred people, divided among four villages and their offspring hamlets. Atimelang is on the eastern side of the valley and has two hamlets, Folafeng and Faramasang, attached to it. The entire population is about 180. The village of Lawatika is closely related through marriage to Atimelang, and its population is distributed among three hamlets on the difficult slopes of the Limbur Ravine below the valley floor. On the western side of the valley there are three adjoining villages—Dikimpe, with a population of 114; Alurkowati, with 95; Karieta, with 56. The remaining fifty people live in isolated field houses.

The dance place is the area about which the houses cluster and from which a trail leads on to another dance place. Some villages have only one dance place, others three or four, as each lineage has its own. Fields lie between the houses and also behind them.

Three types of houses are constructed: the lineage house is the largest and most carefully built, sometimes taking as long as five years to complete; the ordinary family house which is built in a season; and the field house which is an extremely flimsy structure, hastily put together. In the lineage houses feasts are generally held and the gongs are kept here. The family house rests on four poles, guarded by great rat disks, as rats are a menace. The floor is square, and the thatched roof comes down to form a dark verandah; in front a ladder goes up to the living room. There is a small entrance corridor with a hatchway from below. A fireplace extends the length of the living room. The posts and the floor are of wood. The rest is bamboo.

The men wear a coarse, rough loin cloth wrapped about the waist, made of a mixture of cotton and kapok. They are quite careful to avoid exposure. In addition, men wear a shawl thrown over the shoulders. They get much pleasure from their dress and ornaments. The women wear many coils of cord around the waist and attach in front a triangular piece of bark cloth to the bottom of this corsetlike affair. A tubelike garment of bark cloth may also be worn by the women.

When they sleep indoors they use heavy mats for covering, which give much protection. Generally the people sleep in pairs, lying side by side.

Men pay more attention to decorative articles than the women do. They have bow and arrow, a rattan belt used as a quiver, a basket, a back shield, rings, arm bands, anklets, etc. The decorations of the women are more restricted. As dance costume they wear the tubular shawl and necklaces and anklets. The men's headdress is long and cylindrical, and attached to it are many small dangling objects. Both men and women smoke native tobacco cigarettes habitually.

Water must be carried to the house, in bamboo tubes, from springs several hundred feet away. The water is exceedingly cold and as they have no means of drying themselves, bathing is infrequent. Young people, especially boys, bathe in streams. Bathing is segregated, and, though their clothes are scant, they are modest. A woman who bathes often, if she is married, is suspected of making herself attractive to another man than her husband.

Infants and children protest a good deal about being bathed. The mother's hands are hard and calloused from field work and no care is taken to handle the children gently. In addition, almost all children have yaws and the water irritates the ulcers. As a result the children complain vigorously, but to this their mothers are singularly indifferent.

Subsistence

Alorese diet consists of farm products and meat. The former are the mainstay but require much labor to raise, owing to a constant struggle with weeds. The soil is generally fertile, especially in the valleys.

The fields are cut and burned at the end of the dry season. This is a big job and requires the labor of all, men, women, and children. Then follows the planting of corn, the chief everyday staple because it is easy to raise, then peas and squash. Next to be planted is rice, the feast food and the only food stored which requires biennial planting. The battle with the weeds begins soon after planting and lasts from September to January. By February corn is ripening, and second and third crops can be raised. Eggplant and cucumbers are also cultivated; tobacco is a specialty. Bananas are plentiful all year round but are considered children's food. Mushrooms, eels, shrimps, and crabs are also eaten. For meat there are pigs, chickens, rats, and some dogs. Rodents are a great nuisance to farming, and men and boys hunt them. Meat foods, especially pigs and chickens, are for feasts. There are few feasts connected with farming.

All fields are owned individually. The amount of land and the actual subsistence of various families differs considerably. The plots owned by a family are not necessarily contiguous, a condition which often means hardship for the woman. Ownership may be divided between the father, mother, and children.

Fields are given to children, especially girls, between ten and thirteen. Though the produce is nominally the property of the child, it usually goes into the family larder. However, some concession may be made by selling a portion to purchase something for the child. But until adulthood the ownership of land and produce is entirely subject to the parents' wishes.

Vegetable foods are considered property of the woman, regardless of field ownership or labor spent in the field. All meat, on the other hand, is controlled by the men.

Labor in the fields requires some teamwork. Usually a field is shared by lineal kin; two to four people may share equally in the work and the harvest. In addition, bands made up of from ten to fifteen women and children sometimes work one day in one field, one day in another, until each of the group has benefited. But some Alorese never enter these partnerships, because "You work in other people's fields but in your field they just sit around and play." Work in the fields is chiefly the woman's responsibility, and she is prized for her industry. There is, however, little surplus; but some corn and rice are saved for feasting and for seed.

Some of the Alorese attitudes to food are worth mentioning. Care is taken not to waste it, and though stored food is prized, it is not reckoned as wealth. Actual scarcity is relatively unknown; when they speak of "hungry" times they mean that favorite foods were not available.

Feasts are frequent, but the food is rarely eaten on the spot. Each woman brings a basket of food to the common pile, then the whole collection is redivided and taken home to be cooked and eaten. Meat is distributed on the basis of the number of males in the family. A woman who has neither husband nor sons is not entitled to meat.

Meals are frequent but not large. People often eat during the night; a man may wake up from a dream, go and tell his friends. They may then eat before going to sleep again. Children tend to be undernourished and seem to be hungry much of the time. Older children may supplement their diet by systematic foraging for bananas and mangoes, and the hot meal which is prepared for the workers in the field is also an inducement to the children to work.

It is the woman's duty to bring food to her husband wherever he is, and children are fed wherever they happen to be. In general men and boys eat first, the women and girls eat separately. Each person gets about the same amount of food, but young girls learning to cook are apt to obtain more than the boys because they are closer to the food. Only a grown man has the right to prepare a meal at home, which he might do during the day while the women are in the fields.

As a rule there is little generosity about food. The habitual sponger is disliked and discouraged.

Male Activities

The manipulation of finances is the man's chief occupation. These are related to man's control over the meat foods, especially pigs and chickens, sometimes goats or sheep. Just as the woman is in charge of vegetable products whoever helped raise them, the man controls meat irrespective of who helped feed the animals. Pigs are slaughtered only for feasts; if a pig is killed accidentally an impromptu feast must be held.

Finance

Financial transactions permeate every phase of social life: marriage, death, the building of lineage houses. There is a standard of value, the florin, and a currency in three forms: (1) pigs, (2) mokos, and (3) gongs.

No one raises more than one or two pigs by himself. For the greater part, pigs are raised in partnerships. These partnerships are the chief financial preoccupation of the men. A poor man may have five, a rich man twenty pig partnerships. To obtain partnership in a pig, about fifteen payments, plus an equivalent of three days' work, must be paid. Arrangements of payments are variable and flexible, the labor may be paid for with a piglet. The owner gets the first and second litter, the raiser all succeeding litters. When a pig is slaughtered for a feast, each partner gets half, or one partner may accept a currency equivalent for his share. These pig partnerships serve to place a lien on a younger man who is entering his financial career and are also an effective way of concealing wealth and assuring it against claimants, for the partner is obliged to protect the joint property. In spite of these advantages, partnerships lead to endless complications and quarrels.

Mokos are bronze vessels of Javanese origin, of various sizes and designs. Their value in florins is fixed, that is, 1, 2, 3, 5, 50, etc. up to a reputed 5,000. But there are hagglings and disputes over the worth of those of higher value.

Gongs are also used as currency. They are prized musical instruments, kept in the lineage houses. With hard use they wear out, and the fragments are used as small change.

All financial transactions are made in the expectation of profit. One florin interest is considered due on a deal involving a five florin moko. Sometimes these transactions lead to a potlatch situation—a public reckoning and pig-killing throughout the whole valley. Innocent bystanders and kin of contestants become involved and may be obliged to contribute pigs to each contestant to avoid partisanship. Usually, however, these quarrels are resolved by a public counting of tallies, the last to hold tallies being acknowledged the winner. Hostility may continue nevertheless, though a public reconciliation can be effected by the winner's inviting the loser to a meal.

To enforce payment of a debt, litigation is a last resort, for it deprives the litigant of a potential financial ally. More commonly the debtor's pigpen is raided, but this is awkward as other pig partners may be involved. Another way is to take the debtor's *moko,* and this can lead to a fight. Still another method is to accept part payment, or the promise of a daughter in marriage, in which case the debt is considered down payment on the bride price. This last procedure is not the preferred one, for the young man in question may be undesirable, or the girl may refuse to go through with the marriage. If a poor man accepts a girl in payment of a debt, he generally lives in the girl's household and is expected to work hard to make up the balance of the bride price. This is contrary to the usual rule of patrilocal residence.

Marriage

Marriage in Alor is the beginning of a series of exchange relationships between affinal groups. There is a monetary bride price and a dowry, in the ratio of 3:1. If the average bride price is $60, the average dowry is $20.

A marriage agreement is reached either by mutual consent of the couple or as an expedient to aid the finances of the parents. In either case the financial arrangement is the same. Lengthy negotiation sometimes precedes the actual transaction. The first gift is a preliminary down payment of a moko of about $2 for the girl's father, and a shawl worth about $1 for her mother. The bride price and the dowry each consist of six regulation payments, extending over a long period. Actually, the agreement is made in accordance with the money available from kin. The engagement gift and the first and highest priced moko must be paid before marriage. Then the girl goes to live with the man, signifying her consent to the match by arriving at her husband's house with a bundle of wood or a basket of corn, symbols of her readiness to join his household. However, a girl will often deny herself sexually to her husband for some time after marriage.

After the bride has come to the groom he is free to ask her family for the first dowry payment. The rapidity of liquidating these mutual obligations depends largely on other responsibilities, such as death feasts or the building of lineage houses which either family may be called upon to undertake. The severity of these debts often deters a man from entering marriage relations with families who are too wealthy.

In addition to these formal exchanges there are a series of free gifts. They show a man to be either generous or niggardly; they may also be considered a man's payments on offspring. The minimum gift is four piglets. The wife's parents usually will make corresponding gifts of vegetable food in return. An ingratiating groom begins these informal gifts before paying the bride price. All these arrangements are agreed upon between the groom and the father or uncle of the bride.

Should divorce take place, the bride price and dowry are counted against each other, that is, all gifts except the informal ones just described. The tally for each payment requires substantiation by a witness. These occasions when the tallies are counted against each other are opportunities for airing grievances, and more often than not divorce does not follow. The difficulty of repaying the bride price in the event of divorce helps maintain some stability in marriage. Sometimes the bride's male relatives refuse to repay the bride price. In that event only a new groom may settle the bride price with the first husband. These payments make it very hard for a woman to get out of a disagreeable marriage. The man's chief problem is to enlist his father's aid in raising the bride price. It is rare and difficult for a young man to effect these arrangements by his efforts alone.

These complexities are illustrated by the history of a young girl who married a man from a distant village. He paid her father an unusually high bride price, about $80. The girl went to join her husband but refused him sexual privileges. This is not uncommon at the beginning of marriage, and the husband was not too impatient. After a month, however, he followed her one night when she left the house and raped her. They had quarreled also about which field she should cultivate. So she ran back to her own village to live with her maternal uncle who had brought her up. Her mother had died when she was young, and at her father's remarriage she had gone to live in the household of her uncle.

Her father was greatly annoyed at the breaking off of the marriage, particularly since he had given little dowry as yet. However, the husband forced him to repay all of the bride price except a $13.50 moko which the father refused to return until the husband returned a $5 moko of the dowry. This the husband refused because of a dispute as to what precisely was owed. In addition, the uncle was angry because he had not shared in the bride price, and so he refused to help repay the husband. The girl refused to seek another spouse to assume these obligations. Both of her male kin were furious at her behavior; her father took back a shawl he had given her, and her uncle refused to pay for a seer to counteract poison witchcraft which the girl said her husband had directed against her. She had been ill for several months and was sure it was caused by poison her husband made over a piece of areca nut shell she had discarded. The young woman was thoroughly depressed and apparently felt herself in a trap.

Social Organization

The dance place is the center of the lineage group, and the separate family houses cluster around it. A village is made up of from one to six such dance places. Theoretically the in-group expands from the biological family to the patrilineal group, then to the village; so kinship affiliations are usually also affiliations by contiguity. But this is by no means always the case. A family of five brothers may be scattered in three different villages. Residence is patrilocal by rule, but there are exceptions.

Kinship is reckoned bilaterally. Marriage between first and second cousins is disapproved; third cousins occasionally marry. The kinship system is fairly loose, and kinship terms may be extended as an ingratiating gesture. Of chief importance in the system are: (1) Patrilineal lineages and (2) Male Houses, the latter of six varieties, as is shown in the accompanying chart. The Alorese are not good genealogists and often have difficulty in tracing the various Male Houses.

These relationships carry with them definite obligations connected with marriage, death, war customs, etc. Male Houses 1 and 2 make the largest contributions to financial transactions and obtain also the greatest return.

KINSHIP CHART

Household: Each biological family has a separate house. The houses cluster around the dance place (center of lineal group). Therefore households around dance place are approximately groups of brothers and male descendants.

Village: One to six dance places.

Male Houses

1. Mother's brothers, and offspring
2. Father's Male House 1
   Father's–mother's brothers and male descendants
3. Mother's Male House 1
   Mother's–mother's brothers and male descendants
4. Father's Male House 2
   Father's–father's–mother's brothers and male descendants
5. Mother's Male House 2
   Mother's–father's–mother's brothers and male descendants
6. Father's Male House 3
   Father's–mother's–mother's brothers and male descendants

Female House

All kin not in patrilineal lineage or designated as Male Houses.[1]

These relationships show their importance primarily in the complicated financial obligations connected with so many Alorese institutions which seem to preoccupy the people to an extraordinary degree. Some idea of the complicated character of these mutual obligations can be gained from the following description of the happenings after the death of a man of some standing.

A wealthy man, M., was ill with dysentery. For ten days there was much gossip: "Would he die, and was he being poisoned, and by whom?" His friends and relatives were divining the outcome by killing three chickens. Everyone gathered in his house, and for six days before death he slept in the arms of one of his sons. While this was going on the Male Houses were busy trying to decide what contributions they would make, and how to raise the funds. When he finally

[1] Du Bois, *The People of Alor* (Minneapolis, University of Minnesota Press, 1944), p. 21.

died gongs were beaten, and according to custom his female kin, not his wives, wailed. During the illness his wives had withdrawn from the house. At noon his three sons, their affinal kin, and the Female House of the dead man presented themselves at the house of his Male House One. After much discussion this Male House handed over a shroud and a pig and gave food to the visitors. In return for this the Male House said he expected a 100-florin moko, though his gifts were not worth more than 20 florins.

There was more wailing, and boasting of wealth, while the shroud was being taken back to the house. On the way the sons collected a few more gifts. Then clamor started for a big feast. An immediate funeral was demanded by the donor of the shroud. But the burial was not being hurried, because one son of the deceased let it be known that he did not have enough to pay off the gravediggers since he had not approached all the Male Houses for their contributions.

The next day collections began, not without friction and hard feeling. Male House Two contributed a moko, but did not feed the sons when they came; they were outraged and made no arrangement for repayment of the moko. Before the funeral a member of this Male House came forward with a seven-florin moko to atone for the offense. About noon the gravediggers arrived; they were six members of the Male Houses. There was gong beating and wailing, and the diggers were urged on by gifts of prized bits of cloth. Children were driven away from the burial, which, like wealth displays, was considered no place for them. Then the gravediggers rushed into the house and bound the body in the shroud. As they came out with the body, a son of the deceased cut the throat of a pig as a sacrifice to the dead so that he should use his good offices to help them in pig raising.

In the grave they put his areca basket, eating pot, drinking tube, and sleeping mat. After the burial the diggers washed themselves free of contamination. The wives, in the background, cut a rope in two—a symbol of severed relations with the dead. To keep the ghost of the deceased away, they carry an unsheathed knife over their shoulders for several months after their husband's death. They do not return to the house of the deceased. The sons show no grief during the funeral; the women do all the wailing.

After the funeral, debts are paid off and the guests are fed. Again dickering and discontent accompany the payments; everyone tries to get the best of the situation. For instance, Male House Three complained that he did not receive enough for the grave-digging. Reluctantly a son raised the fee. Male House signified his satisfaction, but the sons said "Not yet," took a plate of food and added, "We are hungry." This meant they wanted more in return for the gift they had just made. Male House was reluctant to make a return, but finally gave up a three-florin moko.

Next the sons gathered the contributions from the other Male Houses. The first burial feast was given on the fourth day; the second, four days later. In both, the Female House fed the Male Houses. During this time the sons, brothers, and parents should observe three taboos: (1) eat no salt; (2) have no intercourse; (3) abstain from bathing. The first is to prevent the body from disintegrating, like salt in water. The second taboo is frequently broken; they explain that some women are lucky, so no harm is done by sleeping with them.

About two weeks after the burial the sons announced that they would now give their first pay-off feast. A pay-off feast requires a good deal of wealth and may be delayed anywhere from one to fifteen years. Consequently it seemed rather ostentatious to hold it so soon. Actually the sons did not have the necessary means. They gave the feast anyway, not calling it a pay-off, but a preliminary feast. However, subsequently they claimed they had given a pay-off feast. In fact, they had returned some gifts so that debts would not accumulate too much.

Sons inherit their fathers' wealth, but much of it is dissipated through the death feasts. The mokos must be used to repay obligations, and before the death feasts are completed most of the pigs have been consumed.

In this case, during ten days, pigs worth 57 florins were eaten up, half of them furnished by the Male Houses, half by other lineal kin and the Female Houses. At another such death feast over fifty persons were involved in financial arrangements, either as contributors or as creditors, some of them in eight transactions lasting up to ten years.

Through death, a man in Alor is forced into a debt situation which may be extremely embarrassing, even to a person of wealth, and the financial aspects of death and burial have an effect on his life that extends over years. The death of a poor person creates no such complications. It receives little attention, the corpse is simply wrapped up and thrown away outside the village.

Some other attitudes of the Alorese may here be noted. In addition to concealment of wealth, lack of ostentation, there are beliefs that large accumulations of wealth may cause death without apparent cause. This is due to the anger of the wealth-giving familiar, who is angry when he gets no gift from his human protégé. To prevent this a wealthy man may give a feast and toss food into the weeds. This, though really a sacrifice to the familiar, is anyone's find who happens to be there.

Warfare

Warfare among the Alorese is practically non-existent today, but even before pacification by the Dutch it was not a large-scale affair. In view of the greed and chicanery involved in finances, it may not be surprising that disputes sometimes lead to physical violence. But a murder may have wide reverberations, large groups of kin become involved, and finally whole villages engage in open warfare. So even children are warned against fighting, because, through group responsibility, both in terms of kinship and territorial affiliation, one fight could give rise to a long series of retaliatory acts of violence among their elders.

Their wars are neither bold nor bloody. Rather, they are characterized by the long-term bearing of grudges—a war may drag on for years—and by ambush and treachery, admired as shrewdness by the Alorese. Violent death, like death from natural causes, involves groups of kin in complicated financial arrangements.

Disputes may, however, lead to wholesale destruction of property. For instance, Padata the Leper set fire to Maliseni's house when the latter refused to pay his $17.50 moko debt. The entire village burned to the ground and general pilfering by all ensued in the course of the confusion.

A review of the last series of head-hunting raids will illustrate the actual progress of a war. The series of retaliations listed below covered a period of about thirty years.[2]

1. Manisenlaka of Kewai killed Motlaka of Lawatika. No one seemed to remember the reason for this first murder.

2. Lonmani, a young girl of Lawatika, was kidnapped by Padakafeli of Atimelang and sold to Kewai, and there killed in revenge for the first death. Padakafeli was motivated by the profit involved in selling a head.

3. Lanpada of Kafakberka was killed by Kafolama of Dikimpe at the instigation of Padamai of Lawatika. Padamai was the father of victim No. 2. Kafolama was his friend and was paid for getting Lanpada's head. Lanpada seems to have been completely innocent in the matter except that

____
[2] Quoted from Du Bois, *The People of Alor*, pp. 126–28.

he belonged to a village allied to Kewai. He came to Dikimpe on a dunning trip.

4. Padakalieta of Dikimpe was wounded by the Kewai people in the course of a general skirmish in which the villages of Kewai and Atimelang fought those of Dikimpe and Lawatika.

5. Likma of Kewai was killed by Manimai of Atimelang. At this point, Atimelang had changed sides without notifying Kewai. The change occurred because Padakalieta, No. 4, had kin in Atimelang and the Dikimpe people persuaded the Atimelangers that they owed Padakalieta vengeance. The killing of Likma is particularly instructive. He and his murderer were friends. The murderer visited Kewai while Kewai was still under the impression that the Atimelangers were allies. Likma was persuaded to return to Atimelang by his friend who promised him protection. As the two approached Atimelang, Manimai, who was walking behind, shot Likma in the back and brought his head to the village.

6. Kafolama of Hatoberka, a village allied with Kewai, was killed by Manipada of Atimelang in a general swirmish resulting from death No. 5.

7. and 8. Two women of Alurkowati, a village which had been relatively neutral, were wounded by a group of Lakawati men who ambushed them as they went for water.

9. Lakamau of Alurkowati was killed by Padakari of Lakawati in a skirmish.

10. An old woman of File was killed by a group of Alurkowati and Dikimpe men who were out to ambush a Lakawati person. The men had gone to an area where Lakawati people had outlying fields, hoping to ambush some unsuspecting and unprotected person. They failed to find anyone from Lakawati and took the head of a File woman instead.

This "war" terminated when the villagers of Dikimpe took the initiative and paid for the murder of the old woman of File; a payment of thirty dollars in mokos and gongs bought off the File people. Although active warfare ceased, suspicion between the Kewai and Atimelang people lasted twenty years.

In connection with each of the killings in the course of this "war" financial responsibilities were incurred by the kin of the deceased and the obligations were not completely discharged for many years. The bereaved kin do not necessarily take direct revenge on the murderers. However, it is their duty to buy a head from the actual avengers. Any head, even a stolen one, may be used for this purpose. Or even the mere fact of a killing may be "sold" to the kinsmen, without producing the head. The price the kinsmen must pay for the head may be as high as $112 in gongs, mokos, weapons, and pigs; actual payments may be delayed for years. At the pay-off for the head the dickering goes on as at a death feast. When financial claims are settled, the "head" (represented by a shell or stone) lashed to the end of a pole is "danced" into the village by a procession headed by the buyers and the female kin of the deceased. This symbolic head is beaten by the buyers and discarded, as a precaution against the malevolence of the spirit of the head. The dead kinsman has now been avenged; he has a "spouse," as the head is called, and will not return to trouble his relatives. The final ceremony is a mock feeding of both buyers and sellers, a gesture of appeasement to the souls of both the dead kinsman and the "spouse."

The cost of revenge must have acted as a check on excessive head-hunting. The Dutch authorities put a stop to it altogether, and the Alorese substituted for the "head" ceremonies the spirit bird ceremonies used in cases of death from accident or disease. In these ceremonies small birds, killed and dried, are sold as "spouses" in place of heads. The kinsmen of the deceased must buy the bird from others, thus maintaining the financial aspects of the head ceremonies. Had this substitute not been available when the Dutch put an end to head-hunting, the Alorese would have been exposed to serious conflict between fear of their dead kin and fear of the living Dutchmen.

In the provoking of war and violence and in the moderation of hostilities as well, wealth and financial transactions play the same prominent role that they do in other Alorese activities—marriage, death and burial rites, etc. About one tenth of the adult males stand out as men of financial power; those less successful tend to group themselves as satellites, or allies and servitors, about the wealthier men. Such satellites have no formalized role, but they are depended upon when a show of strength is needed, as in the ceremonial delivery of a dowry payment or at a burial, and when labor is required. Physical exertion is considered fit only for women and underlings, and beneath the dignity of an important man. Satellites in their turn receive protection from those they aid, particularly help in meeting their financial obligations as adult, married males.

Religion

Attitudes concerned with the supernatural are revealed by many aspects of this culture. Finances and warfare cannot be discussed without mention of death ceremonies. A consideration of craftsmanship would reveal a relationship, somewhat casual, to "sacred" carvings, ceremonial procedure, and knowledge of ancestral kin. In the biographies and elsewhere one finds references to village guardian spirits, Good Beings, sacrifices, and seers. It is of interest to review the Alorese relationship to the supernatural in terms of attitudes toward illness and death, burial, the "hereafter," benign and malignant spirits, insanity.

When an Alorese succumbs to an internal illness, such as headache, colds, influenza, he usually collapses completely into depression, inertia, and hopeless moping. The sick person sits in the dark, smoke-filled house, without bathing, often refusing food, with no exercise or air for days, certain that he is going to die. Relatives, much concerned, consult divinatory omens and often increase the depression of the patient by reporting unfavorable omens. When a person is dying, his grown son or close kinsman will hold him on his lap as a parent holds a child. Criteria for death are the death rattle, or cessation of heartbeat and breathing. In addition, prolonged delirium or coma is considered evidence of death, and whatever signs of animation the dying man shows are attributed to possession by an evil spirit. Under stress of fear and distaste, delirious persons may occasionally be buried alive—especially when, as the Alorese say, "their flesh has begun to rot away," that is, when skin lesions aggravated by lying on filthy sleeping mats have become noxious infections.

In connection with this fear of the disintegration of normal conscious personality such as occurs in delirium or coma, it is worth noting that no trance conditions are deliberately induced or culturally prized. In theory, seers are supposed to be unaware of what they are saying; their tutelaries are thought to perch on their shoulders and speak through their mouths. However, the procedures of the seers seem to be managed by fairly obvious and inept sleight-of-hand, their movements and speech give no impression of actual possession. Fear of losing one's normal personality seems also to act as a check against the use of the intoxicating palm wine which the coastal people drink. Delirium, coma, intoxication, and insanity are regarded as spirit possession, evil and dangerous. Several instances of acknowledged insanity show the behavior of the sick persons as aggressive and destructive, homosexual, obscene, and suicidal in intent—for instance, a request to be buried alive, or a challenge to soldiers to shoot. There is no form of institutionalized suicide, however.

No exact criteria of insanity have been defined by the Alorese, though individuals with unusual habits are suspected, as, for example, a woman who would run off alone and spend the night hidden in the field rather than return home. States of marked hyperexcitability and of maniacal behavior are not uncommon; in them the individual is extremely aggressive, destructive, and violent. For instance, Lonmanima as a young girl began to steal food openly. She would enter houses and snatch food from under people's eyes. At feasts she ran off with calabash serving plates full of meat. In spite of these early outbursts, she married and raised a family and during this time she appeared normal. Her difficulties returned when her children were grown. Her most characteristic tricks were to grab up children and run off with them, and to attack people indiscriminately with clubs or stones. She lived with her married children. Sometimes when offered food she would throw it away and return her dish broken or filled with feces. She went on in this fashion until she was quite old. Finally, she was chased away from a field in which she had been destroying corn. As she ran, she fell over a cliff and was killed. For years apparently she had had recurring maniacal attacks during which people threatened her with death or actually tied her up with ropes.

Burial

Most of the important features of the treatment of the dead were illustrated in the case of M.'s burial (see page 111). The shroud is the object to which the greatest value is attached, and since cloth is scarce those who furnish it expect a large return. A high rate of interest must be paid, but how much may be the reason for lively haggling for years after. Many of the best pieces of cloth go into shrouds, and out of circulation, because shrouds are such a sure investment.

While the male lineal kin seek the shroud, the female kin prepare rice and corn, leaving one or two women to wail over the corpse. The spouse of the deceased is thought to be in great danger from the dead, and he (or she) leaves the immediate vicinity of the corpse for fear the ghost may carry him off. He does not sleep the following day or night.

Usually burial takes place from twenty-four to thirty-six hours after death, and it is good form for friends to hasten the proceedings by comments on the stench of the corpse. Sometimes there are delays caused by financial arrangements (see page 112). When these are completed, the gravediggers begin to the accompaniment of much wailing and gong beating. When the grave is ready, the corpse is flexed and wrapped, hastily thrown into the grave, and quickly covered. Children are kept away from burials. The bereaved spouse cuts a cord in two to symbolize the severing of relationship with the dead; this confers some immunity against molestation by the ghost. An unsheathed knife is carried by the living spouse for some months as a protection against the spirit. This does not mean the complete absence of grief though the Alores are poor in sentiment. On one occasion a woman was mourned for two hours, then her relatives went on about their other duties. A woman who lost her third successive child mourned for a day and then went back to work.

The dead are thought to have malignant power and the nearest kin are the most feared. Yet there is much delay in the holding of death feasts. This is striking, since the purpose of the feasts is to placate the dead relative.

The Alorese think that each individual has two souls. One of these goes to the "village below" if the death was natural, and to the "village above" if death was violent. In the latter case a spirit bird ceremony must be held. The second soul is the one that loiters about the village, and protective devices must be employed against it, for at the time of burial the deceased wants company. The feasts on the fourth and ninth days after burial, the minor taboos observed by the family, and the night-long vigils of gong-playing, at which food is passed around, all serve to placate the spirit. Throughout these nine days many pigs are consumed and great debts are incurred. The last of the feasts, for which a sheep or carabao is bought, is for the purpose of permanently banishing the dead from the village and from human affairs. These feasts are usually given under pressure of creditors, to enhance prestige, or because of the illness of some relative. It is supposed that the dead may become impatient at the delay and cause trouble for the living. When illness is diagnosed as due to the displeasure of a deceased soul, a preliminary offering of rice in a container raised on a pole is made. At the same time plans for a pay-off feast begin. But these are apt to take some time; the preliminary offering is therefore necessary to keep the ghost quiet. The dead may also withhold good crops in the fields which they had worked unless the smaller garden feasts are properly made, offerings of corn presented them, and their names called out. Primarily it is the dead parents or grandparents who demand these observances from their offspring.

Ceremonial feeding rituals are common both for the dead and for other supernatural beings. It is noteworthy that these rituals are instituted under pressure of direct threat—that is, the anger of the deceased or of spirits—to preserve health or prestige. There are no permanent shrines; such shrines as they have are usually constructed in haste and are used for the moment. The carvings in which they represent their supernaturals are hurriedly and carelessly prepared and are discarded immediately after use.

When the death feasts are completed and it is felt that the soul is placated and has left the village, all interest ceases and the deceased is forgotten. There is no consistent theory as to what happens to the second soul when it has left the village. Perhaps the soul migrates to a low, uninhabitable coral island; but the Alorese have little interest in elaborating such speculations. Rilpada, the seer, gave the most systematic account of this future existence. He said: "People have two souls, a long and a short one, both called *hanoting*. When a seer sees a ghost, he sees the eyes which have fallen out and travel alone. He may also see a soul which looks like a human being but which grows taller and taller. When it is very tall, it falls over and gets up short again. That is how it walks. Some seers see souls as very tiny spiders which float through the air. These are often called *boiboi* but they are also *hanoting*. When a man dies, his breath has already gone, but two eyes linger here around the village until all the death feasts are given. Then the soul goes to Hamintuku. Not many people get to Hamintuku in this way; most of the dead are around the village. Some old people went to Hamintuku once and saw torn mats, broken pots, and drinking tubes like those broken on a person's grave, but we don't know anything about how the dead live in Hamintuku. The souls of the violently dead go above but we know nothing about that." [3]

On another occasion he said: "People who die go down a slope and come to a level place where there is a big ravine with a bridge across it. The feet of those who cross become slippery. Those who are young and swift get across and go off a long way to Hamintuku. The people who fall go to Sahiek, which is Karfehawa's village. They say to Karfehawa: 'Grandfather, I lost my way. Give me just a little water to drink.' Then Karfehawa looks at them, and if he likes what he sees, he invites them up on his large verandah and his wife cooks millet for them. She asks them to enter the house to eat. As they start up the ladder she pours millet on them. Then the burial rope, shroud, and maggots all fall. They pick up the bones, cover them with cloth, and Karfehawa's wife, who is called Masingbal, takes a fire tube and hits her husband's legs. He jumps and there is an earthquake. When young people die there is no earthquake; they occur only when grown and rich men die. Those that Karfehawa likes are given a field house and allowed to stay. If he does not like those who come, he spits in their mouths instead of inviting them up on the verandah. He orders them to follow the river down to the sea. There they turn into salt and lime rock. When lime bites our tongue we say: 'This is our dead forebear turned into lime.' "

[3] See Du Bois, *op. cit.*, p. 164.

Naturally, these beliefs and customs are related to their other ideas about supernaturals. In myths Good Beings are the supernaturals mentioned most frequently. The abodes of these beings are not related to the places to which the dead migrate. They seem constantly present in the people's expectations. A great war over the murder of the rajah was precipitated by some of his followers' disrespectful treatment of a woman who was regarded as a Good Being. Once Malelaka (see page 185) caused much excitement in five villages by his predictions of the imminent arrival of two Good Beings. Two guest houses were built, the grounds around them were cleared, and two stone basins into which rejuvenating magic water would flow were prepared. Death and death feasts would disappear, Malelaka told the people. So great was the disturbance in the villages that the Dutch sent troops to break up the guest houses and took Malelaka off to jail.

Good Beings are conceived of as humans with extraordinary powers; they revive the dead and travel through air and water. People who disappear are often thought to have become supernaturals. Once when four young men were drowned but only three bodies recovered, the fourth was supposed to have become a Good Being, and it was thought that he inspired the prophecies a five-year-old girl was making. Summaries of three myths illustrate the character of these Good Beings.

Masingbal went to the coast with his six brothers, who deserted him there. He went to sleep so hungry that he chewed the fringe of his shawl. As he slept, his mother and father appeared to him and told him how to get food and how to avoid a village of cannibals on his journeys. When he awoke, Masingbal followed his father's instructions and reached the village boundary of Farik, a Good Being. Farik's two daughters met the hero and reported to their father that the stranger resembled him. Farik, fully armed, went to meet Masingbal, and was convinced of his good intentions. He invited the young man to sit on his verandah and ordered his daughters to prepare food. When it was ready, Masingbal was asked to enter the house. As he climbed the ladder, the sisters poured a pot of millet on his head and he fell back on the verandah, shedding his shroud, burial rope, and maggots. They covered his body with a shawl, and the older sister sat near his buttocks, blowing on them with a fire tube. The younger sister sat at his head, fanning him with a fire fan. When Masingbal awoke the two girls fed him and Farik ordered Masingbal to sleep that night between them. Masingbal obeyed, but did not have intercourse with the two women, saying: "You two are good. I am fortunate to have met you but, my sisters, I shall not embrace you." The girls reported this to Farik who then ordered Masingbal to have intercourse with them.

The three thereafter worked together in the fields. After a time the two wives discovered that Masingbal was not working, instead he stood crying all day at a hole which he had made when uprooting weeds and which permitted him to look down on his own village. The girls told their father, who then insisted that all three should descend to earth and visit Masingbal's village.

Masingbal was alone when he reached his village. By bathing in a spring he turned himself into a person covered with yaws. He asked four women who came to fetch a drink of water for him. Three rejected his request and made insulting references to his condition. The fourth gave him a drink and spoke sympathetically. He sent her back to the village and promised to come in six days with a bride price. On the sixth day, people were dragging in the posts of his lineage house. Masingbal appeared with gongs and pigs which he deposited on the verandah of the Dry Land Woman, the girl who had been kind to him. He ignored all the invitations offered by the others.

The two supernatural wives now came to join Masingbal and his new wife, the Dry Land Woman. There was a shortage of food. Dry Land Woman asked Masingbal to help her climb for mangoes. When he was up in the tree, she took away the ladder, leaving him stranded. He was rescued by his two supernatural wives. On another day, Dry Land Woman killed Masingbal by dropping a heavy stone on him when he was down in a pit digging tubers for her. Again his sky wives found him and with the help of their father, Farik, were able to revive him.

The third time Dry Land Woman tried to kill Masingbal by sending him up an areca tree whose roots she had cut so that it toppled over with him. Again the other wives and his father-in-law revived him.

That night Masingbal called a dance. Toward dawn both he and his father-in-law seized the gongs and rose into mid-air with the two sky women. Half of his village also rose with them and came to rest in Farik's village. The other half of his village, containing Dry Land Woman and all the people who were quarreling, slipped down the mountain side into the sea.

Another tale is that of Masingbal and his son Metinglaug. Masingbal had six sons and an adopted male slave. When his wife was pregnant once more, he left, telling her that if the child was a male, he was to be killed, but if female to keep her until his return. The woman bore a son, but instead of killing him, she hid him on a mountain top with a large supply of food and male adornments. Meanwhile she buried a coconut and sacrificed a chicken. On his return, the husband thrust a spear into the grave, and the coconut milk seeped out. The husband was convinced until a rooster told him of the ruse.

Masingbal then set out with his seven boys to kill the youngest son, Metinglaug. He sent each of his sons in turn up the slope to kill their youngest brother. Each was offered food, accepted, and then could not find it in his heart to slay his young sibling. Each returned and confessed his inability, saying that the young man's face resembled that of his father. Finally, the father went up, refused the proffered food. While the son passively submitted, his father successively blinded him, slashed his mouth, cut off his hand, and slit open his abdomen.

Three days later two women, as they fetched water, saw Metinglaug's reflection in the pool. They searched for him and having found his body, replaced his organs with those of a dog and brought him to life with a fire fan and fire tube. When he was revived they fed him and instructed him in what he must say when he met his father. From here on the tale proceeds much as did the foregoing one except that it is Metinglaug's father, instead of his earthly wife, who tries to kill him on his return to his native village.

In the Tale of Momau the Crow Being, Momau and his brother went on a trading trip to the coast. The coastal people charged Momau falsely with theft. They bound his hands and feet and dragged him behind their boat for three days. Finally he freed himself and suddenly found that he was seated on the top branches of a mango tree. He climbed down the tree and was discovered by two supernatural women. As in the two other myths, Farik, the father of the women, made sure of his intentions, and then invited him to the village where he was revived by the usual millet treatment and the use of the fire tube and fan. After his marriage to the two women, he began to feel homesick. With the help of his father-in-law he went back to the surface of the sea and from there to his own village. His two supernatural wives had been transformed into a conch shell horn and a green glass bottle. These he neglected after securing a third wife in his own community.

A wild pig began to root up Momau's sweet potatoes. He went to guard the field. In an attempt to shoot the animal he was disembowled. (This is presumably a punishment for the neglect of the two sacred objects—his transformed wives.) The villagers all pursued the pig, which escaped by flying into the sea and changing into a porpoise.

Meanwhile his father-in-law, Farik, disguised as a Kebola man, went to Momau's village and healed him miraculously. The following day Farik transformed Momau into a crow, and back again into human form. Thereafter Momau himself possessed the power of healing severed bodies; this he demonstrated on his dog and child. He was also capable of assembling a shattered ax by simply blowing on it. His third wife was alarmed by these powers and said he had become a witch whom all would avoid. Momau then turned into a crow and flew back to Farik's village, taking with him the first two wives in the form of a conch shell horn and glass bottle.

Malignant Spirits

Another group of spirits are malignant; they may be either male or female witches. They gain control over their victims by inviting them to have sexual intercourse, and while the victim sleeps the witch steps over him and urinates on him. Now the witch has the victim in her power and may eat his liver. On this account, abdominal pains which are felt after contact with people who live in areas suspected of harboring witches may be interpreted as a sign of being bewitched. Witches also may take the form of civet cats or of streaks of light, and they have the power to detach their heads and roll them in the dark. They are a particular danger to children, whom they may devour. (Cannibalism is completely abhorrent to the Alorese.) Witches also have a peculiar liking for snails and snakes.

There are frequent stories of people who have had encounters with witches. The death of a man who had recently been married to a woman from Kewai, supposed to be particularly the village of witches, was attributed to his wife's having bewitched him. Hallucinations frequently concern witches: women without head or arms, with flies coming from the mouth, women who turn into bats, etc. For instance, there is the story of a young man who was entertained by a woman one night. When he slept she stepped over him and urinated on him. This bewitched him and he stayed with her and did not go home with his comrades. Some days later he went hunting. He shot an animal which turned out to be a snake. The woman became pregnant. As they walked back to the village she turned into a bat. A child from Kewai came into their garden. The woman changed into a snake and killed the child by eating his liver. The child's kin were angry and set fire to the hero's house. The woman turned into a bat and flew away, but the hero was shot as he tried to escape.

Although stories of witches have some currency here, there is little preoccupation with them. Poisoning also is feared, but there are few tales and little talk about it. Poisoning can be effected by powdering a dead man's tooth and putting it into the food or tobacco of the victim. Such food will kill a fly; therefore finding a dead fly on food makes it suspect.

Anxiety about being poisoned is not an obsession in Atimelang, for witchcraft and poisoning are not thought to be the major causes of illness and death. There is no fear that excreta, nail parings, spittle, will be used as magic bait. Yet one woman thought her husband had poisoned her by using a piece of areca nut shell she had carelessly tossed away. This shows that the idea of using things that have been in close contact with the victim as vehicles for poison is present. But it illustrates as well that there is no overt anxiety about these things, else the woman would not have been so careless.

A common form of malignant magic is to place a curse on someone, not secretly but openly, as a public announcement of hostility. There is also a curse directed against an unknown thief. Most commonly these curses are against those who rob young children or steal from fields or coconut or areca palm trees. A bamboo pole with insignia denoting illness is erected either before or after a theft, to overtake the culprit or to discourage the attempt. Once a child of two had a coin stolen from his belt. His father sent for a man who was noted for his courage in burying lepers. The next day a bamboo pole six feet high was set up. Into a slit in the top of the pole a piece of a leper's mat was inserted. The man who sets up such a curse may not chew areca, smoke, or have intercourse on the night preceding the ritual. The reward for these services is very small and scarcely an incentive. On the day the pole was erected, the little boy's father took a smoldering brand and rubbed it against the foot of the bamboo pole and invoked the soul of the leper to pursue the thief and give him leprosy. The chief purpose of the procedure is to frighten the thief into returning the stolen coin. But in this instance the coin was not returned, and in general thieves are not so easily frightened. The next night a firefly near the pole was assumed to be the soul of the leper in quest of the thief.

A curse can be removed only by the person who put it up. However, these poles usually fall down by themselves and are disregarded and forgotten. The effect of these curses is slight, for generally, even though a person falls ill of a disease specified in one of the curses, the connection will not be made. Confession is not considered as having any curative effect.

These curses are chiefly intended to safeguard property. But mechanical as well as supernatural means are used to this end. Coconut trees are banded with sharp downward projecting collars which require considerable time and effort to take off. They are intended to delay a thief so long that the owner will have a chance to discover him. Ripening crops are guarded by the owner who will not hesitate to shoot marauders; many houses have trap doors at the head of the entrance ladder which can be closed at night. Dependence on supernatural protection is therefore not exclusive.

Relationship to other supernaturals, such as evil spirits, wealth bringing spirits, and familiar spirits, is likewise generally casual and expedient. Everyone has at least one of these spirits whom he should placate to enjoy their favor. But except for the seers and prophets, who are constantly occupied with these supernaturals, people ignore these relationships until some misfortune such as illness occurs or some benefit is required, such as wealth and harvest successes. The village guardian spirit of Atimelang has had no carving or sacrifice made for it in sixteen years. Even when relations with the supernatural are imperative, they procrastinate and delay sacrifices, and when finally a carving is made, it is used for the occasion, then ignored and allowed to rot away.

Status

There are no formal gradations of status by rank, inheritance, or financial position. Wealth, however, is the chief determining factor in status, though age, sex, and kinship enter in. Women, who have no direct access to wealth, have no independent status, but share that of their husbands. Children have wealth only through paternal consent. Inherited wealth is negligible because the death feasts require most of it. As a rule, no man acquires any substantial wealth until he is middle-aged, and to maintain it he must be constantly aggressive, vigilant, tricky. The prestige gained by wealth must be consistently guarded and persistently validated. So difficult is this that most older men retire from competition.

Every man must enter into the conflict for wealth. Otherwise he may not have a chance to marry, he may be threatened by dead kin clamoring for feasts and punished by them if he fails in his obligations. In this connection, the sensitivity of the Alorese to comments on personal defects or status should be noted. To be called by some derogatory epithet, to have physical defects or poverty attributed are grave insults. Fines are often imposed as compensation. On the other hand, the Alorese are secretive about acknowledging the extent of their wealth and they do not praise physical attributes. Everyone must be granted equal status when addressed. Their vocabulary has no superlatives, only intensifiers. They are extremely sensitive, easily hurt; preservation of face is considered a mutual responsibility. A man who comes to dun cannot be sent home with nothing; he is given a token payment which will be reclaimed the next day. Shame provokes the greatest rage—and fear of being shamed is the chief sanction, in the absence of police or other formal government.

Skills

Prestige is not associated with physical strength, nor do the people have skills which bring honor to the possessors. The only skills are carving, fencing, making bows and arrows and wooden mortars. But all these are crude in workmanship and devoid of aesthetic quality. In addition, men may specialize in genealogy or calendry or may become seers or poisoners. The crafts bring no great monetary rewards. Even the seer has little power. Payments for curing are small and can only be a supplementary source of wealth. Choice of a career as a seer is generally due to failure in the struggle for wealth.

Their mythology is unstructuralized. Their genealogies are defective. Ceremonial procedure is fumbled and subject to debate.

Good craftsmanship is not appreciated and there is no pride in workmanship. The houses are carelessly built and do not endure. These people have never acquired the arts of weaving, pottery, or cire-perdue casting known on other parts of the island.

The only aesthetic skills pursued with some vigor are gong-playing and versification. The latter is stylized but permits some creative elaboration. These verses are recited in conjunction with dancing.

One poem, called The Spirit Bird Dance,[4] is a versified dialogue between a debtor and his creditors, with occasional interpolations by a guest. One creditor begins with a gleeful statement that "creditors will ask for large wealth." Another creditor sings:

> When the earth is at dawn
> When the world is light,
> Fani, my chief, ask for large wealth;
> Request long treasure.
> Your creditors, standing in file,
> Will hang the roar of a storm on their shoulders.[5]

The debtor host replies that at dawn tomorrow he will hand his creditors tallies and set a date for payment; adding that when the last tally has been torn off he will return to his dance place and give a dance—this protects the debtor from illness caused by his dead kinsman's ghost. The ghost is appeased when payment is made. Again the creditors gloat over their prospective gains. But the debtor retorts that nothing but disappointment awaits the creditors.

> My creditors, you have spoken truly; correct is your tale.
> At dawn tomorrow you will see nothing tasty;
> Nothing sweet will appear for you.[6]
> I shall give you tallies.
> When I set a date, return.
> Meanwhile, go to Latawati,[7]
> Sit upon its verandah.
> When the last tally leaf has been torn off,
> When it has been destroyed,
> When the intervening days have passed,
> Come back; return to my level home [8]
> To open the hand of illness,
> To pry apart the teeth of disease.
> This place is devoid of wealth,
> There are no treasures in this spot.
> But Lakamani, that small man,
> Has run ahead to ask for large wealth,
> To request long treasure.[9]

4 See Du Bois, *op. cit.*, pp. 137–39.
5 That is, gongs and mokos given in payment; this refers to the sound which gongs and drums will make when they are beaten by satisfied creditors.
6 He does not plan to pay them when the dance ends at dawn.
7 Name of the creditors' lineage house.
8 Literally, "placenta," a figure of speech for dance place.
9 The dead are expected to precede the living kin when they set out to collect debts and to dispose the debtor toward generous payments.

> Your bows will be struck; your shields tossed.[10]
> You shan't sit long.[11]

A GUEST:

> When the sun like a shrimp bursts on the hill
> Shields will crackle with dryness.
> I shall become very sleepy.
> I shall take the memory [12] of your dance to my house.
> Because of you I shall eat heartily.[13]
> The wealth for which you scratched,
> The treasure for which you scrabbled,
> The wealth for which you dunned,
> The treasure for which you asked,
> Your creditors will gather together and carry away.

The Life Cycle

Infancy and Early Childhood. The Alorese distinguish the following stages in the development of the child: (a) birth to first smile, (b) to sitting up or crawling, (c) to walking. There is no calendar reckoning of age. The child is believed to be the result of the union of seminal and menstrual fluids; this fluid mass gradually solidifies from the feet up; repeated intercourse is necessary for the development of the fetus. Because of this last belief, transient affairs are taken lightly.

Pregnant women report the usual backaches, nausea, food preferences, and so forth. They also know that exertion may cause abortion, and, if the husband is considering a second wife, they may induce abortion by heavy labor. Women are known as either long or short conceivers, depending on how long it takes to impregnate them. They have medicines for retarding or accelerating conception, and barrenness is always considered the woman's fault.

There are few observances associated with pregnancy. Intercourse should stop; men who have second wives have intercourse with them. The woman works in the fields throughout pregnancy, though some precautions against overstraining are taken. There are some prenatal taboos: The woman must not place a new pot on the fire, for if it blackens her child will be discolored; she must eat the internal organs of rats; the man must not straighten arrows, for then the child would be born with eyes rolled to one side.

10 That is, creditors will be well paid.
11 That is, the payment will be so large as to be immediately satisfactory and require no dunning on the part of the creditors.
12 Literally, remnant.
13 Refers to the morning meal after the night dance.

When labor pains begin, the woman goes to a female relative, the husband generally stays away. The umbilical cord is left long and the afterbirth is put in a basket and placed in a bamboo thicket. Stillbirths, and human heads and spirit bird bundles as well, are also hidden away in thickets. The child's name is selected if he happens to urinate when someone's name is mentioned.

Men stay apart from the place of the child's delivery and refuse food served by a woman who has been present there.

The midwife is given a small fee, commensurate with the difficulties of the birth. In general, delivery is not regarded as a strenuous affair.

The woman stays in the house four to six days, or until the umbilical cord drops from the child. This time she spends feeding, fondling the child, and bathing it in warm water. These warm baths are continued every two or three days until the child walks.

The mother's needs are looked after by her relatives. The father meanwhile refrains from vigorous work, for this would affect the child's health. If he transgresses, he picks some leaves at the place of his misdemeanor, confesses, and bids the soul of the child enter the leaves. He then strokes the child's head with the leaves. The straying soul of the child returns.

Six days after birth, mother and child go out of the house to the accompaniment of a small ceremony in which the maternal grandmother plants sweet potatoes and piles stones near the verandah, an act which signalizes the end of restrictions on vigorous labor for both mother and father. The mother is bathed, and the father gives a small feast to repay the wife's kin for services.

After the descent from the house, breast feeding is supplemented by vegetable gruels and premasticated banana. The child is passed about from hand to hand. The young men seem more interested in the baby than the women; they have more time. The contacts of the child vary according to the location of the house. Fondling consists of rocking, joggling, mouthing or mock biting, but not kissing.

Before two weeks are over, the mother returns to work in the fields, for she is responsible for the vegetable crops, the mainstay of diet. She does not take the infant with her, but leaves him in the care of the father, older sibling, or grandmother. If birth takes place during the dry season, the mother has a chance to devote more time to the infant. But, for the greater part, the infant is fed by a surrogate, the regularity of the breast is interrupted, and premasticated food or gruel—from different people—is a poor substitute, judging from the fact that infants often spew this food out. When a man holds a child he is disturbed to find the child search for his breast. Sometimes other nursing mothers feed the baby, but there are no arrangements to make such practice regular or dependable.

Before he learns to walk, the child half-sits and cries in a shawl slung over one shoulder of his guardian. Generally a baby is not left alone to cry, or left on the ground to be annoyed by pigs, dogs, pig lice, etc. Late in the afternoon the mother returns and takes the child to feed and fondle. At this time the child suckles whenever restless. Women do not seem to enjoy breast feeding. At night the infant shares the mother's mat until he can crawl about, and continues to share the parental mat even after intercourse is resumed. This resumption takes place at a variable time, depending on the sexual opportunities of the husband. Most feminine complaints are about the haste of resumption, which makes more work for the woman.

The mother masturbates the child to keep him quiet, and the siblings do the same when they are his guardians. No effort is made to teach the child to talk. Sphincter control is disregarded in the pre-walking stage. Walking is not urged or encouraged; crawling is possible only when the child is not being carried about. They learn to stand erect by pulling themselves up on the leg of an adult. Anyone can aid in these unsystematic attempts.

As the toddler grows more sure-footed the carrying shawl loses importance except for long trips. It is discarded after the child is three. Then the child spends the day playing near the house under the casual supervision of an older sibling or an aged adult. Under these conditions, the mother being absent from eight in the morning until five in the afternoon, feeding is sporadic. During the day the child shifts for himself. He gets scraps from older children.

Feeding frustrations increase as the child grows. Weaning may be hastened by the mother's second pregnancy. She weans the child by pushing him away or slapping him. The mother will sometimes deliberately stimulate jealousy in a child by taking another infant to feed. Children often try to make sucking substitutes out of other things, such as toy balloons. But in spite of these feeding troubles, there is not much finger sucking, not more than in our society. Parents do not interfere, but rather encourage thumb sucking to keep the child quiet. In connection with this a teasing game is made of the finger sucking, whereby desire for food is stimulated, but not satisfied.

Toilet training is gradual; the mother takes the child to the privy and watches his performance. He is taught to use leaves for wiping, but all are remiss in this, and the result is considerable irritation. If the child is first taken to the privy at nineteen months, he can be continent within two months. Between three and five they are all continent. No play with feces was observed. Constipation is uncommon.

Bladder control is taught later than anal control. Children from three to five urinate openly and adults treat it casually. There is little effort to control flatus. Bathing is extremely painful because of the cold water and the caustic medicines used on their skin ulcers. Childhood tantrums are most often connected with bathing, and these tantrums are often violent and long.

Sexual activities of childhood are confined to masturbation, started by the parents to quiet the child and continued by the child himself. This goes on freely and publicly. The child has the opportunity of observing parental coitus, and conversation about sex is not toned down in the presence of children. By the age of five children seem to know about intercourse and birth.

Children's sleep is much disturbed; a good deal of activity goes on at night, dancing, wandering in the village, narrating dreams and eating. Many of the dances last all night at which children of five are often present. Children take cat naps when they can, on the verandah or leaning against an adult. In other words, the sleep and rest of the child is a matter of small concern to parents.

Cries of distress are usually addressed to the mother. The word for "give" is early learned, and by five children have a good collection of imprecations, such as "Evil spirit, may you have smallpox." In angry moods the children are talkative, though generally they are shy and silent. There is no formal speech training, but ridicule is used as a corrective.

Children are sent on errands very early, and are sent off in a peremptory manner. There is no permissive, encouraging, nor even deliberate training; they learn by restrictive injunctions, shame, ridicule, and intimidation. They are not taught many avoidances or taboos. A boy often has his penis tugged, or fingers and arrows poked into his distended abdomen; if the child is irritated by this, he is greeted by cries: "Hit him. Kill him." The children do not have open fights, but slyly pinch and run.

Frightening children and threatening to cut off hands or ears are common, but never for sexual misdeeds. However, the severity of discipline or fright is not as decisive a factor as the fact that the child may be punished on one occasion and consoled on another for the same offense, and consequently he can form no consistent picture of what adults expect of him.

The following tale shows the deep and lasting impression such harsh and unorganized parental care creates. Pada was playing with another child whom he hit and made cry. Pada's parents came and asked who had struck the child, and the other children said "Pada." So his parents slapped him and took him home. He slipped out and went back to play with the children. (This episode is repeated three times.) Then his mother gave him a water tube with a hole in the bottom and told him to fetch water down in the ravine. While he waited for the tube to fill, he wandered up and down the stream catching lizards and eating their legs and tails. Then he went back for the fourth time to the tube, only to find it still unfilled. He said: "What kind of water is this which I am fetching?" A bird spoke and said: "Ru, Ru. Your mother made a hole in the tube." Pada refused to believe it. Later the bird warned him that his parents were collecting their valuables and planned to go away. Again Pada berated the bird and refused to believe it. This continued until finally, as the parents and grandmother were leaving the village, he called after his parents: "Mother, father! Wait for me!" His grandmother looked back and urged him to follow, but his parents only said: "We were all gathered in one village, but you were very bad so you can't live with us."

When they reached the sea, his parents went on walking across the water, but his grandmother was sorry for him and waited at the shore. She dug a pit in the sand for him to sleep in, and while he was asleep she followed his mother and father. Pada awoke and looked, saw his mother and father were already near Hamintuku and his grandmother was halfway there. He cried hard, saying: "Grandmother, mother, father, I am good now."

His grandmother called, telling him to return to the village. He went back crying; he cried all the way from the coast to the village. He had no loin cloth, he walked naked.

In the village a rooster told him where his grandmother had hidden rice, fire pots, and other supplies for him, so that Pada was able to plant a garden and cook for himself.

Pada grew up, but he was still naked, so he was ashamed and hid in the house most of the time. One day two girls and their father passed by and their father sent them up into the house to borrow fire. Pada refused at first to let the girls come in, but they insisted. When they returned to their father, they said the young man was naked, but that his face resembled their father's. So the father gave Pada a loin cloth and then insisted that he marry the two daughters.

Again the rooster told him where his grandmother had hidden mokos so that Pada was able to pay a bride price. Next Pada wished to build his lineage house. When he gave the feast for thatching the house, his father, mother, and grandmother came. When they left, he presented each with a bamboo tube of blood sausage and a basket of rice. However, when the three stopped on their way home to eat, the mother and father on splitting open their tubes found them filled with feces and discovered that their baskets of rice held only hulls. The grandmother, however, had been given good food.

Another tale runs as follows: A boy was left alone at home while his father, mother, and everyone else went out to weed the gardens. There was in the garden a squash flower, which turned into a woman. In the evening she turned into a squash flower again. She returned again the next day. The boy courted her and took her home. The boy's mother found the girl and insulted her. The boy finally married the squash flower girl. The mother boiled squash flower blossoms and fed the dilution to her daughter-in-law, who died. The boy said: "Oh, my mother has an evil heart." He then took the squash flower and asperged his dead wife with it. She revived. He then cooked millet and called his mother and as she came up the ladder, he spilled the pot of millet over her head. She died.

Meanwhile the girl's father and mother hunted for their child and wept with joy when they found her. But they turned her back into a squash flower and put her into a pot. Then the boy, his wife, and parents-in-law were reunited.

Temper tantrums are prominent in the child's behavior. The commonest cause is the mother's daily desertion. At first the child may try to follow his mother; then, as she outstrips him, he may roll over on the ground and beat his head on the earth. The mother is not consistent; once she comforts, another time ignores, and still another time she may beat him. Promises of reward for good behavior are never kept, and rarely made. Older siblings who care for the child are not more dependable. The child may be placated and fed, or struck and deserted for the same provocation. Tantrums are commonest before five, but occasionally occur up to seven.

A constant stimulus to which the child is exposed is quarreling between parents, in which the child is the pawn. In these altercations the child is often separated from his caretaker and given to some unfamiliar person. Children subsequently learn to play off one parent against the other.

Residence is unstable for the child. There is constant moving from house to house, village to village. The houses are perishable. A field house lasts only two years; a village house, five to six.

Late Childhood. This period is from five or six years to adolescence. Naturally this period differs for the two sexes; the boys are generally less shy, more mobile and more in evidence than the girls.

At this age food is less of a problem to the boy. He is given a meal at home in the morning and in the evening. In the intervening time he forages for himself in the play groups of children. He may scrape remnants from a cooking pot; he can hunt insects, or forage for papayas, bananas, sweet potatoes, corn. Parents tolerate these depredations unless the crops are scarce or the child's labor is needed in the fields. In addition to permissible foraging, there is institutionalized stealing which is greatly feared. Sometimes the boys also get meals as guests when an adult is on a visit. Boys may also attach themselves to older persons, do errands for them, and begin to learn about the men's business and secure a little food besides.

Boys of this age also form work groups of from three to twelve boys who work in each other's gardens. On these occasions the mother of the host-boy will get a meal for the group. Girls are more likely to take to this work than boys. During feasts, the boys help with the butchering and are given undesired parts of the animal to do with as they like. Rats are another source of food for the boys; they shoot and cook them in the fields.

The girls' routine is somewhat different. Their play period is neither long nor free. They copy the activities of the mother and are inducted into responsibility for cooking by the time they are ten. Having more access to food, they are less tempted to steal, though they do not escape the accusation altogether. The girl has no guest privileges, and doesn't get anything from the butchering. At feasts the women get meat for their husbands and sons, but not for themselves or their daughters.

The girl is made aware at an early age of her responsibility in relation to the vegetable crops and works in the fields much more than her brother. She is also taught to fetch water and collect wood. Until marriage, however, the girl cannot make a contribution of food displays in her own right. In addition to her role in food, the girl is taught to weave baskets and mats, and to make bark cloth.

Except for this difference in training and responsibility, young children are not segregated and do a good many things together. They forage together; but boys emphasize hunting, girls food gathering. They have a good many games and toys of considerable ingenuity. Adults play no games and their entertainment is limited to dancing. A good deal of imitation of adult activities goes on among children. The responsibilities for younger siblings is shared by boys and girls alike—the infant in the family is the one who suffers if too much is asked of an older child.

In general, the boys have less training and fewer duties. The boys have some special privileges—for example, they are the main actors in the corn ritual, in which they drive the rats away. Women are excluded from this ceremony. Boys also participate in the communal pig hunt. They imitate death feasts, and beat imitation gongs. They learn skill in hunting by play with bows and arrows. They share the rat hunting and roof thatching with the men. When they reach twelve or thirteen, they may be sent on errands connected with wealth. But generally the activities of boys are those of hangers-on, not of participants.

However, children are held responsible for their misdeeds. Once a boy playing with his gang called out to a man that he had six fingers— a deadly insult. The man started litigation and demanded a $2.50 moko as compensation. The parents of the boys made no effort to condone the guilt and punished the boys by destroying their toys. There is group responsibility for misdeeds. Moreover, children are often blamed for the misdeeds of adults.

Teasing and ridicule is a favorite device of adults toward children. This is a special sport of young men, who delight in sending children on fools' errands, and deceive them with false promises of rewards. A child returning from such a mission is the butt of a great deal of laughter. It is not surprising that lying is taken as a matter of course. Any statement by anyone is always doubted. Many words in the Alorese vocabulary indicate deception.

Occasionally the threat of being sold into slavery is used against children, though in actual practice such an action is not common. Kidnaping a child as vengeance for a misdeed of his parents is rare, but not unknown. Sometimes children are held as hostages for debts. In such instances the vengeance and prestige of the parents is of higher value than the child himself.

Gossip about supernatural malignancy and about witchcraft poisoning teach the child at an early age to fear the supernatural, and they learn how they can become the victims of their parents' religious neglect, either through delaying death feast obligations or through failing to sacrifice appropriately.

The children's reaction to what discipline there is—and the above account shows it is not great—is significant. Children protest by running away, for there seems always to be some relative who will offer the child sanctuary. Children quickly learn which of their kin they can depend on in emergencies.

Corporal punishment may be administered by parents, siblings, uncles, and aunts. The child most frequently has his head struck with the knuckles, or his ears may be pulled, his mouth twisted, and occasionally he may even be tied up with a rope. It is interesting to note that children are never spanked or struck at all on the buttocks, and that the buttocks lack erotic significance or stimulating power compared with breasts. The young married woman may be punished in the same way as a child by her mother-in-law. Children may vent their aggressive tendencies on younger children or on helpless old people.

The fact that children's property can be confiscated by the parents and that the child has no redress causes added frustration. For example, adults often appropriated toys given to the children by the ethnographer. On the other hand, parents show a good deal of solicitude for their children and give them many gifts. The most formalized is the gift of the loin cloth; the most important is the gift of the field. Either parent may bestow these presents. The gift of the field is really only symbolic, for the produce may be claimed at any time by the parent. Children receive only the token assurance that they are contributing to the family and occasionally they are given some produce to exchange for the highly prized cloth. That children must constantly be reminded of the virtues of industry indicates that the ownership of fields in itself does not carry great feeling of value or of independence.

During this period of from about eight years up to adolescence, sex activities change considerably. The free masturbation of childhood disappears after the acquisition of a loin cloth, when children imitate the modesty of the adults. Ripping off the loin cloth of the object of aggression is a common trick to humiliate the victim. There is much clandestine sex play, both homosexual and heterosexual. Girls take masculine roles in play. The only overt sexual activity between girls that was observed was mutual masturbation. Overt homosexuality of any kind is disapproved of in general, but mutual sex play of boys five to seven was observed. The threat of castration is only rarely used against children; and then only against older children and for offenses which are not sexual.

Play groups of boys and girls sometimes mingle for days at a time. In these gatherings sex activities are attempted. Though this is frowned upon by adults it is not treated seriously. Children's behavior in play situations indicated definite awareness of the sexual situation and also a knowledge of the relation of copulation to conception. Obscene words are common in children's vocabularies.

The children imitate their elders by using obscene words in anger. Words for genitalia are common epithets of derogation. Violent cuss words are: "Sleep with your mother, your father can't,"—which incidentally reveals a high value placed on potency. However, as the child grows, he is expected to curb not only overt aggression but these verbal equivalents as well. There are relatively fewer fist fights; actual violence makes children shrink from the scene of action. They imitate their parents in this, for the Alorese seem unable to intervene when violence does take place. They cannot interfere with something which has started—either to alter or arrest its course. This is true of watching two people in a fist fight, or watching a house burn down.

Children are not considered to be actual participants in society. It is assumed that they know nothing and feel nothing. Full adulthood is not achieved until a man is a father; in other words, the child confers status on the adult. Occasionally a child's status is elevated because supernatural powers are attributed to him, and in this case parents and other adults may be subject to the child's whims.

Adolescence—Marriage—Sex. In adolescence, the two sexes are treated quite differently; the preadult period for the boy is much longer than for the girl. There are no rites of transition; no men's clubs, no secret societies, no tribal initiation; no ceremonies or restrictions associated with first menses. The only equivalents for such customs are tatooing for girls, letting the hair grow long for boys, tooth blackening and filing for both boys and girls, and these are optional.

The time for tatooing the girls is the first day of the four-day communal pig hunt, at the end of the dry season, when most men leave the village. The girls are from ten to fourteen years old. They accompany the men to the first hill crest and then remain quiet until the men return. The tattooing cannot begin until they see smoke of fires started by the men. The tattooing is considered only as a means of beautification. It is of inferior quality and not durable so that tattoo marks are scarcely visible on middle-aged women. Men are not excluded from tattooing and may be tattooed if they wish.

At about sixteen the boys begin to let their hair grow long. At this time they begin to acquire male dress adornments: sword, shields, areca basket, wide belt, bow, combs, and head plumes. This is ridiculed by the women, who hoot the men, and scoff at this manifestation of masculine vanity. At this time a boy also breaks away from his gang and becomes more solitary, partly in imitation of the behavior of the wealthy man. He begins to speculate on his chances of entering the financial system or of ingratiating himself with older men of influence. He also begins visiting young girls, while adults tease him. In addition, he may insist on a midday meal, or cook it himself.

Tooth blackening and filing make for a prolonged picnic, free from adult supervision—the period of preliminary sexual courting. Strict parents will forbid their daughters staying out in the field houses with the boys and even warn them not to cohabit. The picnic is arranged when the girls can get away from their field work. Young men who like the sport go along. The procedure takes six or seven days. The boys hunt some rats, the girls gather vegetables, and they cook and eat together. The filing process is painful, for it consists of filing the upper and lower incisors in half. As a result, when the molars are occluded, the tongue shows through the gap between the incisors. This is considered attractive.

The formal aspects of financing a marriage have already been discussed (pages 108–10). The management of these arrangements varies widely, from sons who are on good terms with wealthy fathers willing to help them, to those who have no solicitous kin and must break into the system by themselves. This is the point in the society at which many complications arise.

A lad who becomes involved with a woman may precipitate a scandal and be forced to marry, thus putting his parents in a bad bargaining position. The following case illustrates the uncomfortable position in which both boy and father may find themselves.

Atamau was a young man about seventeen. His elderly father, Mobikalieta, had found it financially convenient, about a year before, to accept as part payment for a debt the immature daughter of a friend, who was to marry his son. Atamau resented the girl because, as his age-mates said, "He wants someone old enough to sleep with." The matter had been in abeyance for about a year when, at a house-building feast in which the old father was a partner, the young girl was sent along with a food contribution in her own right. This constituted a kind of public declaration that the marriage was valid. When she arrived at the dance place, Atamau flew into a rage and knocked her basket of food to the ground, saying that she was not his wife and had no right to contribute the food. The father was angry and turned on his son, who then openly repudiated the marriage and said that the girl's parents were willing to give back the bride price. The father, in spite of his age and feebleness, flew into such a tantrum that he began dancing in a challenging way back and forth across the dance place, shouting as loud as his aged voice permitted. The son sat quietly at one side, looking distressed but stubborn. Bystanders tried to intercede, but Mobikalieta turned on them in rage and threatened to leave the feast, although he was a building partner of the lineage house which was being erected. After Mobikalieta had made various extremely boastful challenges, he suddenly recalled the original cause of his anger. Turning on his son he said: "Perhaps you had better find another father." This was the equivalent of "throwing away" his son, one of the most drastic pressures a relative can bring to bear. Atamau began to cry quietly, but refused to give up his point. When the ethnographer asked a bystander if Atamau would really seek another man to help him marry, he smiled and said: "When a father and son quarrel, they don't remember their words" (that is, hold no grudge). However, this was merely the traditional response. Atamau and Mobikalieta were not reconciled. Five months later Atamau persuaded a rich financier, called Maliseni, to take up his case.

For two whole days Maliseni negotiated with the father of the girl, with Atamau's father, and with the chief of Atimelang, who was considering buying Atamau's repudiated childwife. The negotiations reached a climax one night when Maliseni paced back and forth on the dance place for two hours, discussing the matter with a sympathetic audience and shouting his conclusions up to the dance place on the ridge where the supporters of the girl were gathered.

All this difficulty centered around a series of interlocking obligations in which Atamau was being squeezed. The situation was complex, but in brief it was like this. Mobikalieta had already paid the girl's father a ten-dollar moko, a five-dollar moko, and two pigs. The father was notoriously poor, and direct repayment from him was out of the question. The chief of Atimelang who was bidding for the rejected girl was willing to pay back the five-dollar moko and the two pigs. Still unsettled was the repayment of the ten-dollar moko. The girl's father and the chief stated that they would not repay it until Atamau made a dowry payment on a kinswoman of his, married to a relative of theirs. Matters were at an impasse for another month until the divorce of another of Atamau's kinswomen, through Maliseni's good offices, put him in possession of a moko. This he could use as the demanded dowry payment, and thereby get back his ten-dollar bride-price moko. With that in hand he could begin to accumulate a new bride price, lending it at interest to Maliseni. So he would be one step nearer to buying the girl on whom he had set his heart. The financial complications and delays must have been highly frustrating to Atamau and to the girl on whom he had set his heart. The frustrations and delays created, and expressed as well, hostility between father and son. They also laid the rejected girl open to a good deal of sly teasing by men, about her desirability and the reasons for her marriage to an older man.

The Atimelangers have a definite conception of romantic love, but for the man such love becomes rather a liability which renders him more susceptible to financial pressure. In courtship women have a tendency to take the initiative. It is they who ask for an exchange of tokens, shawls, etc., and they look forward eagerly to going to the dance places. The men appear to be pawns of the women on the one hand, and of the ambitions of their own parents on the other. Initiative by women is accepted even in native theory. On the other hand, it is not uncommon for the woman to deny sexual privileges to her husband, even after a common residence has been established. Such refusal is rationalized on the basis of unsatisfied financial claims. The men themselves are often extremely inhibited sexually. It should be noted that men while engaged in feast finances are often continent and even sleep in male guest houses. Marriage comes earlier for the girls than for the men, though this hardly implies an explanation of the young women's sexual resistance.

Beauty in a woman consists of light skin, small eyes, wavy hair, prominent breasts, and also of cleanliness. The last, when excessive, may be interpreted as coquetry. Intercourse is solicited of young women by touching their breasts. A common euphemism for intercourse is "to pull a girl's breasts," since it is supposed that no woman can avoid being aroused by such a solicitation. Opportunities for this sort of approach are offered at dances and in the horseplay that occurs among young people when they are away from their elders. In describing this situation one young man said: "Our hands move about at random and touch a girl's breast. That makes her spirit fly away, and she has to sleep with a man." For a woman to touch the man's genitalia is considered completely shameless. A less intense form of suggesting intercourse is to tug at either a man's or a woman's hand. In marriage, people usually wait until they think everyone else in the room is asleep. Then either partner may indicate desire by giving his spouse a short tugging pat anywhere on the body. The woman is supposed to remove her loin cloth since contact with it would be distasteful to a man. The position in intercourse is ventro-ventral with the woman below, or with both partners on their sides. Any other position is considered rather "nasty." In fact, one divorce was precipitated partly, according to the wife, by her husband's demands for the dorso-ventral position. One informant said: "We hear that the soldiers on the coast know how to have intercourse while standing, but we don't understand such things." Inquiries about fellatio brought negative responses.

Cunnilinguus is shocking to them, and kissing altogether unknown, but biting is practiced. Wrestling and mock fighting are often preliminary to intercourse. Anal intercourse is unknown, though they have stories about anal birth. As previously noted, infidelity by a man causes his child to be sick. It is rarely cause for divorce, though a frequent source of quarreling.

Instability of marriage is one of the conspicuous features of Alorese society. The following chart gives a picture of marriage and divorce.[14]

MARRIAGE AND DIVORCE RATIOS

	Males	*Females*
Total number of cases, 252	112	140
Adults never married	14	0
Adults who have at some time contracted a marriage	98	140
Contemporary widows and widowers	5	25
Number of additional wives	..	25
Undivorced but married adults	49	93
Number of divorces among remaining	49	47

These figures are of some significance. There are twenty-eight more women than men in the community. This indicates a higher mortality among men, since out of 108 recorded births the sex ratio was 1 to 1. However, in spite of the surplus of women, there are none who have never married, whereas there are fourteen men who have not. This may be viewed in the light of plural marriages, and of the financial difficulties the men face in contracting marriage. It should be noted that of these fourteen unmarried men all but one are young and still hope to contract marriages. Therefore the woman seems to be at an advantage in acquiring a spouse. A woman's expectancy of losing a spouse through death is, however, higher than a man's. On the other hand, the expectancy of rejecting or being rejected by a spouse is one to three for women, whereas it is one to two for men. In other words, the figures suggest a less secure situation, in some respects, for men than for women in marriage. The figures probably understate the actual expectancy of broken marriages; in spite of repeated checking there were undoubtedly instances which were forgotten by the several informants consulted. Furthermore, many of the adults listed were still young and had not yet run their full course of marital readjustments.

In the choice of mates, marriage with kin is thought to be improper, though some relationships are accepted which in other societies border on the incestuous. Second cousin marriages took place. Mother-son, father-daughter, and brother-sister marriages are denied. One brother-sister incest case is known, but comment was: "That's

14 See Du Bois, *op. cit.*, p. 97.

bad, people don't get gongs and mokos in a marriage like that." Sexual relations with a stepmother or sister-in-law are also disapproved, but are not interfered with. A case of stepmother incest was discovered. The father ordered his son tied. The son refused to submit, armed himself, and challenged his father to a fight. The father dropped the matter and the boy moved away. But the son later returned to give his father's death feasts.

Illegitimacy is rare, only one case being known in five villages, the child of Matignma, known as the "crazy woman." She earned this epithet through alleged promiscuity.

The woman is decidedly less eager for children than the man. Many men express displeasure because their wives do not conceive. Notwithstanding the desire for children by the man, and that having children elevates the man's status and guarantees his death feasts, jealousy of a man toward his own child is known.

In marriage there is a good deal of mutual jealousy, especially on the part of the man. Theoretically, adultery is punishable by death; actually the injured husband is satisfied with a fine and the removal of the offender. There are some magical devices for securing the love of a desired person. A woman will mix love magic by putting at the bottom of the man's food pot shreds of her loin cloth, nail parings, pubic or axillary hair, or by putting certain plants into his food.

A man may take more than one wife; however, the first wife always quarrels with him about it. She may want to know how he can afford a bride price for a new wife; or she will claim that the pigs given for the bride price were raised by her. Then she will seek out the second wife, and a free-for-all fight follows, which may involve all the women of the village. The men as a rule stay out of these fights, and watch them with amusement. Occasionally, the slighted wife may make the new one very uncomfortable, or get a divorce. The only time such quarrels are absent is when a wife is inherited through the levirate.

When there are plural wives, the man must divide his labor, time, and pleasures equally among them. If he does not, there is more quarreling. The senior wife retains the responsibility for contributing the food to his feasts, and these take place at her residence. Not all wives remain hostile and jealous; many get along well.

The status of the women in Alor is rather anomalous. They are the actual providers, also the pivots around which much financial exchange takes place, but actually they have an inferior position and do all the hard labor in the society. Yet they can obstruct a man effectively by refusing him food and sex and can block his financial career. A woman may even occasionally trounce her husband. In many ways the woman has more mobility and is less bound to status requirements than the man, and she is freer to give her allegiance where she wishes.[15]

[15] The reader is urged to consult the fuller account of the institutions and practices of Alor contained in Dr. Du Bois' book. The analysis which follows was naturally based upon fuller data and impressions gained from about twenty seminar discussions, personal contacts with Dr. Du Bois, and reflection on all aspects of the culture for several years. Some of the data were elicited during seminar discussion and are accordingly placed in context.

CHAPTER VI

ANALYSIS OF ALORESE CULTURE

DURING the study of this culture some confusion arose because certain matters of fact could not be definitely settled. These concerned aspects of sexual disciplines, care of the child, some aspects of their rituals and religious concepts. This confusion was not due to inaccuracy of observation, but to the fact that these matters were really unsettled in the minds of the Alorese, and this tolerance for inconsistencies in their religious beliefs and their concepts of ritual was really characteristic of them. The features which stood out conspicuously and served as guides for the establishment of the basic personality were: that the subsistence technique was top-heavy on the female side, with only sporadic and unorganized aid from males and children; the looseness and disorganization of religious concepts; the fact that there is much talk about witchcraft and that no one really takes it seriously; the fact that there is a poverty of sentiment as against the tendency to settle all claims by finance. The poor religious concepts, the disorganized aggression patterns, the conspicuous absence of co-operative techniques, the prevalence of general anxiety, the unstable marriages, all these point to defective personality integration. We note the religious patterns and whereas they seem very like many others we have studied, there is an absence of idealization of the supernatural. We also note the frequent motif of parent hatred and revenge fantasies in their myths, the low tone of the superego mechanisms, and the low aspiration level of everyone.

There is little hope of establishing the relation of these features to each other without following through the course of integration in the life cycle. It may then be possible to reconstruct this seemingly confusing picture.

Parental Care

Prenatal taboos and precautions are not conspicuous. There is no definite couvade, though there is some concern about the appearance of the child, which might be spoiled by this or that activity by either parent. The fact that they do not bury the afterbirth indicates that there is no covert hostility to the child. It is really wanted, for it is destined for a career of caring for parental needs, especially after the parents die, and for a prominent role in the status struggles of the parents while they live. The meaning of the paternal taboos against hard work is not clear.

Good maternal care ends the fourteenth day after birth, though it may last longer if the child is born during the dry season. From this time on maternal care is sporadic, inconsistent, and undependable. The unaided struggle with hunger and other tensions begins for the child.

Tensions created by hunger and other discomforts may be relieved by others while the mother is away. Older siblings are pressed into service to carry the child in a shawl, and some attention is given to keeping the infant from being annoyed by animals and insects. The child probably gets enough food as measured in terms of calories; but it lacks the consistent image of one person with whom it can associate relief of hunger tensions. Tensions which can be relieved by fondling and caressing accompanied by consistent feeling tones in response to parental affective solicitation are also absent. These are both powerful stimuli to responsive activity. The breasts of three women under such conditions are not as effective as one, because the whole relaxation conditioning becomes confused by nipples of different shapes, breasts of different size and consistency, and various body odors. The feeding of premasticated food adds more confusion, for that can be given by anyone who takes a notion to do so. The fact that children are often observed spewing this premasticated food indicates that it is a disturbing influence and not a help; and that the donor of the food and her emotional attitude is as important to the child as the food itself. On the other hand, a stranger who appears from nowhere may bring relief. (In their folklore Good Beings also appear from nowhere.)

All this means that during the helpless period of the child the maternal care fails. And failure in this instance can only be interpreted to mean that ego resources are not aided, but the effects of continuously unsatisfied tensions are permitted to take their toll in defensive inhibitions and confusions. The parental image as a reliever of tensions from hunger or other sources does not have a chance to be formed. These tensions are not of the kind to which the infant can get accustomed, for they create persistent pain, and no effective clear-cut integrations can be erected on a foundation of pain. Painful tensions can only initiate avoidance techniques; and since escape from hunger tensions is impossible, only incessant crying can result. The intermittent appearance of the mother in the morning and at night cannot relieve this situation. In fact, it must in the long run act as an additional irritant, because the only image of the mother that can emerge as a consequence of her intermittent attention is the emphasis of her tantalizing and frustrating aspects to the disparagement of the kindlier side. Hence, satisfactions from the mother must be fraught with rage.

The use of masturbation to quiet the child is not an ego-enhancing factor, but a distraction in the wrong direction. It is clearly not an evidence of erotic interest in the child or an effort to stimulate erotic patterns, but an effort to make the child less of a nuisance. It is done primarily in the interests of the guardian. In the presence of so many other unsatisfied tensions, masturbation cannot become the center of any organized fixation upon anyone. It may however persist in the form of a distraction to children whenever unsatisfied tensions from other sources arise. The ethnographer's observation of abstracted children playing with their genitals is in all likelihood pertinent to this point.

This childhood picture must be subject to a good deal of variation, depending on accidental circumstances, such as whether a grandparent is at hand to take over the maternal role persistently, or whether an older sibling can do the same, whether they have any interest in the child, etc.

It must be parenthetically observed here that this early integrational chain is noted not because in itself it is capable of doing permanent damage but because it is the earliest in a consistent chain. If a decisive change were introduced at the walking stage or at three or four, its bad effects could in a measure be undone, and the later integrational systems might escape the unmitigated damage wrought by the earliest experiences.

In connection with these unpleasant tensions the early illnesses of childhood—especially yaws with its itching sores—must add their share of distress and thus augment the need for a kind parent. The rough handling of the child and the irritating bathing and medication can only aggravate the already bad situation.

In the walking stage we find another traumatic factor. This time it is also the absence of help. The child gets no assistance in walking, in the form of comfort for its failures, encouragement, or urging. Here again is the absence of consistency. Such help as is forthcoming is sporadic, unpredictable and not offered by any one person the child can learn to trust. In this instance, however, the biological forces that impel growth are stronger than any obstacle; but since failures create inhibitions and lack of confidence, this neglect robs the child of the stimulation and encouragement so necessary for the development of enterprise. Not only is walking not taught; talking is likewise subject to no systematic training.

The sphincters are not subject to special training at an early age. Anal control is taught by example and delinquencies are not too harshly treated. Bladder control is introduced later. So that in connection with sphincter control no constellation is created which relates cleanliness with obedience and ultimate rewards. In this connection it must be noted that the anal zone or buttocks never acquire any erotic value with the Alorese. They are never beaten on the buttocks, and anal erotic play is unknown. Neither do hips or hind parts play an important role in fetishistic sexual fixations.[1] The Alorese do not attempt to control flatus in children or anyone else. The anal zone therefore does not take on any meaning adventitious to its chief evacuating function. It has no connection with morality or manners. The irritation caused by faulty cleansing apparently does not alter this situation. In connection with this we can also note that cleanliness has no special significance to the Alorese. They are apparently impervious to bodily odors, and bathing has the significance of a beautifier and indicator of coquetry. On the positive side of this anal situation we can say that the child is not prematurely burdened with responsibilities he cannot understand. Responsibility is a late acquisition, if at all.

Weaning is irregular and is effected by pushing away or slapping. But the most significant thing about the weaning is the introduction of a new and damaging disciplinary measure—teasing, of which the child gets a great deal later on. The deliberate stimulation of jealousy both by taking another child to the breast and by playing tantalizing games in which often food is promised but not given—all these add to the tensions. This pattern is persistently followed throughout childhood. The adults who engage in this teasing consider it very funny. This laughter is in part their unconscious revenge, and partly an indi-

[1] The biography of Fantan is an exception to this (see p. 192).

cator of repressed cravings. The fact that children attempt to make sucking objects of male breasts or of toys with protuberances is an indicator of the unsatisfied hunger cravings. The strong fetishistic character of eating probably originates from this source. That is, the emphasis falls on the eating and not on the early emotional relationship with the mother with whom it is first associated.

The rest, recuperation, and sleep of the child are likewise unplanned. The persistent nocturnal activity must interfere with rest. In addition, the use of ridicule, intimidation, threats, and, on the other hand, the absence of permissive, encouraging, or deliberate training must create a good deal of confusion. The absence of definite landmarks for consistent development is shown by the fact that children will be punished on one occasion and consoled on another for the same offense.

What are the lines of character formation under these conditions in early childhood? Two interesting observations by the ethnographer from early childhood point the general direction for us: the fact that in the vocabulary of the young child there are a good many imprecations, and that generally shy and reticent, they become talkative when angry. The second indicator is the prominence of the tantrum. They both indicate the presence of a great deal of aggression, mostly of a disorganized character. This is a sure indicator of the presence of a preponderance of unsatisfied wish tensions, together with a lack of organized techniques for mastery. This is a general condition of all childhood. In Alor, however, this situation seems particularly intense, because there is so little opportunity for the formation of constructive and expressive constellations or action systems.

The most lasting and dominant effect of all this is the conception that is thus formed of the mother. It must be a confused and ambivalent one. All factors conduce to the preponderance of hatred and aggression toward her and the absence of an affectionate and helping image of her. In the creation of this image the preponderant weight must fall on the feeding frustrations. The only assertive attitude that the child can take to this situation is to take by force what is denied it, that is, to steal. The foundation is laid therefore in earliest childhood for stealing—which ought to be regarded in a very general sense as taking from someone something which you want given to you, but, since you know that it will not be given, you take it anyhow, but without the kindly effect of a gift and without idealization of the donor.

Under these conditions, the mother cannot be idealized as a benefactress. The early use of imprecations by children against their elders is an indicator of this hostile attitude to the mother, or her surrogates. The tantrum is another indicator of the helpless rages of these children. The fact that these tantrums are ignored or even evoke violent retaliatory measures must lead eventually to their suppression, but at the expense of certain defenses.[2] The suppression of these rages, that is, the conviction of their ineffectuality, lays the foundation for the later fear of any aggression, for a lower self-esteem, and for an incapacity to sustain effort, the tendency to give up easily and collapse readily in the face of danger and to aspire to little. It is not unlikely however that the wish to subjugate the mother or anyone from whom they have similar expectations should be retained as a strong unconscious incentive.

In the face of these facts, the question of what happens to their erotic development presents some equivocal features. We are accustomed in our society to observe the consequences of this development under the conditions of good maternal care, of a more or less consistent disciplinary system which places high emphasis on obedience as a condition for being protected and loved. These conditions do not obtain in Alor. The absence of consistent disciplinary measures in the anal or sexual domain fails to establish the constellation of reward for obedience or conformity. The opportunities for observing sexual relations of parents would have the tendency to stimulate erotic tendencies. The constellation created cannot, therefore, be one of a desired parent who forbids sexual activity, which must be abandoned in order to remain in the good graces of this parent. In other words, the emphasis must fall in another direction. The inhibitory influence must take the form of making the object from whom the gratification is expected into one to be feared and avoided. The basis for strong tender relations with the mother is therefore seriously undermined in childhood and never corrected, an attitude which is strongly reinforced later toward women in general by the mores governing status marriage. This situation is quite clear as regards the development of the boy; but the effects of this situation on the girl must be quite similar, although the path of development is somewhat different.

[2] Thus Kolangkalieta (see Du Bois, *op. cit.*, p. 479) mentions an episode in which her uncle stuffed feces into the mouth of a crying child.

The systematic teasing and deception also destroy the possibility of forming a consistent frustration-reward balance. They can only aggravate the child's depressed ego feeling, completely destroying all expectations from its elders, laying a basis of profound general mistrust, together with an incessant unconscious effort to find the kind, loving parent. The proof that this constellation exists in the Alorese is to be found in the striking fact that affection is expressed by them in the unusual manner of the impulse to steal. Thus in the biographies of all the men the affectionate impulses toward the ethnographer showed itself repeatedly in their dreams by a repressed impulse to steal from her. This comes about in the following way. The impulse to love, esteem, or admire arises. This is countered by the recollections of so many previous frustrations that the impulse is automatically repressed, and is replaced by the impulse to take by force what is denied. But this must also be repressed. It can therefore only express itself in a dream. Consciously it can only be represented by a vague tension of expectation and an irritation at the object who arouses the tension. This illustrates a blocked action system. It means in effect that the overt behavior, stealing, already represents the result of repressed feeling tones for which no direct avenue of expression exists. Whereas the intention which unconsciously motivates the stealing is an affectionate impulse, the form it takes must elicit a response directly opposite to the one desired; it leads to further rejection of the child.

The attitude of the child to the father must be of a somewhat different character. The father does not play the role of provider to the child, hence he is not the source of so many expectations. For the greater part, he is absent, and plays little role in the socialization of the child. What he does is sporadic, unplanned, and unsystematic. No strong sense of responsibility can develop toward him, nor any great expectations. The important role of the father, the financial aspects of life, do not become known to the child until very much later. The sexual role of the father must, however, be known to the child very early, and this may create the impression on the child that the father is the successful possessor of the mother, who is so inaccessible to the child. Frequent quarrels undoubtedly disturb this picture. There is a good chance in this situation for the development of the conception of the father as the hated rival, that is, the Oedipus complex. The role that the father plays later is uniformly despotic;

he is in a position to subordinate the child's independence to his own ends. There is little opportunity for the child to greatly inflate the importance of the father. The absence of adequate reward systems makes the likelihood of the development of ingratiating attitudes very small, whereas the continued effect of repeated frustrations by him can only increase the hostility to him.

We see therefore that in relation to both parents there is no opportunity to form strong attachments which have a stimulating influence on character development. The bearing of this on superego formation in Alor is quite remarkable. We have the following factors operating: The suppressed hatred of the mother cannot lead to the acceptance of her as an ideal to follow; there is no incentive for the child to do as the mother wishes, first because it is not directed, secondly because there are no inducements in the form of anticipated rewards. Commands arbitrarily given by her are therefore not binding in a positive sense, that is, to do something "for the sake of" or to preserve boons already enjoyed. They are followed mainly in response to force, or threats. We shall later see that the child has other means at its disposal to defeat or escape from the parent. The sense of shame, fear of ridicule, is much less satisfactory than punishment in superego formation, provided that the latter is not too severe and that the child has some opportunity to establish a correlation between what is disapproved and what is expected and also some quantitative evaluation of degrees of disapproval. Frightening the child is of no more value than shaming it, for it can only add to the already heavy burden of anxiety which the child has to bear. This situation is not much altered in the relations to the father. Since the tonicity of the superego is maintained by the capacity to internalize the parental ideal and since this ideal causes the child so much discomfort, the only termination of this situation can be the failure to develop a real conscience. This is of course a vicious cycle. The child who suffered from his parents does not try to revise his behavior toward his child when he becomes a parent, but mistreats it in the same way. That is, he emulates the most undesirable traits of the parent, and those which, as a child, caused him the greatest suffering.

The situation between siblings offers some opportunities for amelioration. The rivalries we are accustomed to see in our society cannot possibly develop to the same degree because little is expected from the parent and so there is little to fight about. On the contrary, the opportunities for strong attachments between siblings are very great. There are, however, many factors that militate against such attachments. The oldest sibling undoubtedly has the worst time of it, because it is compelled, as soon as it is able, to take over the maternal role without having enjoyed its benefits. The effects must be very uneven. A strong bond must undoubtedly be created by the fact that the siblings have common enemies and common grievances.

The question arises now about whether there is any foundation laid in childhood for later homosexual attitudes. This seems not to be the case. The chief reason for this is that as a love object the father is no better for the boy than the mother, no more dependable, and as the child grows older the father is likely to become more and more frustrating. Ingratiating techniques are of no avail to the child, and the father at no time is in a position to take on a maternal role. His control of subsistence economy does not take in the stable articles of diet. His role as a meat provider—which is really a luxury—is appreciated rather late in childhood. As regards the possibilities of female homosexuality, these are also very unlikely, because of the general interference with development of affectionate attitudes by the maternal frustrations. The chief factor in the sexual situation of childhood here is the general attitude of hatred that is generated toward those to whom the child's first affectionate impulses are likely to be directed. This spoils the whole sexual development, lays the foundation for strong distrust of the man to woman. The woman on the other hand cannot develop any strong love for the maternal role, and so all the forces seem to pull in a centrifugal direction. The facts are that homosexual practices are observed only in young children, but at no time later. Unconscious passive homosexual attitudes are therefore likely to develop in this society only when there is a combination of good maternal care and a strong father. Such is the case with Ripalda (see p. 177).

It is difficult to determine from this childhood situation how much interference there would be with sexual potency in both male and female. We would expect some. But there can be little doubt that the early integrational systems point toward a lively antagonism between the sexes. There is a strong likelihood that sex activity is overvalued, but that its chief unconscious objective is the fetishistic emphasis on the breast (that is, food). The hunger tensions are therefore bound to be exaggerated and to serve as carriers of emotional tensions unsatisfied all along the line.

Late Childhood

Late childhood is characterized chiefly by the channelization of aggression. At first it could only take the form of tantrums; it is now directed into permissible forms of foraging and stealing. This activity is particularly the outlet of choice for boys, whereas the girls, who at this time begin to be inducted into household activities, have greater access to food than do the boys. So far as the boys are concerned these activities are permitted, particularly if the foraging and stealing take place in the gardens of their own parents. These predatory activities are really the first bit of constructive ego development in the boy. It would be an error to regard this purely as an effort to make good the deficits in parental care which persist throughout this period. It is also partly an expression of vengeance against the parent and a bit of self-assertion in that it implies the attitude toward the parent: "I really don't need you any more." This tendency to forage and steal is a trait which persists for a long time, and a certain general feeling of guilt about the deprivation of youngsters exists in the form of a universal fear of being robbed without any too strenuous efforts to suppress the activity. There is some such effort, but punishments are not severe.

In late childhood also both sexes are prematurely inducted into the role of taking care of their younger siblings. The performance of this role is undoubtedly subject to much variation. In general, however, a child who is robbed of the care essential for growth and development will not bestow such care upon a younger claimant without resentment. The result is that the older child, who is now the mother surrogate, is no more dependable than the mother herself. So the situation for the younger child is not greatly ameliorated by this institution. On the other hand, the older sibling is likely to be given attributes which were prevented expression toward the mother by the strong ambivalence to her. This attitude is furthermore facilitated by both older and younger sibling having a common claim. This is a factor which in some would tend to ameliorate the situations of sibling rivalry and render the hatred toward the parent still greater. In others it might terminate in intensified sibling rivalry and hatred.

A third point is that although no formal training exists for the boy, there is a continuance of coercive measures, a continuance of the practice of fooling and misleading and of lying to the child, which only generates more distrust and can only end in a complete inability to believe anyone. This circumstance perhaps more than any other in this culture is responsible for the very weak libidinal ties and the internal sense of isolation that each individual must have. It is at this time that the child also learns that none of its rights in the family are inviolate, that gifts given to it can be revoked arbitrarily, and even gifts such as fields, gardens, and pigs are really only nominal. This is a continuation of teasing.

To all these circumstances, the child, particularly the boy, had an additional institutionalized channel of expression, perhaps the best outlet which the culture permits, namely the practice of running away. This is the most extreme gesture of defiance and independence that the child is permitted and offers both a safety valve for pent-up aggressions and an opportunity to sustain the hope that the child may find in one of its other relatives the long-sought-for kind parent. More often than not the grandparent is chosen.

In contrast to all these untoward influences, there is one advantage of their childhood, namely the rather lackadaisical attitude toward sexual practices in children. In this respect they can, surreptitiously to be sure, but without fear of serious punishment, indulge in this activity. However it must be noted that sexual activity in children is tolerated rather than encouraged or permitted. The acquisition of the loin cloth is an exhilarating experience and probably serves to buoy the hopes of the child of achieving some of the advantages of adulthood. The meaning of sexual activity at this time probably contains elements of breast fetishism derived from maternal neglect. The stealing activities of the child plus the opportunities for sexual activity with other children may in some measure serve as vehicles for those constellations already formed in childhood. It affords some constructive expression for stifled self-assertion.

It is not likely that the suppressions imposed on overt forms of aggression or the gradual diminution in the use of obscene words injure the child in any way. However it must be noted that the self-esteem of the child is in no way improved from that of earlier childhood; it still remains low. The child must still have the idea that it is supernumerary, that it is of no account, and only grudgingly is the boy permitted to participate on the fringes of adult male activity. In this respect the position of the girl is distinctly better, but for reasons that we shall presently see, the prejudices accumulated in childhood do not make the maternal role any more acceptable to her than it is to him.

In late childhood the culture therefore permits an active form of self-expression in foraging, stealing, running away; but these activities all point away from emotional solidarity within the family.

Before leaving the subject of late childhood we must note that in poor parental care the strongest foundation for superego systems has been destroyed. Discipline without rewards can lead only to hatred, and if no real dependency constellation has been created, no superego of any vigor can result.

Adolescence, Marriage, Sex

From this point on, the basic personality structure of the males and females must be separately pursued.

Male. Induction into adulthood for the boy is not accompanied by any puberty rites which mark the introduction of new and serious restrictions. It is not infrequently the case that in societies in which puberty rites are severe the boy is compelled to surrender certain advantages of immaturity and is given new ones which he heretofore did not enjoy. As a matter of fact, in Alor puberty does not introduce the boy into any strikingly new experience; but it is the beginning of a long and arduous struggle for the achievement of manhood. The control over this achievement is vested largely in the father, who by virtue of his control over the property, or of the opportunities for gaining control over property, can indefinitely delay the boy's achievement of status. Nor is there any necessity for binding the child to any rigid sexual taboos; these are left in the same status as in early childhood, that is to say sexuality as such is not forbidden; only status marriage is rigidly under control. The theoretical advantage of free sexual play is thus actually canceled. The time eventually comes when the father actually interferes, not with sexual gratification or the opportunities therefore, but with the admission to the status of paterfamilias.

In the hands of his father the boy continues to operate under a system of coercions without rewards, notwithstanding the fact that the "potestas" of the father is only virtual, and actual control of the subsistence economy is largely in the hands of the woman. The paternal splendor and the father's "important" business is played up to a striking degree on the side of prestige which the boy can in no way share except in that the entire family shares it in part. The status of the father, thus artificially inflated, becomes the envied objective of the boy.

In order to evaluate the boy's approach to the woman in marriage, we must bear in mind those integrational systems which have already been formed up to puberty. From the maternal frustrations we surmise that the boy contracts an unconscious hatred and distrust of the woman. Up to now he has moreover had the opportunity, through the care of the younger siblings, to identify himself with the mother. In addition he has likewise been compelled to aid her in her gardening. The roles suffer by comparison with the accepted prestige of the male role. The boy's longer experience with hunger frustrations and the fact that the mother is knowingly responsible for them give the boy a very strong fetishistic attachment to the maternal breast, so that the approach to the woman is likely to be associated with the same inhibitions, fears, and hostilities that he had contracted toward his mother. Although the sexual impulse itself has not been seriously checked, the approach to the woman is filled with shyness and anxiety. The woman generally makes the first sexual advance. It is also of significance that rape is unknown. The feminine image is bound to be associated with mother, breast, objects which the male both longs to possess and fears. The boy's attitude to the woman is therefore controlled by two powerful forces: the first, that the father can obstruct his legitimate access to the woman; this is conscious. Secondly, that the woman herself is a source of anxiety; this is unconscious. The infidelity and frequency of divorce, almost always at the initiative of the man, is therefore no surprise; for he is constantly in quest of the good, kind, nourishing mother, which the wife has no disposition to be. The man therefore emerges from puberty with a drive toward the woman impelled by the sexual impulse itself and by the hatred of the father but checked by his anxieties toward the woman herself.

The effects of this upon ego-ideal formation in the boy must therefore be an exaggeration of the value of potency—which incidentally is appreciated by the Alorese woman—but more important still an enormous exaggeration of the value of status and wealth, which is essentially masculine. The first represents the means of acquiring the good mother; the second, the means of being equal to and opposing the despotic father. In the difficulties that he has had in eventually acquiring this status we have an additional motive, reinforced strongly by his own experiences, for abusing his own children and for using them, when the opportunity arises, as pawns in his own status conflicts. The overvaluation of status-wealth leads to extremely keen competition among the men for the woman, a reinforcement for the motive of desertion, infidelity, and divorce. The ideal of the man is therefore decidedly fixed upon the reaffirmation of his self-esteem through excessive sexuality as a status symbol and through the quest for wealth. The attitude toward children and wife must remain deeply hostile.

The difficulties and discomforts of this position of the male cannot be overemphasized. In this connection the fact is important that in a society where there is some preponderance of women the incidence of bachelorhood is considerable. The weakest must fail in the struggle to achieve masculinity with status, and in this failure there are three avenues of possible solution: (1) evasion through a state of bachelorhood, a status which is held in great contempt; (2) latent homosexuality, which is really a continuation of the puberty identification with the maternal role, and (3) becoming a satellite of a stronger male, which in practice is also a perpetuation of the state of childhood.

Although the opportunities exist in childhood for the expression of sexuality, thereby diminishing the intensity of the Oedipus complex, the great burden of the conflict with the father comes in adolescence and in young manhood. By this time the boy has had too little opportunity to exercise any really effective aggression against his father, so that expression through sexuality may become the avenue of choice. The systematic playing down of overt aggression is hardly necessary; it is rather the result than a cause of this internal situation. The aggression patterns have been frustrated long before.

As a consequence of all this, the superego formation is necessarily very weak. The boy gets too few rewards for obedience, and hence threats of punishment cannot become very securely internalized. It is therefore no surprise to see that the two expressions of superego formation, in their religion and in the technique of maintaining social cohesion, are not much internalized. There remains the sense of shame (really an external agent) and the sense of impending punishment, neither of which requires any internalization.

One final point must be mentioned in connection with the masculine ego ideal. The dependency upon the woman is all too well known. Hence the playing up of maleness by exaggerating the importance of these unproductive activities of finance is largely a form of denial of the dependency upon the woman.

Female. The induction of the female into adulthood is much easier and is accompanied by fewer necessities for changes in attitude, and fewer conflicts. Here too we must review the experience of the child with the mother. Like the boy she also has a hatred of the mother and a resentment of the maternal role, which she is prematurely asked to undertake with the younger siblings. She is not likely to be disposed to give to others what she herself did not get. By the same token her wish to abandon herself sexually to the man is accompanied with internal resistance; likewise the resentment at bearing children and caring for them, a fact which leads to the consequences of indifference to having children, the frequency of abortions and the maternal neglect of children. This completes the cycle. As far as the feminine ego ideal is concerned, the masculine role seems decidedly preferable from her point of view. It is devoid of the arduous responsibilities and the actual hard labor that goes with being a wife and a mother. It is this, together with the internal rejection of the feminine role, which culminates frequently in the assumption of masculine attitudes. These two factors undoubtedly are responsible for the attitude of vengeance upon the male both for his liberty to engage in the socially approved status objectives and because of the resentment she has for having to carry the larger share of the economic burden and for the thankless job of being a mother.

Under these conditions it is difficult to understand why the female so frequently takes the aggressive role sexually. This forwardness of the female must be provoked largely by default of the male. Nevertheless the status of marriage is, notwithstanding its hardships, infinitely more desirable to a woman than would be the state of spinsterhood. As a matter of fact the record of marriages among females is one hundred percent. Furthermore if the maternal role is accepted, the woman has many compensations for it. She actually can dominate over the male by the threat of the withdrawal of food and she exercises a powerful check upon his infidelities by making the financial obligations associated with bride price infinitely greater. In other words, the whole financial arrangement in connection with marriage acts as a powerful check in keeping the tottering structure of relations between the sexes in some kind of balance. The actual beneficiaries of bride price and dowry are the bride's relatives. However, the hostility between the sexes is extremely acute, and great intimacy and friendliness between them must be the exception and not at all the rule.

It is difficult to formulate any opinion about the attitude of the woman in being so evidently a pawn in the status conflicts of the father. From this position she may derive some sense of importance. On the other hand she might get from it serious frustrations if she were to form a strong sentimental attachment to some man. There is little evidence to prove one way or another the nature of the infantile attachments to the father. However, the evidence indicates strongly that this attachment is much stronger than is that of the boy for his mother. It is freer of ambivalence in childhood, and most of the prejudices against femininity must come from the influence of the mother. From the study of the basic personality of the male and female it would appear that the female has a more comfortable internal situation.[8] She enjoys a much higher degree of security, and the actual control of the household lies in her hands. She does not however have the nominal advantages of status. It is therefore theoretically possible to see two types of female: a masculine type who exercises her masculinity largely through dominating over the male through the permitted channels; and the completely adjusted female with acceptance of the feminine role. Perhaps the chief source of her security lies in the fact that through a complicated series of factors she is actually the most sought-after object in society. Few women are however likely to have enough internal security to enjoy this advantage.

However there is another side to the female picture. If her unconscious goals are the same as those of the male, then her chances of establishing an internal balance are much lower. Because of his struggle for power the male has a better chance to keep trying to find the good kind mother in the quest for new women. He also has an opportunity to achieve the unconscious objective of really exploiting someone, of compelling him to yield to his wishes, which is essentially what the relation of creditor to debtor is.

[8] This opinion had to be revised after studying the biographies.

Adulthood

What we see in adulthood is merely the working through of the old constellations in some new situations. Perhaps the most important of these is the social goal of status and prestige.

In studying this phenomenon the factors of greatest importance are not the forms that it takes but rather the sources from which it gets its motive power. The social configurations in Alor show one important fact: that the fixed statuses are male, female, child, old person. There is an absence of rank or of fixed social hierarchies. Status in this society can be maintained only by a process of continuous validation through the exercise of aggression in the form of ingenuity and chicanery. In fact no man's status can be considered fixed at any time, and such prestige as can be achieved is rarely consummated before middle age.

The particular objects in which prestige is vested are wealth (that is, capital) and interest or profit. Perhaps one could also mention in this connection a form of "conspicuous consumption" through death feasts.

In studying prestige it would be convenient to divide it into three subheadings: What do I think of myself? What claims do I have for social regard? What institutionalized insignia are there for the tenure of status? We have noted that the third is completely absent, which means that the claims for social regard can be only through the acquisition of wealth, which in turn means only the ability to have liens on other people's economic activities.

It is the answer to the first question. "What do I think of myself?" which can supply us with some information about the source from which the quest for prestige derives its motive power. True, this quest is a specialized form of self-assertion. The incentive for this type of self-assertion can be greatly enhanced by the social checks and balances, provided that the need for validation serves to counterbalance, to check or to deny an underlying strong feeling of unworthiness. The wish to be equal to or better than another is really a reflection of an internal need to think well of oneself, to approve of oneself, to like onself. Or it is an effort to guarantee that one enjoys more or suffers less than the other fellow. Both these goals are impossible to achieve in Alor because the entire constellation of self-love, self-esteem, and confidence are injured at the very start of the integrational chain in early childhood. In this regard the Alorese quest for prestige has a very strong internal function. At no time in his life cycle does the individual have the opportunity to think highly of himself. Maternal neglect, and its consequent blocking of ego development, the misrepresentation of elders, and the insistence on conformity without rewards, lay the basis for a very profound feeling of unworthiness.

The struggle for prestige looks much the same in any culture we study. There is evidence for belief, however, that its unconscious fabric is a variable factor. The factors which are likely to intensify all prestige struggles are low self-esteem and blocked action systems. In Alor both are conspicuous. The only successful form of action for the male in late childhood is foraging and stealing, which we concluded was highly symbolic as well as hunger relieving. Stealing thus becomes a devious method of soliciting affection; it is not "criminal," but an expression of affect hunger. This constellation is bound to be stronger in the male than the female. For if the latter accepts the feminine role, she can realize her unconscious goals by becoming the provider for both husband and children. This role is, however, difficult in Alor not only because of the hard labor involved but because the role of motherhood is soured by her own experiences as a child. We cannot tell precisely how this works out for both male and female until we examine the biographies. It would be reasonable to expect to find in the male very strongly repressed predatory trends which are absent in the female. To bear this out, it was observed that it is the men who steal and ask for presents; the women do not. Women return gifts; men do not. Women share with others; men do not.[4] The man is the chief beneficiary of the bride price dealings; the mother much less so. The male needs compensation in dress and regalia; the women don't. The sensitivity to personal defects—that is, the touchiness—is enormously exaggerated in the men as compared with the women. It is the male who is predominantly mortified to have any derogatory epithet directed at him. The men eat first when guests are present and the women eat later. The men are wary about making payments to the maternal side of the house, that is, the side from which they really expect to get things. It is therefore no wonder that the need for security is much greater in the male, and that accordingly every opportunity is exercised both through the rights over children or through

---

[4] This information was elicited in seminar. It will be observed subsequently that resignation in the female takes the place of the stronger self-assertive tendencies of the male permitted by the society. Neither male nor female is subject to depressions.

chicanery to get this extremely necessary compensation to cancel out the deep feeling of unworthiness.

As evidence of this general insecurity there is the characteristic unwillingness to waste anything though there is actually no food scarcity. This is illustrated by a folk tale told by the ethnographer. It is the story which deals with a little boy who wastes his food, and his mother punishes him by serving him a food container filled with feces. So angry is the boy that he gets his regalia and wants to go away. The repentant mother wants to retain him but the boy says no, he cannot stay because his mother deceived him. He goes away and becomes the Morning Star, and the story continues with the idea that the older brother takes the place of the bad mother. This story shows very clearly the relation between maternal deceit and the impulse to conserve food. It is really a defensive attitude of resentment.

Money plays an important role in the struggle for security. Interestingly enough it is not in the form of an actual accumulation of gongs and mokos. The emphasis falls rather on the ability to control someone's activity. A debtor is a person whom you can compel to give you something at your behest. This is one occasion when you can be insistent. The inability to control the mother was the most signal defeat of childhood. If we can allocate any zone, it is really an oral craving, for it is accompanied by intense feelings of greed and envy. The general stinginess about food is evidently derived from oral frustrations, a fact which is strongly supported by the consideration that there is no coercive anal training in childhood.[5]

But the accumulation of wealth is obviously not free of dangers. The fact that large accumulations of wealth can cause illness which in turn can be remedied by giving a feast indicates the very great anxiety that attends the accumulation of wealth, because it means that the individual has a very strong awareness of the power of other people's envy. And hence the giving of a feast by satisfying their oral appetites diminishes the envy. It is this remedy which tells us the origin of the whole insecurity feeling. The remedy is an antidote to the envy of others which the wealthy person fears. This probably is also the source of the necessity for evening things up—a compulsive

---

[5] This evaluation of the economic system refers only to the unconscious gratifications derived from it. But one must conclude from a survey of this system that the emotional aspect of it is paramount. The finance economy is given over wholly to non-productive ends—in fact production is almost completely divorced from it, just as the men are removed from any real productive activities.

trait probably derived from the necessity of sharing with hungry siblings. In practice the whole prestige economy in Alor is one in which the actual material goods are fairly divided with continuous squeezes on the part of those who can control the action of others through financial obligations.

It might be said that the actual accumulation of wealth in this society is an extremely cumbersome process, but it is very doubtful whether a more fluid form of currency would alter the situation to any great extent. It is also to be noted that the whole prestige conflict is quite divorced from the subsistence economy, which, with the exception of animal food, is entirely in the hands of the women. A man who is "broke" always has his wife. This again points up the fact that the woman is the pivot of security in this society. The whole financial system is a series of obligations which purport to satisfy the unconscious cravings of the creditor. And this does not end with death, because the death feast obligations form an onerous part of the financial overhead, and the individual after death can continue to behave like an insistent creditor.

The uses of this financial system are largely to channelize the enormous amount of intrasocial hostility, and it takes much of the brunt off all the other methods. The fear of exercising overt aggression in the form of striking, killing, or even use of magic is likewise traceable to the faulty ego development in childhood. It is an error to regard aggression purely as a form of reaction to frustration. In order to react to frustration with aggression, a high degree of effective organization is necessary. In the Alorese child this organization fails to take place. It is to be remembered that the tantrum is the expression *par excellence* of the childhood frustration, and this is characterized chiefly by its lack of organization. It is, so to speak, a spinal discharge and not one directed by the higher centers. As was noted before in the discussion of the relations of men to women, the inability to be aggressive toward an object that injures you must lead eventually not only to a fear of the object but also to an inner feeling of paralysis. The control over aggression is certainly not due to any superego interference in Alor. It is due purely to an ego defect; they do not know how to put it together. In other words, the fact that overt aggression in any form is feared in this society is merely a late consequence of a situation that began in childhood and which there showed itself in the hopeless futility of getting any response by this method. The whole system of organized aggression or self-assertion becomes blocked, and the individual has a life-long struggle to contain these impulses within limits. He thus lives in constant fear that they will spill over and then get completely out of hand. Hence he must avoid all intoxicants which diminish the powers of control, and has the same fear in projected form of all those whose conscious control mechanisms are in eclipse, as in coma or insanity. It also shows itself in morbid fear of fights which threaten to become serious. The struggle with these amorphous aggressions requires ceaseless vigilance. The only time when overt aggression becomes a form of expression is in the insane. Another psychotic reaction was observed in which the chief content was, in addition to overt aggression, the assumption of the feminine role by a man (see p. 117). The warlike activities are very rare, and the general tendency is to call it off and accept compensation before any serious damage has been done.

This failure of the development of organized aggression patterns is also related to the other characteristics so conspicuous among the Alorese, namely the imperfection of their mechanical techniques, their lack of persistence, their low aspiration level, their easy surrender to difficulties, and the general confusion that they exhibit when confronted with a task that is somewhat unusual.

The Supernatural and Folklore

In their dealings with the supernatural and in their concepts of it the Alorese do not differ very strikingly from other primitive societies studied. The general mold is the same. But if the concept of basic personality structure means anything at all, we should be able to see a reflection of it in the projections that are used in representing the supernatural and dealing with it. And in this we are not disappointed. What is distinctive about their ideas and techniques for dealing with the supernatural are their negative features. They do have a supreme being who has some general attributes as the originator of life. There is also a cultural hero, who makes men from food with the breath of the supreme being. However these figures are of no great practical significance.

In their practical religion there is the general framework of a family cult. This is not the significant feature. The family cult lacks precision. The powers of the dead for good are not exaggerated. The dead are not to be placated by suffering and renunciation, nor is there any attempt at restitution through penance in order to be reinstated into the good graces of the deity. Good things are not sought for by an appeal to deity, only relief from immediate and pressing distress, such as illness. What we do find is a purely formal arrangement. The ancestors are angered through failure to be fed. They will perform some wicked act against a neglectful individual, that is they will cause an abortion or they will annoy a child, because it was not named after its grandmother, and as soon as the name is appropriately bestowed the annoyance ceases. There is, in other words, no great inflation of the parental imago for doing good, owing to the poor frustration-reward balance in this society. The universal form of sacrifice, with which they are well acquainted, is the sacrifice of food, and in this connection it is to be noted that the sacrificial feeding of the ancestors takes place reluctantly and under great pressure of some actual emergency. So slight is the tendency to idealize the parental imago that the effigies by which the Alorese represent the ancestral spirits are made in the most careless and slipshod manner and are used in the most perfunctory way and then forthwith discarded. There is no tendency to give the deity permanent housing or idealized form. The dead are merely pressing and insistent creditors who can enforce their demands through supernatural powers. This is precisely the experience of the child with his parents. Hence he obeys reluctantly and grudgingly. This is one of the most startling distortions to be found in primitive religion. The constituent elements are the same here as in any other religion. There is a superior being whose functions are, however, only nominal. The real executives are the ancestral spirits. They have the power to inflict hardship and in great emergencies can ward off or call off an evil which they themselves have set in motion. There is no trace of the god who is essentially bountiful—though some of the familiars have that character. Like the bountiful stranger who relieves the discomfort of the crying child, their good beings appear from nowhere. There is no effort to insure the good will of the deity in advance by good or exemplary behavior. Religious practices are not a form of insurance. The fact that the image of the deity is modeled after the bad creditor is a proof that the kind parental ideal has not been incorporated into it, though it retains the attribute of power to do harm. All this is a consequence of the faulty and undirected disciplinary systems.

In their folklore we have additional opportunity to see what the products of the imagination of the Alorese are. For this purpose we can examine three stories. First there is the bogy-man story, which is told children to keep them from crying too hard. (See p. 133) It is clear from this story that the parental image is a frustrating one and that the deceits and misrepresentations which parents practice upon the child do not go unnoticed and that they foster an attitude of disillusionment and a vain hope for revenge. The fantasy naturally replaces the bad mother by the idealized grandmother, who is theoretically a good provider; but she also abandons him. And this in turn is followed by a third image, that of the father-in-law, who gives him his two daughters. When the boy has gained his independence he is kind only to those who were kind to him. But toward his parents he has an everlasting hatred, and unrelenting thirst for revenge. The story also points to the fact that the male feels particularly indebted to his father-in-law because through his consent he has a chance to renew the quest for the good mother. By the same token he gets sexual satisfaction only by consent of the older man.

A second story deals with a boy deserted by six older siblings and left to starve. (See p. 121) Here again we find the motif of desertion, starvation, and rescue by the father-in-law, who in this instance is idealized in that he gives the boy his two daughters without a bride price. The infidelity of the male and the punishments for infidelity are present in this story, also the jealousy between women over men and the motif that a good wife compensates for the treacheries and failures of siblings and parents. In this story we must note that the father kills the son rather than the reverse. In several other tales the Oedipus motif is prominent; but the hostility of the father to the son is extremely persistent, as in many instances it is in real life.

The woman does not always appear in the stories as a rescuer. There are many representations of the mother as a witch who steals and eats the food of children. The story of the little squash flower (see p. 134) is a good illustration of how the mechanism of mother hatred seeps into the relations between the man and woman. The squash-flower girl represents the attempt to find the good mother, who is killed by the real mother. The hero wishes to obliterate the deep unconscious hatred for the mother and to renew his relations with her on a more amorous basis. In the story this happens. In real life it ends in the ceaseless quest to find her in repeated discordant marriages.

The attitude toward magic is quite striking. The practice of magic is rather rudimentary. There is no great frequency of its incidence nor is there any great fear of the evil wishes of others. Magic, in other words, is not used as a form of aggression. Nor is there any great anxiety about being injured in this way. Likewise there is a scarcity of ghost seeing, and hence seers have no great prestige. This can be explained by the fact that their aggressions are too poorly organized to be expressed in fear of magic, or in any highly systematized magical systems.

We can now examine the Spirit Bird Dance as a literary production of Alor. The situation represented there is one between debtor and creditor. The verses ring with their animosity toward each other. The creditor looks forward to big payments; the debtor host promises only that at some future date he will overwhelm his creditor with his wealth and pay him with such alacrity as to shame the greedy creditor. The creditor has a suitable retort in the promise to rob his debtor host thoroughly and leave him impoverished. Both derive satisfaction through enjoying the disadvantages the other fellow has in relation to his own. At best, the score can only be a draw; for each is both debtor and creditor.

Conclusions

The derivation of basic personality in Alor presented considerable difficulty in some details. Some matters of fact were unsettled because the evidence was inconsistent. This concerned certain details of infant care and the sexual development and disciplines. From the evidence so far (without biographies) it is difficult to come to definite conclusions. It actually proved (as will be seen from the biographies) that some of our guesses were wrong.

However wrong our guesses may be in detail, there can be little doubt about the main trend. Such a combination of influences acting from birth to adulthood must create a deeply insecure and isolated individual; but correct as this conclusion may be, it is not precise enough. We find in this strange personality emotional combinations with which we are completely unacquainted in our society. But they are made a little more intelligible as we follow the integrational systems from infancy on. The personality gets off to a bad start. More tensions are created than discharge avenues; there is a vast predominance of painful tensions, which begin so early in life as to prevent the formation of effective action systems. This can be seen especially in the aggression patterns, in which the affect predominates; the executive capacity is, however, very low. The individual, therefore, is in constant dread that this aggression may break its confines. Hence the defenses against anything that will relax this vigilance—the desistance from intoxicants, fear of comatose conditions, etc. Although their war patterns are influenced by external pressures—from the Dutch—the Alorese show violent explosive and indiscriminate aggression, together with the desire to have done with the aggression altogether and to accept token forms of placation. Such aggression patterns are found in our culture only in deeply psychopathic characters. Another consequence of maternal neglect germane to the disorganized aggression patterns is the strangulation of all action systems which pertain to interest in and mastery of the outer world. Hence they cannot construct, systematize, plan or forestall; have little mechanical ability or interest; fail in aesthetic development; give up enterprise easily; and allow themselves to die without a fight.

The effect of this affect strangulation must be that it prevents tender and coöperative relations with others. In their place are deep predatory and exploitive wishes, with all the mutual anxiety thus created, because the predatory trend must be repressed or expressed through financial channels. This is probably why finance becomes the chief emotional vehicle.

In their projective systems (in religion and folklore) we find the remnants of the childhood constellations, with special emphasis on parental hatreds and revenge. The same emotional constellations dominate the relations between the sexes—hence the generally discordant marriages.

The basic personality in Alor is anxious, suspicious, mistrustful, lacking in confidence, with no interest in the outer world. There is no capacity to idealize parental image or deity. The personality is devoid of enterprise, is filled with repressed hatred and free floating aggression over which constant vigilance must be exercised. The personality is devoid of high aspirations and has no basis for the internalization of discipline. Individuals so constituted must spend most of their energy protecting themselves against each others' hostility. Coöperation must be at a low level and a tenuous social cohesion can be achieved only by dominance-submission attitudes, not by affection and mutual trust.

CHAPTER VII

PERSONALITY STUDIES

HAVING MADE our conjectures about the kind of personality likely to develop under the conditions furnished in Alor, we now pass on to a study of these personalities themselves. This can serve a threefold purpose. First, it is a check on the correctness of our conjectures; second, it gives us a living picture of how the culture looks from the inside looking out and how the institutional picture is integrated in the mind of the individual; third, it gives us an opportunity to study the relation between this abstraction of basic personality and the individual's character.

These personalities are here presented as sketches, drawn from a detailed report recorded in the subject's own words. These are not autobiographies in the conventional sense; they are rather cross sections of the subject's life over a span of several months and include such data as dreams, reactions to the ethnographer, stories from the past as they occur to the subject when invited to talk about anything he wishes.

Are the Alorese truthful about themselves? Fortunately we do not use the subject's veracity as our only guide, for we depend on dreams and the sequence of ideas, the significance of which these natives do not know. Needless to say, they are guarded. They will discuss nothing that will injure their standing in the community or with the ethnographer, whom they all hold in great awe. This means that the data are distorted in only one direction. The sex of the ethnographer was undoubtedly a powerful influence, as was the presence of the interpreter.

Notwithstanding all these limitations, it is remarkable how revealing these autobiographical sketches are. There is however some difference between the men and the women. The former are much more articulate, less guarded, and really much more coöperative. There are undoubtedly many reasons for this. The women are not as intelligent; but, more important, the men have a much greater emotional stake in the adventure, apart from pay. A strong, "rich," and influential woman is attractive bait for an Alorese male. The unconscious appeal is very strong. This probably accounts for the greater success of the male personality studies.

These characters are described as far as possible in psychiatric terms and not by value judgments. Hence the question "According to whose standards is the particular character described?" has no validity. Psychiatric descriptive terms can claim some universality. It is only when we use a concept like "honest" that the issue can be raised that this concept is contingent on a value judgment which is not the same in Alor as it is with us. There "honesty" may have the connotation of "simple," and "dishonest" the meaning of "shrewd." These terms are used with the meanings they have *in our society*. Any other procedure would be confusing.[1] If we were to use Alorese value judgments, their meaning would be apparent to the Alorese, but not to us.

Mangma, the Genealogist

In studying this autobiographical account of Mangma two factors must be taken into account: first his reaction to the ethnographer, and secondly the presence of the interpreter. Mangma is an extremely insecure, sensitive, easily hurt person, who has deep unconscious cravings for being loved, together with a conviction that this will not be fulfilled. He regards the ethnographer as a very rich and powerful individual and he wants to impress her. The interpreter is a disturbing influence which distorts Mangma's story. Mangma will not tell anything about himself that will be very disparaging either to his manhood or to his general standing.

Because of these two factors Mangma's story is full of gaps; what he tells is probably the least objectionable part of his life story. The material of his biography takes us up to eighteen years before the narration. His story deals almost entirely with his past, and almost nothing pertaining to his current life is mentioned. We can therefore expect that his representation of himself will be calculated to hide his inadequacies, of which he is in his inarticulate way quite well aware, and to emphasize his skills. He spends much time on irrelevant matters, proving his memory of unessential details. There is something

---

1 Those who wish to consult the original biographies will find the study of them a difficult exercise in empathy. It is recommended that the men be studied first. They are easier to understand. All the women, with the exception of Kolmani, are well-nigh unintelligible. Their associations are more disjointed and, apart from the fact that the subject matter is quite unlike the conversation of Western man, are not revealing until they are read several times. See Du Bois, *The People of Alor*.

compulsive about the way in which he digresses from the essential point of his story to emphasize his knowledge of detail. Notwithstanding these difficulties in the narrative, Mangma's life history is of great value.

He is a person in good standing in the community and is considered a strong, active man, but one who does not participate much in the society. He made an attempt to become a seer, but apparently without success; he then set up claims to being a genealogist. But in this his accuracy is dubious.

Mangma is the second child of a family of nine. This means in effect that he received a minimum of advantages of parental care and was in turn expected to assist his mother materially both in her gardening and in the care of the younger siblings. His father is generally represented in the more benign role—also a common trait in Alor. Mangma evidently did not adjust very well to this situation because the story of his late childhood and early adolescence is one of continual quarrels with his parents and siblings, as a consequence of which he ran away repeatedly. He did not settle down until late in adolescence, when he was already a beaten man. He encountered many hardships in establishing his claims for recognition as a member of the society. He had great trouble with his father about getting married and collecting the appropriate bride price. The development of his relations with women is not altogether clear but it is quite evident that he is decidedly inhibited and backward. He married only once and in his own peculiar way he was faithful to his wife. With her he had an extremely troubled and difficult life which was repeatedly broken up by her leaving to live elsewhere. He tried several vocations—seer, genealogist—but the one in which he persisted and in which he took great pride was gardening. This is a most unusual occupation for a man in this society. However it was a virtue that was appreciated by the women, who thought that they could thus induce him to alleviate their own tasks.

What interests us most in Mangma is his character. He is a man whose wishes, desires, and ambitions are far in excess of his capacities to realize them. This is true from his earliest childhood. He is an extremely vain person, a trait which he shows by boasting about trivialities, but most frequently by exaggerating the injuries and wrongs he had suffered at the hands of others. This emphasis on his sufferings, this excessive vulnerability and touchiness, is the expression of a very deeply frustrated feeling, covered up by pretentiousness. Coincident with this he has a strong tendency to minimize pleasant things. He never has the courage to acknowledge his wrongdoings, always imputes evil motives to others, unscrupulously blames other people for his own misdeeds. The violence of his feelings so far outstrips his capacities that he knows of only one way of solving his difficulty and that is to run away from the situation entirely, a technique he continued until very late in life. These runnings away were utterly ineffectual and did not contribute in any constructive way toward solving any of the difficulties in which he was immersed. His distrust of others is profound. At the same time there runs through his story a persistent current of underlying longing for the good, kind protector. His life is one endless series of quests to find the good friend, the good parent, longings that are always frustrated. This frustration is due not so much to the injuries that other people do him as to the fact that at no time in his life did he learn to make any kind of strong attachment to anyone. Like every paranoid individual, he does not know that he is largely responsible for the bad behavior of others to him. In addition to these traits must be mentioned his enviousness. His aggression is deeply repressed. He shows this repeatedly by crying profusely when he is hurt, but laughing heartily when someone else is hurt. He thus has a combination of viciousness and vulnerability, a combination frequently found in Alor.

At the age of seven or eight there were already indications of his future character. He and his younger brother once decided to kill a chicken and eat it, but to do it in such a way that the father would not detect it. The father, however, did apprehend them. For this Mangma refused to take any responsibility. One day he worked in the garden with his mother. She punished him by tying his hands, which even in Alor is severe treatment. He ran away to a classificatory grandfather, where he was set to gardening. The general weakness of his ego structure is shown particularly in the ease with which he is discouraged, the ease with which he abandons enterprises and then lapses into a complete black hopelessness. For example, he once built a field house which burned down. Then he built another, which also burned. Then he gave up entirely and said that from then on he would live in a cave, a most unusual resolution for a man in this culture. On another occasion he raised pigs. Someone killed a pig or two, whereupon Mangma stopped raising pigs. As a matter of fact this killing of the pig by one of his relatives was not a wanton destructive act at all, but merely one of the conventionalized forms of feast making. Mangma made a great to-do about it, exaggerated its significance as a tremendous wrong and ended by abandoning the whole enterprise. Later a tax was levied upon him which he resented so much he ran away. With this last running away to evade a tax, Mangma's life practically came to an end. He was thenceforth a beaten man.

It would be interesting to see whether the study of his actual productions in the report can give us some clue as to the structure and significance of these character traits. We lack enough data to be able to reconstruct it historically. It will have to suffice to describe some of the dynamic interconnections. The opening interview with the ethnographer may be taken as typical. His associations run as follows: (1) hunger; (2) stealing; (3) mother gave me bad food, unripe cassava, and refused me good food—resentment; an earthquake occurred; (4) I shoot a dog, the owner breaks my bows and arrows and beats me; (5) mother wants me to cut the fields, I refuse, she ties my hands up; (6) I run away from home; (7) I begin gardening on my own; (8) I won't let mother get my harvest; (9) he boasts of his gardening exploits; (10) fights with his friends; (11) fantasy about raising bride price; (12) planting a garden and the father and mother eat it; (13) is falsely accused of sleeping with a girl by people who want to get his money, and this starts a financial war with the family; (14) I'm cheated again, etc. . . .

His first association is that of hunger. However, from our experience with this culture we cannot take this at its face value. "I was left hungry" means that he suffered from bad care. The association from hunger therefore means that the wish to be loved by the mother in terms of being fed is frustrated. He therefore reacts by taking by force what was not given to him—stealing. In this particular case he remembers taking some wild bananas which his mother was pounding in a mortar, some of which had fallen over the edge of the mortar. His attitude toward his mother remains one of hatred plus the deep suspicion that she will never do anything for him and merely wishes to exploit him. His vengeance upon her is therefore to refuse to obey. This is followed by running away in an attempt to find a better parent and winds up in his learning to excel in gardening, whereby he takes over the role of the delinquent parent. The attitude of expecting nobody to do anything for him and the fear of being exploited lead to extreme touchiness and vindictiveness. His low self-esteem based on this original constellation must express itself in compensatory activities in the form of pride, lying and boasting about trivialities, and in profound avarice and envy of what other people have, upon which he unconsciously has persistent designs. Another persistent attitude is that of feeling constantly injured, which is another way of saying that his expectations of other people are enormous but that the tension between these expectations and the conviction that they cannot be realized is so great that it ends in an impasse. His low self-esteem leads off into another series of constellations, the most constant of which are the expectation of failure and the conviction of his own ineffectuality. The abandonment of all constructive enterprise and incapacity for any persistent effort follow.

The unconscious hatred of his mother gives rise to the distrust of women in general, and this, together with the obstructions to manhood offered by his father's procrastination on the bride price, results in an insecure feeling of his own sexual value. Hence he has to permit every woman to make the first advance. The number of platonic relationships that he has carried on with women is also noteworthy. Furthermore the frustrations suffered through his mother constrain him to assume a feminine role, and toward his father he takes an attitude of limp and helpless passivity, which leads only to more hatred toward his father and everyone else and finally to an increase in his own distrust of himself. The constant longing for a protector is illustrated by a dream of the ethnographer toward whom he shows his longing by robbing her garden. His marriage shows no evidence of actual disturbances in potency, having produced seven children, but he is wary of approaching any other woman except in a platonic way and winds up his life by a kind of marriage to his sister, which has been the most satisfactory relationship in his life. This relationship is probably consummated on the basis of identification, that is, he gets along with her so well because they are two of a kind.

These conclusions are borne out by some of his dreams. One dream deals with stealing; to this his association is dying. This probably describes the dominating constellation of his life. His father and mother are now dead. He dreams of being cared for by his dead parents, but this he expresses in his now constant method of robbing them. The next dream is of being attacked by women who give him a stick. From this dream I should be inclined to question his confidence in his own virility. It confirms his very divided feelings about women. All his associations following this are about the fights between men and women. He feels compelled however to be masculine, according to the pattern of the culture, but feels strong misgivings of being able to validate it. He resolves this dilemma, as he usually did those in the past, by going away from women altogether and working alone. It is interesting to note that he blocks decidedly at this point and begins to speak about gardening, and how his father obstructed his opportunities for being a man.

This is followed by a dream about his sister, who is burning weeds in her garden. Then follows another dream of stealing from a man but of denying the guilt. In the dream another man is accused of the theft which he actually perpetrated. This excites his laughter. This is an abstract dream and without more help we can only venture a few guesses. It suggests that his relationship to his sister is an erotic one based upon an old attachment. He winds up this series with a dream about robbing the ethnographer's garden, which leaves the story in the situation of his continuing his quest for the affectionate parent, a longing he can express only in predatory activity.

Rilpada

This man furnishes an excellent contrast to Mangma. He lacks the pretentiousness of the latter, but shows a character trait which it is surprising to find in Alor, that is, a high degree of imagination, a most vivid and varied fantasy life. Considering some serious physical handicaps, he made a successful adjustment in certain aspects of his life. He comes quite close to the characteristics of neurosis in Western society.

He is about thirty-six, the middle of five siblings, married to a woman ten years older, who had two daughters by a previous marriage. He has no children. He is a seer, has some standing, but no wealth. Physically he is blind in one eye, crippled, emaciated, and has a deforming skin disease. He is a dreamer and an interpreter of dreams.

His father, now dead, was a prominent seer, who had risen from a slave child by dint of persistence and enterprise. His father was the dominant influence in Rilpada's life; for he not only follows his father's vocation of seer, but is constantly occupied with the latter's finances rather than with his own. He takes pride in his father's sexual prowess in having had nine wives. Rilpada is the offspring of his father's second marriage. His mother is still living.

The feeling tone of Rilpada's biography differs notably from the others. We deal here with a contemporary picture that differs strikingly from the childhood picture. His story differs from the others in emphasis. Whereas the general culture picture is the same as the others, it is safe to deduce that he had better than average care as a child, but especially from his father. He felt the influence of both maternal care and paternal guidance, and both seem to have been intelligent and directed. The description of maternal care is however true to the cultural pattern. The difference lies in the character of his father, who was much more attentive than is usual. Rilpada's discipline was more directed, so that he could make direct connections between offense and punishment, and thus be assured early in life that his parents were not vicious. Thus on one occasion he insisted on eating with guests and cried when forbidden. His father explained the matter to him and the boy promised not to act that way again. Such an incident would—even if it had occurred—never register with Mangma. The evidence for this more systematic education is that he is actively partisan, now of his mother, now of his father. He tells how, when his mother went out into the fields, he had to take care of his infant brother Senmani. The child began to cry. Rilpada tried to feed him, but he vomited the offering. Rilpada then cried too, and asked his mother to nurse the child. This she refused to do. Rilpada then took the child home and put it on a mat and ran off to play. He does not remember what his mother did, but next day she took the child to its grandfather, tried to shame Rilpada for his delinquency, and also beat him. Whereupon he ran away and stayed with his grandfather for a month, when his mother came and "talked nicely" to him. He returned, and with her cared for his younger brother. He even looked after another woman's child on another occasion.

He had plenty of quarrels with both parents; but Rilpada always adds a forgiving note, indicating that both his parents made persistent efforts to placate him and to understand his feelings. He was always reconciled to them, and his story abounds in episodes of gratitude to and solicitude for them. His earliest recollection of grabbing and spoiling a rice cone which his mother had prepared is followed by the comment, "She told me not to do that, and gave me a coconut dish with rice which was left in the pot." It is natural therefore to find that he behaved the same way toward his friends, with whom there were plenty of fights, but always followed by reconciliation without the chronic maintenance of destructive grudges. Only in the case of women were his reactions true to cultural type, and even worse; he has a decided neurosis on this score. There is some likelihood of his being impotent, though his childlessness is not evidence of this, since he is married to a woman now forty-five. There is however decided evidence of great shyness; he was constantly running away from women, and finally married one whose chief virtue was that she could work well and be a good caretaker—a maternal replica.

Rilpada seems to have been crushed by his father's greatness. He has a great reverence for him, and, save in the matter of sexual activities, tried hard all his life to emulate his father. This is all strong evidence of great attachment to his father.

In short, in Rilpada we have a man who had parental care above the average, resulting in an enormous inflation of the paternal ideal, which he seeks to approximate, and of consequence has more than the usual inhibitions concerning most of the manly activities. Rilpada therefore has a constant need to justify his inability to be like his father, and this seems to be the significance of his constant emphasis on his physical injuries and handicaps. "How can I be like him, when fate doesn't permit me—strikes me down again and again!" He is not trying to win sympathy but to justify his mediocre achievements. What he fails to do in deed, however, he makes up by invention, which likewise comforts him on the same score.

He begins his narrative (at age eight), with the desertion of his father to another wife, his solicitude for his mother, and his efforts to comfort her by shooting a pig for his aunt's death feast. This desertion enrages the little boy, and he seeks immediately to take his father's place but he is stricken down with an injury.[2]

In his relations with playmates he shows a healthy self-assertion. He quarrels, but he values their friendship more than the opportunity to be angry. He does not discard the object that displeases him, though he may get angry. His father always stands between him and his misfortunes with advice, which he takes.

Of pertinent significance is Rilpada's reference to food. The emphasis is not on nutriment—which is a confirmation that food hunger in this culture stands for poor parental care—but rather on the prowess side, since he is a good rat hunter, in which the paternal ideal is

---

[2] What is recorded here refers to the sequence of ideas, which does not necessarily mean chronological sequence.

easily identified. The influence of the paternal ideal is shown more clearly than this in his early leaning in the direction of contacts with spirits—very exciting and anxious dreams. Yet he was an unusually fearful child and was constantly getting hurt, sometimes quite badly, from the age of three to twenty-five.

His fears include all kinds of phobias, some of which are common in Alor. But some clue to his anxious dreams of childhood are contained in his story that he had these dreams when he was staying in the field house, so he had to go home. The dreams were of being pursued by men. Though their chronology is not definitely indicated, these terror dreams must have occurred after his father's desertion. He follows the culture pattern and steals a good deal up to his seventeenth year, often using as his justification that others put him up to it.

With but one exception, he was at no time malicious; he once set fire to some fields, which according to Alorese standards was a decidedly pernicious act. But he went home and dreamed anxiously of the spirit of the field saying, "See what you have done, you have killed my wife and animals." He woke up in distress and confessed to his parents and brother. His brother decided that the dream was prompted by a spirit. They shot a hen and fed the spirit. The next night he dreamt that the man in the last dream reappeared and said, "You are good. You transgressed but you paid a fine." In short, as has already been indicated, Rilpada had a conscience and was consequently educable. He is repeatedly losing consciousness and having long, moralizing visions. He once went rat hunting and injured a rat, who ran up a tree. Rilpada followed it but lost consciousness. In his "vision" he developed a "conscience" about rat killing. These were probably hysterical trances. The spirit warned him that the rat is his child, and the tree his house. A child who bore his mother an unmitigated grudge because of the effects of early privations could never have such a fantasy. Rilpada seems always to have a good deal of free-floating aggression, which he has some difficulty controlling.

He is decidedly passive, is never a leader, and is never a financial success. He has been living on his father's glory. The story of how his father was ambushed by an enemy, but nevertheless challenged his adversary to bring out his pig and sheep and he will kill them with one stroke, and how his father validated his threat—this is the kind of episode to impress a child with his father's fearlessness and strength. When he was twelve Rilpada was witness to another impressive episode. The father was a guest at a feast, and when served he saw a hair in his food—a sign of poison. He broke into a rage, broke the pots and serving dishes, seized his weapons and shouted. Rilpada says, "I was afraid and I took father's hand." The old man compelled his hosts to pay a fine, kill a fresh pig, cook a fresh meal, and give him a live pig to boot! In other words Rilpada grew up under the influence of an overweening, self-assertive father. But Rilpada used his father as someone whose strength is to be used for his, Rilpada's, benefit; he sought to be protected by this strength rather than to emulate it. His father is always mentioned as the curer of his ills. If he got into trouble his father got him out. However his father did not condone Rilpada's lack of skill; he gave him many scoldings. On one occasion his father threatened him with castration, not for a sexual misdemeanor but for a lack of skill in rat hunting.

Rilpada's relations to his mother are less distinct. There is the usual story of neglect—of running after her when she went to the fields, and the usual compensatory stealing. But his account of her is without rancor. He slept with her until he was six or seven. He often disobeyed her, and once shot a bird arrow at her and injured her. This was the occasion of his running away. But his father coaxed him back after two months' absence and he found both parents forgiving and understanding. He attacked his father once when his sympathies were aroused by unjust treatment of his mother.

His father died when Rilpada was twenty-seven, and only on this single occasion was Rilpada an important person, because of the death feast obligations.

His attitude toward siblings is nebulous. He did not mention his two older brothers until he was asked about them. He refused to take care of his younger brother, but he does tell of one episode in which he was getting the worst of a fight when his younger brother, six years his junior, came to his aid. He likewise neglected his younger sister. On one occasion when the younger sister created a great to-do by refusing to marry the man to whom she was contracted, Rilpada attempted the role of paterfamilias (age thirty) but failed badly. He was totally ineffectual.

His relations to women are decidedly bad. About preadolescent relations with them he mentions four episodes, and in connection with three some untoward incident occurred. He entered into a serious relationship with a girl for the first time at seventeen. He offered to build her a house and she proposed to him. He accepted and stole a moko from his father. His father detected the theft but nevertheless offered to help Rilpada collect his bride price.[3] But he lost the girl to another suitor nonetheless. He denied having intercourse with her, and we may well believe him.

The next occasion was with a girl with whom he exchanged areca. She sent a go-between and again he was willing. His father again helped him with bride-price arrangements. Five days later the girl came to sleep with him. He happened to be away on an errand and when he returned he found her in his home. He was overcome with scruples because it was only five days after the bride price was given instead of the customary seven, and he ran away to the chief's house to sleep. Despite reproaches by his father, Rilpada broke up the projected marriage if he could get the bride price back. In this he failed at first. He nevertheless refused the girl. His father recognized Rilpada's abnormality and said, "You are afraid of women. You didn't sleep with her. You aren't your age." His father was right. This girl died shortly after and there followed a great fuss about bride price because the girl's brothers accused Rilpada of having slept with her, and hence the bride price was forfeited. However, he got his mokos back.

Later he had another episode with a girl, with whom he had no intercourse, but he sent her away too. He finally succumbed for a small bride price to the advances of a widow with two grown daughters. Rilpada justified to his father this strange marriage by saying that it is better to have an older woman who knows how to take care of the garden. His father held out for the younger woman. This choice is quite telling. He feared forward women and finally married one who was a maternal replica. So that after marriage the general life situation hardly changed for him at all. Nominally he was paterfamilias; actually he was again one of three siblings.

Rilpada was a voluminous dreamer. Most of his dreams deal with litigations and ceremonies in which he is in reality only a spectator. He represents himself as discharging all financial obligations. Actually he doesn't. In his dreams he is a great and generous person who feeds

[3] In several of the biographies very inhibited men make an early effort to get a bride price as if in preparation to marry. These efforts usually occur immediately after adolescence and represent impatience to acquire status rather than a need for a sexual mate. Several of these precocious efforts are followed by a long history of troubled relations with women, largely due to deep anxiety provoked by them.

the needy, fixes everything, acts as judge, and sees to it that wrongs are punished. He also cures people, and receives gifts in token of his good deeds. These are all compensatory fantasies, in pursuit of his paternal ideal.

The relation he has to his familiars in dreams is quite revealing. They take his side in fights, and they are injured in his stead. They therefore replace the dead and powerful father. In one dream his father denies he is dead and promises Rilpada that he will be rich. It is with the aid of his familiars that he is thus able to be important and to overcome his physical handicaps. "My familiar has good eyes and legs; my soul is lame, my eyes are blind." But despite the fantasy of protection by these supernatural creatures, he is often threatened by an evil spirit.

He evidently cannot tolerate guilt feelings. Many of his dreams deal with litigations in which he is always judged right by some superior judge. Another version of the same situation occurs in dreams in which he is made to pay damage for other people's wrongdoings— more evidence of repressed envy and aggression under strong super-ego control. Thus his wife commits theft. Rilpada is humiliated and made to pay a fine. He pays the fine for her sister's adultery. This was probably in response to some sexual temptation of his own which is not recorded. This point supplies us with a valuable bit of insight. He cannot, even in a dream, formulate his own sexual wishes. He must accuse someone else of the same thing, but he pays the fine. His martyrdom is really a sense of guilt and inadequacy.

Concerning his sex life one dream gives us a valuable clue. In this dream his dead father has intercourse with his mother (living) and has a child. Rilpada wants to throw the child away, but his father says, "This is my semen; do not throw it away." Rilpada takes a club and beats his father. His brother and Rilpada then kill the father, who turns to dry leaves. They proceed to burn the dry leaves and scatter the ashes. In the hearth appears a snake. His brother and he are frightened and he wakes up. In another dream he sets traps to catch rats. But instead of rats he catches a snake, who speaks to him. Rilpada promises to build an altar for the snake and they become friends. But when he tries to catch it, it runs away and then bites him. His father as snake is again discernible.

It was pointed out before that Rilpada admired his father's power over people and also his sexual prowess, in having had nine wives. The father's sexual power is easily seen in this dream when he impregnates Rilpada's mother after he dies. This causes great anger in Rilpada, and he and his brother (he confesses to being too weak to do it alone) kill the father. This is a typical Oedipus dream. But he cannot have done with his father; after he kills him a snake (penis) rises out of the ashes. In other words, just as his father's influence on Rilpada was to stunt his growth—for he could not emulate his father—likewise in his sex life he cannot do what his father does. He succumbs to his fear of his father, despite the jealousy. The result is complete passivity to him, and consequent fear of women, and sexual inhibitions.

That power and importance always fascinate Rilpada is very clearly shown in a little episode bearing on the ethnographer. Two children in the village jumping over a fire were badly burned and were brought to the ethnographer for treatment. He dreams, "People carry me to you. You took medicine and put it on me and you [ethnographer] said, 'Another time don't step over the fire.' " Then follows more flattery of the ethnographer's kind and wonderful deeds. Then he reports another dream of the same night. A girl (Foepani) dies and Rilpada diagnoses that an evil spirit had entered her mouth. He takes a knife and cuts off the skin of the evil spirit possessing her. His wife boils rice and feeds the girl. Then follows a dream of the ethnographer giving a feast, and another in which he visits his dead father, much to the latter's annoyance.

This sequence is quite remarkable and checks on our original conclusions about Rilpada's relations to his father. He now repeats the same pattern on the ethnographer. He is injured in order to be the recipient of her bounty, he flatters and idealizes her in the same way. Then he takes over her role as a healer (which he is not) and performs a miracle too. Then he is feasted by the ethnographer and visits his father. It is therefore no accident that Rilpada always mentions his father in connection with his injuries. In this instance he clearly walks right into an accident to satisfy his passive longings. In another dream at this time he dreams he has a large boil on his thigh. The ethnographer lances and treats it, but it recurs. She lances it again and a stone falls out, etc. The motive is quite the same. It is a solicitation of love, and an extenuation of his weakness. It is of great significance in Rilpada's character that the predatory motif is almost entirely absent. In its place we have the motif of being injured in order to be the recipient of the father's or ethnographer's kindness, and the frustrated attempts to imitate both. In this phenomenon we have a confirmation of Rilpada's better emotional development; he wins love through weakness or the possession of admirable traits.

Malelaka

The subject of this biography, taken at the age of forty-five, is the most obscure of the four men. He is indirect, shifty, insinuating, cowardly, grandiose, distinctly paranoid, circumstantial, internally deeply insecure, hypocritical, unconsciously cruel and destructive, but actually timid and pretentious. In other words a pious fraud. He resembles more closely than any other of the men an epileptic constitution. There is little doubt but that this man's life was complicated by a chronic illness dating in all likelihood from childhood. It might well have been malaria or yaws, or both, with his unmistakable recurrent febrile attacks accompanied by a good deal of delirium from time to time. His frequent vomiting attacks and gastric disturbance point to chronic liver or biliary disorder. But he makes the most constructive use of his illness and his destructive tendencies find outlet in his fantasies about the end of the world, which he is constantly predicting.

He is not a successful man, his standing as a seer being very questionable. What little he had was injured by his conflict with the law—he has served one and a half years in jail—for his monotonous prophesies of a doom which never materializes. He tells the story of his life with ulterior motives; he is so occupied with impressing the ethnographer in the hope of convincing her of his high mission that he takes little interest in the narrative of his life which is our paramount interest. In spite of the fact that many crucial sequences of his life are lost in his disconnected account, Malelaka nevertheless reveals himself and gives us a consistent picture of the structure of his personality. The connections and causal relations are however lost.

Malelaka was exposed to the usual childhood situation of being neglected by his mother; but she apparently provided two substitutes, Loma, his cousin, who cared for him until she was married, and then by a paternal cousin. At five or six he remembers an episode typical for this society, of his mother's going to the gardens to work and of his trailing after her and crying. She asked him to go back, promised to give him food and gives him an egg. Malelaka makes much of this episode to show how generous he was in offering to share the egg with all his comrades. He seems also to have tagged around a good deal with his grandfather, accompanying him on errands. He had the usual obligations of caring for a younger sibling, which he did badly, was scolded and hit by his mother, and as a consequence he ran away to his grandfather. There is a good deal of mention in childhood of illness both febrile and the result of injury. During one of these illnesses he could not eat and rejected food offered by his mother, but remembers that his father cooked a rat for him which he did eat. This motif is not, as one would expect, consistently followed through. He at one time regards the man as helper, at another the woman. He had many reasons to fear each and no definite constellation toward either ever developed. The contrast to Rilpada in this respect is striking.

The repeated loss first of one cousin and then another to men who take them away must have made a deep impression on Malelaka; for this constellation of the loss of women to men seems to have dogged him all his life. He was constantly giving up his women, whom he fears on other grounds, to men more powerful than himself, or who appeared to be so. He is mortally afraid of the men to whom the women belonged. He says he has never had relations with any woman other than his wife, and we can well believe him. The entire chain of events which led to his sexual inhibitions cannot be reconstructed, but a few situations can be clearly identified. When he was very young he heard his grandfather (or heard it about him) threaten to castrate any man whom he caught having relations with his wife. He believed his grandfather actually castrated a man and put the severed member into the slit vagina of the woman. At all events he had a dread of infidelity. At an early age he witnessed intercourse between a boy and a girl. Malelaka decided to uphold the public morality by informing on the girl to her older brother. On another occasion, age twelve, he was witness to the infidelity of another couple, and he refused to tell what he saw, probably fearing the man. There were no direct threats of masturbation in childhood. Once he saw a boy, who had stuffed a pea into his penis, being reproached by his father for having done something bad. But masturbation was apparently regarded as a sign of indolence, for one such boy had his hands rubbed on stones to teach him to be industrious. The emphasis falls here not on the wickedness of masturbation, but that it is a distracting influence. Malelaka once stuffed a pea into his ear, much to his father's annoyance, who observed, "Why do you hurt yourself when I don't."

From all factors combined we can deduce that Malelaka's childhood was more than usually traumatic as far as his relations with his mother and her surrogates were concerned. This was undoubtedly aggravated by illness. This laid a foundation of distrust of the woman herself. The fact that women were taken away from him by men laid the basis for a fear of men, with whose strength he could not compete. Not only did he refuse to do anything himself but feared to tell what he knew about others. These are approximately the constellations with which he entered puberty.

This period of his life was likewise typical. After a period of rebellion against the task of caring for younger siblings, he later does so with more grace. He says he often cooked for them. He began playing house with girls, boys' sports occupied him, and he gradually began to enter the economy by way of cultivating his own fields. He was reproached by his parents for looking after his own fields before those of his elders. On the other hand, he represents himself as extremely generous about disposing of his crops and on several occasions his thrift and saving brought him great praise. His luck with establishing himself independently was not very good. As he began raising pigs in partnership, his father kept taking them from him and replacing them with very young pigs, thus compelling him to start all over again. He finally protested against his father's behavior. This inability to establish himself because of the prior claims of his parents evidently affected him very badly and ruined his already low self-esteem. His father finally permitted him to begin raising pigs for a bride price, but here his sexual troubles began.

His serious relations with women began at about eighteen. During his life he has had some kind of relationship with seven women, only one of whom he married. Several of these relationships were purely platonic. He entered into betrothal with five of them but ran into innumerable obstacles in connection with them. These betrothals were always at the instigation of the girl and generally against his wishes. He broke off because he discovered they talked to other men, were evil spirits, or undesirable for other reasons.

The earliest of these relationships took place after he began a financial career. Saving money to buy a wife is the conventional start. He worked hard and made enough for a down payment on the bride price. After he had made arrangements with the girl, she refused to have intercourse and then declined the marriage altogether. Malelaka had some difficulty getting his investment back. Apparently this was a severe setback for a man with his deep insecurity. The fear of women was never to leave him from then on. His next adventure was with a woman who made all the advances, taking his bracelets and giving him a necklace in exchange. She tempted him sexually, and then he discovered that mosquitos were coming from her mouth, which meant she was an evil spirit. He had a good deal of difficulty getting free of her because she was insistent on marriage. His reactions were phobic, for he not only feared the woman, but feared the litigation involved in being falsely accused of having had relations with her, in which case his bride price would be forfeit. Later he became involved with another girl, who proposed marriage and compelled him to accept a necklace. This he promptly gave to an aunt. She invited him to have intercourse but he refused, stating that this would cause his financial ruin. She tried again to seduce him at a tooth blackening, and he again refused. This time she became enraged and beat him with a stick.

On another occasion he became engaged to a girl, F. He had to leave to do corvée labor, where it is customary for the wives to bring the husband's food. She did not do so and he felt hurt by her neglect. He ran away from the labor camp for food, and on the way met F., who was on her way to Kalabahi to sell some of his corn. Later he wanted to have relations with her; she refused and he turned her out.

His constant association concerning his fears of women is the fear of impoverishment. This is of course possible; and undoubtedly timid men were often tricked by girls for financial gain. He married only once, but his relations with his wife were indifferent. He doesn't speak of his children or of his siblings until asked to do so.

Malelaka dates his career as a seer to his puberty. When he was about twelve he had his first encounter with spirits. One day he was alone in the house. He remembers leaving a shawl lying about. He left the house and when he returned he found two red fish in the shawl. He was amazed at this experience and rushed out to tell someone of his great discovery. When they returned to see the fish, they had disappeared. That very evening Malelaka says that he began to have second sight. He saw two strange beings who informed him that they were kind spirits and that they were two men from the sea, that is, Good Beings.

On another occasion, while visiting a man and his daughter, he had a hallucination that her arm was suddenly amputated and that there was no bleeding from the stump. Later, at about seventeen or eighteen, after an illness which followed the eating of fish, several good spirits announced themselves to him. They said that they were not evil creatures and asked him why he had not abstained from sea food. Whereupon he knew that his familiar spirits were sea spirits, which meant wealth-bringing spirits. Before he identified these spirits as sea beings he had a vision of the sun speaking to him and promising him that he will not get sick, and ordering him to build a house. This is a promise of supernatural aid. Later he had a vision of the mountains suspended in the air.

His dreams are constantly occupied with supernatural beings; in them he is always foretelling doom: earthquakes, the end of the world, pestilence, etc. Some of these dreams of doom took place at a time when there was a storm raging on the island and there had also been an earthquake, which did very little damage. On such an occasion he dreamed that the world was coming to an end and that all the dead were waked, but the dead reassured him that he would not have to feed them.

Another dream described his relations with the ethnographer quite vividly and was very revealing about Malelaka's character structure. He appeared for his interview one day looking quite depressed, stating that he had had a dream in which the Kapitan had beaten him for not working. In associations to this dream he described an accident of falling off a swing as a child. Then he recalled another dream; he saw a chain hanging from the sky and he proceeded to climb upon it. As he came near the sky he saw a tree with its roots in the air and as he climbed it he found himself feet up and head down, and he feared that he was falling. Then he found himself in his own house. He then went to a near-by village and saw people who were tying a python to a pole, and he was told that it was for the ethnographer. "But," said Malelaka in his dream, "she already has one." (This is a fact; the ethnographer had actually bought a python skin.) So he suggested in the dream taking the python to Kalabahi to sell; then two people carried the python off and sold it.

His first dream about being beaten is evidently a dream of guilt for not working. Then follows a fantasy of being pulled up into the sky, that is, lifted into mother's arms. His own association to this is, "ascent to the sky is a sign of hunger." But he found himself falling; in other words, he is rejected. The ethnographer did not give him anything. Whereupon he proceeded to rob her. He had noticed that she had bought a python skin; in his dream at his direction the python skin was sold. The implication obviously is that he appropriates the money. As a matter of fact he needed money at this time. He was in difficulty about paying taxes. He therefore expected the ethnographer to take up his burden for him. The dream says, "You buy luxuries while I am in need. Since you do not give me what I want, I shall steal it."

This dream reveals Malelaka's infantile adaptation. He is too indolent or too inadequate to be successful and he is always looking for some superior being upon whom he can throw the burden. It furthermore reveals a very powerful, envious, and strongly repressed predatory trend.

In another dream he is relieved by the dead of responsibility for feeding them. Malelaka wants to play the role of the great prophet but feels too poor to be the benefactor and great man that he would like to be. In the dream he has the honor but does not have to pay the price. The dream of not feeding the dead is really a dream of stealing, for in his associations he turns this impulse into a text for moralizing that one must not steal; that one must pay for what one takes, and then he expatiates on what would happen if one stole, especially from children. The implication is: "They would hate you as I now hate you." These impulses are largely directed toward the ethnographer. He is really threatening her.

His relations to the spirits are of a similar character. That is, they are parental surrogates through whose power he is able to be someone of importance in the world. His attitude to them is, however, entirely passive; he merely tells what they inspire him to do. He cannot materialize any of the power he covets and so has to be satisfied with empty claims.

An excerpt of one of Malelaka's dreams, together with the spontaneous flow of ideas following is a good representation of his character, relation to superior beings and to the ethnographer.

"Last night I went to the village of the dead. Someone's familiar spirit took me. Karfehawa [chief of the village of the dead] was sitting on a chair. He didn't look at us but just hung his head. Then the familiar spirit said, 'I have brought a man.' Karfehawa said, still not looking at us, 'Why did you bring him?' The familiar answered, 'I just brought him.' Then Karfehawa said, 'You must take him back.' So the familiar took me to an island, a little one with the ocean all around it. I looked and saw five villages there. I asked where he was taking me, and the spirit said, 'I'll take you to your village.' Then we went to Batulolong. There I went to the kitchen, but the people didn't feed me, they just gave me tobacco to smoke. There it was very bright and hot. Then we went down the ravine and there was a big spate. I asked what we were to do and the familiar said, 'Don't be afraid, sit on my shoulders.' I did and he jumped across the ravine. Then he shook his shoulders and tossed me off so I landed on my feet. I was very hungry and told my friend. He took someone's tubers which were growing there and gave them to me. I bit into one and it was raw. I said, 'This is raw and I can't eat it, let's just take it along.' "

This dream took place during the early part of the interviews, when his anticipations from the ethnographer were much aroused. He was accustomed to wait for his interview at the kitchen door, and the ethnographer's was, moreover, one of two kitchen houses in the mountains. While waiting he was given tobacco, but not food. The sunshine and heat referred to in the dream denies the existing reality of heavy downpour of rain for days, which apparently made him feel ill.

The rejection by the chief spirit is not elucidated, but that he expects a great reception and doesn't get it is quite plain. What it is that he expects is made clearer by the succeeding images; it is food, or what food represents to him. But he complains that he is again badly received, getting "only tobacco." That this is the ethnographer he is complaining about is made very clear by the reference to the kitchen house, hers being the only one about. This is followed by a picture of disaster—a spate—from which he is again rescued by the spirit. (This succession of food frustration followed by disaster is frequently formed and supports the contention in the previous chapter that poor maternal care lies at the basis of feeble ego development.) Then again his hunger asserts itself, but his predatory impulses (to steal—I want to be cared for by you) get the better of him. It is not he who does the stealing but the spirit. But the tubers are raw and he cannot eat them.

The whole configuration of the dream is a continuous struggle with an overpowering wish which goes only part way toward satisfaction. It is channeled into the direction of a hunger craving, which is the manner in which it is universally represented. Children want to be fed, the dead want to be fed; only the latter are obligatory. Malelaka cannot carry this responsibility; he himself wants to be fed and carried around. Whatever the cultural situation, this is the dream of a man who feels himself devoid of resources. The role of the spirit is assuredly a parental image.

His associations to this dream are very enlightening—"When I was small (two to three) I was sick and I couldn't eat. I almost died. My mother cooked rice and I didn't eat it, she pounded corn and I didn't eat it . . . my father hunted rats. He roasted one. This one I ate. Whenever I cried, father took a rat and fed me. Mother stayed home to take care of me because I was so thin. Then Lonmani came to take care of me." Then follows a tale of a good deal of shifting about, staying here and elsewhere.

By his associations following the dream Malelaka wants to impress the ethnographer that he was able to compel his mother and father to look after him by virtue of his illness. He still considers himself in a similar position with respect to the ethnographer. It is hard to reconcile this very infantile dream with a man of forty-five, who is married and has children. Yet it is obvious that these roles do not alter the infantile constellations at all.

The tension in Malelaka is greatly heightened by the fact that he cannot be confronted directly with his repressed wishes. When he has a desire to steal he must dress it up in the form of a moral discourse against stealing. His particular reproach is about parents who take from their children without due compensation and also the dead who do the same thing. It is the necessity to deal with his impulses in this indirect manner which makes Malelaka such a hypocrite; it is his inner sense of helplessness which makes him assume his grandiose role; and it is general hostility to everyone which makes him seek his revenge by destroying everyone in his predictions of doom.

Fantan

Fantan's biography differs from those of the other men we have studied much as that of a city "slicker" differs from that of a farmer. He is sophisticated and has had more than average experience. Though it is not entirely clear whether he has accommodated himself to whites, within a certain range he knows their ways of thinking and knows how to get along with them. He knows particularly how to play upon their sympathies and try to get as much as he can out of them. Fantan differs from the other men also in that he has a slightly more cosmopolitan air. He has been to school and has traveled a good deal more than most of the other men. In other words, we have here an extremely independent, shrewd, somewhat educated young Alorese. His story also differs from the others we have undertaken in that it is largely taken up with concrete activities, difficulties, and problems of his current life. There are very few fantasies, and such as he does indulge in are colored very little by the ritual aspects of this culture. Notwithstanding all these features, Fantan is a true Alorese, for he is compelled to live within the circuit prescribed by the institutions. About some of these he has his tongue in his cheek, but from others he has no opportunity to escape, and his enlightenment avails him nothing on that score.

Fantan is the youngest of six siblings. At the time the story is told he has only two older sisters living, two of his brothers having died before he was born and one sister when he was young. The story of his development is sparse. What follows can, however, be gathered from his narrative. His parents while not wealthy were apparently well-to-do. His father was obviously an enterprising person. Fantan received good care, that is, good in so far as this culture permits good treatment of children. He admired his father, feared him, respected him, accepted his ideals but had some difficulty in being the kind of person his father was. He declares that his father's magic powers were so great that if he hit a tree it would die. This exaggeration speaks for a tendency to idealize the father, which in turn means that he had something to expect from him. It speaks for a good relationship with the father, who must have helped him grow into manhood. This is borne out by the absence of stories in which the father deprived him of rights, or put unusually great obstacles in the way of his acquisition of status-marriage. The fact that Fantan has to exaggerate his own exploits shows that he is imitating the father as well as living up to a cultural ideal. This is shown definitely in the fact that Fantan likes to boast about exploits of physical courage which are obviously lies, for he is known about the village as a coward. His father was not a coward. On the other hand, Fantan apparently puts his education on the side of his identification with his father and presumably puts it in lieu of physical courage. Now at the age of twenty-five, his parents having been dead three years and one and a half years respectively, Fantan speaks about them with a great deal of emotion. Though it is obvious that his story in so far as it deals with his parents is exaggerated somewhat for the benefit of the ethnographer, nevertheless the feeling is undoubtedly genuine. He had the usual frustrations in childhood and mentions a good many kindnesses from his parents. He follows the usual pattern of childhood of having to cry to be fed and then tells of incidents in which he has water poured on him for crying. However these episodes are dwarfed by the predominance of incidents in which it is clearly shown that Fantan's parents fostered his self-esteem very early in life and encouraged him in performing exploits. For example, when he was about eight he was sent by his father on an important errand, namely to fetch a moko. His father dressed him appropriately and when he consummated this errand, his father praised him and called him a rich man. His father sent him to fetch a pig from a relative for a new house that his father had completed. Although the pig was almost as big as he was, he finished the task to his own great satisfaction.

In other words in Fantan's life we find that he participated actively in the lives of his parents. Accordingly he was eager to grow up, but his fantasies about growing up are clothed in those of accomplishment, rat hunting, premature fantasies about being married. Moreover his father encouraged him at the age of ten or twelve by making a gesture in the direction of already buying a wife for him. Fantan had an interesting reaction to this situation, for he noted that the girl was rather big and he was somewhat terrified of her.

A very good indicator of Fantan's development is in the fact that in childhood his anger always was readily expressed, at times toward his father upon whom he once threw a coconut and got soundly beaten for it. On another occasion he accidentally shot an arrow into his mother, but he got complete forgiveness for this accident. The words which his mother said on that occasion indicated a very deep affection for her boy.

There is one relationship of his childhood that is unusual, or at least it is unusual in the sense that Fantan unlike all the other men speaks about it with a certain degree of candor. This relationship concerns his sister. She was his next older sibling. It seems that when he was very young he had a great deal of sexual curiosity about her. Interestingly enough, he tried to satisfy this curiosity by observing his sister defecate. She once caught him in these peeping activities and smeared his mouth with feces. His mother rescued him and settled the quarrel by assuaging his rage against her. In this connection the first dream that he has about the ethnographer is about watching her activities in the toilet. As the story unfolds it is obvious that Fantan had a very strong sexual attachment to his sister which she did not encourage. Whether it is on this account or whether other rivalry situations complicated the matter, the fact is that Fantan carried a very deep grudge against her, but at the same time tried to enter into friendly relations with her. In this he was not altogether successful because she was constantly taking advantage of him, at least so he says. Fantan's story ends with a litigation that he brings against his sister for refusing to share the produce of a field upon which he had a legitimate claim through the labor that he expended on it with her.

At the present time Fantan seems to be sexually quite a mature and aggressive person. His attitudes fall within the cultural mold. He boasts that women were eager to have him as a husband. But toward the end of his story he seems to be uncertain about finding a new wife should the divorce with his present wife, to whom he has been married for four and a half years, materialize. There are the usual stories of being wanted by women and the usual efforts to deny that he ever had anything to do with any woman other than his wife. However a few slips of the tongue here and there indicate that Fantan is quite a philanderer and takes advantage of any opportunity that presents itself.

In his courtship of his wife he showed himself to be extremely aggressive; he wanted to have intercourse with her before the legitimate time. She held him up for a while until he had given a sarong to her mother. Then they had intercourse. In his willingness to break the convention in order to satisfy his sexual interest Fantan differs from every other man we have studied.

Much of his story is concerned with the current problem of whether he should get a divorce or not. Fantan is very reticent about his emotional relations to his wife. It is also very clear that his wife was very much interested in him, but that the relations between the two were constantly spoiled by the intervention into his affairs of her relatives. Her parents are both living and she has a large family, and the relations of Fantan to all of them are quite complicated. So that the impression he creates is that his relations to his wife are also very bad. However in some of the retorts that his wife makes to him in their quarrels we have some indication of what the root of the trouble is. Apparently Fantan put on airs about being an educated man and looks down upon his in-laws; so that his wife has by this time a feeling of inferiority toward him. On the other hand, his in-laws really try to exploit his education for their own ends. Fantan pictures himself as being very gallant toward his wife; that is, he never strikes her and he never philanders. But he tends greatly to exaggerate every trifling injury that she inflicts upon him. This may indicate a sense of guilt. He probably does philander but says, by implication, that he only does this when he wants to avenge himself upon his wife. This is probably not true.

His marriage therefore seems to be a typical Alorese marriage with constant quarreling and bickering about jealousy and property. He is constantly on the verge of divorcing her. After the death of his first child—that is, about a year and a half after their marriage—he wanted to separate from his wife. His parents-in-law insinuate that he has an evil spirit in his family which kills all the men. When he is on bad terms with his wife, Fantan undoubtedly does a good deal of philandering. In the final story of the "divorce trial" it proves however that his wife's specific accusation about Fantan's infidelity is wrong. Fantan probably had a narrow escape here.

It is clear from Fantan's domestic life that the financial obligations of marriage act as a decisive check against wholesale divorce. Without this check Alor would be a completely disorganized society from the point of view of the relation of the sexes. Fantan is greatly intimidated by the fact that if a final reckoning were actually made, a procedure necessary for divorce, he would find it impossible to marry again, being financially ruined. On this account he is obliged to stay with his wife. On the other hand the vindictiveness of the woman is likewise very clearly shown in this story. So violent were her feelings about their quarrel that his wife actually placed a leprosy curse upon him. This threat would sound very serious to anyone but Fantan; and although he had not the slightest actual fear of it, he professed to be afraid of this curse and insisted upon its removal before he was reconciled. In other words Fantan was beaten into submission by the fact that his parents-in-law were clever enough to cheat at the reckoning so that he came out a debtor instead of a creditor. However he stays with his wife; and that is really what the institution is aimed at. What is important about Fantan's relations to his wife and in-laws is that his difficulties do not in any way interfere with his sexual appetites or interests. The foundation for a healthy sexuality has already been laid. This is not disturbed by his external difficulties, as we saw to be the case in the other three men.

We have in Fantan therefore a man whose childhood was noteworthy for good care. The parental images stand out very sharply and Fantan's attitude toward both parents is good. He was encouraged into many activities, received the very unusual advantage of an education. But Fantan did not follow through. He has to boast, and to cover his inadequacies with falsifications. He must lie and give himself the benefit of every doubt. In spite of these traits he develops into a sexually mature person and even under these conditions he finds the financial complications of marriage extremely irksome.

Perhaps the key to his character can likewise be discovered in the reactions that he has to the ethnographer. His first dream is one in which he imputes sexual curiosity about the ethnographer to another man whom he beats off. However the incident of peeping at the ethnographer's toilet activities is the replica of an experience he narrates between himself and his sister. The ethnographer stands for a sexual object about whom he has much curiosity but he recognizes that this impulse must be repressed. If we take the ethnographer as a sister, then the narrative of his life bears out the fact that this relationship was not a good one, that he was constantly being punished by his sister, his sexual interests rebuffed and finally cheated by her. This analogy with the sister must be translated. He does have a sexual interest in the ethnographer. Secondly the imputation that the ethnographer is cheating him is merely another way of stating his claims upon her, that he would like to get more from her than she is giving. Whether or not Fantan was being well paid for his work is beside the point. The ethnographer likewise stood to Fantan as a powerful person with endless resources, and he therefore expected her to share them with him. This is shown by his efforts to induce the ethnographer to make various purchases for him. Thus on one occasion he offered a ridiculously low price for an object, a way of proclaiming his poverty, and the ethnographer's wealth. In this attitude toward the ethnographer Fantan differs from none of the other male subjects. He does differ however in another respect. Fantan is the only male subject who had a sexual attitude toward her. There is another possible explanation of this peeping dream. He has several associations about defecation; of being scolded by his mother, of defecating on men's heads and being beaten off by his father. In view of the fact that urinating on people is a method witches have of getting other people in their power, this dream may also represent a great awe of the ethnographer and her power over the people in the community. This long series of attitudes about feces is decidedly atypical. He is the only Alorese whose biographies were studied who has such a constellation of ideas about defecation. There is no way of determining how this came about, because the culture does not emphasize this zone either erotically or otherwise.

His other dreams are not very transparent. He dreams of a stone ball which falls from heaven and misses him. This is followed by a dream about catching birds, crayfish, and eels (he gets a small eel and someone else a big one) which seems likewise to refer to the relationship to the ethnographer. Dreams of large, round objects falling are common breast symbols. The transition between the two dreams, however, contains an important idea—namely, "I would like to have the ethnographer give me things, but I really don't need her. I can do things for myself." There is however a catch to his self-confidence, namely that someone else gets a bigger eel than he does. The ethnographer was not very successful in eliciting any material that would point up his interest in eels and crayfish or why these particular objects should be thought of in connection with hunting. The actual associations to this dream—of being robbed, of his father's catching the thieves and making them pay compensation—only confirm the previous impression. The ethnographer is a thief by implication; that is, if she does not give him all he wants she is thereby taking things from him, and to this attitude he is very sullen and promises to avenge himself upon her.

The manner in which Fantan handles aggression is well described in the following circumstance. Fantan had inherited from his father a fifty percent share in a valuable moko, the other part owner being Malikalieta, a rich kinsman. One day Fantan got word that the moko had been sold by his partner. This infuriated Fantan. Meanwhile the moko had been placed with the ethnographer for safe keeping. One night Fantan and his wife seized the moko and secreted it somewhere. Fantan appeared for duty one day in a very agitated frame of mind. He had heard bats wheeling and squeaking in the house and both he and his wife were frightened. He says he saw a dark figure trying to seize his wife when she stepped out of the house. As an antidote to these anxious factors Fantan burned some medicine and went to sleep in another house. He was certain that he was the victim of malignant spirits. On the day preceding Fantan's anxiety attack it was noted that a grave had caved in at Karieta. Rilpada the seer divined that the dead man was dragging into the grave the souls of several living men. The seer recaptured the souls and returned them to their owners. But Fantan was worried. He went to his father's grave and noticed that it too had settled. As between the services of Rilpada or another seer, Padatimang, Fantan's wife and sister chose the latter. The seer corroborated Fantan's worst fear: his soul had been dragged in. The seer returned it but warned Fantan that he had found the soul of Malikalieta in the grave. The seer who now had control of the soul of Malikalieta could now enter into an alliance with Fantan, who turned the moko over to him. Now Fantan, having a seer as an ally, felt safe. Fantan committed a theft, but he couldn't tolerate the anxiety it generated. He cured the anxiety symptomatically by an alliance with someone who could control his partner's soul.

This situation is typical of the profound distrust he has of everyone, and at the same time the concealed predatory impulses of everyone toward everyone else. This predatory impulse takes the form of stinginess and procrastination in the performance of death feasts as well as in the payment of debts. This type of aggression, in the form of withholding, is also associated with a good deal of guilt. Thus after Fantan's child dies, Fantan warns his official kin not to kill one of his pigs and thus force a death feast on him for the child. His excuse is that he has already killed six chickens. But these latter were for divination feasts, which did not at all discharge his obligation. Though Fantan was really grieved by the death of this child, he was infuriated when told that his brother-in-law had shot his pig. This turned out to be untrue. The pig was not killed. That night he had a dream: he is at a pig-hunting feast where there are also a renowned poisoner and his brother (a shrewd financier), who are pursuing a pig. He finds himself holding a strange child which he lifts into a tree, which turns into a house. The pig charges and Fantan jumps to one of the rafters. It is about to bite him, but instead turns and kills the child. Then he hears that his pig has been taken by his female relatives. He takes the child, which disappeared. He then goes home and finds that his pig has really been stolen.

Fantan feels quite guilty about his child's death, and in the dream atones for it with the sacrifice of his pig. He sacrifices the child to his voracity, otherwise he would not have to even the score before he could get some peace of mind. He identifies himself on that account with these two vicious characters, the poisoner and the financial sharper. From these impulses he shrinks, only to attempt a refuge from his voracity by jumping to the rafter of the house—a maternal representation. (Alorese houses must be reached by ladder—and trees, houses, and the sky have appeared repeatedly in the dreams of others as maternal symbols.)

Fantan has therefore the same basic constellations as the other men. There is, however, more sophistication and a stronger ego formation.

There are several association sequels which follow frequently in his biography. For example, a powerful man hits him and then fondles and feeds him; there is much reason to believe that Fantan's father was a strong and at times a violent man and that Fantan feared him. He was early conditioned to fear irate people, especially men, and tends to greatly exaggerate their powers to harm him. He shows also the usual constellations of a strong wish to be dependent on women, but a deep distrust of them, and a tendency to be very quarrelsome with them on that account. The ethnographer is no exception.

Tilapada

This woman seems to be as well-adjusted as this society permits. She is a woman of about forty, comes from a family of six brothers and two sisters. She is married, has five children, and has evidently been able to make a success of her marriage, judging from its stability. She differs from several of the other female characters in that she is more than usually affable and self-assertive and has for a long time been accustomed to take an active share in the running of her household.

So far as the facts of her life are concerned as they emerge from her narrative, the following are most significant. As is typical of this society, her chief caretaker during her childhood was a sibling, in this case her second older brother. The treatment that she got from him was apparently very good. She took her induction into household duties with considerable grace and married at about sixteen. It is quite evident from her story that most of her childhood was spent in the company of other children, chiefly siblings, and that her encounters with her parents were few. About the latter she has more things to say about beating and punishment than she has about favoritism and kind deeds. This is what we would be led to expect. However, her story is not devoid of pleasant encounters with her parents. Punishments are mentioned chiefly in connection with her mother, though her father is also occasionally mentioned as a disciplinarian. There are repeated references to her trailing after her mother when she went out into the fields and insisting on going along. She frequently succeeded in prevailing on her mother. There is also repeated reference to punishment by her mother for her refusal to do garden work. Later she took care of a younger sibling, and repeated the conduct of her mother to her. She resented the crying youngster, hit her on the head and then fed her.

There are several things that stand out prominently in this biography. First she seems to have been an unusually assertive child and she evidently got what she wanted by sheer persistence and doggedness. Secondly, food occurs a large number of times in her associations and dreams and evidently is one of the constant anxieties of her life. For this there seems to be little rational basis. Thirdly, although her brother was her immediate caretaker, it seems that her relations with boys were extremely bad from childhood on. Part of this quarreling seems to have been that the boys tried to keep her in her status and she wished eagerly to participate in masculine activities. In fact, this wish is the most dominant trend in her life; she is constantly doing unusual things such as killing rats, generally an activity of boys; as an adult she dreams of pig-hunting or riding horseback, the latter an activity reserved for the Kapitan. In her games she showed a decided tendency to play the man; on one occasion she took care of two "wives" at once. Another point was her constant resentment against household duties and responsibilities, and her hostility to her children. She shows this in connection with the illness fantasies about her children and the sense of guilt that she is not feeding her guardian spirit. Since this feeding ritual is such a bagatelle, one wonders why all this procrastination. She is never mobilized into action until she has several dreams of guilt. She furthermore shows her resentment of her present duties by quite frequently and naïvely dreaming and fantasying about the good old days of childhood—which really weren't so good after all. She is always dreaming of being sent away, abandoned, reproached, and robbed.

Notwithstanding that her marriage is successful as far as appearances go, there is every indication of a rejection of the feminine role. There is also very substantial evidence of sexual difficulties. Men are represented in her dreams as brutal, predatory beings of whom she is afraid and in constant danger of being killed and devoured. Her marriage has had the usual history of running away from her husband, his requests that she return, the worry about paying back bride price, coaxing by relatives, reconciliation, and return to her husband. On the other hand there is also considerable good will between them and they assist each other in giving death feasts for each other's dead.

Tilapada's sexual history raises the question of what probable route she pursued to attain her masculine role and what is the deeper content thereof. There are two possibilities: (1) That she came to it by way of identification with her second older brother, who was her guardian; that since she saw much of masculine activities through him she wanted to be like him and do the same things he did. (2) A second and more far-reaching possibility is that the pursuit of masculinity stems from her deeper unconscious sexual attitudes. If the latter is the case then our conclusions about sexual development in childhood as we drew them in the basic personality structure are incorrect. There is much to support both views. The story of her childhood games, in which she makes her "wives" do the chores while she pretends to shoot a pig and play being rich, support the first view that it is purely an issue of status. She even lays it on thick by beating her imaginary wives.

There is also considerable evidence of sexual repression. Thus, she deals with sexual temptation by accusing another woman of adulterous intentions with a man and feels very self-righteous about it. This in itself does not give us much information about repression. No one can tell whether or not the ethnographer's influence was responsible for her prudery and that, free of the responsibility of telling her thoughts, she might have dealt with the problem differently on another occasion. In her associations with the dream she speaks of a strong attachment to her father. She then speaks of making errors and of being punished. The implications of an Oedipus complex here are quite likely and are furthermore confirmed by the fact that on the following night she dreams of being a good mother, of cooking food and feeding her children. That is, she satisfies the adulterous, incestuous wish by identification with the good mother. The same dream also satisfies the wish for atonement. Paradoxical as it may sound, the masculine attitude may really be a cover for the wish to be a protected child. This is really not such a far-fetched conclusion in a society where the woman exercises the role of food provider for her husband. She also makes frequent references in her narrative to how niggardly she was with her husband before the latter had met his bride-price obligations. This speaks strongly for repressive measures in dealing with sex, and the bride-price obligation appears to be merely a rationalization for a more deep-seated unwillingness to accept the female role. There is no way of telling from her account whether she is sexually potent or not.

There is another explanation which satisfies both possibilities mentioned and this one derives from the relation to the mother. The frequency with which food enters into her dreams is quite remarkable and is undoubtedly typical for the culture. In this connection the dream which follows the one just discussed is illuminating. The dream is, "My soul went to Baletmia. There I saw much betel up in a mango tree. When I climbed up there was none there. So I came down and then saw another tree with much betel in it. I climbed it. When I went up the tree there were no houses near. When I came down I found myself descending into a house corridor. The doorway was closed and there was no ladder. I wondered how I could get down. Then I saw a woman come up on the verandah. It was T——— (a woman whose child had died). I said, 'It is fine that you have come . . . there is no ladder here. I was wondering how I would get down.' She said 'Why not come to my house?' I thought people might suspect me of stealing, so I opened my areca basket for them to see I had nothing but the betel I had picked. Then Tilapada said, 'Mother, you have been gone long, you had better go now.' She was eating a big fish and another old woman was eating lumpets. But they did not offer me anything. So I went away." Her associations are: Picking betel is getting wounds; Tilapada and the old woman were from the village of the dead. Going into the house—I will get wounds and die. The house —place where placated spirits stay—they are not malignant ghosts.

The mother appears quite decidedly as a food frustrator and the motif of desertion and of being alone is also basic. The dream confirms strongly the conclusions reached in the derivation of the basic personality. The longing expressed in the dream is not necessarily for food, for there is really no food scarcity in the culture. However the constellation is apparently formed in childhood of a food scarcity created largely by the neglect of the mother. Furthermore, the significance of food in these dreams is expressive rather of a hunger for affection than for nutriment. The importance of this cannot be overemphasized, because it is apparent that the whole pinching of affectivity which is so prominent in her story is rooted in the inability of the child to respond to the rejecting mother. Children do not know anything about love. They measure this only in terms of impulse or appetite gratification or frustration. A woman who unconsciously regards herself as a rejected—that is unfed—person cannot meet the sexual situation fully. The masculine fantasies must therefore be compensations for this incapacity. This fear of rejection is also corroborated by the constant death fantasy if it is judged by the frequency with which she dreams of visiting the village of the dead. In the associations with this dream we must note that all her responses to stimulus words refer to death or injury.

It must also be noted that in a woman of forty who has five children it is very strange indeed that the most vivid memories and those which are most highly tinged affectively pertain to her childhood. She has a great deal more concern over the death of her brother than she does over the death of her own child. In fact, references to her children are almost conspicuously absent. Her resentment to maternity is clearly shown in her refusal to have children in the first years of her marriage. She takes abortive agents and shows extreme embarrassment when she is obliged to talk about it.

Tilapada's biography is very striking in the almost complete absence of affectivity, and no coaxing by the ethnographer was able to elicit any. There are very few positive feelings listed, but in addition to greed, resentment, fear of being isolated, punished, wronged, and deserted, there is a strong feeling throughout that she does things largely because of pressure of the fear of not doing them, rather than because of strong positive feelings.

Tilapada is the most articulate of the four women studied, and at the same time is a well-adjusted person in this society. It is therefore possible that we may get from her biography the clue to the problem which can be stated thus: What is there in the position of the female in this society which facilitates the perpetuation of the vicious cycle of bad maternal care, poor personality integration, bad motherhood. There is little hope of recovering this from the other three women; the only other possible candidate, Kolmani, is so occupied with her social ambitions that we cannot get a glimpse into this particular facet.

Tilapada formed only one significant attachment in her early life, and that was not to her mother, but to her older brother. If we take this as a starting point then her attachment to him follows normal lines, first dependency, idealization, identification. The end result, identification with her brother, is incompatible with the role she is biologically predestined to follow, namely, motherhood. We can therefore expect some deep difficulty on that score. We cannot use the same standards in evaluating this identification that we use for women in our society, because her brother was not primarily a sexual object but a mother surrogate. But he becomes such a surrogate only after the real mother has failed her and after the pernicious effects of maternal neglect have already become consolidated. We know that this was only a second-best solution from the fact that her dreams betray a deep insecurity and a constant longing for feeding, for being lifted up—as we see in the dreams of climbing trees with the expectation of finding a choice morsel, only to be disappointed; to recommence the quest, and then to be followed by the fear of being apprehended stealing. This situation is therefore quite the same as we find it in the men. Another corroboration of this conclusion follows from a study of her free associations, in which the need for food stands highest in frequency and achievement lowest. And the associations about fear and failure occur almost always in relation to food frustrations. This is also present in all the men except Fantan.

The relationship to the brother therefore has a therapeutic function, and the fact that Tilapada can cling to it is a manifestation of her emotional verve. It is natural, therefore, to find the activities associated with motherhood just as eagerly avoided. But since she cannot avoid them she performs them with very divided feelings. As a child she did these undesirable chores to avoid being punished, but never developed any real interest in them or in the ultimate purpose of such labors, to feed her husband and children. She cannot do that because she still wants to be a child, and, failing that, to be a man. Nothing else can explain the fact that the greatest emotion in her story is related to the period before adolescence, in which she spent much of her time in masculine play.

At the age of ten she was already an adult, and at sixteen already married. It is safe to say that at no time after sixteen has there been any opportunity for her basic character to change. If, when an adult, this woman behaves like a child, runs away to a dance, for which her husband refuses permission, and plays children's games, we can be certain that it is this childhood period of irresponsibility which she is trying to recapture. What kind of an attitude can this woman have to a child or to a husband? It can only be an attitude of resentment—perhaps not conscious—but at the same time a feeling that her obligations are inescapable. She therefore does them in a perfunctory way, but without feeling. The blocking may therefore be toward any form of organized activity, be it in the form of affectivity, or of sexual or garden activities. Nothing else would account for the persistent and ubiquitous anxiety in her dreams. These anxieties are attached to fear of soldiers, illness of children, loss of wealth and, most common of all, fear of death. She also dreams constantly of being away from home and having great difficulty in getting back, taking shelter in a house which proceeds to burn down. These dreams vividly describe her deep resentment to her inescapable responsibilities of wifehood and motherhood; she wants to be a child herself, a wish completely incapable of realization in the actual world in which she lives.

In comparison with the men, the woman is therefore at a great disadvantage. The man can channelize his wishes in the direction of recapturing these childhood boons from the woman sexually and in his financial dealings with men. In this respect the woman has no outlets at all, for she proceeds at once from a frustrated childhood into motherhood, and if Tilapada is representative, the woman has no preparation for this role. The emotional blocking caused by this situation may account for the consistently low intelligence of the women. But there is little doubt that it is the nodal point in the frustrations of the child and husband in the woman, and therefore pivotal for the whole society. A woman like Tilapada cannot teach an infant free emotional response, having none herself. And so the cycle is renewed indefinitely.

Lomani

Lomani, a woman of twenty-six, was the youngest of seven girls. Her father died when she was an infant, and her mother when she was fifteen. In between, all but one of her sisters died, and the survivor was so deformed by a skin disease that her nose had completely disappeared, thus diminishing her chances for a desirable marriage. Lomani grew up in an environment exclusively of women. Moreover, owing to her mother's impoverished state, the family was constantly on the move from one village to another, or she had to stay with one relative after another. One of the reasons Lomani gives for her mother's frequent change of abode is that she was envious of her relatives who had males about and hence much more meat food. Lomani quotes her mother as cautioning the children against envy of other peoples' better diet, by stating that those who had the superior dish might resent the envy. On another occasion the moving took place because her mother was bitten by a pig. This is the usual Alorese trait of abandoning everything because of one untoward incident. The family did not starve, having enough vegetable food. Pigs were scarce however. The family was poor in wealth and connections, and the influence of men was nonexistent.

This poor and constantly changing environment never gave Lomani a chance to develop any constant feelings to anyone, apart from her mother and one friend of her own age, Kolata. After her mother's death she went to live with an uncle. After a year he died and she had to shift again. She married, had one child, but her husband died shortly after. She contracted two other marriages with shiftless characters, but these unions terminated. At the time her biography was studied she was practically alone. She had two nieces, three nephews, and two paternal cousins in the village. But she made no effort to associate with anyone. She surrendered her child to her mother-in-law, though Lomani had considerable fondness for her daughter.

In the opening remarks she made to the ethnographer spontaneously, we see the dominant trends in her personality. She tells that her father died when she was very small; that after his death her mother moved to three different places; that her mother built a poor house and raised a pig for her grandfather's death feast. Then her mother died. Then she hunted husbands; she went to her husband's village and he died. Then she married again; the new husband did not help her with the gardening, so she ran away. She married a third time, but her third husband deserted her for another. She was asked to marry again but she refused, saying it was better to stay where she was and work, and wait until her daughter should grow up when she could cut weeds by her daughter's side.

In these first two hundred words are recorded three deaths, two unhappy marriages, endless moving around, hard work, loneliness, resignation of all life goals except waiting for her daughter to grow up.

She lived constantly in the company of poverty, illness, and death.

The early conditions of her life were not conducive to any capacity for strong emotional ties, and hardly for creating a well-integrated personality. Humility, hopelessness, a sense of being without value or worthy of claims on anyone—these seem to be her dominant traits.

Nor does she take kindly to the biographical interviews. After the first interview she has a dream in which the ethnographer is about to return home—"but only for two months"—the duration of the interviews. This is apparently her way of being through with the interviews, by wishing the ethnographer away. She reassured the ethnographer that she would be missed. Obviously this was no indication of ill-will to the ethnographer; but that she finds the situation of being interviewed distasteful. Accordingly her narrative is stilted, unspontaneous, and perfunctory and she must be continuously urged and prompted.

Lomani's narrative is more scattered than the other three; she seems to be less intelligent, more distractable; she contradicts herself many times, is extremely poor in affect, especially about aggression. Hence she must be prodded to talk. But even her affectionate impulses are blocked. She hesitates to describe or even acknowledge her feelings; and probably the chief reason for her distaste for the interviews is that they confront her with the necessity of making some emotional orientation. The part of her narrative with which she has least difficulty is that which refers to her late childhood and preadolescence, and her play with other children at this time seems to have been the happiest period of her life. From these episodes we get the only pleasant feeling tones. These references to childhood play are her chief escape, during the interviews, from the necessity to offer an opinion, to express resentment, or to recall quarrels.

In this flight from affect, angry or tender, we see Lomani's distinguishing character trait. It shows partly an emotional disorientation, partly a low opinion of herself, an almost incredible passivity, underneath which there is an all-pervading anxiety about anything and everything. She seems convinced that she has no rights that anyone is bound to respect or any legitimate claim to happiness. Hence she is devoid of drive. In its place there is a vague longing for someone to rescue her, and this wish must be throttled because too many traumatic experiences in her past show this to be a vain hope.

Beneath the ruins of this personality one finds fragments here and there of traits which might have developed. She begins with a strong attachment to her mother, but is subject to the usual desertions and has the customary resentment. She was no more fortunate with her older sisters who acted as maternal surrogates. She is left with a terror of being alone and has all sorts of imaginary fears, of being robbed, of being deceived, of dangerous animals. These later become fears of men with hostile intent to kill her. She narrates but one quarrel with her mother, who beat her. She ran away and decided to sleep in a mango tree. But her friend Kolata coaxed her to come and sleep with her. The following day her mother brought her food and "spoke nicely" to her and she was reconciled. She showed a good deal of reluctance to learn gardening, but after an unskillful start, she improved.

We see therefore in Lomani a typical mother-child relationship, in this instance complicated by the absence of men in the household. Her maternal attachment was spoiled, but she retains not too unpleasant a feeling about it. The strongest tie of her childhood is not to any of her older sisters but to a friend, Kolata.

There are a few episodes of her childhood which indicate some obstinacy and an occasional outburst of uncontrolled rage. On one such occasion she tore off the loin cloth of another girl; she then began to have the most exaggerated fears of retaliation, even to being killed by the father of the girl she offended. She had to take refuge in the home of a friend. This is another indication of how deeply repressed all her aggressions or self-assertions are. She pictures the most dire consequences. This unconscious significance of self-assertion as violent aggression which will provoke retaliation is probably the secret of her limpness and passivity. Hence every aggression, self-assertion, or wish must be abandoned, and in its place is a fear of being robbed, a feeling of being abandoned and unprotected. Having food stolen from her is a common theme in her association. Hence at an early age she was already devoid of initiative. She is always led and acquiescent, and generally uncritical of the advice she usually follows.

There is a strong likelihood that the absence of males in her household also had a decisive influence on her character. She was frequently reminded of this deprivation by her mother, both in the direct complaint that there were no men and by the occasional demonstration of how helpful a man can be in alleviating the burdens of life. The household was helped from time to time in the building of houses by male relatives. The superior skill of boys in hunting was also a feature of childhood play. But the subtle insinuations of her mother not to envy other people's meat diets was really an admonition not to aspire to have men around. "Mother thought we had better not go on living there (with Lanpada who had plenty of meat feasts) because the children were looking at the meat and people might be angry. In their mouths they weren't angry but one doesn't know what thoughts they have in their hearts." So they moved away. Her own father's death while she was an infant and the presence of sick siblings, all but one of whom died, again must have created a feeling of hopelessness. She emphasizes in her childhood play that there were no boys, though on one occasion she speaks of playing in the water with boys without her loin cloth. She was constantly admonished against playing with boys, lest some harm come to her, that she might desire them or they her.

In adolescence we find her very timid about boys. At the tooth blackening (at about fifteen) she sleeps with Kolata, and permits no familiarities with boys. The awareness of her poverty—meaning that she could be had for a small bride price—could not have increased either her aspirations or courage. Her first marriage was terminated by her husband's death, thus repeating her mother's experience. She was apparently attached to her first husband. This she intimates by saying that had it not been for his death she would not have married the other two. From then on she seems to have felt completely defeated about men. When she gets into a quarrel over a man who already has a wife Lomani retreats humbly. She contradicts herself on precisely who her second husband was, on one occasion claims that he was her deceased husband's uncle, with whom she went to stay. She left him because he refused to help her or give her food. Going away from it was her mother's method of dealing with any difficult situation.

Her dominant attitude to men is the fear of deception. This she describes aptly when talking of how she overheard her third husband speaking about her to a third person, indicating that he wanted her to leave. Whereupon she leaves without a fight. We must not overlook the dignity of this behavior. Her next topic is about a piece of deception perpetrated on her. However, though she left her third husband, she joined with his first wife against the woman for whom he deserted them both. This is conventional behavior; it was also an insistence on her status as a wife, although her kinsman took her away from the quarrel by questioning the legitimacy of the marriage since no bride price was paid for her.

At twenty-six she is already through with men. It is difficult to say whether this is due to her feeling of not being able to command the devotion of a man or to an accurate appraisal of her social chances—for under her present conditions she could marry none but a poor or shiftless character. The weight of evidence is in favor of the first motivation. Her fear of abandonment—to her death must have that connotation as well—is her dominant attitude toward men, which is only her special version of the deep distrust she has toward all human relationships. She is left with only one human contact, that with her daughter, in whom she has the opportunity to idealize her own unhappy childhood. She lives in the hope that this relationship, over which she has lost direct control by surrendering her child to her mother-in-law, can some day become a meaningful one.

As for her other aspects as a social being, they simply do not exist. She conceives of herself as isolated. She rarely speaks of the common form of socializing, participation in feasts. At least one can say of her that, though she is limp, passive, and devoid of aspirations, she prefers resignation to exposing herself to an endless series of degradations.

Lomani thus shows us the structure of a character composed of blocked action systems. Her character resembles Tilapada; but it is compounded by a severe dose of adversity which was continuous throughout her life. This could only add to the deep mistrust, easy abandonment of enterprise, lack of continuity of goals, low achievement aspiration, isolation, resignation, and a straw on which to clutch in the form of recapturing her own childhood through her daughter. Even for Alor, Lomani is a crushed human being, having nothing but a flight into reality in the form of preoccupation with the sheer mechanics of living.

Kolmani, the Seeress

Kolmani is a woman between thirty-five and forty. Her parents both died when she was very young. She had one brother, who died, and many uncles, aunts, and cousins. She had two youthful marriages which did not last long and one marriage which was permanent. By this last union she had three children; the first died at the age of two. She now has one boy of fourteen and a girl of three.

Kolmani sought out the opportunity to become a subject for study.

She evidently regarded it as a great honor. But although she volunteered her biography, her first dream tells us some of her motivations. In this dream the ethnographer seeks her, to whom in turn she gives areca, a sign of friendship, and gets money in return. She cannot resist the temptation of seeking money and honor, but she must make it appear that she is sought after. This is one of the dominant constellations in her character. We learn later that she is extremely jealous of any woman who gets the ethnographer's attention during the time she is giving her biography.

The wish to be important has a long history in her life. Her father died while she was an infant and her mother when she was about two, and, although she received fairly good care from her uncles and aunts, she was constantly complaining about it. She used her orphaned state as a justification for feeling very sorry for herself and as a reason for persistent claims on others. The basis for this attiude was laid in her childhood. After she was orphaned, she was cared for first by her grandmother, then by a series of aunts and uncles. She was apparently remiss in doing what was expected of her, and she narrates several incidents in which she was upbraided and called either a sponger or a slacker. These disparaging remarks evidently accentuated her feeling of isolation, and, together with her frequent changes of abode and guardian, did not give her much of basis for a high self-esteem or strong ties of affection. In fact it gave her an additional incentive to try to cheat on her obligations. This was her mechanism of revenge. At the same time it set in motion the need for compensatory attitudes, such as trying to get the most out of those around her, never being satisfied with what others did for her, complaining and even misrepresenting. There are several glaring discrepancies in her story. She tells two versions of a story of how her aunt cheated her out of the proceeds of her field. Two cloths were bought with it. The first version was that her aunt appropriated the cloths; the second that her aunt gave her both, but that she, Kolmani, gave one of the cloths to her aunt out of gratitude for her care. In other words, her complaints about her poor care by relatives are undoubtedly exaggerated, probably for the benefit of the ethnographer on whose sympathies as an orphan she wishes to play. The purpose of this is undoubtedly to get something from the ethnographer.

In childhood she had a bad case of yaws, the scars of which incapacitated her. She went through an exceedingly trying period during the 1918 epidemic, when relatives were dying all around her. Her early environment was therefore unstable, giving her little opportunity to form strong attachments to any parental figures. In this connection it must be observed that bad treatment by a permanent parent has a more decisive effect than indifferent treatment by a long series of parental surrogates. Her earliest traits were apparently formed as a defense created by her sense of isolation. The strong wish to be loved took the form of discontent, and eventually the attitude of exploiting others by compelling them to give her what she wants.

From her dreams it is also quite apparent that these fears of being without much value and of being exploited and mistreated are compensated by the illusion that she is possessed of supernatural powers. She has a dream in which three male figures steal her pig, which she reclaims with the aid of her female spirits. The things she talks about after this dream suggest a strongly defensive attitude to men, though there is no evidence that it ever took on a masculine tinge, as was the case with Tilapada. The supernatural powers seem to stand in the same relation to her that masculinity does to Tilapada. Her social position of being an orphan exposed her to the risk of being given away in an undesirable marriage so that her guardian uncle could profit by the bride price. She escaped from this obvious exploitation by claiming immaturity and refusing the sexual advances of the man. On another occasion, when a marriage was already arranged, she discovered that her suitor and she were cousins and hence could not marry. By these devices she got out of two marriages and left both her suitors and uncle in the lurch.

In other words, we find in Kolmani a series of defensive attitudes which serve to bolster her self-esteem. These devices are all assertive at the expense of others. She enhances her value by these direct means and through supernatural powers. But it is obvious from Kolmani's talk that she is discontented and filled with ill-will. She must give a benevolent picture of herself as a hard worker, ill-treated by others. She must depreciate others and gossip about them, and thereby lift herself. She must impress the ethnographer by dreaming prophesies, one of which foretells her husband's death. Her husband is frequently used by her as a scapegoat, in her dreams as well as in real life. She narrates incidents of quarrels with boys in which she always gets the upper hand. She is exceedingly vindictive, and invokes her "supernatural powers" to avenge herself on those who incur her anger. Thus when she was still quite young she was humiliated by the woman who was her guardian and who called Kolmani's attention to the fact that she didn't pound rice for her grandmother's death feast. The fact is that she had yaws at the time. But it is equally true that she has always tried to evade her obligations. On this occasion she had a vision in which her grandmother threatened her guardian's child. She thus avenges herself on her guardian by making an ally of her grandmother, in her obligations to whom Kolmani is remiss. She is not forgiving, is always planning revenge; if that is not possible through ordinary means, then she turns to the supernatural, and that failing, she promises herself to even the score after death. In spite of her great expectations of others, she is remiss in her obligations to her dead brother, who has to threaten her repeatedly in her dreams before she finally feeds his spirit.

On the other hand, while her brother was alive she coöperated with him in their marital arrangements. She offered him her bride price to enable him to buy a wife. Judging from her dreams he was probably the strongest attachment in her life. She feels guilty about her negligence in feeding his spirit.

Several aspects of her life come out with some clarity, her role as a seeress, for instance, and her relations to her husband.

Her mother and her paternal great-uncle were both seers. When her mother died, the supernaturals were taken over by her great-uncle. She undoubtedly heard much about this, and in becoming a seeress after her supernatural experience at fourteen she thus identified herself with her mother, and at the same time preserved her as an ally in need. However the role of the great-uncle in this connection is that of exploiter. He told her to placate her dead mother's spirit and get her powers; but then he expected her to hand over the fruits of her powers to him. This situation is somewhat difficult to evaluate. We are obliged to treat this whole relationship to the supernaturals and the great-uncle on the basis of a fantasy, which in this culture can be implemented in a practical way in the role of seeress. She had more dread of the exploitation of men than of women. Perhaps this was impressed on her by the child marriages she was almost obliged to contract for the benefit of her guardians. In one instance she refused sexual advances. The men whom she had to regard as paternal surrogates were people who really tried to use her. The opportunity to develop any real tenderness for the man was therefore lacking. This situation is clearly shown in her fantasies in regard to her supernatural powers; they are to be used for the benefit of her great-uncle. She had some success as a seeress, though it was not remarkable. Her relation to the supernatural is therefore quite typical of her whole character structure. It is first an identification with her mother. Secondly, it is a means of getting power over others; but it is not entirely successful; it is somehow under control of a man (great-uncle). Thirdly, it is a means of protecting her against a sense of isolation and it implements her defenses against exploitation and abuse.

Her sexual attitudes, though not described in any detail, are now intelligible. Unlike Tilapada, she does not identify herself with the male; there was no relationship with any male in her childhood sufficiently strong to serve as the vehicle for such a fantasy. She is constantly on the defensive against men from childhood on. She currently has dreams of anxiety and of quarrels with men and fears them. Her refusal to learn to make baskets (she is the only woman in the village who cannot do this) is likewise a part of this defense. It is not femininity that is so distasteful to her as that she fears men—and fears them in a specific way, she fears being abused by them. Her two early marriages give us no important clues. But her last marriage is quite in accordance with what we would expect. She married a man whom she could easily dominate. She tries to frustrate him at every turn. He wants to buy a sheep; she puts every obstacle in his way. She dances with other men at the dance place and makes him feel slighted and unworthy. She separates from him and wants to pay back his bride price. She is constantly browbeating him. Yet in her peculiar way she is quite dependent on him. He appears as a rescuer in several dreams. This constant bickering is one of her ways of assuring her own internal security.

Although she accepted marriage as an inescapable necessity, her inner distrust of men was too great to make any marriage with her a pleasant one. It is impossible to tell which of her versions of her husband's courtship is correct, whether she affected coyness or whether she took the initiative. The very fact that she has two versions of this tale indicates the strong division of her attitudes. She uses her supernatural powers to browbeat her husband into doing as she wishes. She is constantly making him do things for honor and pushing onerous financial burdens on him.

Her relation to her children is nebulous. It is obscured by the difficult relations with her husband. He resented her first child; it was apparently jealousy on his part. After the death of this child she left him for three years. After a reconciliation she took a contraceptive preparation and remained sterile for a long time. She seems to have regretted this step. After three years she conceived again. Then there was a gap of eleven years before the next child.

In her relations to the ethnographer we get again a picture of a rather complex individual torn between many contradictory trends. She wants to draw a picture of herself as a powerful seeress and again dreams of the ethnographer in the role of a rescuer. She doesn't quite know how to represent herself, and in several episodes of her life we get two contradictory pictures. Her dreams at the time of the interviews show her to be extremely apprehensive, their sources not being very clear from the content or associations. She often thinks of herself as small, insignificant, threatened, demanding aid of supernaturals, dead relatives, the ethnographer, and as a last resort her husband. Nor is her confidence in herself as a healer very great. In one dream she visits a sick person and the house burns down. This does not indicate any great confidence in her abilities.

One little episode and the dream that followed it is very typical of her character in so far as it is brought out in relation to the ethnographer. One day she appeared for her interview and began at once to converse in an irritated tone with the interpreter. It seems that on the previous day another woman of the village had visited the ethnographer's house. Kolmani observed this and was apparently much concerned about it. She wanted to know the details from the interpreter. She could not tolerate any other woman edging in on what she thought was for the time being her exclusive prerogative. On this occasion she narrated a dream she had the previous night. In the dream she wants to cut a banana from a tree. Then she observes feces near the banana. She says to an older female companion (undoubtedly the ethnographer), "We wanted to eat those bananas, but some one has defecated near them." She then asks her husband to cut bananas from another tree. He does so but she is still dissatisfied. Her husband says, "Save them and I shall see if I can find a dog to eat with the bananas."

She fears that someone may interfere with her position with the ethnographer. This is represented by an eating symbol—a banana. But bananas are commonly regarded as children's food. We cannot account for the particular representation of the interferences, feces.

From their folklore we learn that feces in place of food is the commonest representation of maternal frustrations (see p. 105). Here she becomes vindictive and starts prodding her husband to satisfy her whim. Her husband has the unpleasant task of acting as a buffer against her deep sense of frustration, which obviously began with her being orphaned. The ethnographer is undoubtedly the idealized powerful mother, whose support is threatened by interference on the part of another woman. In several of her dreams in which she appears helpless, there is always a note somewhere— "But I can strike back." In other words, she is a deeply insecure person; but one who has developed a sufficient number of aggressive defenses to act as counterbalances. In contrast to this biography see that of Lomani, where the collapse of the ego is complete.

If we contrast Kolmani with Tilapada we must note the absence of masculine fantasies. In the case of Tilpada the masculine attitude was fostered by two coöperating trends, one based on her grievances against her mother, the other on a strong attachment to her brother, whom she wishes to emulate. In the case of Kolmani these grievances were spread over a series of guardians. Her dead mother on the other hand, with her supernatural powers, became the idealized protector. Kolmani identifies herself with her mother, and evidently keeps that identification all her life. Besides, her hatred and fear of men was no vehicle to carry an identification with them. She got enough power and prestige through her role as a seeress and hence did not need the masculine compensation.

Thus in Kolmani we find the great weakness of her character rooted in her inability to make strong affectionate attachments. The emotional façade is made up of a struggle for security by means of control and power over others.[4]

---

[4] The ethnographer supplied one other biography, Kolangkalieta. It is not included here because it has nothing new to offer bearing on character formation. Kolangkalieta was apparently overcome by the interviews. Her account is perfunctory. She had a successful career as a woman; but now, being past middle age, she is occupied in a rather defensive way with the externals of living, and much of the material she offers is nothing but details concerning these activities. She does however furnish some interesting details concerning Alorese customs, and the character delineation is included in some of the discussions which follow.

CHAPTER VIII

BASIC PERSONALITY, CHARACTER, VALUE SYSTEMS

THE ORIGINAL DATA from which these biographical sketches were abstracted can be mined for much more than was used in the previous chapter. Our chief interest in this material is the study of the character variations along the lines of the conjectures we made in delineating the basic personality of the Alorese. In addition we can see how the institutions are articulated in the life of the individual; we can study the projective reality systems and form some notion of their value systems.

The Study of Character

When we discuss character configurations within our culture, we have difficulties of a purely technical nature, namely, whether to describe character in terms of drives toward certain goals, conscious or unconscious; whether to describe it in terms of attitudes, such as proud, cruel, vindictive, etc., or in terms of certain interests or tendencies. All these methods are overlapping, and each presents certain dynamic, semantic, and other operational difficulties. Freud tried to derive character configurations from repressed sexual trends (for example, passive homosexuality), from sublimation of certain partial impulses (for example, the derivation of oral and anal character traits), or from reaction formations, which are really special forms of repression. What stands out in this conception of character as derived from sexual components is that they owe their origin chiefly to various forms of repression. Precisely how repression operates to produce these character traits was never completely explained by Freud. The general assumption that sublimation, reaction formation, and repression all accounted for the drive component in character formation had some operational as well as descriptive value. This whole conception of character did a much better job of supporting the libido theory than it did of describing the origins and vicissitudes of character. It is hard to say, for example, whether the so-called "anal character" is constituted so as to perpetuate the original somatic pleasure from which the trait is supposed to originate, or whether the somatic pleasure zone has entered into relation with the character trait in some other incidental manner. Alexander gave another answer to this question of character derivation by use of the vector principle instead of somatic pleasure principle. He maintains that the drive is not toward somatic pleasure, but toward retentive and expulsive tendencies, from which such traits as stinginess or benevolence can be derived. Alexander uses a much broader base than does Freud. At all events, the character trait is an indicator of a certain habitual style of adaptation which has a security function, and that is the chief thing we need to know about it. Equally important features are the integrative nature of the character trait, its tendency to remain fixed and automatic. The adaptive purpose of the character trait often miscarries. The character trait belongs to the executive functions and is maintained by cognitive features determined by past experience and extended to situations other than those from which it took its origin.

When we study biographies in a culture other than our own, in addition to the technical problems just discussed, we have the problem of empathy—that is, of approximating these character configurations in their own culture. How is it possible to render intelligible the character of an individual from a culture so different from our own? In the seven character sketches presented above we have committed a bit of psychological violence on the material. We have arranged the data into sequences meaningful to us, but not to the Alorese. They have no regard for chronological sequence and have no "time sense" similar to ours. We have also here and there used not pure psychological characterizations but value judgments which have validity with us, but not with the Alorese. This was not due to carelessness, but was an attempt to make the description vivid to the reader. Most of the character traits were described in terms of well-known psychiatric constellations. These can stand and would be meaningful no matter in what culture we found them. The type of characterization which is most confusing is that pertaining to "normal" and "abnormal." This characterization is a pure value judgment. According to our guess about the basic personality structure in Alor, Mangma must be considered a normal man for his culture. Rilpada has more aberrant features for this culture, though he tends more to approximate the neurotic character of our culture. Thus in order to make these characters intelligible we were obliged to translate them to some extent into the psychological currency and value systems with which we are familiar. We had no other choice. If we represented these characters as they appear to the Alorese, we would call a "simple" man *honest*. The question "according to whose standards," when asked about a character delineation, thus confuses two issues: (1) sequences and constellations which are valid no matter in what culture they are found; and (2) the social significance of a given combination of traits. This latter is an evaluation; the former is made up of universal constants.

The biographical data give us an opportunity to do more than merely confirm our guess about basic personality. We have in addition the more difficult task of correlating personality types to cultural configurations; of studying their reality systems, projective and empirically desired, their value systems and their ideologies.

The Male Characters

In the four male characters we find that though each follows an individual line of development predicated by the particular accidents that accompanied growth, there are also similarities due to contact with conditions uniform for all. Both the similarities and the differences in character structure must engage us.

For purposes of making this comparison Mangma will serve us best as a norm. As we read his collection of attributes, it is evident that they are not discrete items, but are systematized and interrelated, and can be derived from experiences which can be identified. If we take the sequences he describes himself, the main trends of his character can be represented thus:

Repressed craving for support and affection plus conviction of frustration	*Feeble ego development*	*Compensations*
sensitivity	repressed aggressions	boastful
insecurity	low aspiration level	pretentious
mistrust	abandons enterprise &	minimizes good
inhibitions to women	changes vocations	envy
no capacity for	exaggerates injuries	lying (?)
attachment	feeble superego	vanity
repressed predatory	absence of ideals	gardening
trend	low self esteem	female activity

These traits derive clearly from the early maternal rejection and neglect, reinforced by factors set in motion by his father later in his life cycle. In other words, the effects of frustrated cravings for support and affection run a course unaltered by later mitigating influences. His character is therefore consistent and has some organization. The compensatory traits show an internal organization and are consistent with the basic constellations. Another testimony for internal organization is the direction of his repressed predatory trends. Failing in finance, he takes to gardening. His fear of exploitation is consistently derived from real experience; his inability to form anxiety-free emotional bonds is consistent with the absence of ideals, feeble superego, low self-esteem, and the readiness to abandon enterprise.

The character which most resembles Mangma's is Malelaka's; but the latter is much more disorganized, much more infantile and diffuse. The two poles: on one hand, undisguised wishes to be carried about, supported, helped by superiors and supernaturals; and, on the other, his diffuse destructiveness, stand out with great clarity. His diffuse hatred and aggressions take in the entire world, hence his persistent gloomy predictions. The destruction of the world is clearly his own destruction; it is the constant reënactment of his own eviction from the arms of a protector. Though the same basic constellations are present in both Mangma and Malelaka, their organization is different. Malelaka is completely devoid of judgment and self-control. In these two characters the nuclear characterological constellations are alike; but they are elaborated in entirely different ways.

In Rilpada we have a difference in nuclear constellations. The maternal rejection and neglect appears to have been the same, but a powerful antidote to the devastating effects of the latter was introduced in the form of a meaningful relation with his father. Under this influence there appear traits absent in the first two—ideal formation, conscience, educability, and some capacity for friendly relations. In his inhibitions to women he is like the first two characters, but it is along lines of paternal influence that we find an attempt at identification, which fails. In its place, however, we have an admiration of the paternal example with abundant excuses for failure to approximate it. There is more direction than in the two previous characters to the elaboration of his aggressions against his father, in the form of an Oedipus complex and passive sexual attitudes. The repressed predatory trend, so prominent in Mangma and Malelaka, is decidedly in abeyance, and his relations to the supernaturals are modeled after his relations with his father, rather than on the frustrate relations to his mother as is the case with Malelaka. His aggressions are better formed and more directed. In combination with his better capacity for affection, his imagination has direction and range, and he uses it with some constructive purpose as compared with Malelaka. Withal, Rilpada is an insecure person, with no capacity for leadership.

Fantan's character structure was molded by influences similar to those in Rilpada: the better parental care, especially by his father. But like Rilpada, Fantan cannot live up to his paternal example. He does not claim disabilities like Rilpada, but his defensive system is made up chiefly of denials of his weaknesses. He has most of the characteristics of Mangma, but not the sexual inhibitions. He is the only male of the four to have a sexual attitude to the ethnographer, though it is expressed in anal terms.

The presence of Fantan's anal complex is very arresting for it is not present in any of the other characters. It is an indicator that there was something atypical in his development. Unfortunately he supplies no data on this point except that relating to his interest in his sister's excretory activities. That it is a fixed element in his character structure is shown by the fact that he readily extends it to the ethnographer. This is an aggressive sexual attitude. But the other dependent attitude, so prominent in the other men, is also present, in a different form. He also has the wish to exploit others, to take from them what he can, to give as little as possible in return. Consequently he fears being exploited. It is possible to fill in the wide gaps in the explanation of this anal complex of Fantan, but it would lack substantiation in the data supplied by him. It might be something like this: He mentions defecation with several connotations, being on top or being on the bottom, defecating on someone or being defecated upon; the former being the equivalent of exercising mastery or advantage over someone. Defecation is also used in the sense of giving and producing. In this case the excretory act in Fantan's case may be linked with the idea of retaining, not giving out, of holding on to possessions or wealth. It is in Fantan's case decidedly not linked with discipline, obedience, and cleanliness. If these conclusions are correct, then Fantan's curiosity about the ethnographer is tantamount to the wish to get something from her. This is, however, pure conjecture. How these meanings of defecation became linked with sexual attitudes cannot be recovered from the data. There is one possibility. Fantan is the youngest of six children. His older sister might well have been his caretaker while his mother was away. It may well be that cleansing activities and care were associated with her. The fact is that he is always trying to go into partnership with her—and she always wants to cheat him—at least that is his story.

The conclusion can only be that owing to certain aspects of development not recovered from his account Fantan uses anal symbols (that is, derived from anal activity) to express retentive and taking attitudes which all the others express in terms of oral symbols.

Fantan gives further evidence of a less obstructed development in that he has no sexual inhibitions and does not fear women as sexual objects. But he does want to exploit them and take from them—his sister, his wife, and the ethnographer. The last is the most powerful of all and therefore the one who arouses his greatest expectations, not all of them unconscious. Fantan did not escape the damaging effects of poor maternal care. But as in the case of Rilpada, and a great deal more effectively, paternal support took up the slack. Notwithstanding his advantages the culture caught up with Fantan. The sequences cannot be established from the material submitted, but his character, apart from the adornments of education and some skepticism about the validity of Alorese reality systems, is not so very unlike the others. He tends like Mangma to wish to put everybody else in the wrong and to represent himself as the injured party. He also exaggerates slight injuries into threats of annihilation. Like the other men he is afraid of his wife, who is decidedly more assertive. He compensates for his inadequacies by vanity; is so afraid of being cheated that he cheats first. Fantan's superior development does him little good because of the people around him, and he is obliged to live according to their values; hence his character is deflected in the direction of those around him despite his greater potentialities. He is like the others in that passive longings predominate, though mixed with aggressive ones.

Fantan's biography proves that in a given culture individual deviations from the norm do not affect the personality except in detail. His life illustrates the issue created by "progressive" education in our society, where children are enlightened sexually in early childhood in the hope of forestalling neurotic trends created by these early repressions. To be sure, such explanations do help the child. But a child cannot be taught complete sexual freedom in its home only to encounter the customary taboos in school or with its playmates. The effect of the latter will be decisive in the long run. However, the child which is brought up with knowledge of sexual activity will have certain psychological advantages, in that socially conditioned repressions enforced on the activity can be handled in a more effective manner. In short it is the summation of influences in a culture and not one specific detail which is responsible for character formation.

In these four men we see therefore that different influences due to the different personalities of their parents, their status, etc. influenced their character formation. In three of the men the influence of poor parental care was quite along lines projected from the basic personality structure. Moreover, in each case differential features were introduced which deflected the development in specific directions—Rilpada by a powerful father ideal, Malelaka by serious illness in childhood, and Fantan by education. The institutionalized running away from parents is reified by Mangma, Rilpada, and Malelaka, but not Fantan. The first three are seriously inhibited to women; only Fantan escapes, but all four are unconsciously afraid of women. All are trapped by the serious financial responsibilities of bride price and death feasts. They are alike in their general mistrust, their deep insecurity, their sensitivity and cowardice. All but one have deep predatory trends. All have amorphous aggression patterns and limited capacities for affection.

Thus in our conjectures about basic personality, the role of the father was not sufficiently discounted. This appears to be the variable in the character structure of the males. Rilpada and Fantan show that the devastating effects of maternal rejection and neglect can in a measure be overcome. The earlier influence is not erased; but a unique combination appears in which some attempt at ego ideal formation and conscience development can be engrafted on an ego that has a very poor foundation.

The Female Characters

If we compare the life goals of the men with those of the women we may find some explanation for the blocked personalities of the latter. The four men studied all showed distinctive characters; they were all oriented toward objectives like accumulation of wealth and of status, and all made reactive defenses against their weaknesses; compensations were instituted for defects. Even Malelaka, the feeblest of the four men, had an organized orientation. All were organized toward the passive goals of getting and receiving. But such an organization, filled as it is with inconsistencies, is directed and continuous. All these goals are singularly feasible for the male, but correspondingly inaccessible to the female.

She is essentially the *donor* in the society; she is also the executor of the real economy. She plays no direct role—with limited exceptions —in finance; she is bought and sold; she does not even have the objective of the male to work toward a bride price, which, as we noted, even the most inhibited males have. What goals are left her? Marriage— which presents no special difficulties—having children—which give the Alorese mother too little emotional satisfaction—and for post mortem status through death feasts. The rest is an endless career of work in the fields and an actual position of control over subsistence economy for husband and children, though no participation in the prestige economy of finance is open to her except through marriage. There is an obvious discrepancy in the vigor of the life goals of the two sexes, not because of any intrinsic defect of the feminine goals themselves, which are quite like that of women in our society, but because the goals become internally disqualified by major conflicts organized around them. That is, the unconscious goal of becoming a recipient is vitiated by the social necessity of becoming the donor. Not that the objective of motherhood or marriage cannot become a vital goal to these women; it does. But this goal does not enjoy an unconscious emotional resonance. This is assuredly the case with Lomani (and Kolangkalieta), although in the former case the objective was finally abandoned. The two other women have their main goals in life organized about masculine and socially ambitious pursuits. The acceptance of the feminine role in this society is synonymous with being exploited and worked to exhaustion. But even this would not be a disqualification or cause for rejection of the female role. The real reason seems to be that the woman remains tied to her own passive infantile goals, that she never gets any encouragement to abandon these objectives or any real psychological preparation for the role of wifehood or motherhood. This seems to be for the woman the real source of major conflicts.

These conflicts seem to be made up of two contradictory attitudes. The impulse to motherhood is completely canceled out by a corresponding impulse against motherhood. This is what is commonly known as ambivalence; yet this term is not precise enough to describe the process, because the concept ambivalence presupposes two precise and well organized contradictory attitudes like love and hate. This does not fit the circumstances. The chief factors in the case of the Alorese woman is that neither of the constituents of the ambivalence is well organized. The hatreds or acceptances cannot even be formulated precisely. Hence the only attitude that emerges is a confused, anxious state. The most extreme form of this state we find in Lomani. (But a not dissimilar disorganization exists in Kolangkalieta, although the form it takes in her is a shallow but sticky preoccupation with superficialities, the concrete but insignificant details of living. This shows itself especially in her dreams or fantasies.)

There are certain points in which all the women, excepting Lomani, seem to have some organized attitudes. All tend to boss their husbands, fight with their rivals, and fight to keep their man. This is conventional behavior. They are all aggressive with their men; all tend to resist sexual activity. None of them has a maternal attitude of anything like the quality we find in our society. They all have a deep resentment toward work. Lomani and Kolangkalieta have an attitude of resignation to it; Tilapada and Kolmani both seek other objectives to embellish their lives. Their sexual attitudes cannot be ascertained; to guess that all four are sexually frigid is probably correct. It is difficult to conceive that the kind of intrapsychic picture which Tilapada, Lomani (or Kolangkalieta) present can be associated with sexual potency. Kolmani is more likely to be potent.

Thus the psychological picture which the females present is one of utter internal confusion. It is possible that this is the factor responsible for their consistently lower intelligence as tested by the Porteus method. It is not in the data; but there is ground to suspect that the wide discrepancy in intelligence between males and females would not exist in children of the preadolescent stage. This lack of intelligence is probably an emotional blocking. The woman in Alor is caught in a much tighter web of incompatible factors than is the man, and is infinitely more frustrated. On the other hand lower intelligence in the females of primitive societies is very common. It may not therefore be a differential feature in Alor.

Perhaps we can demonstrate some of these incompatibilities in the material from the biographies (See Du Bois p. 396.) In the very first interview Tilapada reports a dream, "My soul went to my mother and father. They asked, 'Why are you here?' I said, 'I have just come to see my mother and father.' They said I must go back. Father stayed but mother brought me part of the way. From there we flew to T . . .

where we fell in a tree top. We ran from there to M . . . In a short time we were at F. Then mother turned back and I went on alone." Her parents are both dead; but she is rejected. She is accompanied by her mother part way, is driven from place to place and finally deserted by her. That she is tied to a childish objective is not the least in doubt, though she herself has five children. But this wish is frustrated. In this dream the wish for protection is prominent, but there is hopelessness and fear of desertion. This is followed by another dream in which she holds rice in her hand and her husband says, "That rice is not good, it is evil spirits' rice, you can't take it." Her obligations to her husband prevent her from satisfying her craving for food, that is, her craving for protection, an additional incentive for discord with the husband, envy of her children, and masculine activities.

At the ethnographer's invitation to talk about early memories she speaks of playing with her younger sister, tells stories of civet cats, and continues to repeat childhood nonsense syllables, "oa, oa, ing, ing, Kanale, aug, aug Kanale." Every dream she brings has a similar anxiety. In our society such a group of associations would mean schizophrenia; but in Alor it does not have this significance.

Kolmani, though she rates low on the Porteus test, tells the most integrated story. She shows a wish for distinction and deference, to be on familiar terms with the ethnographer, a very appropriate fantasy anticipating her first encounter with the ethnographer. The dream that preceded her visits to the ethnographer indicates, apart from its content, that Kolmani has at least some decisive orientations. She wants recognition and glamour. She is something of a work shirker and there is much reason to suspect that much in her story is edited so as to place her in a favorable light. But the emphasis in her story does not fall on the femine aspects, but on those of status and discontent with the treatment she received. Affectionate attitudes she displays not at all. References to the death of relatives are chiefly concerned with the formal aspects, death feasts, etc. But this is common to all Alorese. Her vocation as seeress can be considered a masculine equivalent, though she came by it through her mother.

If we take the three women, Tilapada, Lomani, and Kolangkalieta as most typical, then we are obliged to conclude that the women fail to achieve the same degree of effective integration as the men. And the only reason we can assign for this is the crucial change from a brief childhood to adulthood, the latter being filled with arduous tasks which they are in no way prepared to carry out. The absence of definitive character formation in the female of this culture is crucial because it is through her that the low affectivity, the confusions and incompatibilities are perpetuated in the offspring.

Character and Basic Personality

The question can now be answered as to whether the seven Alorese whose lives and character structure we have examined have enough in common to justify the concept of basic personality as a useful operating tool. It does. But this does not mean that one can add all the character traits and derive an average. The one defect in our data is in that most of the characters come from the same status, and the really successful individuals in this society are not available. In a society where, despite absence of fixed statuses, there is a good deal of mobility, where the tug and pull for advantage is so strong, small differences in character structure will greatly influence the success of the individual, and it would have been instructive to know the formula for success in this society and how these constellations were integrated. It must however be emphasized that character variations, apart from influencing the immediate fate of the individual, have no relevancy to Alorese culture and its institutions. It is not the kind of a culture in which a great man could arise or make important innovations.

Basic personality only indicates a certain range and certain modalities within which great differences can arise, depending on "constitution," the specific characters and fortunes of the parents. Within these limits, the delineation of basic personality came very close to what the actual biographies reveal. The factors common to all are the low range of affectivity, the distrust, the low aspiration level, the amorphous aggression patterns, the limited capacity for strong attachments, the sensitivity with all varieties of defenses it mobilizes, the repressed predatory trends. The variations come in the degree of integration achieved, the capacity for idealization of parental example, the character of the aggression patterns, and the specific defenses against anxiety and inadequacy. Factors not adequately predicted from basic personality are the depth of the anxiety that the men have concerning women and the extent to which paternal influence can overcome in a measure the effects of maternal rejection. However in the latter cases, that is, where the father's influence was strong, the engrafting of these positive features complicates the picture greatly. Mangma is a relatively simple character to understand; Rilpada and Fantan very complex. In these two latter cases the effects of maternal rejection are not canceled; but new combinations are engrafted on the old base. What kind of a conscience, for example, can be erected on a base of poor affectivity and disorganized aggression patterns? It must terminate in a form of servility or abjectness; it must yield to uncontrolled outbursts of aggression; or both may take place alternately.

Affectivity is commonly regarded as inborn. This view is not incorrect except for one detail. Affectivity is inborn, has a demonstrative function, and is intimately tied to appropriate executive functions. However, affectivity may fail in its demonstrative function. A tantrum will eventually disappear if it fails to elicit any response compatible with the tension it serves. The ease, the appropriateness of emotional response is a part of training which begins in the cradle, and affective responses can be encouraged, deflected, or completely blocked. Furthermore, affective responses tend to become habitual along the lines of most frequent exercise. The Alorese infant may be affectionately fondled for two hours in the morning and two hours in the evening. If in the meantime the child is left to the care of older siblings who have other interests, the predominant affective experience will be in the direction of the unpleasant tensions arising during the day. It is a quantitative matter purely.

Furthermore, affectivity is related to executive functions like curiosity to investigate and master the outer world, and to attitudes such as regard, affection, or hatred in relation to the human objects who are the source of the emotion. We can expect therefore that the diminished and blocked affectivity will affect not only interpersonal relations but will influence the creation of institutionalized practices consistent with the lowered emotional tone.

It is a striking fact that in Alor there is a complete absence of anything that can be called government or even status. This is no accident, but is intimately related to the factors we have just considered. No one has ever heard of a strike by the inmates of an insane asylum. The analogy is not perfect but is close enough. For concerted action by a group the constituents must be able to have some kind of affectionate ties and be able to identify themselves with each other and have a common ideal. This has long since been pointed out by Freud. Such organization is impossible in Alor; there are too many hostile trends in each individual and too much eagerness on the part of everyone to subject the other fellow to his own infantile needs. This problem is solved by the financial system, which is the vehicle by which the lowered emotional tone of interpersonal relations is carried.

Another similar fact is the complete lack of systematization in their thinking and acting except in connection with finance. The ability to tolerate inconsistencies without taking the trouble to find out which is "correct" is typical. This concept must be quite foreign to the Alorese. This entire complex is related to the failure to create an organized picture of the world, because their curiosity is not stimulated and because there is no great emotional stake in finding out which ritual or religious idea is "correct."

Other Features of Basic Personality

It is therefore evident that the characterological substratum of the personality exercises a polarizing influence over all other systems in the personality. It is for this reason that in considering basic personality we must include more than those features which enter into the creation of the character of the individual. From a purely descriptive point of view many of the characters seem like those we find in our society. This idea is quickly dispelled when we examine them closely. The differences are found in their unique system for handling drives; in activities where no drives are involved; in their taboo systems; and in their reality systems derived from both projective and empirical sources. All these put together make the socially relevant mental and emotional equipment of the personality.

In connection with drives we found a unique aggression pattern difficult for us to comprehend. In our society we are accustomed to find an aggression pattern which, though it can be arrested at any stage before it becomes completed action, is nevertheless so well constructed that its force is not dissipated, although it may be deflected against the subject. This phenomenon is known as masochism. But we tend to overlook the fact that masochism rests upon a well-integrated pattern. A less effective form (from the point of view of the economy of the individual, though it presents a better social façade) is to be found in psychosomatic discharge phenomena like migraine. We encountered an absence of true masochistic phenomena in Alor. Lomani is a case in point. She is not masochistic; her aggression patterns are too amorphous. Her method of handling aggressions is either complete avoidance of anything that calls for aggression, or what looks like resignation. There is no guilt, no self-injury and no destructive grudges or self-reproach. She is the most extreme instance. Fantan's and Mangma's aggressions are better formulated than are hers.

The controls associated with the sexual drive were very different from those to which we are accustomed. Though this aspect of Alorese culture is lacking in important essentials, this is not due to any oversight by the ethnographer. The natives would not discuss it. And this fact is difficult to evaluate. In all probability this is due to a blocking similar to what they encounter in connection with stimulus words related to eating (see page 247). It is assuredly not modesty. We do know that masturbation in children is not taboo. Later it is considered a type of indolence. The split between tender and sensual relations must be very great in Alor. One of the best bits of evidence we have that their value systems connected with sexual activity are not like our own is to be found in the fact that very inhibited men like Mangma and Malelaka do not have potency disturbances—at least not of a blatant kind. Sanctions are not against the pleasure function of sexual activity; they apply only to the status aspects.

In connection with anal activity we found no similarity to the values that obtain in our society. The absence of punishment on the buttocks, the absence of erotic stimuli, and the absence of ideas concerning cleanliness, obedience, and discipline or orderliness were likewise striking.

Their taboo systems are not especially prominent. They are chiefly connected with the supernatural.

They have a reality system derived from empirical sources, contained largely in their subsistence economy. This is not very elaborate. Their reality systems of projective origin are much more in evidence. The following illustrate these latter systems.

Mangma reports that one day he began to talk irresponsibly and did not eat or drink for three days. He says it was because he hunted rats near a place where a spirit lives. The spirit follows him and presumably possesses him. It seems that another male spirit gets mixed up with the situation and that they begin fighting each other. Two people make a medicine for him, but he does not improve. Then someone has to rub his body so as to make the male spirit come out of his windpipe. Thus he gets well.

On another occasion he feeds a Kuya hearth and then says, "Now let me eat my corn and cucumbers and squash and not be sick. May my shoulders and thighs be strong." Then on still another: "My father, mother, and brother died because we did not give our death feast for our ancestors rapidly enough. We built an altar but did not feed it. Then the village of Karieta burned down."

Rilpada reports that his brother had boils. The sacred hearth is fed, but the child does not get well. Alorese culture supplies an answer to this difficult diagnostic problem. His father, also a seer, divines that the reason why the boy failed to recover from boils was that a pair of carabao horns had been stolen. His father therefore proceeds to get another pair of carabao horns, make another hearth which they feed and the child gets well. His father remarks with professional pride, "If we had remembered those horns the first time, Senmani would have gotten well the first time. If we had forgotten them altogether he would have died." The reasoning is very logical.

The interpretation of illness as due to spirit possession is decidedly not new, neither is the extraction of the spirit by some procedure— in this instance rubbing. Feeding a hearth as a means of placating either spirits or the dead is not new. But there is one distinctive feature which is peculiarly Alorese about these conceptions of certain phenomena like disease, and the method of dealing with them. That is, there is a great reluctance to do it, and hence endless procrastination. This feature seems to be based on the same emotional rationale as any of the other financial arrangements on which they enter. This is Alorese.

Another series of data common to all Alorese are certain conventions and specific connotations—for example, giving areca and betel as a sign of friendship. To peel the skin off a person is to make him immortal. To sleep with an evil spirit means to die. Hence people who die from causes that are not obvious have slept with an evil spirit. These are all different facets of the projective reality systems of Alor. It would take a long inventory to catalogue them all. This is hardly necessary; but they are an integral part of the basic personality structure.

We might however dwell on two aspects of these reality systems: (1) the particular configuration of the feeding ritual and (2) the procrastination in relation to it. The ritual is one in which the spirit is fed; not one in which the subject is fed, as is the case with some types of ritual cannibalism or with the Eucharist. The adaptation of this widespread idea is influenced or polarized toward certain direct experiences, and in this instance the poor maternal care seems to be the subjective origin of the rationale in accordance with which these "empirical facts" are treated. The Eucharist is based upon a direct maternal longing, and the Alorese on the negative of the same idea, its repressed form. How does such a transformation come about? It is not so complicated; it is really nothing more than a projection of a direct experience, which is being rejected by the mother as far as feeding is concerned. The concept "mother" has now acquired a specific connotation, one of rejection. And the impulse to be fed by the mother is a powerful one in childhood; the frustration becomes an integral part of the concept "mother." It is inconceivable that the Christian concept of the Madonna should make any appeal to an Alorese, and no less inconceivable that he should be able to invent such an idea or representation. In short, the Alorese need not have invented the idea of feeding the spirit—this is almost universal. But Alor has added a particular attitude to it, expressed in procrastination. This attitude of procrastination is also expressed toward debtors. This undoubtedly comes from the same source and represents an extension of the same constellation derived from real experience.

With respect to these projective reality systems we must note the absence of those based on obedience as we found in the case of Tanala. These projective reality systems were almost uniform in all the biographies. There was one possible exception to this in the case of Fantan. He is ostensibly much disturbed over the leprosy curse his wife puts upon him. But his persistence in his fears after reassurance that the curse has been lifted raises the suspicion that he does not believe in the efficacy of this particular curse, but continues the pretense because it serves other interests.

The projective reality system is taught to the individual. It supplies him with ready-made interpretations of natural phenomena and a ready-made method of dealing with them. By the time he receives them these precepts have been subjected to a long process of "proofs" about their validity. But each individual can behave toward these facts in a way that is influenced by his own subjective experiences. This is what gives the cultural imprint to these beliefs. Thus the idea of deity is absent from no known primitive people—that is, of a superior being whose aid can be enlisted under certain prescribed conditions. This is the universal experience of humanity, to have a superior being to look to its needs while it is helpless. In many religions this idea is not abstracted into the concept of deity, but as a continuation of the actual life situation where the departed parent continues his assistance under prescribed conditions. How this help is solicited or forfeited differs in different cultures—and this is determined by the specific experiences of the child.

The reason why we attached so much importance to the projective systems is that they were the unconscious source of so many derived (secondary) institutions, which have a reinforcing effect on the institutions or practices from which they arise. It is a well-established fact that religion will reinforce the existing morality, or when accidental circumstances produce forces which tend to disrupt existing morality, skepticism about the existing religious dogmas is bound to arise. Likewise there is little need to change religious dogma in a stable society.

Whereas all aspects of basic personality structure apart from projective systems are directly imparted to the individual, there must be a certain compatibility between the projective and conscious or learned systems, and vice versa. In Western society we find the conscious, rational, and empirically derived reality systems exercising a strong pull away from projective systems (see page 438).

In Alor we derived the following features as being of projective origin: (a) folk tales; (b) religious dogmas and practices which were noteworthy for the absence of idealization, no expectation of good from supernatural, but freedom from persecution; (c) the special attitude of procrastination and action only under threat; (d) absence of conscience and generally low tonicity of superego; (e) lack of interest in conquering the outer world; (f) lack of confidence; (g) easy abandonment of enterprise; (h) low aspiration level; (i) anxiousness, mistrustfulness; (j) poor affectionate fixations; (k) ill-defined aggression patterns and fixation of life goals on derivatives of breast fetishism through financial transactions. This takes in the most distinctive features of Alorese culture.

Value Systems in Alor

A value system can be defined as a generally accepted appraisal of patterns of interpersonal relations (e. g., honesty), achievement (e. g., heroism); goals (e. g., salvation, success); approved types of gratification (e. g., aesthetic, those pertaining to order, systematization, efficiency), and pertaining to social ideals (respectability, status, strength, skill). This list is not complete. All value systems are conscious directives and by implication also involve avoidances. They contain all aspirations, ideals, and morality which are publicly sanctioned. The value systems of a culture are among its most conspicuous features; the most violent incompatibilities between individuals and groups arise from clashes in value systems.

Whereas all value systems are conscious, they are end results of a complex of constellations deeply rooted in unconscious factors. Alor gives us our first opportunity to examine the structure of these value systems and to track down the unconscious roots of some of them. As a text for discussion, we can recapitulate some of the prominent features of the value systems of the Alorese scattered throughout the discussion.

They have no "interest" in permanence or durability. Their buildings, lineage houses excepted, are built for immediate use with little care for the future. This is true of field houses, dwellings, representations of spirits. The exception of the lineage house is due to the fact that they have a post-mortem stake in it. Dilapidation does not annoy them.

Strength does not rate very high; neither does skill; nor are these qualities greatly admired. They have no skilled artisans who take pride in achievement and special talent, which, even if it did exist, would get no special esteem. Their seers are not held in high regard, and Rilpada, a successful seer, does not enjoy high status. This is a reflection of the low regard they have for those things which his efforts govern, notwithstanding that much divination goes on all the time. If they tend to just give up and die when ill, the seer cannot enjoy high prestige. These attitudes reflect the hopeless attitude they have toward the intervention of either human or even superhuman agencies.

Honesty is not an admired trait; it is doubtful whether they have any connotation for it. Shrewdness and chicanery are in better repute and probably have the connotation of competent or able.

Their aesthetic sense is limited; they have no interest in beauty in the graphic arts; but they do have some interest in music by gongs and versification.

Personal beauty has an equivocal standing. Adornment is practiced more by the males. Tattooing, tooth blackening are efforts at adornment, but they are optional and no effort is made to give them permanence.

In their folk tales heroism is not the conspicuous feature. The hero is generally a rather helpless creature dependent on the bounty of women or of his father-in-law. Vengeance on the parents for mistreatment in the past supplies the chief emotional release of the hero tales.

They have little investigative drive, and the concept of "correctness" (as against incorrect) holds little interest for them. They tolerate inconsistencies (Lomani, Kolmani, Mangma) and have therefore no interest in systematization.

The chief positive values are those associated with food and power over others, here closely related to wealth.

Though not a value system, government is a formal codification governing interpersonal relations. But in the character of a government the chief values of a culture are to be found. There is no government to speak of in Alor (except that supplied by the Dutch, whom the Alorese fear). This absence is not due to conquest or acculturation. Religious ideologies are inconsistent and fragmented.

This collection of values is not arbitrary or disconnected. The values can all be easily derived from the projective systems we have described. The key to the value systems is to be found in the low emotional character of the interpersonal relations of the Alorese, and their deep lack of self confidence and enterprise, which we traced to the poor parental care. Since they have no concept of delegated authority, but only of enforced authority, we find no authority delegated to a government. But they do understand externally imposed authority by the Dutch. There is no evidence that the Dutch have any such delegated authority; but the Alorese fear them and submit to coercion. There is no idealization of the father, except in the case of Rilpada, because the Alorese do not feel his protective influence. They have no real dependency; obedience is not rewarded, deception by parents can lead to no ideal of honesty. Hence their heroes are not noted for achievement by which they profit. The Alorese do not idealize deities, but only try to evade their anger.

Since the ego is crippled in childhood, they have no conception of achievement, have no investigative drive, do not admire strength, and tolerate dilapidation (by our values). For the same reason they have no interest in order or systematization. From their cramped emotional and manipulative capacities can also be derived their absence of aesthetic sense; they cannot manipulate the environment, take no pride in what they do and cannot idealize nature.

From their deep lack of confidence and their tendency to give up easily can be derived the low standing of their seers. The absence of capacity to idealize a helper has something to do with it. The absence of direct solicitation of boons from the gods comes from the same source. The absence of interest in skill is a compound of inability to be effective in mastery and an incapacity to idealize these properties in themselves and in nature.

Only the "positive" values are left—in reality an absence of other values. These are chicanery, shrewdness, the resolution of interpersonal relations by finance, and an overestimation of food. The emphasis is on mastery over others, which here means the ability to compel others to give you food, not support or prestige. Their value systems are thus founded on mutual mistrust and internal isolation.

This collection of values and their origin again raises the question of "taught" versus integrative systems. Value systems are not only conscious, they pervade every activity and relationship in a culture. They are taught, but enjoy a deep compatibility with projective systems from which they are derived. The value systems of Alor show conclusively that one cannot impose new value systems which are incompatible with the personality structure. If they are to be changed, all systems from which they originate must be changed. The life of Rilpada is a case in point. He is one on whom a Christian missionary might make some impression, because he "understands" something about idealization, conscience, and expectation of help from an agency more powerful than himself. To Mangma and Malelaka and all the women this would all be completely unintelligible. The diffusion of value systems can therefore take place only on the basis of compatibility with basic personality. The exceptions to this are material culture and aesthetic values, which are more easily diffusible providing features in basic personality furnish the necessary *Anlage*. These considerations also hold for intrasocial change; value systems can only change when the growth pattern is altered.

Conclusions

The relations between basic personality, value systems, and personal character, as found in Alor, may not be typical for societies in general. But there are certain conclusions that can be safely drawn. The following chart describes the relationship:

Female division of labor: women work fields, neglect children;

↓ Maternal frustrations

> Mistrust; unstable marriages
> Lack of interest in outer world
> Lack of constructive ability and systematization; no interest in crafts, absence of idealization, poor aesthetic development
> Easy abandonment of hope and enterprise; religious ideologies, low standing of seers

↓ Reinforcement of repressed cravings for maternal protection: release through predatory trends; dominant value of financial competition.

The value systems and the reality systems of projective origin are the systems encountered at the periphery of any culture. Upon these value systems, which are deeply rooted in the personality, devolves the chief burden of supplying the emotional directives in a culture.

What then is the place of personal variations in character apart from their influence on personal destiny? This is a subject that cannot be treated at length from Alor. But some definite clues emerge. The places where a character like Rilpada differs from the others can be precisely located. Rilpada's conscience and educability could have no decisive influence on the culture as a whole unless there were a good many others like him. Under these latter conditions any innovations he might conceive, echoed by others like him, might exert a gravitational pull. As the matter actually is now, it is Rilpada who is drawn into the ambit of the main currents of the culture, and his unique characteristics are freakish in their isolation, and devoid of influence. It is safe therefore to conclude that isolated characters in a culture can have no decisive influence until their ideas and attitudes can be echoed by a sufficient number of others similarly constituted. In other words, if one wished to modify Alorese culture in the direction of Rilpada's character, one would have to make his experiences with his father common to all Alorese.

CHAPTER IX

NEW MATERIAL, SYNTHESIS, AND GENERAL CONCLUSIONS TO ALORESE CULTURE

THE PROCEDURE followed to this point was first to guess what kind of personality emerges from the institutional ensemble; second to corroborate this from the study of actual individuals in the society. We are now in a position to check our results, and the first thing that strikes our attention is that the two procedures do not lead to agreement in all details. Some of the results are rather surprising and could not be anticipated from the institutional picture alone.

Generally our conjectures about the basic personality structure are borne out in the biographies, allowing for differences in the personal fate and the character of the parents of each individual studied. It is decisively established that our conjectures about poor maternal care have not been exaggerated; that the constellations established in this crucial period of life are consistently followed throughout the entire life of the individual, by poor guidance in the walking stage, the crippling of interest in the outer world, the deep lack of confidence, the pernicious effects of lying and misrepresentation by parents and elders, the absence of consistent reward-punishment systems, the premature burdening of the child with parental responsibilities while they in no way participate in the society, the genesis of deep mutual distrust, the exploitation of children by parents, the delayed participation by the males and the premature induction of the female into adulthood. But the biographies have helped us further to appreciate reaction types that could in no way be anticipated from the institutional picture. It was a great surprise to find that the men were as deeply afraid of the woman as appears to be the case, that inhibitions so strong can exist without the influence of severe sexual restrictions in childhood, where masturbation is not interdicted by castration threats, and where familiarity with sexual activity begins so early. Furthermore it is quite apparent that these inhibitions in Alor do not take the form of impotence in the males; this could not be established even in the weakest of the four males, Malelaka, who had a brood of children, and Rilpada. It is obvious that the orientation derived from our society does not exhaust all the possibilities in sexual development. We are safe to qualify these inhibitions of the male by saying that potency is not disturbed as such, but that the tender relations are seriously interfered with. The reasons for this have already been covered.

But the chief surprise that emerges from the study of the biographies is the great discrepancy in character formation between males and females. This could not be anticipated from the institutional picture alone. The only conjecture we can make about it is that the residual life goals determined by the culture are more capable of realization by the males than by the females. The character constellations found in the men can be compared with those formed in our society; but those of the females cannot even be formulated. They present a disorganized character to be found in our society only in very severe mental disorders.

We can now compare the results of the procedures followed in this book with several other techniques for which the ethnographer brought back the data.[1]

The Rorschach Experiment

The reading of 38 Rorschach tests was made by Dr. Emil Oberholzer.[2] This was the last evidence submitted in seminar, and the results of our studies from the institutional set-up and the biographies was not known by the Rorschach experimenter. Dr. Oberholzer's report can be divided into (I) reactions which are present in all Alorese, (II) specific character estimates.

I

They are all suspicious and mistrustful, not only to everything known to them, but distrustful and suspicious among themselves, constantly on guard and always defensive. This distrust dominates their lives and must affect their social relationships.

Fearful, timid, uneasy, insecure; no neurotic anxiety and no neurotic feeling of inferiority; a feeling of misgiving and apprehension, an unde-

---

[1] *Porteus Intelligence Test.*—The men average a score of 91 by this test (12.76 years). By another reading, which eliminates answers predicated by imperfect comprehension of the test, the average male score would be an I.Q. of 97 (13.7 years). The women's performance was decidedly inferior to that of the men. The average I.Q. is 67, and only two (of twenty-eight) reached the 14-year-old level. (See Du Bois, *op. cit.*, pp. 552–55.)

[2] See Cora Du Bois, *The People of Alor*, pp. 588–640. The following is a condensation of Dr. Oberholzer's report. It follows the report given in seminar, supplemented by his more lengthy account in the book.

fined feeling of being threatened and endangered; of never feeling positive and sure of their safety and intactness, therefore never outspoken, straightforward and direct; never outgoing and expansive, but self-contained and suppressive. They are shrewd, cunning, and astute, at least careful and cautious.

What they fear is hard to say, perhaps the things they feel unable to master. But they have the same suspicions and uncertainties among themselves.

They have an attitude of letting things come and accepting them just as they are, in a passive way putting up with them, surrender and submitting up to inertia and lethargy, drooping without being depressed, being submissive and resigned. This attitude they have not only toward the big things in life such as death, catastrophe, and disaster, but as well toward illness, mishap, and little things which they might tackle in an active manner so as to forestall, to prevent the worst, or make up for it. This they do not do; they seem not to care; they just let things slide and go, allow things to dilapidate and run to ruin where we feel the necessity of making repairs. They have an easy-going attitude, prefer calm, and evade big effort and strain. They live from day to day and for the moment, not worried about past and future.

They are self-centered, egocentric, and encysted, each concerned about himself and concentrated on his own belongings, keen and greedy for advantage, often unrestrained and deceitful, cheating and overreaching each other, using crooked means when they can do so without being caught, barely adjusting to the community in which they live. These traits all follow from the extreme amount of egocentric affectivity which finds no adequate offset by other factors such as enthusiasm or self-sacrifice, sublimation, introversion, contemplativeness, or creative power. These are all barred out. The organization of conscience is inadequate; in its place there is caginess and cunning.

They are easily upset and frightened, easily startled and puzzled, easily scared and put out of coutenance even to the point of helplessness. They are subject to emotional outbursts and tempers, anger and rage up to violence, then becoming immediately submissive and shrinking into themselves. They are in a permanent state of excitement without adequate stabilizers. Hence there is no self-control. There is therefore a permanent readiness for emotional discharge, and hence are at the mercy of their feelings.

They lack capacity for personal contact, living beside one another but not with one another. They know little about each other; they know little of what is going on within themselves; and there is no need of knowing more about themselves, as there is no need to give much of themselves. They are strangers to one another throughout life. They are incapable of being aware of others' feelings, they are not without need of contact, but they are unable to have an echo and to give response. There is no deeply rooted friendship or relatedness. But without getting close to one another they need one another and pull together on the basis of their community, because none of them (except perhaps Fantan) could live alone. They have no introversive inwardness.

Sixteen men and twenty women studied show no neurotic traits, but instead conscious suppression. They are much given over to their instincts, but have too great capacity for abreaction to produce neurotic symptoms by way of repression and regression. For the same reasons there is no depression or suicide. The Rorschach cannot reveal what amount of non-pathological repressions they establish.[3]

They show restlessness and fussiness that takes the place of more important activities; they keep busy but do little. They keep pottering with things of little value in an aimless but seemingly intellectual fashion. This feature is due to the lack of introversiveness which affect chiefly the kinaesthesias. Hence the introversiveness disappears while the emotions persist. The kinaesthesias are probably nipped in the bud early in life. There is no inward concentration, and hence their niggling activities and emotional oscillations.

They are not of a theoretical turn of mind, little given to synthesis, constructive thinking, synopsis and correlation. They could not build an organized cosmology and are unlikely to show artistic achievements. They are not inventors, make no contribution. At best they adopt.[4]

The women are more squeezed and timid; but once their confidence is gained, they can establish better rapport than the males. They show more stereotypy, stability, endurance, and stamina. Perseveration is common, but confabulation is absent. The women are less alert, less quick, and don't see beyond their noses; but they are more industrious, stick to routine, and don't shy away from work.

II

Rilpada is the nearest to autistic tendencies, most given to fantasy thinking, meditation, and contemplation. He has a good deal of introversiveness and intuition. He does not go so far as mysticism. He has too good a footing on earth, and his introvertedness is mixed up with traits of confabulation. In his manners he is agreeable and sweet, modest and submissive, even humble. He is too submissive to be a great prophet, but has just the right qualities to be a bit of a saint of the village without being secluded from the world. In his affectivity he is egocentric, of a rather passionate nature, easily worked up, subject to swings of mood, impressionable and suggestible. He is not however without self-control; is able to master himself and make adjustments. He is of average intelligence, but has little discipline in his thinking. He loses himself in detail.

Mangma does not rank high in intelligence but apes the thinker and scholar. He soars too high and dares too much; he jumps to conclusions, does not discriminate enough between essentials and accidents. He lacks common sense and self-criticism. He is not incisive and sharp, self-sure,—

[3] Du Bois, *op. cit.*, p. 602   [4] *Ibid.*, p. 633.

he is even smug and cocky. He stretches a point, begs questions, and is only seemingly factual. He is not very scrupulous as to truth, nor reliable as to statements, not particular or exacting, and hence neither apt nor keen on learning from experience. He is a dazzler who has not much to say when it comes to the point, and tends to show off his knowledge and scientific activities. On the whole, a pseudo-scholar; but he has some composure and balance, is without outbursts, is even somewhat reserved and dignified; however under his dignity he conceals a great deal. He is devoid of intuition and inspiration, but has ambitions and aspirations to which his abilities are not equal. He is haughty, high-handed, condescending, and presumptuous. He has no empathy, is egocentric, opinionated, suspicious, distrustful, and resentful. He fears for his dignity and has no real balance.

Fantan rates high in intelligence. He is more practical than theoretical. He is not incompetent, but is not given to abstract thinking. He goes after tangible things. He has good, even detached judgement, and also has the will to use it. He profits by experience. He has no discontent or uneasiness. Introversive features are also shown by his affectivity and behavior. He tends to live within himself. He has difficulty in emotional approach, in making contacts and adjustments. He is reserved and distant, not seeking contact and rapport, though not shying away from it. He is self-contained and undemonstrative. He is not without self-control and has good mastery of affect. He is not expansive or likely to be carried away by emotions. He is easily puzzled and upset even to the point of perplexity, when he becomes helpless. He lacks self-confidence, is timid, on guard, and not free from fear and mistrust.

Lomani is self-contained, encrusted, encysted. She is neither pleasant nor sweet. She is not easy of access, is distant, shy, reserved, fearful, frightened. She is neither nagging nor spiteful, but has no cheerfullness or gaiety. She never dares to be spontaneous or warm. She has no daring, but is not despondent. She is too staid, stolid, and passive to be so. She never gives offense, never puts herself forward, is never conspicuous, and makes no demands. She is acquiescent, meek, submissive, and humble, without resistance or revolt. She is resigned without grumbling or complaining, as if there were no alternative. Her poise is unwilled. She is burnt out, dead in life. There are no surging emotions and no conflicts. She lives a simple day-by-day life with no interests except domestic surroundings. She is not attached to or wrapped up in anything. She works without pleasure or displeasure, without enthusiasm or antagonism, without inner participation, without striving or ambition. She wants nothing and expects nothing. She has no wishes. She does what she is told, and lives a joyless, eventless, monotonous existence.

Discussion of the Rorschach Experiment

The Rorschach experiment by Oberholzer is, to the writer's knowledge, the only technical device that can supplement the technique described in this volume. It is not known how much the element of skill and intuition enter into the final formulations, or how much variation there would be if the same data was submitted to several operators independently. The use of the experiment for our research is twofold: we can check it against the findings of the analysis of the projective systems, in which case we can examine the discrepancies and try to account for them. Secondly, the Rorschach is obviously able to discover constellations not likely to be found by the examination of the projective systems alone. On the other hand, the Rorschach does not pretend to be able to show the sources of these emotional constellations. It is also questionable whether the interconnections between the various constellations can be adequately reconstructed. But it can surely identify the main constellations, which are end products.

If we compare the constellations identified by the two techniques, we find that they are almost identical in essence. But since they use different vehicles of description, there is bound to be some difference in the degree of generalization and in the level of abstraction. The analysis of the projective systems furnished many more basic traits than did the Rorschach; but the latter described many more of the refinements and derivatives as they are found in the periphery of the personality. In addition, the Rorschach picked up traits that were not indicated by the first procedure—the prominence of suppressive tendencies and the absence of introversiveness.[5] Although not identified by name, the existence of these traits was indicated in simpler forms in the projective analysis.

Naturally our interest in the Rorschach test is directed chiefly to those traits which were found to be common to all Alorese, for this corroborates or contradicts the conception of basic personality. It must be remembered that all Rorschachs were done on adults. Hence it is most remarkable that the salient features identifiable by this test should be composed of those constellations already recognized as having been established in early childhood. The Rorschach showed some very interesting elaborations of these basic constellations, such as the absence of enthusiasm, self-sacrifice, sublimation, or creative power.

[5] The Rorschach experiment in Ojibwa demonstrated many traits that could not be predicted from the study of the institutional influences integrated genetically, and could only be verified in part in the material found in the projective systems. This kind of finding at once proves the value of the Rorschach as a source of new data which cannot be elicited from any other source. The Rorschach may also be used as a check on the completeness of the ethnographer's report. When too many new traits show up in the Rorschach I would be inclined to question the thoroughness of the original description.

These latter are all end results of more basic patterns, such as general impoverishment of affectivity. It is well nigh impossible to tell in advance what particular elaborations will take place in a given culture of such a basic pattern. However, once we are told by the Rorschach that certain end results can be identified, it is a relatively easy matter to reconcile them with more basic traits. It would be an easy matter to derive all the Rorschach findings from the maternal frustrations, which qualify the affectivity patterns, and the aggression patterns, both of which we found devoid of organization. Once these basic patterns are established, others, like tolerance for dilapidation and easy surrender to difficulties, can be easily derived. However other traits identified by the Rorschach are more difficult to track down, for example, absence of enthusiasm. This trait is highly complex in organization, and though its relation to a basic trait like affect impoverishment can be surmised, the actual path of development to this particular end is very difficult to reconstruct. We do not as yet have psychological notational systems accurate or delicate enough to follow the organization of such a trait.

We can therefore conclude that the Rorschach experiment will help us identify important elaborations of basic traits to be found at the periphery of the personality, and to express them on a higher level of abstraction than can be done with the findings of the projective systems. This is an important contribution.

Dr. Oberholzer's report does not confine itself to the identification of these peripheral traits; it also attempts to reconstruct some of the dynamic interrelationships between these traits. It is at this point that we run into some real difference of opinion; it is in this connection that we think the Rorschach has decided limitations. For example: Dr. Oberholzer finds no evidence of neurotic traits, no neurotic anxiety, no feeling of inferiority, no repression—only suppression. To this statement we cannot subscribe. If the concept of basic personality is at all correct, then one of its implications is that repressions do not fall in the same place in all cultures. Hence the neurotic configurations that we will find in different cultures will of necessity be different in organization. We do not therefore know how to read the statement that they have no neurotic anxiety. If all Alorese are subject to the same anxiety, then the trait must be considered "normal" for Alor, using the term to connote *common* or *general*. This does not mean that this general trait is not based on a repressive factor, common to all Alorese. In the autobiographies we had the opportunity to establish beyond cavil that there was plenty of repression, and that some of the peripheral traits owed their origin to these repressive mechanisms. This was assuredly the case with the common predatory trend found in the men. We were also able to establish that the repressed impulse responsible for the predatory trend was the normal craving for affection, so frustrated by the mother. A craving of this kind cannot be handled by means of suppression by an infant, who does not have the control necessary for suppressive activity. The source of the trouble seems to be that the Rorschach is able to see that in connection with an activity motivated by a predatory impulse the suppressive mechanism may be set in motion. But the Rorschach is in no position to see that this impulse is the result of a previously instituted repression.

In other words, the discrepancy between the two views can be reconciled if we can account for precisely where the repressive and suppressive dynamisms are instituted. The craving for maternal affection is repressed. This will not necessarily show up in the Rorschach. What will appear is the remote derivative of this repressed trait. This latter can be handled by suppression. Perhaps the repressed craving for affection belongs to the category of "non-pathological repressions" which Dr. Oberholzer says he cannot identify in the Rorschach. This test clearly reveals the need in the Alorese for contact, but also the inability to respond. This combination of traits cannot be accounted for on the simple basis of repression and regression. This is too narrow a base to account for the establishment of such complicated action systems.

We have a similar difficulty in accepting Dr. Oberholzer's statement that the Alorese have too great a capacity for abreaction to produce neurotic symptoms by way of repression and regression.[6] For this reason Oberholzer claims they have no depression and no suicide. Here again we must complain of the narrow base on which the dynamics are conceived. In our discussion we attempted to account for the absence of depression as follows: The earliest relations of the child to the mother prevent the formation of constellations normal to Western man—the strong attachment to the mother, the capacity to idealize her, the capacity to introject her and the formation of strong and organized aggression patterns. In Alor none of these are well developed. Hence the aggressions directed against the mother do

6 Du Bois, *op. cit.*, pp. 601–2.

not ricochet back on the child in masochistic form. For this reason there is no depression and no suicide. The whole mechanism is related to poor superego formation, limited idealization, and disorganized aggression. However, in place of those mechanisms we find in Western man, which form the constituents essential for the depressive mechanism, we find passivity and surrender, spinal rages (tantrums), and all kinds of devices for indirect aggression. It is in the control of the latter that the control mechanism of suppression is invoked.

As regards the specific Rorschach reports of Rilpada, Mangma, Fantan, and Lomani, the correspondence between the two techniques is close enough.[7]

Synthesis

All the data being in, we can now appraise the relative value of each type toward establishing the relations between personality formation and social configurations.

There is no substitute for actually living with a people, participating in their daily lives, learning their values from personal contact and empathy, and observing their emotional reactions at close range. The role of informants should be limited to what cannot possibly be recovered by direct observation. The most valuable features of Alor were elicited in the course of discussion, as side remarks, or as recollections of events in the life of some specific individual. Perhaps more

---

[7] *Word Association.*—The value of word associations has long since been discredited as too inaccurate to diagnose the operational constellations in the individual. But one ob servation recorded by Dr. Du Bois is of some interest. There is a high degree of blocking on words referring to *food consumption*. For example in our society, in a sample test carried out under comparable conditions, the food staple "bread" yielded 22 percent *eat* responses. In Alor the word "corn"—a corresponding staple—yielded no "eat" responses. Only one of 107 responses to test words *corn, rice, beans,* was *to eat*. Of 28 responses to *fish,* 2 were *to eat*. To the words piglet, dog, wild pig, chicken, rat and pig, 207 usable responses in all, only 4 meant *to eat*. This is very definite evidence for blocking. The reasons for this we already know. This blocking is incidentally a confirmation of the repression mechanism in relation to maternal frustrations. (Du Bois, *op cit.,* p. 556.)

Children's Drawings.—Dr. Du Bois collected a large number of drawings made by 33 boys and 22 girls ages six to sixteen. The data are analyzed in her book. These drawings were analyzed by Mrs. Schmidt-Waehner, who has made a study of children's drawings in relation to personality. Of these drawings she says in part: "They have a feeling of aloneness. They look like children who have good abilities but are apart from each other. Their relationships are poverty stricken. They cannot bring themselves into effective contact with others. They have no resources for realizing these wishes for contact with others. They lack creative approach." In other words the wish and need are there, the executive capacity is blunted. The reason for this we have described. In this analysis by still another psychological approach we see a confirmation of some of the main points in basic personality structure. (Du Bois, *op. cit.,* p. 566).

data recovered by direct participation may diminish the discrepancies between overt and covert culture.

Alor proves conclusively that personality studies are indispensable for the coördination of the institutional configurations. More status variation in the subjects selected for study than is available in Alor is desirable to establish the precise role of character variations in maintaining social equilibrium. Concerning the technique of recording personality studies, that followed by DuBois [8] is probably best suited for our purposes. The procedure of allowing the subject to tell his life story as curriculum vitae in terms of current values and life goals is to be avoided. How such values can differ and how such a story can be distorted to conform to the conventional standards may be seen from a comparison of the Confessions of St. Augustine with those of Rousseau. Such a curriculum vitae has some value, but it is not what we need. What is indispensable in a personality study is to retain thought sequences in the order in which they occur in the subject, dream material in the context of daily life and current preoccupations. Reactions to the ethnographer and to the procedure should be carefully recorded; they furnish valuable characterological indices.

The intelligence test, that of Porteus or any suited to illiterates, should be routine. Children's drawings, though interesting for the record, give no new information. Perhaps more can be learned with greater standardization. Word-association tests yield no information not covered more adequately by other techniques. A synthesis of the various types of evidence need not therefore go beyond those which give real information, and these are projective analysis, personality studies, and Rorschach tests or others of a similar nature.

The real technical problems therefore reduce themselves to a coordination of projective analysis with the personality studies, and with both of these against the Rorschach.

The personality studies show conclusively that the basic personality, with some allowance for variations, can be recovered there. As pointed out by Oberholzer, the character variations in Alor run higher than in our culture. The reason for this is that the greatest variable is the factor of maternal and paternal care; and this means that the earliest integrations are most subject to variation, and hence the entire subsequent development is decisively influenced. Such radical variations in basic integrations are not likely to take place in our cul-

[8] See Du Bois, *op. cit.* p. 193.

ture; the differential features occur much later in the life cycle. It is unfortunate that we do not have in Alor a better description of the neurotic and psychotic disturbances. But there are enough to indicate that the end forms which these take are different from psychoses in our culture. It may be pointed out that the specific forms of neurosis and psychosis in any culture are functions of the basic personality.

The confirmation of the projective analysis in Alor by the Rorschach is to date the most startling confirmation of the technique. This being the case, can one work with either of these two techniques alone? The evidence is that the projective analysis is the least dispensable because it furnishes the key to dynamics. The Rorschach is of great help in diagnosing the constellations existing at the periphery of the personality, some of which might be passed up in the projective analysis. Another question is whether it is so necessary in the future to work the Rorschachs "blind." Now that we know that both techniques mesh, it is hardly necessary to make every culture a *tour de force* for the Rorschach experiment. It can be put to the use of working out more delicate coördination than was done in Alor. The question as to whether we can use the Rorschach without projective analysis answers itself, since it was accurate on diagnostic features, inaccurate on dynamics. Hence, when used alone it could be of no more use than the "culture pattern."

The crucial problem in technique remains the refinement of the use of basic personality as an operational tool. Alor completely vindicates the claims made for this technique and removes all doubts that followed upon the exposition of its uses in *The Individual and His Society*. Considerable extension of its use is illustrated in Alor, more in the discussion on Plainville, and still more in the application of the concept to problems in the history of Western society.[9]

9 The problems connected with the use of this concept of basic personality are technical in nature, and the refinement of this technique is an achievement of psychopathology and psychodynamics. This aspect of the problem is belittled by some. It is claimed by some that all that psychodynamics did was to show us how "it can be done." It must be pointed out that the technical problems will not be solved by changing the name of the operational concept from *basic* to *modal* or *communal* personality, or to *social* or *primary* character. The problem is not to devise a catchword but to forge a usable technique. Those who seem so eager to change the name seem to accept without question the technique of deriving basic personality, the whole theoretical basis for the technique and the conclusions which it yields—in other words, a red herring.

The real difficulty in connection with this technique is that it requires an expert knowledge of psychodynamics, and it can be expected that much mumbo-jumbo will

The technique of projective analysis is by no means completed; there is room for difference of opinion. Some of the difficulties can be illustrated by the following: It is submitted that the women work in the fields all day; that the gardens are not contiguous; that the women neglect and ignore the cries of children; that the folk tales contain the motif of revenge on parents; that the marriages are unstable; that the Alorese are careless in their observance of rituals. These are all factual data supplied by the ethnographer. Other crucial characteristics, like poor superego formation and disorganized aggression patterns, were not reported as such, but were inferences. What if these inferences should be wrong? These can be easily checked. What is done under these conditions is to try one hypothesis and then another and to settle on the one that fits the facts best. By the time we hear the life cycle we are already attuned to what will make psychological sense. Nothing would be gained by hearing the life cycle first; we might even be more confused. Hence it is quite misleading to write up an account of a culture from the life cycle outwards, to include in it the results of the projective analysis, and to give the reader the impression that the ethnographer knew all the time precisely what effects each vicissitude in the life cycle created in the personality. A culture studied in this way would be prejudiced from the start. When we finally hear in the life cycle that maternal care is poor, and get the specific details, a great many facts we had previously heard but could not place, now fall into order. For example we had previously heard that they abandon themselves to illness, make no fight for life, that they lack constructive ability and tolerate dilapidation—these all fall into line as consequences of maternal neglect. But how? For these emotional combinations are unknown in our society, and we have no precedents to guide us. We have to bring another series of facts into relation with the known fact of maternal neglect. The revenge stories, the absence of idealization of the deity, the absence of expectations from the deities, the procrastination of sacrifices—these are all of one mold. They signify that the affective tie to the parent is poor. But this inference alone does not

---

result from attempts along this line by dilettants. Moreover each culture presents unique combinations of emotional complexes, for the unraveling of which no previous culture is a guide. Some of the crucial deductions from projective sources in Alor, subsequently proven correct by the weight of evidence and by Rorschach, were originally contested both by the ethnographer and by the students. In some instances the conclusions of the projective analysis compelled a reëxamination of the facts originally submitted. The answer to this question seems to be that a knowledge of psychodynamics will have to become prerequisite to original work in this field.

satisfy all the related facts. There is still another series of facts that must be brought into line: that all aggression patterns are poor in organization, that there is no guilt and no masochism, no depression, no interest in construction or systematization. This new series supplies us with the new lead that there is a definite temporal relation between the poor affective ties and the aggression patterns. It means that violent aggressive attitudes were mobilized before organized aggressive patterns were established and before strong emotional ties to the parent were formed. And this is the combination which supplies the crucial information that the integrational series whose projective manifestations we have used as guides were started in the nursing period. Nothing else could account for this particular combination.

Once we know this, we are in a position to understand some of the features which appeared in the Rorschach, the absence of introversiveness and the predominance of suppressive mechanisms. When the strong tie to the parent is interfered with and there is no introjection of the parental imago, the foundation for an adequate superego is spoiled. The social equilibrium has therefore to be maintained by conscious or suppressive mechanisms and not by an automatized internal control. This conclusion satisfies most but not all of the facts. Much evidence points to the fact that the individual, in spite of frustrations, never abandons the infantile claims on the parent. This is shown clearly in the dream life of most of the subjects studied. In other words, the claims on the parent are repressed, and this repression in turn gives rise to another compensatory or restorative predatory impulse, which in turn makes more work for the suppressive controls. This basic repression saves this society from complete disintegration. On the other hand, the predominance of suppressive controls is a recipe for ceaseless discomfort and anxiety. The psychological advantages of this arrangement are that the individual is freed from the dangers of depression and guilt, but he pays for it by having to live in a society where the social cohesion is lost and coöperative endeavor is at a minimum. A further price is exacted by the necessity for universal mistrust, by the necessity for endless vigilance to control the aggressions always ready to spill over.

The upshot of the precise delineation of basic personality is that it furnishes a key to understand what specific values and life goals can be formulated within its ambit. If the interest in constructive activity is nipped very early in life, and there develops no interest in crafts-manship, aesthetic expression cannot become one of the social goals. If the superego is inadequate and there is no internalization of dis-cipline, we cannot expect the society to have any interest in social justice, in a judicial system, or even in government. We can also now answer the question why the Alorese do not have imposing religious shrines. A complex of factors is responsible. First in importance is the absence of idealization, the absence of expectations, the absence of constructive interest. Their lack of technical knowledge for the con-struction of shrines is a secondary factor. We must also observe that in Alor the interest in hoarding, property, and so forth, supposed in our culture to be a derivative of anal erotism, is greater than in any culture so far encountered in these studies. But we found no evidence of anal erotism, repressed, sublimated, or otherwise identifiable, with the exception of Fantan. Moreover this interest in property (in Alor) is not associated with meticulousness, orderliness, or any of the traits associated with the anal character.

It is to be expected that with a basic personality organized like that in Alor the psychosomatic patterns will likewise show unique traits. But we do not have enough evidence to draw definite conclusions.

The study of Alor offers us an opportunity to clear up many moot points in personal psychology which cannot be solved from the study of individuals in our culture alone. Isolated instances of child care similar to Alor can be found in our culture; but these isolated in-stances cannot influence the culture as a whole. It is a startling socio-logical fact that so many of the major integrations so characteristic of Western man can be so decisively influenced in the first few years of life. If the conclusions on Alor prove to be correct then it can be safely said that it has opened up a new chapter in the understanding of human society.

Alor as an Effective Form of Social Life

Apart from questions of technique the culture of Alor warrants some reflections on whether it is an effective form of social life. No citizen of Western society can approach this problem without preju-dice drawn from the particular issues current in our own social and scientific world. It may be pointed out that all value judgments used in the appraisal of Alor were drawn from our culture. This needs no special apology. There is no need therefore to maintain the pretense of disinterestedness, since there are no absolute values which we can use as a yardstick. However, the value judgments which were used were based not on *moral* issues but on purely psychological grounds. We can call an adaptation effective or ineffective without lapsing into moralization. This we have a right to do, for social life is the most effective means that man has consciously devised to aid and abet survival in an agreeable form, and some types of social life help toward this end while others do not. We can take this stand without being obliged to answer the charge of moralization.

The first thing that can be said about Alor is that it survives, and gives evidence of being an old culture. This is already saying a good deal; for to survive, a culture must have a sufficient number of staying qualities and compatibles to keep it going. However, in the case of Alor the continuance of the society must hang on a very thin thread, chiefly because of the low level of coöperative possibilities and because of its tenuous grip on the external environment. This culture has no place to go, not that progress is an essential factor, as we seem to believe in Western society, but because it must remain completely immobilized. Its survival can be accounted for largely on the basis of the absence of external enemies.

Yet there must be a sufficient number of gratifications for the individual. Dr. Du Bois tells us that they have plenty of good times and there is a good deal of socializing. Are they happy? That is very hard to answer; but it is certain that they are not aware of their wretchedness. This culture can be used as a text for the thesis that human beings can tolerate any conditions if they are born to them. On the other hand there is much evidence that this is not the case. They tolerate the conditions and function within them; but they are not effectual as human beings or as a society.

The arresting feature of Alorese culture, as seen through the individuals studied, is that difficult conditions do leave a mark on the development of personality, and we are helped by this evidence to point out specifically at which junctures these failures arise. And this is where the specific lessons of Alor for sociology lie.

A culture which sacrifices adequate maternal care for infants to other interests starts a cycle which never ends. Adequate maternal care, as judged by Alor, means assisting the ego in the early years to the formation of adequate executive capacities to deal both with the outer world and with other members of the community. This is a necessity for man because of certain peculiarly human traits. Man is an exoparasite, and adaptive capacities are not complete at birth. They are acquired, irrespective of inborn drives, because adaptation is not created by the existence of the drive alone, but by the learning of adaptive maneuvers which have perceptive, conative, cognitive, and executive elements. If this integrational system is shaky in its foundations, then what is lost is not only the grip on the outer world, but affectivity, the emotional basis of social life. This is adequately proven by Alor. Of what use is the "maternal instinct" if the affective conditions in the mother are such that she cannot yield the child the interest it needs, not for survival, but for effective social functioning. The development of the child is deflected from what would other-wise be an effective growth as seen in our culture and shunted into a direction which by-passes this effectuality and causes the formation of a new integrational system completely divorced from that end. It acts like a scar tissue formation. Of what use is the innate drive to the parent if this is frustrated? This whole situation appears all the more absurd in view of the fact that the women do not need to take over the subsistence economy and tend the fields instead of aiding the child in the normative years. The men do not contribute, save very sporadically, to the subsistence economy and they do nothing with their time but dun for debts in what seems to us a meaningless though complicated financial system. It can be safely said of the Alorese that they are totally devoid of social insight and have no idea about the effects of the institutions by which they live. However, in that regard neither are we concerning our culture.

The system of substitute parents, intended as a stop-gap in caring for the infant, fails completely of its purpose. It even creates more confusion and prevents effectual growth. Only one of our subjects gave evidence of a real attachment to a surrogate parent (Tilapada). What individual studied showed that the system of teasing and mis-representation to the child had any effect but to aggravate the already bad situation? Which of our subjects showed that they liked the role of parent to a younger sibling? The boys all ran away from it to seek better foster parents. The girls had no choice. Which of the men showed that the delayed participation in the society helped him in any way? Out of all this how many men showed any preparedness for sexual life at maturity? One out of four. How many of the women showed any love for their work, or an attitude of eagerness for the feminine role? None. The only two successful women were essentially masculine, Tilapada and Kolmani. It is evident that the crucial points of this society are eroded at the very places where social life should show the greatest cohesion, the tie of children to parents, of the sexes to each other, and of the men in common enterprise. Of the latter there is none at all; such a conception does not even exist except on the shallow basis of exchange of labor in which everyone tries to cheat everyone else anyhow. The financial system is totally meaningless and is merely an excrescence of the coveted wish of everyone in the society to get the other fellow in the position where he can compel him to give him something.

By dint of all these blind alleys created, the capacities for expression become blunted—to wit, their religion, folklore, and poetry, and their mastery of the external environment marginal. They do not even have the psychic advantage enjoyed by a schizophrenic in our society, that is, they cannot even introvert, an extremely valuable point made by Dr. Oberholzer. The only one who shows any capacity in this direction is Rilpada, and he differs from the others in that he had the opportunity to form a strong attachment to his father. Without this capacity, the fantasy life becomes stunted, and the only thing left is a feeble and superficial attachment to the externals of living. There are a sufficient number of exceptions to be found in the biographies to show that these characteristics of the Alorese are not constitutionally determined but are ontogenetically integrated; for wherever a chance was offered to a child for a more meaningful relationship to either a parent or a sibling, the influence on character formation was much as it is in our culture. This strengthens our case.

But as between the males and females in this society, the women are the more crushed, sometimes, as in the case of Lomani, to the degree of sheer vegetation. Such an uneven distribution of advantages must injure the society as a whole. And the advantage of the male in this society is not his freedom from labor and lack of other responsibilities, but lies in the fact that he has a much better psychic economy. He is able much more effectively to exploit the women and children for the consummation of the passive goals formed in his personality. The woman has no such opportunity. The psychic incompatibilities in the female must lead to a kind of deterioration, though their low intelligence is too common a feature in primitive society to be used as evidence on this score. Tilapada, the most successful of the four women, describes this internal confusion in unmistakable terms. It is due to the complete blocking of passive goals—the wish to be cared for, carried around, fed, protected—by the necessity to become the donor in the society. This is a role from which she cannot escape on penalty of being completely removed from the society. The masculine compensations of Tilapada and Kolmani are not organized on the lines we find in our society. The content is entirely different. There is found in both women the significance of superior adjustment, as compared with Lomani and Kolangkalieta.

This society—if it must be described by any epithet—is best termed *marginal*. It is not even anarchic, because to be anarchic strong destructive forces must be unleashed which have a firm psychic underpinning. While everyone is against everyone else, this attitude cannot be implemented by enough organized aggression to do any real damage. This is probably the secret of the survival of this culture. It is the fact that all unconscious goals remain passive goals. This was clearly seen in all the characters—but less so in Fantan than in any of the others.

The relation of institutions to one another presents no special problem in Alor. The division of institutions into primary and secondary is less essential than it was in previous studies. This is obviated by our access to the individual and our opportunity of examining his mental processes. We need not therefore ask the hen and egg question all over again: Which came first, the institutions or the personality? History would clarify the issue for us to some extent. But our researches up to now indicate that institutions change first and that personality changes follow. While not inaccurate, this formulation does not establish the continuity and interrelatedness of institutions and personality; both change each other in a continuous cyclic process. Man has a peculiar inability to foresee what changes in personality are effected by alterations in institutions. This is probably the most destructive bit of ignorance in human society. With our social insight, we are today unable to make reliable forecasts, or to endow them with sufficient authority.

Does Alor point to any specific lesson with regard to the dynamics of social change? To answer this question we must free ourselves of the objections that are likely to be raised by students of the social sciences. They will say that we have been guided largely by value judgments, that this or that institution creates effects which are "bad," and that is not a scientific but an emotional valuation. Our primary interest in this study is driven by our own social discomforts, which we are trying better to understand. We have no standards other than expediency; there are no absolutes to guide us. To be sure, we are attuned to the values in our own society, and the directives in research we get are attuned to them. These value judgments have a validity according to the issues in our culture. Once this objection is out of the way, we can say that Alor teaches a definite lesson in social dynamics. During the past few years suggestions have been made that the way to alter society is to alter the family organization. This is a trite suggestion. Alor shows definitely how complex and closely interwoven and systematized the ways of living are. Hence we cannot expect that by introducing the papoose into Alor or making the men do the gardening, the whole society would change. In the latter case, if the change were abruptly introduced, the men, having a common interest, might present a united front and protest that their "rights" or "liberties" were being taken away; that things are fine as they were; their forefathers did things that way, and what is good enough for them is good enough for us; that the children are getting along fine; what would the women do if they didn't garden, and so forth. What we are here describing is what is known as cultural lag; the lag is not, however, in the culture but in the habits and practices and their allied emotional gratifications. Good maternal care could not be introduced abruptly through any external agency. Nor would it, if introduced by force, yield immediate results. It would take generations. Then and only then would some of the organized derivatives peel off by losing their functional value. There is little chance that either of the systems which create the discomforts could be spontaneously identified by the Alorese. If this were pointed out to them, they could not possibly believe it, and to educate them up to seeing how it works would be a matter of generations. By the same token, if we were to enforce some of our peripheral mores on the Alorese but leave the normative institutions intact, we could only anticipate that those mores we introduced would slough off and be drawn into the ambit of Alorese values.

We are speaking of only one institution—parental care—which we have identified as crucial. To attempt changes in the peripheral institutions, like religion, would be hopeless. Teaching the Alorese Christianity is a quixotic undertaking. It cannot take, can have no significance, when the personality is built on values with which Christian doctrine is in complete disharmony. That is surely beginning at the wrong end.

CHAPTER X

PLAINVILLE, U.S.A.[1]

By James West

PLAINVILLE is a small town in the central part of the United
States of America. The town is near the edge of a little prairie in
a locality prevailingly hilly. Both culturally and geographically Plainville is in the "North-South Border." [2] It stands between an American
"hillbilly" region and the richer farming plains of the Midwest. The
culture of the Plainville region is therefore a composite, in historical
origin, in the everyday attitudes of the people, and in technology, of
two ways of life—the way of the hill people and the way of the Midwestern prairie farmer.

As a town Plainville depends wholly upon the produce and trade
from about two hundred and twenty farms which cluster about it.
The Plainville farmers unlike many European farmers dwell on their
farmlands in the open country. Those who live in Plainville are the
merchants, the retired or partially retired old, a number of odd-jobbers and other wage-earners, and a handful of professional people,
including a doctor. Plainville is near the geographical center of Woodland County, which is about four hundred miles square and has a
population density of fifteen persons per square mile. Woodland
County has a total population of 6,700, of whom 275 live in Plainville.
The county seat, Discovery, five miles east, has 250 people; Discovery
is on the Apple River, which runs through the county to join a still
larger river about 100 miles northward.

Stanton, eleven miles west, has 450 inhabitants. There are several
other lesser towns and some country stores.

[1] The data for this partial description of a rural community were collected in 1939–1940
on funds provided by the Social Science Research Council of Columbia University. The
field research was done under the supervision of Professor Ralph Linton, to whom I
owe much for help toward understanding the material. Plainville was tentatively described in 1940–1941 at the Psychoanalytic Seminar in Anthropology conducted by
Professor Linton and Dr. A. Kardiner. The materials collected have since been analyzed
more fully and published separately (in *Plainville, U.S.A.*, Columbia University Press,
1945). For various reasons anonymity is desired, of place-names and all persons, including
the writer.

[2] See A. R. Mangus, *Rural Regions of the United States* (Washington, 1940).

The main local trading and social center for Plainvillers is Plainville, though most of them also rather frequently visit Stanton and Discovery. The only bank in the county is at the county seat, and all legal business is also transacted there. But Plainvillers also "go outside" nowadays. They go to "X," a county seat of 1,000 inhabitants, situated thirty miles north of Plainville on the gravel road which runs through Woodland County, and more often to "Y," another county seat twenty-eight miles south, likewise "on the gravel." They often go to Largetown, a regional metropolis of 65,000 people, in the hills seventy miles south; and they sometimes go to Metropolis itself, an important Midwestern city with a population of nearly half a million. Metropolis is 135 miles north. Once Plainvillers knew little of the outside world, but most of them now have cars, and "have been out and seen things."

Early Settlement; Population

The white settlement of Woodland County was part of the main westward migration of a century ago. The sparse Indian population of the region was moved further westward by governmental decree about 1825; the first wave of white settlers began to occupy the newly opened lands during the 1830's. These came mostly from the hills of Kentucky and Tennessee, with a sprinkling from the Pennsylvania mountains and a few others from Virginia, West Virginia, and New York. These were the pioneers, and most of their fathers had been pioneers before them. By 1870 most of the bottom land had been either "preëmpted" or (after 1862) "homesteaded." Later, when it was discovered how to plow up the prairie bluestem, another wave of immigration occurred, and the prairie third of the county was settled. The town of Plainville was founded about 1870. The present population around Plainville is almost entirely "English" or "Scotch-Irish" in name.

The population peak for Woodland County, ten thousand, was reached in 1900. After that it declined gradually to a minimum of 6,300 in 1930 through migrations westward and to cities, but especially to one region of the Sacramento Valley in California, where several hundred people from Woodland County now live. The great depression of the 1930's brought a new increase in the county's population.

Natural Resources

The only excellent farmlands in the county are the river bottoms, which range in size from 500 to 600 acres in wide bends of the river down to small bottom patches of only a few acres each. A man who "owns a big bottom field" is considered "well off." Even years of careless farming practices have not depleted these alluvial deposits. The next best land is the prairie. When first settled the Plainville Prairie produced annually forty to fifty bushels of corn per acre. Its present productivity averages per acre: corn, 19 bushels; wheat, 14 bushels; oats, 12 bushels. Most farmers erroneously attribute this lowered productivity to diminished rainfall. There has been a 52 percent erosion of the prairie topsoil, originally only about 8 inches deep, and much of its lime has leached away. The poorest land—over half of the land in the county—is thin, rocky hill land. Much of this hill land is waste —brushwood and scrub timber—or serves as poor pasture; much of it is farmed. The poorest farmers are generally to be found on these shallow hillsides.

The timber of the region is poor, consisting chiefly of scrub oak, black oak, poor hickory, and some cedar. The fine hardwood black walnuts which once grew in the bottoms were cleared away early and were burned or used for early log buildings, a few of which are still extant. Most of the houses of today were built later, however, and mainly of native lumber. Several old men still alive once made their living from sawmills, and few trees large enough for lumber are now left. In the early days there was an abundance of game—deer, wild turkey, prairie chickens, and many small fur-bearing animals. There are still many fish, quail, squirrels, and rabbits, and much wild fruit, such as blackberries, gooseberries, plums, grapes, persimmons, and pawpaws.

Technology

In discussing, however briefly, the present-day agricultural technology of Plainville, reference must be made to the technology of the early settlers. The tools, animals, and techniques which they brought here were those that people took to new frontiers anywhere in America a hundred years ago. They brought horses, cows, pigs, and chickens; wagons, plows, guns, hoes, axes, and the art of home-smithing; simple furniture and textiles; techniques for weaving cloth and tanning hides; garden seeds and pits of tame fruits; and grain for seeding corn, wheat, oats, and other cereals. All of these except corn were European in origin; but the pioneer's way of life had been "Indianized" on earlier frontiers. With his ax he girdled and burned trees for a corn patch—then he lived off the wild game and fruits until his first cereal crop came in. After that only gradually he became a "farmer," and even today some Plainvillers live more from the natural products of river, timber, and "patch farming" than from conventional field farming and livestock raising.

It is impossible to list all the implements on Plainville farms. What is important is that nearly all of them are manufactured; few are homemade. However, at present almost all types of modern agricultural technology coexist with practices dating from the first settlement and before. One farmer still "cradles" his wheat patches, and until recently flailed out the grain. Others harvest with combines. The "average farmer" harvests wheat with a binder. It is the same with the magical aspects of the early technology. Side by side with efforts to utilize the advice of agricultural experts there still exist many magical practices for planting crops, castrating livestock, weaning, gardening, girdling trees. Most of these relate to the "light" or "dark" of the moon or to zodiacal signs. Sanctions are in general much stronger for "doing things the old way" rather than "the new way," and there is widespread criticism of the government's effort to teach people how to farm their mediocre land "rationally." The "acreage payments," as well as admirable organizational skill on the part of the government men, however, are accomplishing very great cultural and economic changes in Woodland County.

Communications

The earliest communications were by water or overland wagon trail. The Apple River was too shallow for navigation, but freight and passengers came by water as far as "X" (thirty miles north). A railroad was built through Stanton a few decades after the first settlement. Today, however, the highways are by far the most important means of communication. Most people travel, even to California, by car or bus, and trucks now carry to larger market centers most of Plainville's produce and bring into Plainville most of the merchandise sold there. A network of local roads connects each farm in Woodland County with neighboring farms, with its own trading center, and with all the other towns in the county. Most men know almost every other man in the whole county.

Electricity is rather uncertainly supplied to Plainville by a high line which serves a number of small towns. Two thirds of the houses in town "have lights." The rest, like nearly all the farm houses, are lighted by kerosene lamps. Plainville has had telephones, including farm party lines, and rural mail delivery (now serving two hundred Plainville farmers) for thirty years.

Newsprint is another important form of communication. The county weekly (the *Discovery Beacon*) has one thousand subscribers, two thirds of them within the county, the rest forming an important link between natives and those who have gone outside. A number of city newspapers come into the community. The favorite daily paper is the *Largetown Bee,* which distributes some fifty copies among the seventy-five homes and the stores. The *Bee* is a very conservative and region-conscious organ. Only a few "dailies" go out on the mail route to farmers, most of whom subscribe to one or both of two well-known weekly farm newspapers. Most farmers also take a number of 25–50 cents-a-year farm and "story" magazines. A few farmers take the *Saturday Evening Post* and other nationally known magazines. The Plainville liquor dealer sells about twenty copies weekly each of *Life, Look,* and the *Saturday Evening Post,* and a number of detective story, Western, movie, "dream romance," and confessional magazines.

Radios are now considered almost a necessity; over half the people own them. The programs favored by adults are livestock and produce markets, hillbilly music, religious programs, and war news.

Thus most Plainvillers are potentially linked by roadways, cars, the press, mail-order catalogues, telephones and telegraph, and the radio, not only with every neighborhood and town of their own local region, but with all corners of the world. Their reception, understanding, and interpretation of traits and news from outside, however, are limited and colored by the local environment.

Occupations

Plainvillers are in a sense aware of the whole range of American occupations. In each generation about half of their children migrate to the outside world. These write home, come home on visits, and sometimes return home to live. A great number of Plainville males make at least one trip to California. The press, radio, catalogues, and hearsay inform them further about the rest of the country. They subscribe in the main to the American credo of vertical mobility and believe that a man (but hardly a woman) can become anything he wants to. Actually, opportunities are very limited for them, even if they go away. Opportunities at home are quite limited indeed. A WPA survey of occupations in Woodland County in 1935 listed 1,949 men and 177 women as earning a living: 1,234 men and 39 women were farmers; 339 men and 5 women were farm laborers. There were 7 blacksmiths, 9 printshop employees, 13 seamstresses and tailors, 1 glass and clay worker, 3 bakers, 1 miner, 2 automobile mechanics, 12 filling-station hands, 15 postal employees, 1 railway worker, 5 telephone and telegraph workers, and 21 truck and bus drivers. Twelve people were engaged in banking and brokerage, 6 in real estate, 7 as car agents or salesmen. Ninety-one men and 8 women were in wholesale and retail business; 15 men and 2 women in public service; 53 men and 55 women in professions (teachers mostly); 8 men and 14 women ran hotels or rooming houses; 10 men and 37 women did laundry work; the occupations of 35 men and 92 women were unspecified. This listing divided by six probably represents Plainville.

One must include trading, as a form of barter outside the commercial system. It is the most approved channel for male aggression, and also a release from the stern sanctions for hard work. One point of trading is to profit but another point is to outwit. Trading follows a complicated procedure, and any deception must conform to rigid rules.

The main local opportunities are: (a) Farming, as owner or renter; a poor start in farming can be made on $300; $1,000 gives a good start. (b) Local business; an investment of $300 will start a small new business. Many such attempts fail. A town boy may inherit his father's business. (c) Some men become wage earners or odd-jobbers. (d) Many migrate.

At age eighteen or so "the average boy begins to want to see the world." He often wants also to "sow some wild oats" in fields beyond the critical view of his neighbors. Kin, friendship, and economic factors generally determine what part of the world he decides to see first. He may travel to kin in California who write that "there is plenty of work around here," or a group of young men may together "make the Western harvest" or the "Northern corn-shucking season." From kin or others he may hear of jobs in Largetown or Metropolis; many

Woodland County people live and work in both cities. At any rate most youngsters go away, get a job, stay away, or return home; those who come home often set forth again. Most who emigrate become day laborers on farms or ranches or in cities.

The ramification of Plainville kin bonds into the Sacramento Valley, Metropolis, Largetown, and other regions is fascinating and offers many interesting possibilities for studying the structure of American society, both rural and urban. A Plainviller arriving in the Sacramento Valley finds a replica of his social situation (kin, neighbors, intimacies, securities) at home. He is welcomed as a visitor and newsbearer from home, and lacks financial obligations until he finds a job. Emigration opportunities on the "new land" pattern began to slacken about forty years ago when good western homestead land grew scarce.

Half the Plainville boys (and more of the girls) now go to high school; so much education might be expected to suggest emigration for further training and professional life. The high school hardly accomplishes so much, except for a few farm boys who acquire from their excellent vocational education teacher a vision of becoming soil chemists, county agents, vocational education teachers, or scientific farmers. For these few, family poverty and parental hostility to "higher education" usually blast the dream.

For the girls the situation is different. Plainville girls know that "women are supposed to be the equals of men nowadays" yet few occupations except teaching are traditionally open to them, nor can they migrate as easily as the men, except as wives. Some do get jobs outside but with more difficulty. When a girl becomes a "hasher" (waitress) or hotel maid she is generally assumed to have become also a prostitute. More girls than boys are sent away to normal school to become teachers; a few go to business schools and "beauty colleges." Almost all Plainville high school girls say they would like to become beauty operators, stenographers, or teachers, but not farmers' wives.

This section on possible occupations cannot be left without mention of WPA, and even direct relief, as ways of livelihood. The average monthly case load of persons receiving general relief in the county during 1937 was 90; it was less in 1939 and 1940, but had been much higher in some previous years (and applicants had greatly exceeded recipients). Perhaps 60 or 70 men in the county (10–15 of them Plainvillers) and 12–14 women were working on WPA. About 200 people in 1937 drew old age "pensions" averaging about $12 each per month;

in 1938 an average of 15 families (with two to eight children each) drew aid for dependent children; others drew NYA checks and disabled war veterans' checks.

Formerly charity was apparently fairly well handled through neighbors, lodges, and churches. Except for the Plainville church lowliest in prestige, charity is now left entirely to government agencies, all of which (including AAA) are utilized nearly to the fullest, and "cussed" constantly for (1) "ruining this country," (2) "making people unwilling to work and ruining people's characters," (3) "meddling with business" and with "the way farmers know how to do things," etc. The produce man said, "If this New Deal had just been put in by Republicans instead of Democrats, everybody here would have liked it." Actually the New Deal does disrupt many "values" in a "traditional" community like Plainville. For example it tends to disrupt the entire value system of the subsistence economy. A man who leaves a farm for WPA draws $34 each month in cash; this is more cash than most of his still "independent" neighbors have ever taken in. He sells his milk cow or cows and stops gardening. He doesn't understand why he is now poorer than ever, nor can his neighbors understand why he can't "save money." People think they live in a money economy; their real living, though "unvalued," is more often in what they produce and consume.

Houses

Housing varies widely from log cabins and shacks made of rough native lumber to modern houses with flush toilets, bathrooms, and hot running water. Not many log cabins are left and there are few modern homes, but there are plenty of shacks. The smallest houses are generally the oldest or the very new ones. The early houses usually contained a low attic into which boys, in the days of large families, were crowded for sleeping.

The newest houses are generally built in a perfect square, with four small rooms. They are usually constructed of cheap or second-hand frame materials, covered with commercial rolled roofing and inexpensive prepared surface board. Such a house often costs no more than $200–$300, including whatever construction work the owner hires done. A neat cottage will rent for $8 to $12 a month.

The largest houses, the one- or two-story houses containing seven or eight large rooms, were built in towns and over the countryside (particularly on the prairie) during two periods in the past: (1) thirty to fifty years ago, when local sawmills provided cheaply all materials except weatherboarding, flooring, and doors and windows; and (2) the period of First World War prosperity.

The "average" is perhaps a frame house of four or five rooms, built in a square, an L, a T, or a double-T shape, with or without a porch, but without running water or any other "modern convenience," except that more houses in town have electric lights than lack them.[3] Stoves are used for heating and cooking. The windows and doors are generally screened in summer against flies. Water is brought in buckets from a well in the yard, from which it is pumped up or drawn up by a bucket and pulley. Many people living back in the hills and timber still get their water from springs.

Each house is set absolutely square with the four directions. Any other orientation would be unthinkable.

In front of each house is a "frontyard," where there are often flowers—roses, lilacs, hollyhocks, smaller flowers—planted at random or in flower beds. Behind the house is a "backyard." The whole yard is usually fenced off as one large space with the house near the center. Toward the rear of the backyard stands a privy, called "toilet" or "backhouse."

The garden is either behind or to one side of the yard, and the chicken house is generally behind the house, sometimes in a special "chicken yard." The barn and other "outbuildings" (sheds, hog houses, pens, cowbarn, etc.) usually stand at some distance behind the house.

In moving from the woman's domain of house, garden, and poultry yard, to the man's domain of "outbuildings," "lots," livestock, and farm implements, one sometimes feels that he is moving from neatness to disorder, from management to mismanagement, from the family's realm of real "living" and subsistence to its sometimes fruitless efforts to deal with money.

One of the rooms of the average four- or five-room house is a living

[3] And probably an electric radio and an iron; perhaps also a curler, toaster or some other electrical gadget. It seems odd that there are as many electric ranges in Plainville as there are modern bathrooms (three). No one owning a range has also a bathroom. A trait from outside may "take" or "not take." Many people would like to have a range; few want a bathroom. No one wishes (aloud, at any rate) that the town had a water tower. Nearly all have or want a radio. Telephones, once popular, are declining in number and use, and most lines are in poor repair. The car, once considered "impractical for here," increases in popularity despite its great cost in maintenance.

room. Another is the kitchen. Eating is done in one of these rooms. Families generally eat in the kitchen; if it is very large, they often "live" there mainly also. The other rooms are bedrooms, often one for the parents (or for the parents and the "baby," who is the youngest child and may be as old as seven or eight years); others are for the children. Large families often have an extra bed in the living room. Parents generally dislike having children "above school age" sleeping in the same room with them. Another point in sleeping arrangements is to separate the children by sex, preferably in separate rooms but at least in separate beds. No "harm" is felt, however, in putting a small boy to sleep with an older sister. Where there are lots of children a bedroom may have two beds, in each of which sleep two to four children. Even when there is no question of space, children generally sleep together, brothers with brothers and sisters with sisters.

There is the same range in furniture as in housing, though no one any longer cooks on an open fire. The average house has a wood-burning kitchen stove and a wood-burning heater in the living room. The living room is ordinarily carpeted with a rag carpet, a Brussels rug, or a linoleum. Other rooms may or may not be carpeted or linoleumed; the wife wants a linoleum for her kitchen if she has none. The living room "heater" is the center of family leisure in winter; the best chairs are set around it, the two best ones—rockers or "overstuffed"—generally restricted to parental use when the parents are present. There may be a davenport. The walls are papered in floral patterns from Montgomery Ward or from the drug or hardware store. They are further decorated with family "enlargements" (especially of children or of the dead), advertising calendars, and perhaps a magazine cover or two. All these things are attached to the walls with nails and string. There is also a shelf for a clock, bottles of pills (for physic), and other medicines. On other nails in the kitchen are a large-lettered calendar and several farmers' almanacs.

The walls of other rooms are sparsely decorated, if at all, though bed quilts, especially if old, may be very beautiful. The average bed is of the flat-spring type.

In the absence of bathrooms bathing is infrequent, especially for men. The stated ideal of cleanliness is "a bath once a week." Many women bathe weekly, if no more than a sponge bath, and most of them try to keep their babies and small children clean; among men little value is attached to cleanliness. Women consider most men to be "dirty as animals," this criticism applying not only to their "dread of wash-water," but to their use of pipes, chewing tobacco, and cigarettes, their spitting, and so forth. In summer most boys swim in the river, but most winter bathing is done in the kitchen in the large galvanized tub used for washing or rinsing clothes, with water heated on the cookstove.

There are few closets. Clothing is packed into dressers, bureaus, or boxes, or hung on nails or hangers on one wall of each bedroom and often curtained from sight with paper, chintz, or cretonne. Work hats and everyday coats and sweaters are hung on nails in the kitchen or living room.

The staple food (flour, sugar, coffee, spices) is stored in the "kitchen cabinet" or the "safe" (cupboard). The potatoes are kept in the cellar during winter, or are "holed in" outside the house in a straw-lined pit. Meat is hung from rafters to protect it from mice and rats, in a smokehouse not far from the back door of the house. The home-canned foods are on shelves in the kitchen or in the cellar.

Clothing

A first and week-day impression of Plainville people's clothing is one of level uniformity. Overalls are the standard male uniform, but wash pants, union-alls, cheap wool trousers, and slack suits are also seen. Little boys barely able to walk wear overalls which imitate their fathers' apparel. In addition men wear for everyday, in summer, a plain cotton shirt, a straw or wool hat or cotton "mechanic's" cap; cheap work shoes; sometimes ten-cent cotton socks; ordinarily no underclothing. For sleeping, they remove everything except the shirt. In winter they wear the same, except that they always wear socks and long heavy-ribbed cotton union suits. For sleeping they strip to the union suit. Few wear pajamas; fewer wear a nightshirt.

The everyday dress of women and girls is more varied, but the "average" summer dress is a ready-made print, costing from 98¢ to $1.98, or a home-made cotton dress. Cheap woolen dresses and coats are worn in winter. The average woman wears low shoes with moderately high heels, rayon or lisle flesh-colored stockings or black cotton ones. At her work she is "wearing out" an old dress and old shoes and stockings.

Women "dress up" for Saturday afternoon, when country people come to town and town people come downtown. Some of the men also dress up; men are supposed at least to "clean up and wear fresh clothes," even if these are overalls. Both girls and lads "of the sparking age" ordinarily dress up in their best on Saturday afternoon, though lads sometimes wear overalls to town even on Saturday afternoon.

People dress up still more for picnics, "home-comings," or "reunions." They also dress up for church, though this varies with each church: in the Christian Church every one dresses up; the majority dress up for Methodist services; Baptists value dressing up less, especially during revivals; the Holiness faith, while officially stressing cleanliness, places moral insistence upon the utmost plainness in dress. Holiness women must wear long-sleeved and long-skirted dresses without ornament, no jewelry, no make-up, and no "bobbed hair." Holiness men of good faith will "stop wanting to wear a necktie" at the same time they cease desiring to swear, drink, quarrel, or think evil thoughts.

The peak of ostentation in dress is at funerals. This might be expected, since funerals are the most heavily attended of formal rituals except the annual high school commencement exercises.

The majority of men and grown boys "own a suit." A man's suit lasts many years, because it is worn only rarely. One comfortably-off old man bought his "last suit" for his wife's funeral twenty years ago, "and it is still good."

The average woman when dressed up, is practically indistinguishable from women anywhere. Her clothes are cheaper than city women's clothes, but they are neatly cut and sewn or selected ready-made, according to current styles. Some have \$100–\$300 fur coats, smart shoes, and all the other belongings of well-dressed women. Most of them use make-up with reasonable skill and patronize the beauty shops at Stanton, Discovery, "Y," or Largetown.

The difference in appearance between Plainville men and women is very striking.[4]

---

[4] Plainville women are more progressive than men in all ways. They began to acquire "scientific attitudes" toward poultry raising and to try to apply what they read in the farm magazines while most men still thought that "the only way to learn farming is out there between the plow-handles." The county agent said, "If we only had the women to deal with, our program would go over fast. They listen and try to learn and to do. The men won't even listen."

Subsistence

Nearly every Plainviller is in two separate and simultaneous economic systems, a "money economy" and a "subsistence economy." The average man feels himself to be more in the "money system" than he actually is. Even town people raise in their gardens or chicken houses so much of what they consume that a "widow lady" drawing old age assistance of, say, $12 a month (for "food, clothing, and medicine"), if she owns her house and is able to work her garden, lives comfortably according to Plainville standards. Some farmers raise practically everything they eat except flour, sugar, and coffee. Others, more prosperous or less "saving," buy many luxuries.[5] It will be well to preface any discussion of the "money economy" of Plainville with a brief account of the "subsistence economy" and its accompanying techniques.

Food. Food is considered plentiful in Plainville. Three meals a day are eaten—breakfast, dinner, and supper. The typical "good meal" consists of meat (or eggs, especially for breakfast) and potatoes; vegetables in season or home canned; bread and butter; pie or cake; often fruit; milk, if they have it; and jam or jelly. A "very poor" family's

[5] Of over 1,300 farms reporting from Woodland County to the Sixteenth Census on the "Value of Farm Products Sold, Traded, or Used" for 1939, over one fifth reported "under $250." The average for this group was $145 per family, over half of which was the value they placed on home-produced and home-used products. The next poorest group ($250–$399) of 230 families reported an average income from farming of $320; half of this was the value they gave to what they used. The other groups listed are:

Group	Number of Farms	Total Value of Products
$400–599	260	$130,000
600–999	300	232,000
1,000–1,499	128	155,000
1,500–2,499	64	116,000
2,500–3,999	23	70,000
4,000–5,999	6	30,000
6,000–9,999	5	37,000
10,000 & over	less than 3	fig. not given

Such figures are somewhat deceptive; they omit augmentations to real income from frequent or occasional wage jobs and the sale or consumption of most natural products— game, furs, fish, wild fruits; they omit interest payments on mortgages; they reflect also unwillingness or inability to supply requested information to census takers.

Plainville (and Woodland County) society and culture "appears" and "is" much more level and uniform than such figures suggest. There is real poverty, with suffering, in Plainville, and there is real wealth, with sufficiency. There are wide variations in food, housing, education, techniques, religious and magical beliefs and disbeliefs, attitudes, and values. Yet the "wheat-cradler" actually "lives" much more as the farmer-with-a combine lives than might be supposed from the figures.

meals are often limited fairly steadily to "fat-side," potatoes, and bread. The staple meat is "hog-meat," which is home butchered and cured in early winter. A family consumes from three to six large hogs a year. The "best" meats are fried or boiled ham, fried chicken, or game (squirrel, quail or fish—rabbit, since "rabbit fever" became known, is less eaten and little valued). "Shoulder" is also well valued, but "side meat" is "ordinary."

Good eating is very highly valued, but not in terms of the market money value of the food, since it is home produced. The meal is set on the table in platters and bowls and passed around or asked for, without much ritual except for preliminary saying of grace (by many fathers), serving guests first, and so forth. Meals are generally eaten quite fast.

The main vegetable is potatoes. A farmer may raise and store (in cellar or hole) 20–50 bushels of these, as a winter's supply. All other vegetable foods are raised in gardens. These vegetables are commonly grown: lettuce, radishes, tomatoes, onions, turnips, beets, cabbage, green peas and beans, and sweet corn (young field corn is also eaten). Some vegetables are canned for winter.

Orchards do not thrive about Plainville, and while fruit is valued, a small quantity is consumed. The government's effort is to keep fruits and jellies out of a farm woman's available fruit jars, and to get these filled instead each summer with vegetables. Health officials consider Plainville diet, as well as sanitation, poor, pointing out the high though unmeasured incidence of rickets and tuberculosis among children.

Butchering and curing meat is the work of men and large boys. They also raise, dig, and store the potatoes. Women, girls, and small boys usually plant the gardens, hoe and weed them, and gather the produce. All preparation, cooking, serving, or canning of food is woman's work, as is generally the whole care of the chickens or other poultry, and the handling of all dairy products, after the men have brought in the milk from the barn. Women also usually handle the income from the sale of eggs, poultry, or cream. The cream and egg checks can best be considered as lying wholly within the realm of the subsistence economy, since they pay ordinarily for all "boughten food," plain clothing, and other frequent small expenses of "running the household." While actual money ($1 to $12 weekly) does change hands between farm and merchant, all such transactions are only a slight step removed from the earlier days when "women span and wove," and when almost every item consumed on a farm was produced there.

Money. On the farms, the real "money economy" begins with the work of men. Men own the big livestock: hogs, cattle, horses, mules, sheep; and the big crops: corn, wheat, oats, and hay. The man ordinarily also owns the land (though deeds are often jointly in the name of husband and wife), or he rents the land he tills. He is responsible for mortgage and other debts, and for large expenditures. He pays for a car or tractor, farm implements, an "operation" or other doctor's bills, men's and large boys' suits, overcoats and shoes, and often the more costly items of women's clothing. Either the man or the woman (from her cream and egg savings) may buy a washing machine, a cream separator, household furniture, or children's and women's clothing. The man usually handles the bank account, when there is one. He pays taxes and fire insurance.

The man decides what to plant and where to plant it and whether crops are to be sold as grain or hay, or fed to livestock to be sold as livestock or livestock products. From his hogs he supplies the family's meat for butchering. From his cows he furnishes to the wife the dairy products that are consumed in the household or sold for its benefit, but the live increase in pigs or calves is his.

The external legal system imposed on these traditional patterns alters their forms somewhat, yet the way I have described them is considered "the way things are" or "the way they rightly ought to be." A man who tills his wife's inherited farm is considered somewhat less the man for his wife's ownership; a man's status as a man is somewhat lowered by his wife's doing field work, or owning livestock (except as a pet, or just an animal "to claim"), or in any way meddling except as a wifely and private adviser with a man's business.

Once a year or oftener the man receives, if fortunate, a rather sizable sum from the sale of crops or surplus livestock. This cash, aside from such large expenses as I have named, pays his rent,[6] interest or principal on his mortgage, or adds to his operating capital. It is his money which "places" the family in the local and national money economy. What he has measures the family's poverty or wealth in land, savings, securities, interest-coming-in, etc. Beneath this superstructure of money economy, and altered by it, there goes on the sub-

---

[6] If he cash-rents. Otherwise he pays one third or two fifths of his crops. Nearly 40 percent of the farmers are renters.

sistence activity of the family, guided and manipulated by the wife.

The financial fantasy wish of most Plainvillers is "to be rich"; the common real hope is to be "independent." Independence, to a Plainville wage-earner, means having a good job. To some, $50 a month seems a good income; to the average, $100 a month would be "great big money here." To a merchant, profits of $80 to $150 a month above expenses provide a good living; money or real capital of $5,000–$10,000, plus such earnings, would be "independence." To a farmer, independence means "owning your own farm, being out of debt, owning some good stock, and having money in the bank." (The "average farm" has 160 acres.) A tidy sum to have is $300–$400; it is, or rather was until recent years, a common ambition to accumulate $5,000, lend it out at 8 percent and retire to town when too old to work. Another widespread ambition and frequent achievement until recent years was for a man to climb what the literature of rural life calls "the agricultural ladder" from hired man, to renter, to owner with mortgage, to mortgage-free owner.

Confidence in the practicability of the "old-time" farmers' hopes and aims is breaking at present. The depression years began to engrain among farmers the unwelcome notion that the only "independence" they are apt to know when old is old age assistance.

The whole new form of rural social reorganization and security which seems to be implied in the present government's agricultural program is too new, despite the vast changes [7] it has already wrought in Plainville, to have created in the tradition many sanctions changing the aims, or enhancing the personal feeling of security, of the individual farmer.

Social Structure

It is already clear that however isolated or "backward" Plainville might seem to a city "furriner," it has many channels of communication with the outside world. All natives now know that in comparison to many other places Plainville is a very poor community. I have heard people say, "Everybody here has an inferiority complex about their-

[7] Woodland County received a county agent in January, 1938. A part-time agent had served since 1927. A few of the main resulting changes are: (1) A huge decline in the acreages of soil-depleting crops (corn, wheat); a huge increase in acreage of *lespedeza* (a low-grade clover); a resulting shift from grain sales to livestock, and a growing interest in pure-bred stock. (2) The beginnings of "program" planning of crops, gardens, livestock, poultry, soil conservation, diet improvement, and sanitation, by committees of farmers, Home Economics clubs, etc.

selves." Yet natives brag often about the factors that contribute most to their low status: "cheap" soil; the intense churchly stress on morals; local resistance to law, education, better diet, etc. The most highly prized local trait is perhaps "sociability." "We're all just ignorant hillbillies here, but we're mighty friendly people, don't you think?" The most frequent apologies are for "poverty," "this poor country," "poor education," "not knowing how to act," and especially bad English—"not knowing how to talk right."

Such feelings of personal and community inferiority are accompanied by constraint and frequently hostility toward strangers, whom they call "strangers," "outsiders," or "foreigners." (True foreigners are called "Swedes," "Germans," "Poles," etc.) Reassurance concerning a newcomer usually comes slowly. The surest way for a newcomer to gain acceptance is to be friendly and interested in local doings (but never "forward"), and to imitate quietly the average level of native life. He should refrain from all criticism and unfavorable comparisons of Plainville with other places. The essence of anxiety concerning strangers seems to be fear of ridicule, and even of real harm to the local institutions and value system. The commonest stated criteria for judging a newcomer are "honesty" and "morals"; his ultimate full status depends on the number and kinds of linkages he and his family are able to establish in the formal social structure of the community. The local forms of social structure will now be described.

The Family. The salient feature of American kinship is the complex yet tenuous quality of the loyalties, obligations, and privileges related to kin beyond the immediate family. The language transmits to each individual a series of kinship terms, and the culture transmits to him a statement of the prerogatives connected with each term. These terms and prerogatives are ultimately rooted in both rural and city England, and in a day before either horizontal or vertical mobility became commonplace for individuals. They are for Plainville more recently and specifically rooted in the American frontier: in large pioneer families, where the father's control was patriarchal (and enforced enduring respect, even for the aged) and where no one's living was felt in the least to depend upon money. The stated prerogatives of kinship were functional when brothers often tilled neighboring farms, and an aged grandmother, costing nothing to feed, could usefully knit, spin, and mend, or could "mind" and entertain a child. Pioneer "clan" solidarity survives among part of the backwoods sector of the community, but in most families grandparents are considered neither very useful nor entertaining now, even in Plainville.

Migration, machinery,[8] money, have all weakened the functioning of kinship. Brothers lose complete track of each other; one no longer knows where the other one is. The old are considered "cares"; they are less welcome and less respected;[9] they are beginning not "to mind" asking for the pension. A man "fails to help out his own sister with even a cent, and her left alone with a houseful of children to raise."

In Plainville the stated kinship obligations beyond the "own family" have changed little since frontier days. The actual treatment of kin has changed more, and yet not so much as in cities: Plainville people still live "surrounded by kin" and by observing and critical neighbors. One ordinarily keeps in touch also with many emigrant kin (for example, in California) who are potentially useful for hospitality and as intermediaries in getting jobs. People are said to be growing "stingy" with kin where money is involved, but they will "help each other out or put each other up for awhile" in case of need. A Plainviller's conscience is likely to hurt him at any noticeable dereliction from the stated kinship obligations.

The firmest and most essential bonds are to one's own immediate family. The husband "owes his wife a good living"; he should "be true to her" and "kind to her"; he should not "meddle with the house." The wifely obligation is "to be a good helpmate." She should be a good cook, a clean housewife; "saving and not extravagant."[10] Her average conception of her "wifely duties" include also the idea that she should "yield to her husband (sexually) without minding it too much." She should be "a good and patient mother to her children," and a "comforter" to children and husband. She should not "nag"; or "meddle with the farm." She should not even "look at another man."

---

[8] Instead of hand techniques. In the early days an old man could "hoe a little," flail, whittle out a toy or ax handle with his knife. Nowadays he can't plow, pitch grain to a thresher, or "wire up a Ford so she'll run."

[9] This works out neatly: Father and mother "teach respect" for grandparents, but laugh with children at their "old-fashioned ways." Children apply the example a generation lower, thus intensifying the conflict between generations.

[10] Meaning: (1) she should cook mostly what they raise and not waste anything ("not throw anything out"); (2) she should not "spend too much" (on foodstuffs, clothing, household nicknacks); (3) she should ask for as little of "his money" as possible and should make "her (cream and egg) money" extend as far as possible beyond table expenses into the realm of other cash expenses such as clothing.

Parents are supposed to take care of their children until they are "grown," "married," or "able to make their own living." The care and "teaching" of children is considered to be mostly maternal, though actually the father teaches [11] the boys at least as many things as the mother does. What children are particularly expected to learn from their parents at home are morals, honesty, work, and obedience. The ideal child is docile, obedient, and willing to work, never questioning the rightness of parental authority. What children owe their parents is love, respect, and obedience. Grown children owe them love, or at least respect, and economic care in case of need.

The obligations between siblings vary with sex and age. As youngsters, brothers (or sisters) near the same age are presumably leagued into especially tight bonds of "friendship," confidence, and mutual support against aggression from other siblings, parents, or other (especially "bigger") children. They should willingly help each other with chores. Brothers and sisters should "by rights" be bound together similarly; they are considered "odd," however, if so bound. The early separation in a boy's mind of "women's and girls' work" from what it is proper for him to do precludes much whole-hearted mutual help. Yet "any boy will protect his sister" from insult or harsh teasing at the hands of another boy, unless boys are banded for cruelty against girls and he is "with the boys." After marriage, real responsibility ceases, except that a man must always protect his sister's honor or reputation.

Grandparents and grandchildren treat each other with the same affection that exists between parents and children, but more familiarly. The same restrictions on obedience, respect, and mutual care theoretically obtain, but they are actually relaxed greatly. The child "does not really have to mind" its grandparent; the grandparent also "spoils the child" with leniency, candy, and gifts. Grandparents love their grandchildren dearly and are proud of them; the grandparental home is always open to grandchildren, who visit there, not only with parents but alone, to "spend a night" or stay a week or two. It is sometimes used as a sympathetic refuge from stern parents.

Uncles and aunts have few fixed obligations beyond being very warm adult relatives. Children feel little if any distinction between their blood uncles and blood aunts and the spouses of these. The spouses, however, are supposed to feel but not show warmer feelings

---

[11] Much of what is taught in the home, especially in regard to sex-typing is not considered taught material. "A boy just naturally acts differently from a girl." A child "just naturally knows a lot of things that you don't have to tell it."

toward their own blood nieces and nephews. Uncles and aunts treat nieces and nephews affectionately and "give them a lot of nice things to eat" when the children are taken to visit them. An orphan would be taken in and cared for as an "own child" by uncles and aunts, if its grandparents were dead or "too old to do for it." An orphan might instead go to live with a married sibling. Cousins who live near together enjoy very intimate relationships, often like those between siblings. Even distant cousins are considered very close in relationship by children. When they become adults these bonds disappear almost completely.

In short, strict obligations between relatives stop in most present-day families with the one-family home and the parent-child relationship. The "own family" is the unit of obligation as it is the economic unit. At marriage one's "own family" changes. At marriage one also acquires a whole new and duplicate set of kin, the spouse's kin. These are called "my wife's (husband's) family" or "kinfolks," or "my in-laws." One presumably enters into filial (or sibling) relationship with parents-in-law and siblings-in-law almost as warm as those of the spouse. A special relationship of warmth is ideally set up also between all the parents concerned. The mother-in-law myth circulates here as elsewhere, but without much basis in fact. It is a folklore trait much like the stepmother myth. The stepchildren observed were treated about as warmly as blood kin; yet a child with only a stepmother is considered unfortunate. There are meddlesome mothers-in-law, but fathers-in-law are more often troublesome, since fathers often attempt to run their boys' business and postpone their independence. It is considered best for married children to move away from their parents.

Marriages are quite permanent. Only three or four divorces are applied for semi-annually in the circuit court. Of course other divorces are granted elsewhere, but "the better class of people" are nearly as unwilling to solve family problems by divorce as by "wife beating" or the "rolling pin." People say, "Divorces are all right, I guess. They're *legal,* but I wouldn't want one for myself."

For all the looseness in family obligations beyond the one-family unit, there is always an emotional lien on a blood relative. Young people know "who they're kin to," and from any kinsman anywhere a place to sleep or a meal can be expected, if not formally claimed, unless there has been "trouble in the family." In community hostilities the members of extended kin groups tend to line up together.

Another important economic function of kinship lies in the realm of money. It is easier to borrow money on poor or no collateral from kin than from "strangers." Kinsmen most likely to be asked for a loan are, in order, parents, grandparents, a brother, a favorite uncle. The interest on such a loan, if considerable, is ordinarily the same as "bank interest" (or perhaps nowadays "gub'ment interest"), but its collection is less stringent.

Neighborhoods

The word "neighborhood," like the word "family," is ambiguous. Townspeople speak of which "neighborhood" in town (that is, which section of town—the "south part," the "east part," or the "west part") they live in and which one is best to live in. They speak of what people they "neighbor with" (visit, exchange meals, borrow from, etc.) or "neighbor with most." They also speak of their "neighbors" as the people whose houses are nearest their own, whether or not they actually "neighbor back and forth" with them.

Even on the farms the neighborhoods cannot be described in topographical terms only. Each farm family belongs to a series of at least three separate "neighborhoods," only two of which have any remote likelihood of congruence, aside from all the other focal centers which the world may provide for their "neighboring" (such as Plainville on Saturday afternoon).

A farmer's "real close neighborhood" includes geographically his own house and farm (at the center) and the four to eight or ten adjoining or nearly adjoining households and farms. The occupants of these farms are his "near neighbors." They are within easy walking distance for himself, his wife, and his children. These are the people whom he and his family supposedly neighbor most with. Each neighborhood of this type is unique; there are as many of them in America as there are farmhouses. Ideally the occupants of all houses in a given topographical section should be close, friendly, and coöperative neighbors; but feelings of social or moral difference may make two separate (and what might be called "geographically simultaneous") neighborhoods out of the area. An old quarrel (for example, a dispute regarding a "line fence" or "crop damage by livestock," or a children's fight) may cause unfriendliness between neighbors; as may family alliances or misalliances; or a neighborhood division on a tax levy or an election.

Each farm also lies in a larger and named neighborhood, which the farmer often calls "my big neighborhood," and to which he is considered by himself and others "to belong." The margins of big neighborhoods are clearly defined, with little overlapping, by the limits of a rural school district, by some natural feature—a valley, a prairie, a barrier of hills, or a bend in the river—by the arrangement of roads, even by a telephone line.

This arrangement and classification of people into neighborhoods serves many useful functions. Most neighborhoods serve as convenient units for elementary "schooling" and school taxation. Some have a church. But the important function of neighborhoods is to provide "neighbors"—people to know more intimately than anyone else except kin; people to visit and be visited by; people to exchange work with, or the tools and instruments of work.

Important neighborhood groups are the gangs of men who work together year after year in harvesting and threshing, the smaller groups who "butcher together," and the less frequent ones who saw wood together. The first task requires fifteen to twenty men and many teams and implements; butchering requires four or five male helpers. Each man's harvesting, threshing, and butchering are done in a turn decided on informally, and the whole task force works on every separate job.

There is a smaller feminine counterpart to each of these gangs. It requires a good deal of cooking to provide all the cakes, pies, and fried chicken that a "bunch of hungry harvesters can eat," and many of the wives come. At butchering, still more wives "try to come," for women have many tasks in the preparation of meat, lard, and sausage for storage. The social aspects of both harvesting and butchering are very important. These are gay times, in spite of the hard work.

While the neighborly exchange of work, borrowing and lending, help in sickness, etc., tends to be phrased as "duty" or as "neighborly accommodation," careful mental record is kept on a tit-for-tat basis of all such accommodations given or received. Tools should be returned in good condition. A little more sugar should be returned than was borrowed. A general willingness for these mutual exchanges is assumed. Many are indeed willing, but not all. A man returns tools dulled or broken and unmended; a woman "borrows too often" or too often "returns less than she took." An effort is made to judge people "on their average" for neighborliness, not on one dull ax or one skimpy repayment of flour. Yet there is much backbiting and criticism and blaming of neighbors for sins of omission and commission against the ideal of neighborliness. People are now thought to be much more "selfish and stingy and unneighborly" than they were in the old days. They don't want to "visit" or "help" or "borry" or "loan" as they once did. Many blame the "car" [12] for the decline in neighborliness.

Other Forms of Social Organization

Numerous other forms of association or social organization, formal and informal, bind Plainville people together. These include schools, churches, clubs and lodges, and formal political parties, as well as loosely or tightly knit political and business "control groups," groupings by age and by sex, and the loafing and gossip groups which function with astounding importance for both entertainment and social control. All such groupings are interlocked, of course, in personnel and function.

Schools. Eighty-five percent of the children under eighteen are enrolled in school. The schools run eight months a year, from September to April. Attendance is poor: the average child misses, through truancy, sickness, bad roads and weather, parental indifference, or labor at home, 40 of the 160 school days.

The neighborhood log schoolhouse, with puncheon benches that all old people remember, is gone; so are the old-time teachers who thought that "the whup (whip) was the main thing to school." Some of the old regret both puncheons and whips; some consider both a good riddance; many believe that the earlier books and teachers were better than "what childern gits nowadays." As a matter of fact, children still get the whip, despite the law against corporal punishment, in some of the schools; along with "standing in the corner" (or on one foot), and other old-fashioned punishments.

Consolidated town grade and high schools are rapidly replacing the

[12] The automobile began to become frequent shortly after the First World War. On April 1, 1940 (Sixteenth Census), 921 "reporting" farms owned 974 cars; 200 farms reported owning 1936–40 models; 247, 1931–35 models; 469, models of 1930 and earlier (these are "jalopies"). The "coming of the car" is the best endpoint to take for considering cultural changes between "old-time days" and "now." I suggest some of the changes effected or partially effected, by the car: (1) The expense of maintenance, minimally $50 a year even for a "jalopy," is often the biggest single item of cash outgo for a farmer. (2) Faster and more frequent travel has lessened family, neighborhood, and community isolation and solidarity, altering the patterns of visiting, entertainment, courtship, dress, and mutual help. Less value is placed on the horse, on "knowledge of nature," etc. (3) The values and stereotypes of the outside world are gradually replacing local values.

one-room schoolhouses which stood at the center of each country neighborhood a generation ago. Two generations ago these were important community centers for "socials," "literaries," and often Sunday school and "preaching." Only eight "country schools" are left in the Plainville trade area; these eight are "in the hills"—all of the prairie schools having been voted one by one into the consolidation after much neighborhood "friction and fraction."

Educational aims are theoretically established by the State Department of Education. Each teacher is required to follow the state course of study. This is far from being done even in the town schools. In the rural schools a teacher "teaches as much as she can," or "as much as the parents will stand for." All children learn to read, write, and figure—after a fashion; some learn to do all these things proficiently; some are graduated from high school unable to read newsprint with facility. Few teachers dare to "fail a child" from promotion. The most common phrasings of the aims of formal schooling are: (1) "to learn children readin', writin', an' 'rithmetic an' maybe a little joggerfy"; (2) "to give our children the same kind of education and the same chance that children have anywhere"; (3) "to keep children from growing up as wild and ignorant as the animals." Another main function of the schools is to gather the children together from their mothers at age six, into various types of age and play groups—the separate, special, secret, and complex "world of children" in which they live until they leave school. They leave school "upon completing the eighth grade," at the end of high school, or when they "get big enough to work" or to "be ashamed to go to school any longer."

Lodges and Clubs. Recent culture changes in Plainville are especially great in the shifting of interest away from old-style lodges to newer kinds of clubs and cliques. A few years back nearly every formally approved male joined one or more of the well-known lodges—Odd Fellows, Woodmen, and Masons. The attractive features of lodges seem to have been male solidarity, mutual help, "exclusiveness," the horseplay and practical joking of initiations and meetings, insurance and burial benefits, and, especially for the Masons, the solemnity of the rituals, including the public ceremonials for burying the dead. These lodges are all dying in function. The Woodmen and Odd Fellows declined because of increasing dues and assessments to pay insurance policies. Why the interest in Masonry is declining is less clear. I suggest the following main reasons: (1) the decline of interest in all older rituals, including church rituals; (2) the decline in respect for old, hallowed things, including old age itself; (3) the decline in community solidarity; (4) the decline in small town "business" (the older business leaders were relatively "rich"; as lodge leaders they were worth being "brothers" with); (5) the introduction of new forms of entertainment: movies, radio and the car. Young men are no longer anxious to join; the rituals are carried on mainly by the old. The Eastern Star, women's auxiliary of the Masons, is also composed mainly of older women. One of the latest (and shortest-lived) of these organizational forays into local pocketbooks was the K.K.K. "Half the people joined (in the 1920's) and paid up and burnt a few fiery crosses and had some Klan-buryin's, but it soon died down," said an informant.

Some farmers and their wives are being gathered by the county agent into committees and boards which function for agricultural progress and some entertainment. A traveling emissary of the WPA attempted without success to introduce an entertainment program into Plainville and other Woodland County towns. The Plainville school superintendent gave her a cold shoulder. Others thought it wrong and ridiculous for "tax money to be spent just for fun." A WPA library was founded in Plainville in 1940 (with a paid librarian and donated books), in the face of angry opposition. Other towns in the country quickly followed suit. A rural sociologist from the State Agriculture College spent a futile [13] evening in 1940 teaching traditional English morris dances and folkgames to a group of twenty gathered into a schoolroom.

The most stable and active new organizations formed under outside stimulus are the Home Economics clubs, to which over 10 percent of the eligible women already belong. In some of these clubs social or religious activities predominate over the activities for which they were organized; others carry on energetic reform programs. About 10 percent of the farm children have also been induced to join 4-H clubs under the sponsorship of adult local leaders. The 4-H

---

[13] Futile (1) because totally foreign to the concepts as well as to the felt and real needs of Plainville; (2) because nobody who really needs to be persuaded to participate in community life came or would dream of coming, and (3) because the whole attempt, from the point of view of applied sociology, looks backward and not forward. It smacks of the idea of recreating a contented peasantry on thirteenth-century lines, dancing merrily, not even on a green, but on a schoolhouse floor. The word "game," by the way, was substituted for "dance" in these festivities in order not to arouse the antagonism of the many people who consider dancing sinful.

clubs however are less successful than the Home Economics clubs. The children lose interest in their "projects"; parents ridicule them as useless, time-wasters, or even immoral (one 4-H club was criticized because the children "laughed together"); they still disband nearly as rapidly as they are formed.

Both men and women belong to political parties, and are mainly Republican. The rest are Democrats, except for a handful of Socialists—a hangover from the Populist movement and considered rather eccentric, laughable, and "atheistic." "Atheism" and "socialism" are thought to go together. Women, though they generally "vote along with" their husbands, in general express distrust of all politics and politicians and consider that "the whole mess is crooked." Politics is an essentially male preoccupation. Men are *religiously* Republicans or Democrats. "Changes in politics" occur, but they breed suspicion regarding a man's stability of character. Republicans who voted for Roosevelt in 1932 are still labeled "renegades," even if they returned to the fold in 1936. A man is born into his political party just as he is born into probable future membership into a church. Men, like women, all recognize the crooked aspects of politics, but when their party is in power they tend to ignore its misdeeds and gloat over the discomfiture of the rival political moiety.

The party out of power accuses the party in power of incessant sinning: vote buying, "fixing," and favoritism and graft connected with small local contracts for roads, buildings, and supplies.

The simple division of adults into two major political parties represents only the surface of political organization in Woodland County. Republicans win all the local offices; the important local campaigns are the primaries. In and around Plainville alone there are several rival and semi-permanent Republican cliques, interconnected for bargaining power with each other and with other Republican cliques over the county (and beyond it). The Republican cliques also preserve connection with the Democratic cliques. The minor party machine in the county wields tremendous power, not only because it is now "in," nationally, and therefore has central patronage, but also in the local election of Republican County officers. The heads of cliques are the "politicians," who, for money, past favors, "love of party," and the gratifications of controlling people and manipulating events, attempt to accomplish the election of "their candidates." Their work involves lining up influential neighborhood leaders, the most respected members of large kin groups, preachers, church deacons, and the like, all of whom can sway votes. This means gifts to churches, compliments to women, the admiration of babies, lending tools and dispensing "trading-information" to men, subtle threats to debtors and to individuals whose secret moral or financial delinquency is discovered, and the culling or creation of gossip, rumors, or outright lies to circulate via "the grapevine." [14] During the weeks before an election, and especially on election day itself, male feeling runs high. Most women find this amusing and ridiculous. "Why do the men get so excited over nothing, when they know it's all lies?" Until recently anger frequently broke out into fist fights and sometimes knife fights. Nowadays even open quarrels are infrequent. When the elections are over "most fellers soon forget all about 'em and start speakin' agin just like always," and the politicians who lost try to figure out, for use next time, "just what went haywire with their schemes."

Government: Formal and Informal. No discussion of state and national government is necessary here, further than what has been stated or implied concerning relief, WPA, and the agricultural program.

The county government includes the usual county officers, a sheriff and his deputy, prosecuting attorney, county clerk, tax assessor, recorder of deeds, rural school superintendent, and a three-member county court. The functions of these are varied, but have mainly to do with maintaining the formal structures of the property system, including taxation, and with the preservation of law and order. Only the sheriff and the prosecuting attorney have much to do with actual law enforcement and the punishment of crimes and misdemeanors. The sheriff or a deputy arrests a lawbreaker on sight or formal complaint. Misdemeanors are settled by local officials who may release, fine, or jail. If criminal action is taken, the culprit is jailed or "bailed out" until the next term of circuit court, when the action against him is prosecuted in the name of the state, by the prosecuting attorney.

---

[14] One politician extended "complete confidence" during the county primary of 1940, regarding his political machinations. They were bewildering enough, and mostly successful. Each day for a month he stated what rumors he was "starting on the grapevine," about his candidates and the others. He told through whose innocent voice he was starting each rumor, and predicted whose ears it would reach (in how garbled a form and why garbled), and what its effect would be. He also discussed very intelligently individuals' motives for retelling or not retelling. He checked results by the speed and channels through which rumors came back to him. He said he had never before divulged his "teck'nick," not even to his "own brother."

The circuit court is a traveling court, covering seven or eight counties. The presiding judge sits at Discovery two or three days every six months to hear Woodland County cases. All criminal charges against individuals are tried before him, as well as civil actions between individuals (e.g., damage suits, property-partition suits, foreclosures, divorce cases; and condemnation proceedings originating with the state). The circuit court's time is about evenly divided between criminal and civil cases.

The sheriff "delivers to the court" any defendant against whom criminal action is taken, and the prosecuting attorney theoretically attempts to secure a conviction. The cases with advance docketing that were tried during three recent sessions of the circuit court are listed (some of them are duplicates, or carry-overs from one session to the next): Driving while intoxicated, 23; [15] petty or grand larceny, 17; [16] common assault, 8; burglary, 6; disturbing peace, 6; reckless driving, 4; driving without a license, 3; selling liquor on Sunday, 3; possession or display of a deadly weapon, 3; forgery, 3; leaving the scene of an accident, 2; violating the compulsory school attendance law, 2; and one each of rape, maintaining a public nuisance, passing a bogus check, obtaining money under false pretenses, stealing an automobile, creating an affray, assault with intent to kill, failure to provide for wife and children, wife desertion, and malicious killing of a dog.

Twenty years ago, circuit court sessions lasted for a week or two. People filled the town and camped outside it. "It was just like a big picnic or a camp meeting." Today's shorter sessions reflect perhaps a

[15] This is the "catch-all" charge today (supplanting "disturbing the peace") for punishing people of undesirable conduct, because convictions are easy to obtain and punishments are severe. Many "foreigners" speeding through the county have been flagged down and arrested. Those with the smell of liquor on their breaths have received extremely severe punishments.

[16] Most of the stealing (petty or grand larceny and burglary) is petty thievery: chicken stealing from henhouses, stealing of meat, grain, etc. from cellar, smokehouse, or barn. Livestock is only rarely stolen. There is some stealing, particularly of mail-order merchandise, from mailboxes, which are sometimes a quarter or a half-mile from the house.

Much more stealing occurs than the court dockets suggest, but much more stealing is "imagined" than really occurs: An elderly widow who continues to run her husband's store in Plainville, hears footsteps outside her house at night; the neighbor's dog barks loudly, then stops suddenly as he "recognizes somebody"; she misses arm-loads of wood off her woodpile "nearly every morning." "I know who it is, but I wouldn't want to disgrace the family by naming him." One type of stealing is interesting in that it is at least partially approved. "A boy that ain't never stole watermelons out of a patch, to *eat,* or apples off a tree, ain't much of a boy."

slight change in entertainment patterns, but they more importantly reflect both fewer and shorter court trials. Less violence occurs now in the county, where violence was formerly rife. No murder (except the unsolved ax-killing of a socially unimportant hermit) has occurred for nearly ten years; yet fifteen or twenty men were slain within the memory of living men. Fist fights are becoming rare, and "cuttings" almost unknown. Fewer important "land disputes" and "livestock damage" suits occur. The boundaries, land rights, etc., have been established a long time, Livestock are now fenced up and not "given to the range." Likewise the "compounding" of cases out of court and their partial "compounding" [17] in connection with formal legal procedure has lessened the number of cases brought to court and shortened the time which each requires for settlement.

Perhaps the majority of cases are "compounded," either partially or fully, before their legal settlement in court. Some are initiated by legal mechanism and then "settled out of court." A few are played out with full panoply and expense of rival teams of attorneys, changes of venue, and appeals. Such a one, which scandalized the community of Plainville with its obscenity and rocked it with old and new divisions and hatreds, began its court history in April, 1939, and had not been settled two years later. This was a suit for large damages resulting from an alleged adulterous relationship. Both plaintiff and defendant were Plainville business men. About one "sex scandal" reaches the courtroom during each generation.

One gets the feeling regarding court cases and "outside law" in general that "the law" is dreaded and even hated; [18] and that lawsuits should be avoided and are in no wise considered a safe or sure way to justice. "The people with the most money win the cases . . . Only the lawyers make anything out of the law . . . I don't think much of a man that hollers 'law.' " These and other criticisms are frequent. The law seems to be used more often as a threat than a reality (except for its minor punitive use against local "bad characters," in actions against drunken drivers, peace disturbers, petty larceners, etc.)—a threat un-

[17] The sense of "compounding" as used here is different from its American legal sense. As used here the word means "settlement by agreement."

[18] Game laws, for instance, are hated by a great many natives. Few people would any longer criticize the laws dealing with murder, but a generation ago many people would have upheld "feud law." A retired preacher recounted the tales of a dozen murders within his memory. Many reached trial, but there were few convictions, and no convicted man spent over four years in the penitentiary.

der which can be initiated the traditional procedures for settling trouble and punishing violators of the mores. Most petty offenses are settled out of court, or are controlled before their occurrence.

Loafing and Gossip Groups. The role of law among all other mechanisms which force Plainvillers to conform to their society's established patterns of behavior is really very slight. More important mechanisms, both preventive and punitive, for social control are gossip, ridicule, and, in the widest sense of the term, folklore. These function "individually," of course, but they also function "by groups," and it is necessary to describe the organizations which I shall call "loafing groups" and "gossip cells."

Every Plainville group, no matter what its primary function, is of course partly also a gossip and loafing group. The members of a church loaf and gossip together before and after church. A harvest gang is also a center of news, enjoyable discourse, and social criticism. The long hours that merchants spend in their stores are not like long hours at a factory assembly line, because the "assembly line" here is intimates who gather to sit, spit (a particular male gesture), smoke, chew, chat, and whittle together. Actual "business," except on Saturday afternoon and a few other "big days," takes very little of a merchant's time.

Each loafing group, while not rigidly organized, involves a central nucleus of membership, some communion of interest, and frequently an informal "meeting place." The most visible loafing group is the "Old Men," who "put in their time" at loafing. They are called the "Old Men," the "Club," the "Story Tellers," the "real loafers here," or sometimes the "Spit and Whittle (or Argue) Club." These names, used by others (and sometimes by themselves) are arranged in descending order of respect, and suggest the pastimes and the social functionlessness of the old men. Their nucleus is half a dozen men ranging in age from their late sixties to early eighties. The main ones are three "retired" and "respected" farmers (one also a nearly retired carpenter, one now a notary public), an aged "life-time loafer," an ex-"timber man" (woodchopper), and a blacksmith—all leveled socially into the companionship of age. The club "sits" throughout most of the long summer on two iron benches under the shade tree in the corner of the square; in bad weather they move into stores. They are joined at times by other men and boys, all of whom listen and, except the boys, contribute to the conversation. Here the society of forty and fifty years ago is daily reconstructed, as it is remembered. The old times are lived over and lamented (and pitied, for the "ignorance of them days, and the way people had to git along").

The present also interests the Old Men, who are far from being the intolerant and meddlesome critics old men are generally and locally assumed to be. Only one or two are "as sharp-tongued as women," but most of the damage they do is through their wives, not through their loafing club of old men. The rest, while certainly not themselves "reformers" and often ridiculing the efforts and "mistakes" of reformers,[19] have seen too many changes in technology, morals, and taste (and are perhaps too aware of their own social uselessness) to exert a very active influence in community affairs. Their attitudes are more tolerant than they are assumed to be by the women and girls, who on each trip down the street have to pass by the Old Men, endure their scrutiny, and "wonder what they're sayin' now." The Old Men are more tolerant than intolerant. Their chief function is to entertain themselves and other males.

Across the street from the Old Men, and viewing them from concealment behind the glass windows of the Notions Store, sit several old women. These are the "Old Women," [20] the "Widows" (not all are widows and not all the widows gather here), the "Gossips," the "Old Gossips," the "Busybodies," the "Snoops." The owner of the store is a widow and is considered to be "one of the worst old gossips around here." If a man enters the store conversation ceases and all eyes regard him. The proprietress asks, "Did you want something?" The purchase finished, the man leaves, or he pauses a moment standing to chat. Such talk is either "kidding"[21] or news—an exchange of news between the man and the woman, or a solicitation of news from the man

19 For example, the county agent and the vocational agriculture teacher—preachers are not thought of as reformers.

20 It need hardly be said that the majority of old women do not gather here. Nor do most of the old men sit frequently "under the tree." A point is made by many old people of "stayin' at home," being "busy at something useful," and especially not being seen frequently in these groups of the old.

21 The most frequent kidding with men in this place is a form of sexual kidding: The proprietress says, "I thought you were some old widower comin' in to make a date to take me to church tonight . . . anyway, I have a date." She then tells of proposals, rejected and heart-broken suitors, and imaginary intrigues and romances, adulterous or otherwise, among the old, but chiefly among the old widows and widowers. She carries on similar kidding by telephone with certain old men, including frequent impersonations of other women, as a form of practical joking.

It is as if the taboo system on free sexual conversation and relationship is relaxed among people considered too old for real sexual interests.

("What were the old men talkin' about just now? . . . Are your folks all well? . . . What do the children write? . . . Did you see the accident yesterday? . . . Do you know the particulars?")

Women say (and men believe) that the Notions Store is a clearing house for exchanging and garbling all news, especially scandal and other gossip discreditable to individual reputations. Here adult men are condemned for "not working hard enough" or for "neglecting their families"; youths for "wild oats"; women for mismanagement and delinquency in wifely and maternal duties; young girls for the clothes they wear, the company they keep, the certain bad ends they are coming to if they don't "show a change"; children for idleness at home and school, bad manners, disrespect to their elders.

The gossip of these women is hated, dreaded (and often scorned). They are said to "fight every progressive thing in this community." [22] They are said to be "against schools," "against good clothes," "against being the least bit modern," "against anybody's having a good time." Their attitudes "show why young people want to leave here." "They're too old to enjoy anything themselves and they don't want anybody else to." There are other well-known "gossip cells," but they are groups of only two or three women who "work together." The role of old women as gossips is highly exaggerated, but they do collect and scatter a good deal of news. They also exert a great restraining influence against deviation from the stricter and older moral patterns. One man said, "They drive sin into the timber."

A clique that exerts great influence on the community today is a group of young married women called the "Leaders," living in or very near Plainville. They are "exclusive." They "dress nice," "fix their hair pretty," "run around lots," and "like to be up-to-date." They are not the women who behave in the most "modern" fashion, however. Another "young set," of four married couples, whose women dress equally well, drink cocktails together and sometimes even get drunk or gamble. They are a "wild set," and condemned, though one of their women is also on the fringe of the "Leaders." She is sometimes "invited when somebody that was invited can't come and you need an extra person." The Leaders however are not in close relationship with the wild set. The Leaders all belong to the much larger

[22] As many people also say of the churches and as church people often say of "the people who don't respect the law." And as people "who don't have anything" sometimes say of those who do ("they are too stingy to spend it"). Everybody is for "progress."

Boosters Club, which is Plainville's Home Economics Club. Thus they are in close contact with other women in the community, including those guardians of tradition, the older women. These young women "try to be leaders" in all progressive matters. They exchange luncheons, shop together in larger towns, and attempt to set a scale of living like that in larger centers. Yet they try to avoid criticism on all grounds, including that of too great modernity. Though most of the husbands of these women stand high in the community, they participate almost not at all in the social activities of their wives. Men, in general, do not like "parties."

Scores of other adult cliques exist, of course. Families, both close and extended, groups of neighbors, the work gangs, the congregations of each little rural church, and the four congregations that gather in Plainville—all these are cliques, functioning socially both for entertainment and toward social control. Through all this multiplicity of social grouping a great variety of purposes and aims—even incompatible social aims—operate. There are forces under way (with clique leadership and backing) to maintain without change the old mores— morally, technologically, etc. Others attempt to lead, persuade, bribe, cajole, betray, or compel people to abandon old attitudes, scorn old ways, "practice scientific agriculture," "be up-to-date," "become like city people."

Organization by Sex and by Age. In Plainville society, as in all other human societies, "primitive" or civilized, the most fundamental social division is into the two moieties, male and female. Within at most a year or two after birth, the individual is expected to demonstrate the personality traits attributed to its own sex. He (or she) begins even earlier to receive differential treatment in accordance with this supposed inherent difference in personality. At "the walking age," in childhood and youth, throughout adult life, and during the period of old age and decline, Plainville males and females enjoy privileges and are bound by duties, interests, and viewpoints that are theirs by sex alone—or more accurately stated, by sex and their age-status at any given time.

Plainvillers also group themselves by age alone, regardless of sex. A brief listing of those categories follows, given in frequently used local terms: "Babies" ("babes," "infants") are ordinarily infants in arms. By extension the term also frequently applies to toddlers; also to any child of pre-school age. Also, in affection, pity, or forgiveness, to later childhood, or even to middle or late youth. An "infant in the eyes of the law" is any boy under 21 or any girl under 18.

Children ("kids," "young-uns," etc.): These terms connote, by one usage, all offspring of whatever age. ("My young-uns is all grown up and got kids of their own and some of *them's* got childern.") They mean ordinarily however any children big enough to run about and play informally outdoors with other children and not "too big to be ashamed just to play." Children leave off most informal outdoor play shortly after adolescence. "Children," in the ordinary sense, are sub-categorized into "small children," "large children," etc.

There is a gap in clear local terminology for the age between that clearly defined as "childhood" and that most clearly occupied by those called "the young married people." This intermediate group comprises the "young people," who are "at the sparkin' age." For boys, part of this period is likely to be called the "wild oats stage."

At marriage people become "married people," though this phrase includes in primary connotation neither the "young married people" whose functional participation in community life as married adults has not fully begun, nor the "old married couples" whose similar participation has begun to wane. The "married people" are primarily the heads of families: their children are in school; they go to church and take their children to church (or "they should"); they should vote and be interested in the outcomes of elections; they work and "manage" as full adults; they are "in the prime of life."

"Old people" are those whose children have married and left home, whose physical vigor has begun to decline. They are, in order of descending respect, the "old couples," the "old widows and widowers," the "old bachelors" and the "old maids." A term of either kindly pity or respect for the old is to call them "the agèd." A term of pity or contempt is the phrase "the old and childish."

People who pass through life unmarried are "old maids" or "old bachelors" from the age when they cease being "eligibles." People who delay marriage now become old maids or old bachelors later than they used to, here as everywhere else. The age a generation ago was roughly about 20 for girls and 25–30 for men. Now it is about 30 for girls and 30–35 for men; very few people, however, marry at a later age than 20–25.

There is not space to discuss here the implications and meanings of all this verbal stress on juniority and seniority, which is particularly directed toward the younger members of the society. Many of these implications can be inferred however from the phrases themselves and from other sections of this account of Plainville life, especially the final section on the life cycle.

Class

The class system of Plainville provides natives with a master pattern for arranging according to rank every individual and every family, clique, club, lodge, church, and other association or organization in Plainville society. It provides also a set of patterns of expected behavior according to class, and a way of classifying and judging all norms and variations in individual behavior. Yet many Plainvillers completely deny its existence. They are aware of class-distinctions elsewhere but often say, "This is one place where everybody is equal. You don't find no classes here." People tend to recognize the system for what it is, or are at least more able or willing to verbalize regarding it, according to their rank: "higher ups" are clearer about the system than their inferiors. People who "manipulate" other people for personal gain or advance are also quite familiar with the system because they have to use it. The two strongest preventives toward a local full understanding of the system are these: (1) a moral attitude that class distinctions are wrong; (2) the etiquette governing inter-class relations; no one must be reminded overtly of his "inferiority." "Everybody must be treated equal." Few people commit any serious errors in behavior, however, against the rules which govern interclass relationships.

The system, as it appears to the average "better-class" adult, is impressionistically represented in Diagram 1, which suggests a diamond-shaped numerical distribution of the population according to class.[23] The diagram was constructed, except for two compromises, by the simple principle of listening to how people were described by others and classifying them accordingly. The first compromise is unimportant: a very few people who must live in the community without liking it and with few or no social roots there will privately say, "All the people here are just hillbillies (or 'low-class')." The important compromise is with the fact that religious lower-class people tend to place morals, symbolized by "salvation" and participation in church activities,

[23] I am indebted for this concept to Robert K. Merton's review in *Survey-Graphic*, October, 1942, of *The Social Life of a Modern Community*, by W. Lloyd Warner and Paul S. Lunt.

above all other criteria of social distinction. The majority of Plainville people classify others, by behavior and innuendo at least and usually also in outright phrasing, as they are classified here. Only the "better class," however, classify both themselves and others in this fashion.

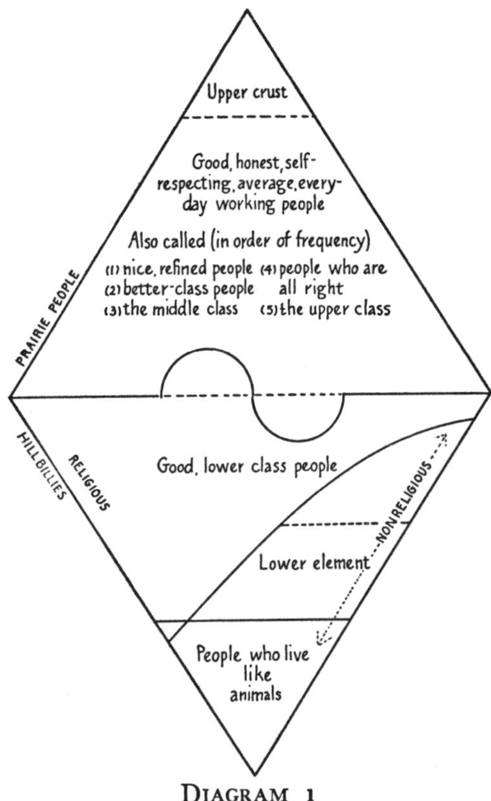

Diagram 1

The "diamond" of Diagram 1 is bisected laterally by a line labeled above, Prairie People, and below, Hillbillies. The first and most obvious criterion of class distinction happens to be geographical. The "better class of people" lives out on the prairie, the "lower class" lives "back in the hills." For farmers this is almost, but not quite, literally true. The very best land is the bottoms; the hills must be traversed to reach the homes of "rich bottom farmers." The bottom farmers, if they "live like prairie people," are "better-class people." If they "live like hill people" they are not. The two curves in the central line, however, refer not mainly to the bottom farmers, who are few, but to certain hill-farm families who are "better people" and to people actually dwelling out on the prairie who are not. The former, again, "live like prairie people," the latter "like hill people," and both rank accordingly.

"Living on the prairie" versus "living in the hills" have come to be the two poles of one criterion of status which we can call the "geography of residence." Since the prairie land is better than hill land, less rocky and better suited for tillage by more modern farming practices, a second criterion is "technology." Modern technology vs. "scratch farming," or "old-style" farming practices (or vs. the older pattern of "hunting and fishing plus a little patch farming," or even vs. "living as a wood-chopper") are the polarities.

A third criterion, as might be expected, is wealth, or "worth." Its extremes are on the one hand "real wealth," or more reasonably "independence" ("they own their own home . . . they have enough"); on the other, "poverty." The average wealth per prairie family exceeds that of hill families in value of land; in size, quality, and appearance of housing and other "improvements"; in size and quality of livestock herds and poultry flocks; and in many other items of use and appearance on which discriminatory judgments can be made, such as tools, cars, clothes, furniture, and food.

A fourth and very important criterion is "lineage." "Good families" (so labeled by any number of synonyms) are opposed to "poor" (or "low-class," "low-element," "no-account," or even "trashy") families. So rigid are the restrictions governing courtship, visiting, worship, etc., and so firmly set are the patterns of behavior expected from each member of the society according to "what kind of family he comes from," that lineage can be described at present as an almost absolute criterion. Since many of the "good prairie families" are linked by kinship with many hill families, and since people have no hesitation in "stating their kin," this criterion, in its present form, must have arisen since 1870–90, when the prairie was brought under cultivation.

A fifth criterion, "morals," is given much local lip service. Some common moral traits which most people agree in stressing are "honesty" (especially the payment of debts), "willingness to work," and performance of all domestic duties. Traits commonly condemned as "immoral," are dishonesty, idleness and unwillingness to work, family neglect or cruelty, drunkenness, and, of course, serious "law breaking." Other, and "severe," moral points frequently stressed but on which there is division of opinion are church membership or "salvation"; and numerous taboos against drinking beer or spirits, dancing, card playing, smoking (especially by women), profanity, obscene talk, ostentation in dress, etc. A good many people, including some who do not stress all the taboos listed, say, and apparently believe, that "to live right and do right" is the one criterion by which people are and should be judged. Actually however no one ever crosses the main class line as the result of moral distinction or moral delinquency alone. Within the upper class morals are a criterion only for approval and "respect," and therefore of relative rank.

Within the lower class morals count more. Except for its lowest and smallest group the lower class is subdivided mainly by the criterion of morality. "Lower-class religious" people are church members. They have all, except some of the children, been "saved." They have mostly been saved in the Holiness Church. The life of this large group is active, neighborly, and moral, by all the positive traits and the taboos that have been named. Though they strive to better themselves financially, of course, no other criterion of status except morals is very important in their social judgments of themselves or others. Non-religious "lower-class" people fall into three subclasses, all of whom "live in the hills." At the top is a group of families who are "good citizens," but lower class because of lineage, relative poverty, living in the timber, old-fashioned ways, etc. Beneath them is the "lower element," a group of families who range, at the top, from breaking a few of the conventional taboos, to, at the bottom, actual criminality. The least respected of these "come to town and get drunk and get into fights," or "get arrested and get into jail" (for fighting, drunken driving, etc.), or "they absolutely won't work," or "they steal chickens and meat."

The "people who live like animals" are in still another category. They "live in the timber," of course, but the main point about them is that they are considered too "ignorant" to be accountable morally or legally for what they do. For example, if a man and woman of this class live together without marriage, others consider the fact comic, not reprehensible. No one would "have the law on" a man of this class for chicken stealing. The owner would instead scold the culprit or frighten him, preferably with a practical joke. There are a few whole families in this class, and several individual men. All are believed to be, and seem to be, somewhat subnormal mentally, though not all mental subnormals fall into their class.

The sixth criterion of class is of enormous complexity, because it involves all other criteria, and in a sense supersedes them. At the same time it governs interclass relationships and is critical in matters of class mobility. This criterion is "manners." What is meant here by "manners" can best be explained by describing the actual shifts in class status which have occurred among people now or very recently living in or near Plainville.

Only three such shifts were observed. The mail carrier rose from "the worst hillbilly stock" to a position of respect, affluence, and full participation in upper-class affairs. He did so through the following main procedures. When he came back from the First World War he got a job in town, showed honesty and "no bad habits," secured the profitable mail-carrying job, lessened his contacts with kin and former associates (except enough to avoid criticism for neglect of kin), acquired the "manners" of the upper class, began to accumulate property, married the daughter of a prosperous farmer, and raised a family of children which he sent to the Christian Sunday School and to high school. Ora Bell, who died recently, was the son of "one of the biggest and worst and most ignorant families in town." He was "bright in high school," "worked every chance he got," showed himself to be "absolutely reliable," "kept away from all bad company except his family," married a "good, moral girl" (from the upper edge of the lower class) bought a home, saved his money, made many friends and finally ran for one of the county offices and won. ("People give Ory lots of credit for what he done, and they helped him. He showed what anybody can do that'll try.") Elmer Simmons accomplished what is even harder—in his own lifetime he descended from the upper to the lower class. When his father's prairie farm was sold and the money distributed among his heirs, Elmer bought a cheap hill farm and moved into the timber. He quit serious farming and "trying to do something," "took up with the lower element," started running hounds, married a backwoods girl, and settled into the hill pattern of life. It is more difficult to lower one's class status than to lift it, because the upper class is varied enough to retain anyone who retains its "manners," and because apparently it is almost impossible to lay upper-class manners aside, once they have been acquired. Perhaps also, more people "rise" than "fall" because people sometimes "try to rise" and no one actually "tries to fall."

In the sense that both "natural endowment" and "achievement" were factors in these changes in status, they can be considered as further criteria of class status. Like wealth and morals, however, they more usually play a role only in relative station or "respect" within the class where one was born. The first two men "rose" and the third one "fell" by a slow process of "dis-identification" with the "born manners" of their original class groups, and a concomitant acquisition of the "born manners" of the groups with which they are now identified.

The number of traits associated with "manners" is nearly infinite, and no effort can be made to describe them all. All relate to the division between the prairie and hill ways of life. To begin with, all the traits connected with wealth already listed should be listed again here, considered only in the light of "manners," because people are often said to "have the kinds of things they have because they want 'em that way." Certainly many "old-style" people are in a better financial position than many of their "betters" to afford material possessions regarding which discriminations are made. "They have that old wagon (house, car, team, food, suit, dress, etc.) because they like it better"; or "because they don't know any better." Knowledge is a very important discriminatory trait. People say of the lower class, "They don't know how to live . . . dress . . . cook . . . take a bath over once a year . . . eat . . . talk . . . talk proper . . . talk to people . . . act . . . act in public . . . act in town . . . act at church." Or it is phrased in another way. "They don't know nothin' except hounds, huntin', and fishin' . . . hoes, axes . . . and doin' it the hard way. . . . Their women and children are afraid of strangers . . . If a stranger goes toward one of them houses, all the dogs start barkin', and then you see the dogs, hogs, chickens, women, and children start runnin' for the brush." The "lower element" is described in a similar way, plus the addition of phrases of moral reproach.

Manners separate the two main classes much more effectually than any other criterion, except lineage, which merely establishes at birth an environment, with its expected patterns of behavior. A "lower-class" individual can only with great difficulty learn behavior apart from the behavior expected from one of his class, unless he migrates, because interclass social activity is severely restricted. Wealth, while important in many ways, is not a valid criterion of class status, because many lower-class families (perhaps a third) are richer than many upper-class families (perhaps another third). One of the two richest farmers near Plainville, Mahlon James, lives on the prairie and is "at the top of the social heap." Mahlon's prestige, as a result of his wealth, political and financial control of others, etc. is extremely high. He is viewed with admiration, fear, and even awe. I have heard him called "Mr. God." The other lives on the river and is at or near the bottom. Both "made it theirselves" and are "credited" for so doing. The difference in their status is essentially a difference in "manners," the outgrowth in each case of residence, technological habits, lineage, and participation (versus non-participation) in community life.

There is no space here in which to modify the class diamond as it would have to be modified repeatedly to show how the class system appears to every Plainviller. For women the class lines are drawn much more sharply than for men, because in business dealings, trading, and informal loafing men cross the class lines freely. For children the structure forms gradually as it is implanted in their minds through home and other training. The "pure money-grubber" sometimes sees only a "respect-diamond" of hard-won wealth. Most preachers, like the entire Holiness congregation, would "represent" it as a "diamond of morals," but the Christian preacher would hardly visit any "lower-element" sick, or "pay his respects" to their dead by going to one of their funerals unless asked to preach it.

Various lower-class groups see the class lines in still different ways. Yet no lower-class child is taught, "You must treat So-and-So thus, because he is better than you" (upper-class children are often taught their lesson in exactly reverse terms). He, like everyone else, is taught, "You are as good as anybody."

Lower-class people "see it wrong," it is said, "because nobody in their class can understand or explain it to them." But they seldom make social mistakes. They accept the received patterns as anyone else does. Indeed, in the lower class certain alternative prestige points occur which are lacking in the better class. For example, hunting and trapping (including the care and training of dogs) are highly respected useful skills in one sector of the lower class. They are scorned or condemned or are respected only within strict limits as sporting skills in the upper class. Physical prowess is respected more in the lower class. So in one sector are certain traits, such as "fighting at the drop of a hat," now become outlaw traits in the main society. Finally there is the phenomenon of "upside-down prestige." An "outlaw sort of a feller" can attain a certain real distinction in the eyes of people by being "just the opposite of what people respect." This may involve mastery of one or more highly condemned traits, such as profanity or obscenity, habitual drunkenness, or habitual loafing. A well-respected Plainviller said one day of "the worst loafer in town," "What would we do for a real loafer if it wasn't for Uncle Darb? He's an institution!"

All local cliques are rather easily "placed" in the class system. Plainville's clique of young women "Leaders" is very near the top of the upper class—almost "upper crust." The Boosters include these and go a little lower in the same class. They are still very "high." The Home Economics clubs are always formed of farm women securely in the better class. The 4-H clubs comprise mainly upper-class children. For the most part, only better-class men and women meet with the county agent to form committees and formulate plans regarding reform. High school children break up into cliques according to class. A boy or girl who can play superior basketball gets on the team, without class favoritism, and in this activity is treated like anyone else—including applause for merit, but his or her dates are very apt to be restricted according to class. Families, even members of the same extended family who keep in close contact with each other, are of a single class. Visiting cliques are of the same class. No lower-class man is a Mason. No lower-class woman is an Eastern Star. Even the churches are arranged in a hierarchy of class.

The description of classes has been confined to country people. Town people belong to one or another class as their way of life, lineage, wealth, morals, etc., fit them in. With them modernity of life (car, dress, extensive use of electricity, for example) and its opposite largely replace the prairie-hills polarities in instances where these are not sustained by active kin ties. In town, professional people stand high; odd-jobbers and WPA workers stand low. Until recent years town people *as town people* outranked country people *as country people,* but this social difference has disappeared almost completely.

Folklore

A meaningful discussion of Plainville folklore would make much more of the techniques, materials, and function of gossip, kidding, and practical joking, than of the traditional stories, songs and superstitions which are conventionally gathered as folklore. The same practical jokes, for example, appear generation after generation, and the discomfiture of their victims is never forgotten.

Many of the favorite stories (told especially by the old men) are "tall tales." The motifs of these are widespread, but the characters are nearly always local Plainvillers, living or dead. One tall tale relates how Uncle John Wisdom, a famous early woodchopper, once planted a big patch of sweet potatoes. One day he went down to the timber to chop wood and noticed a big log across the stream. He chopped into the log and discovered it was one of his sweet potatoes. In another tale a local man's sow disappeared. He found her the next spring living inside a pumpkin with nine little pigs. ("She wintered right good on that punkin.") One informant believes that his father, long since dead but remembered as a great story teller, "made up most of them big stories he used to tell." Another favorite theme of tall tales is "killing many animals with one bullet."

A few old people remember a number of classical English ballads, often greatly transformed. An aged woman, who would not "say" or "sing" the songs she knew to me, spent hours helping her great-grandson, a high school boy, record them for me. She said it would not be "right" for her to give them to me directly, though she insisted on his copying them accurately. The lad took down a score or more songs from her; these included classical ballads, older religious songs, Negro songs, and Civil War songs. These were all, to her, simply "the songs people sang when I was a girl." The only ballad heard on a strictly local theme is about a Baptist preacher named Huddon, who lived twenty-five years ago in one of the timbered sections of the community. As a circuit-rider Huddon was often away from his farm for weeks at a time. A neighbor's hogs and geese repeatedly broke into his garden, while he was away. Once when he came home and found the hogs eating up his garden he caught a hog, tied it, sewed up its eyes, and lifted it back over the fence onto the neighbor's land. A song celebrates this deed:

> Green corn, green corn growing in the garden
> Green corn, green corn growing in the garden
> Green corn, green corn growing in the garden
> > Down in Viney Cove
> Old man Huddon sewing up a hog's eye
> Old man Huddon sewing up a hog's eye
> Old man Huddon sewing up a hog's eye
> > Down in Viney Cove.

In another stanza he buried a goose alive. His granddaughter, now living in Metropolis, says that he actually buried three geese. Returning home from preaching in another community, he caught the geese in his garden and buried them on their owner's property, leaving only their heads sticking out.

More women than men seem once to have known the old ballads. Men used to sing many fiddle songs, like "Sally Goodin," "Cuckoo's Nest," "Sandy Land," and "The Irish Washerwoman." An interesting feature of these songs was that each existed in two versions—the standard version, ordinarily comic, which "could be sung anywheres," and an obscene version which women and girls were never supposed to hear. Young men no longer learn the fiddle songs. Young people are interested in learning only such of these as they hear revived over the radio. Traditional children's folklore that survives includes a few game songs, many riddles, and many "album verses."

Many ancient superstitions survive in regard to planting, weaning of children and livestock, castration of animals, tree-killing, and so forth, according to zodiacal signs and the "light" or "dark" of the moon. Almanacs (distributed free through drug stores by patent medicine manufacturers) are often consulted to "get the sign right." This lore is ridiculed by many farmers and is declining, but many still "foller the signs," and more believe in them than follow them. The agricultural experts discourage "sign farming," but tactfully, so as not to arouse hostility to their work.

There is also a vast, though declining, body of traditional medical lore for treating man and beast. Patent medicines and cure-alls more than medical science have lessened the popularity of home remedies. Many ill-fed cows each year however are "cured" of "holler-tail" (by splitting the tail and sprinkling salt and pepper in the wound). Not many years back every child with measles was made to "break out" by drinking "sheep-nanny tea" (made by boiling sheep dung in water).

Amusements; Aesthetic Interests, etc.

The leading informal amusement for grown people is gossip. Children, especially school children, bring home much news and therefore carry the materials of gossip, but children's talk is "chatter" rather than "gossip." Gossiping amounts really to an art, an art practiced as vigorously as it is condemned by most Plainville adults. Any community happening is "news"; discreditable news is gossip. The subjects of gossip are mostly crimes and misdemeanors, past and present, moral delinquencies, hypocrisies, skulduggeries; what an old skin-flint *he* is, how he cheated somebody out of something, how *she's* no good or at least wasn't before she was married, etc. In other words gossip is concerned with all the unapproved activities of one's neighbors. Favorable comments are not gossip.

The art in gossiping is to retail gossip in such a way as to entertain listeners and condemn victims without risk of getting into trouble as a scatterer of gossip. This requires skill in phrasing and innuendo, as well as complete knowledge of the social and kin connections of all listeners so that nothing said can be carried in definite form to the subject of the gossip or the subject's family. A very common device of self-protection is a request not to be quoted ("I wouldn't want it told that I said it . . ."). Another is a phrasing so careful that only the most knowing listeners can understand who is being talked about.

The three commonest subjects of gossip are the stinginess or miserliness of people, cheating in a trade or other business deal, and illicit sexual affairs. The last are actually very infrequent. During fifteen months in Plainville there was only one full-blown scandal, a second case of adultery which was quickly hushed up, and a third one which did not occur though it was much gossiped about for a while. A woman living in Plainville was astonished at the few adultery stories there. She had been raised in a town sixty-five miles south, where "there was a good new scandal every two weeks."

Another subject of gossip which delights people is the "backwoodsiness" or "ignorance" of lower-class people. Everybody knows someone a little more "backwoodsy" than himself. Traits commonly reported for laughter are personal dirtiness, dirty food, dirty houses, bedbugs, "ignorant" manners, illiteracy, emotionalism in church, backward or old-style language usages, and sometimes even personal defects or great poverty.

"Kidding" is another great amusement, particularly the kidding of children and of the somewhat subnormal members of the society. There is pride in the quantity of kidding given and taken, and in its quality. Gossip and kidding are the two greatest arts in Plainville. The kidding of children is often gentle and affectionate. It is often however extremely cruel. A two-year-old boy was howling in his mother's arms in the doctor's waiting room. She explained, "His father and brothers have got him scared to death, tellin' how the doctor's just a-gonna kill him." Boys are kidded more than girls; the excessive kidding of boys seems designed both to provide entertainment for their teasers (men and older boys) and to develop very early in the victims the desirable male traits of aggressive comeback and ability to "take it." Women, generally speaking, do not do much kidding; and most of them condemn the severe kidding of children. As soon as a boy can laugh off a tormentor or answer him with wisecracks, he appears no longer to suffer from kidding but to enjoy it. Kidding between adults seems to take place on two levels, among equals who kid only as a game and do not take each other seriously, and between groups of men and such individuals as lend themselves more or less permanently to the role of scapegoat. Kidding on the second level may be very severe. Uncle Poley Prouty has been a lifelong victim of a systematic series of lies. His mind has never been quite "average." He believed that the census of 1940 was taken mainly to discover "all the men living with two women" and the "women living with two men," out of a governmental intent to restrict such practices; he believed that many such cases would be found about Plainville. His mental content is the result of having been told just that kind of thing throughout his life. He is seldom told the truth. He was told that the local Liar's Club (non-existent) had been wanting him to join their organization for a long time because he was such a fine musician. Poley has some home-made instruments, including a fiddle made of a cigar box. Although "he can't even carry a tune," people call at his shack to hear him play; he always obliges and is flattered. He is given no insight into the fact that he is an object of ridicule. Poley is by birth and church affiliations a member of the "good, honest" sector of the lower class, and his gullibility neither lowers nor enhances his class status. Another recipient of such lifelong kidding is a mentally subnormal man, about thirty-five years old, of the "better class," who enjoys an equally fictitious "honor" and "fame" as the Bell-Ringer for all the churches in Plainville. All "dim-witted" and gullible males (and a few females) are kidded as Poley and the Bell-Ringer are kidded, regardless of their class status. In addition there is a tendency to treat all members of the lowest class (the "people who live like animals") in the same manner. Such kidding seems to build up a feeling of self-importance in these lowly people, and at the same time to establish a basis of contact by which they become not only tolerable, but a source of social pleasure to other members of the society.

Other amusements for men are loafing hours in town and at country stores, or rest periods at fence rows (between "rounds" of plowing or other field work), to chat with other men. Men also sometimes go hunting and fishing; lower-class men spend a good deal of time at hunting and fishing.

Men and their wives, or whole families, visit other couples or families; families often go home with each other after church for Sunday dinner and an afternoon visit until chore time.

Lodge meetings and church services all should be considered partly as amusements, as should harvest and butchering days, when men work in large groups and their wives and children share in the work, big eating, and other excitement. Other "big eating" times for large groups are the basket dinners given rather frequently by churches. Long tables improvised from boards are set up on the church lawn after Sunday preaching, and loaded with food brought by the women of the congregation. The governmental agriculture office has imitated this well-loved local entertainment trait by initiating an annual Achievement Day, which includes a basket dinner in addition to exhibits of farm products and other educational features.

Shopping trips or visits to kin in other localities provide new scenes and relaxation.

Great gathering times for people of all ages are the picnics. Every town in the county has an annual picnic—an Old Settlers' Reunion, or Homecoming, with many concession booths, carnival attractions, and prizes. The Plainville picnic is held on July Fourth; people attend from miles around. Picnics are times for great "spending" by children, and for almost unlimited consumption of ice cream, cheap candy, and soft drinks. Children are expected to "be sick with the bellyache" after a picnic.

Radios are an amusement to the majority of people of all ages. They are considered an especial "comfort" to the old; and surprisingly there is little opposition to them on moral grounds, not even to beer advertising or Sunday jazz music. The first cars were condemned as "useless here," and "a detriment to the country," and even now car-riding by young people is often condemned; yet the only criticism remembered against the first radios was a general contemptuous belief that "they wouldn't really work."

Adult women visit each other in town and on the farms afoot or by car, and women "visit over the telephone." Women, especially those of the upper class, also meet and enjoy themselves in cliques and formal clubs.

As for movies, nearly everybody except the very old and some extremely religious people goes to them, though older people see fewer movies than young people. More children than grown people see the movies shown weekly in Plainville, which are mostly old Westerns. Better and newer movies are shown every night at "X" and "Y" (22 and 28 miles away). Sometimes whole families drive over to one of these towns to see a current picture, and young people at the dating age often "go outside" to a movie.

Young people complain bitterly of the lack of entertainment in Plainville, which they consider very lonely, unexciting, backward, and restrained in comparison with larger towns. They have almost no parties in homes, though parties for the young, and for people of all ages meeting together for ice-skating, fish fries, candy-breakings, etc. were once frequent. Religious people discourage parties. The Christian preacher said, "The old have shut the doors of the front room on youth." A party "to entertain the young" projected by members of the P.T.A. in 1939 was abandoned because of adverse criticism ("The young will start playing games at parties and then they'll want to dance").

The boys' and girls' high school basketball games are very popular and widely attended—and criticized by many church folk. The most popular local amusement for youngsters whose parents will permit them to roller-skate is the Rink, an enormous transformed cowbarn at the edge of Plainville. Its owner has installed a second-hand and partly improvised amplifying system, over which he plays, to attract customers and as skating music, outmoded phonograph records which he buys in Largetown for ten cents apiece. The noise of the rink can be heard a mile away.

Other social amusements for youngsters of both sexes are riding to and from high school on the bus, chatting together between classes, and annual class picnics. Some lower-class youth occasionally dance in their homes to the music of fiddles, banjos, guitars, or the radio. A few upper-class ones also dance occasionally at road houses far outside the community. The Young People's church meetings also give the young a chance to be together. Some meet there, as the vocational agriculture teacher phrased it, "to rub hands in a holy place."

A great local "to-do" after every wedding is to shivaree the bride and groom the first night they spend in the community. The shivaree party makes a vast amount of noise with shotguns, pans, and automobile horns, until the groom passes out cigars to men and boys and candy to women and girls. If the shivaree is in town, the groom is often obliged to wheel the bride around the square in a wheelbarrow. Occasionally as a variation the bride is made to wheel the groom around. The shivaree group creates as much uproar as possible about the house of the newlyweds, sometimes filling their bed with horsehair or cornflakes.

Aesthetic interests are not prominent. People admire a well-kept house, freshly painted, neat indoors, and well maintained without. The furnishings of the better houses include some overstuffed furniture, a conscientiously polished stove, commercial picture calendars, and framed photographs of deceased members of the family. Women often plant flowers in the front yard or a row or two beside the vegetables in the garden. They like pretty dresses, are interested in hairdos, and sometimes take an aesthetic pleasure in the labeling and arrangement of glass jars of canned fruit.

Men who farm admire a straight furrow better than anything else in the world. It has been part of the government program to try to teach contour farming for erosion control. The idea often meets with incredible hostility; that a man would deliberately plow a crooked furrow is considered insane. Men admire fat, pure-bred stock. Clean fence rows and weedless fields are also admired as "signs of a good farmer." People "who like hounds" consider a well-trained fox or coon hound as very beautiful indeed. Others consider hounds as "just about the ugliest animals God ever thought up." A man said, "You'll notice that everybody here likes something pure-blood and something scrub. People that like pure-bred hounds like scrub stock, but people that like pure-bred stock like scrub dogs."

One hears almost no praise of the beauty of the country, except from a few who have heard from outside sources that hill country is considered picturesque. The word "beautiful" is practically taboo. Once an old man riding with me said of an impressive view, "Them hills ain't hard to look at." Many of those who live "back in the hills," however, have a profound appreciation of the country, its streams, hills, and even its rocks, although they say little about it. Yet with all their disdain for "beauty," people feel a great warmth for their community. They often say, "Anybody that's ever tasted water out of the Apple River will come back to Woodland County."

Colored advertising calendars represent perhaps the highest interest in the graphic arts. Almost no poetry is composed or read except the graveyard poetry, usually copied but sometimes composed, which is often published in the *Beacon* in memory of the dead. The most skillful creative writer in the community is an intelligent backwoods farm wife who is correspondent from her neighborhood for the county paper. She generally adds to her news items each week a short and exaggerated folkloristic satire on "hillbilly ways." The local paper thought them too silly to print until the Largetown daily began printing them. One described a girl's first dance: her escort had a new pocket knife; in dancing barefoot she got splinters in her feet; he removed the splinters with his new knife and she became the envy of all the girls at the party.

An interest in pianos, which replaced many of the older reed organs about 1920, has declined. At about the same time many phonographs were bought, and a taste for records nearly supplanted the older taste for all "old-time" songs except the hymns sung in church. Most of the phonographs have now been turned in on radios or chopped up for kindling wood, and radio broadcasts have somewhat restored the waning prestige of "old-fashioned" hillbilly songs and traditional "ballads." Youngsters sometimes nowadays learn from their grandparents songs which their own parents, when young, ridiculed as "old-fashioned," and several lads play the guitar proficiently. When the old-time fiddlers still living have died, however, there will be no one to take their place.

As for craftsmanship, few handicrafts are left in which people take great pride. Men and women gradually make fewer of the things they wear and use. Men repair implements crudely—bailing wire is their fix-all. (A man said, "Bailin' wire's what holds this whole state together!") Women spend more time in patching worn-out clothing than at quilting, embroidery, tatting, or other "fancy work." Many overalls (and other simple garments) have been patched until "there's more to the patches than there ever was to the overalls." Cars, when washed, are washed to save paint and maintain trade-in value more than for appearance. Most work of repair or restoration has utilitarian value only.

Religion

The number of non-believers in Plainville is surprising. They are
scattered among both broad classes of people; a number of upper-class
non-believers (men) belong to the Christian church, as a matter of
self-advantage or of "good citizenship." ("If it wasn't for churches and

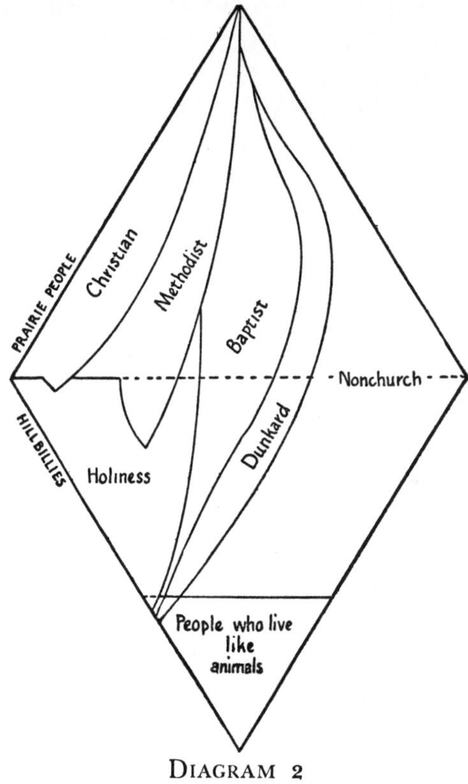

DIAGRAM 2

CHURCH MEMBERSHIP AND "LEANINGS"

schools, land here wouldn't be worth ten cents an acre.") Lower-class
people seem never to "belong to the church" as a conscious matter of
policy. They are generally either emotionally religious or wholly unreligious, and some whole families are unreligious. It is possible to
join the Christian Church but not the Methodist, or Baptist, or Holiness church without preliminary emotional upheaval of conversion. In
the more emotional churches the process of seeking "salvation" is very
painful indeed.

The churches are arranged in an order of social hierarchy (see Diagram 2). The Christian denomination stands highest; the Methodist, next; the Baptist, next; the Church of God (Holiness), lowest. This is the ranking as it appears in the eyes of all "better-class" people and of all non-religious people. The ranking by most Holiness people would be exactly reversed: the vitality of their religion sets their own church highest, since they deny the validity of "worldly" standards of judgment; worship in the Christian Church seems to them so "cold" as hardly to be religion. The same criticisms of the Christian Church are offered by Methodists and Baptists, who however tend to laugh, with the rest of the community, at Holiness people. The Dunkards, who have no town church, stand somewhat apart from the hierarchy.

The Christian Church has not always stood highest. Until about 1925 the Methodist Church was the church of the elite, its leaders comprising three or four upper-class families who owned the Plainville Bank and most of the leading businesses in Plainville. It was replaced in local prestige by a curious set of circumstances. Until shortly before 1925 the "Christians" were a small and unimportant denomination. For a revival, however, they happened to import a preacher who believed that because of cars and improved roads the church of the future must be a community church, attracting members from long distances and furnishing recreation for youth. A building fund was started. A request for money was sent to an ex-Plainviller named Harlow Jackson, who had "made millions in Oklahomy oil." Jackson, motivated by the preacher's ideals, it is said, and also by the memory of how the Methodists had looked down on his family (as members of the Christian Church) in his youth, contributed a large sum of money for the new building, which "made the Methodist church look like a woodshed" (others phrase it more crudely). At the same time, and "on Jackson's money," a Christian bank was also financed to compete with the Methodist bank. The Methodist bank failed, the Methodist aristocracy died off or left Plainville in disgrace, and the new Christian Church triumphed. The Christian bank also expired, but more gracefully. It was merged with the county bank at Discovery without loss to depositors, whose interests were protected at considerable sacrifice by Jackson, the doctor, and another man. The whole spirit of the Methodist Church has changed since the aristocrats left town. It remains more "respectable" than either the

Baptist or the Holiness Church, but it has been over-run by people who prefer the more emotional kind of worshiping. The county agent's wife, a Methodist, complained, "I never did hear people shout in a Methodist church before."

The Christian Church won out in the social-financial competition, but it failed to become the community religious and recreation center that its promoters dreamed. Its main non-religious use is for high school commencement exercises. The Sunday school rooms in the basement are used for classes, but use of the basement for games, young people's parties, etc., for which it was originally intended, is greatly restricted by conservative members.

The Baptist Church is the least active church in Plainville, chiefly because of several very active rural Baptist churches in the trade area. The preacher who conducts services once a month in Plainville preaches to larger rural congregations on the other three weekends of the month than in Plainville. His revival meetings are also more successful in the rural communities, where he sometimes "saves" as many as twenty-five or thirty people during the course of one revival series.

Holiness people, as no other congregation in Plainville, have a strictly "seven-day-a-week religion." The members try to "live out every day" what they hear preached in church on Sunday. They think of the Christian Church especially as a "Sunday religion." Indeed the Christian services are never "hot" like Holiness services. Baptist and Methodist services are nearly as emotional during revivals, but not at "regular preachings." Only the Holiness people meet frequently, in each other's homes, to pray over the sick (they believe that only prayer, not medicine, can cure); all their social life is permeated by religious conversation and prayer; theirs is the only congregation practicing material charity for their poor; and their mutual helpfulness in everyday life exceeds that of all other Plainvillers. Their church, in short, may be said to represent a "nativistic" religious movement which rejects the worldly standards of the outside world and attempts to restore the waning pioneer virtues of rural "neighborliness."

It is difficult to know whether or not hysterical and emotional behavior is decreasing or increasing in Plainville churches. Some say there is more shouting now than ten years ago. Others say that there was little shouting until the last seven or eight years. In regard to the ebb and flow of local interest in religion, one man said, "When people have two or three good crop years, they begin backsliding. When they have several crop failures in a row, they come crawling on their bellies back to church."

Only the Christian preacher is relatively well paid. He gets $30 a weekend at Plainville and nearly as much for his weekend services in other communities. With fees for weddings and funerals, he receives $1,500–$1,800 a year. The Baptist preacher is paid $10 a weekend. For this he preaches at Plainville three sermons: one on Saturday night and two Sunday sermons. At one or two of his rural churches he preaches an additional sermon on Saturday morning. Gifts for preaching funerals and performing weddings do not pay for the gasoline it takes to drive to the funerals. Much of his income goes for gasoline. One church is twenty-five miles from his home; this means a hundred miles of driving unless he stays over night with one of the brethren. Fees and offerings at revival services augment his income somewhat. His main income, however, comes from farming.

The Holiness preacher receives in money only collections. These amount to little because the Holiness Church is a gathering place of the poor. In times of stress Holiness men sometimes make up work parties to cut corn or do other work on their preacher's farm.

An important feature of the church is the revival. The Baptist Church holds two revivals nearly every year; the Holiness Church sometimes holds several. The Christian and Methodist churches ordinarily hold one each. Each revival lasts for about a fortnight, with nightly services and occasionally morning sermons too.[24] Sometimes it lasts longer if conversions are coming in fast toward the end, or if it is felt that a few more sessions might "bring through" a few mourners who are "having a hard time." Attendance at these meetings is not limited to members of the sect holding them. Religious people (and others, for various motives, including a desire to "have a good laugh") go to all the revival meetings in town. The main revival season begins at about the end of the haying season and lasts until well into the fall, that is, from about August 1 to late October. The Baptist preacher

---

24 The Methodist "evangelist" in September, 1939, railed in the pulpit against the superintendent of schools for not dismissing school for daily morning revival services. "I'm not *against* education," he preached, "but I'm *for* God. If the people in this community was interested in the souls of their childern, they'd have 'em here in church." He also railed against farmers who worked in their fields during those "preaching mornings." "God wants 'em to save their souls more'n he wants 'em to cut corn."

probably preaches revival sermons a hundred nights a year, counting all his rural churches.

Many revival sermons are utterly incoherent. The following excerpt from a Holiness sermon is a typical exhortation:

There are ninety-six known anti-Christs now in the United States. One of them is Father X in New York City . . . I am going to spend my first five thousand years in heaven just a-listenin' to the angels sing . . . I have sympathy for the godless. I am agin the things they do but I have sympathy for them . . . The sins of the people in this town—it's enough to run a man wild . . . Some people may be ashamed to come up here [to the mourner's bench] because they're afraid some women will laugh at them, but a woman never turned a man down for being saved . . . The devil says to people, "Sow your wild oats, have a good time, and then settle down" . . . Any woman you see suckin' on a cigarette wouldn't make any decent companion [wife]. It's divorces that's ruining this country . . . Why ain't they been any souls saved at this meeting? It's the cold hearts of the people here . . . Father, truly I'm sanctified, Father, tonight. [Here the speaker in shirt sleeves was punctuating his speech by stamping his feet] . . . See, God, I am trying to show 'em, God, the error of their ways, God. . .

Another passage of the sermon went:

Open your heart and let God in! I am sanctified, tonight, God; and I pity the people that don't know the love of God! This town is full of beer jints and ain't fit for a decent man to live in or take a decent woman down the street.

The words vary but are always rhythmic, and always stress the ideas of an inspirational acceptance of the spirit of God, the terror of hellfire, and strong condemnation of "the sins of this community." The "sins" most commonly attacked are card-playing, drinking, the sale of beer and whiskey, car-riding, cigarette-smoking by women, failure to attend church, and "cold hearts that will not let God in." From afar also the "sins of the cities" are condemned: dancing, red-light districts and "white-slavery," and the "lures and temptations held out for the young." The "going away of our youth" is sometimes attributed, not to economic necessity, but to the "sinful call of the cities" or as "a punishment to parents for not bringing up their children right." Education beyond "what it takes to read and understand the Bible," is often attacked. Holiness preachers attack also with special vigor (for women) bobbed hair, cosmetics, showy clothes, and short skirts; and (for men) tobacco, evil thoughts and language, and sometimes neckties. An odd Holiness taboo is that pop must not be drunk out of a bottle but must be poured out into a glass first. The positive exhortations in sermons are: to "open your heart and let God in"; to "feel the burden of your sins and repent before it is too late"; to "know the greater joy of living with God in your heart than living with the devil there," etc. "Salvation" occurs when one "knows that God has entered" one's heart; at this time the "burden of past sin" rolls away and the convert "knows that he is saved."

Various mental states can precede the revelation of grace, or conversion, depending somewhat on the church and the age of the convert. The most common pre-conversion feelings described were of bearing a great "burden of sin" (the "feeling of a lost condition"), fear of hell, and fear of "death without a promise." Most children in religious families join the church between the ages of twelve and fourteen. Pressure from kin, preachers, and congregation stimulates the required "feeling of sin" at the proper age, and young people are generally "saved" at a revival meeting after appropriate mourning and prayer. People remember the "burden of sin" but few remember any definite sins that burdened them, as children, before conversion.

A good many adults, however, are saved, either for the first time or after backsliding from a previous conversion or conversions. A sickness often precedes adult conversion. One man (Holiness) said that during a long illness he was delirious; he dreamed of seeing Hell as a lake of fire "with just the arms and legs of people sticking out." "I decided right then," he said, "that if I ever got up again I was a-goin' to be saved and not go there. And I was. I'm a changed man." [25] Another (rural Baptist) said, "I joined the church so's my children would be brought up in the church." He (oddly) did not, and does not, believe in the Bible as "anything more than history and morals," though he prayed at the mourner's bench, felt the burden of sin roll away, and has "felt better ever since. When I got saved I felt good all over." The ordeal of conversion is often a device for cutting across status lines. A man who has been considered worthless as a worker, sexually immoral, or dishonest financially can through salvation gain social acceptance by the religious sector of his own class. The road is difficult

[25] The "changes" he listed were these: The Lord delivered him, in turn, from (1) "gittin' mad at people and wantin' to fight 'em ever' few minutes," (2) "wantin' to tell an' listen to them dirty rotten stories they tell in the Garage," (3) "needin' tobacco," and (4) "wantin' to wear a necktie."

however, for a man of the "lower element," who must give up many warm associations and bear the contempt of his old associates for "backslidin' into the church."

A few people are converted repeatedly. Sometimes repeated conversions are the result of repeated backslidings—sometimes they result from the search among the churches for "the truest faith," or the "true baptism." Poorer people are more often converted repeatedly than wealthier people, women oftener than men.

The method of baptism is still a point of concern among the churches, though less so than some years ago, when the "wrong kind of baptism" was considered tantamount to damnation. Christians, Baptists, and Dunkards practice total immersion (Dunkards immerse three times); Methodists ordinarily "sprinkle." An interesting point about outdoor baptisms is that they are performed at any season, even if ice has to be broken from the river. "Nobody ever heard of any one catchin' cold from bein' baptized."

It is difficult in a few words to assess fairly the role of churches in Plainville life. Not even in the Christian Church, which remains proudly aloof from the emotionalism that marks the others, are discussed any problems of economics, ethics, or human relationships that actually face the community. The real resident "reformers" (county agent, vocational agriculture teacher, etc.) all go to church as a way of keeping "in" with the community, but not one of them would dream of attempting to make of any church (or preacher) an instrument or ally of their work. One of them said of the churches, "They control everything. Nothing can be taught in school because the religious people would rise up in wrath. They control all conduct and prevent all progress. But they provide a social center, especially for women."

Many natives share or partly share his feeling. A retired Methodist preacher said, "The Church does nothing. It's bound to a formula; there's no inspiration to do anything except increase the membership. It's just an insurance policy for the old, and a gossip center. Oh, I guess they try to save souls, but even preachers aren't agreed on personal survival any more." An old man (and non-believer) said, "If it wasn't for the churches real estate would be worthless, and we'd all be like the animals."

In the eyes of more emotional religious people, however, the church is the instrument of neighborliness and mutual help on earth and the avenue to eternal salvation, which is worth more than pearls and rubies or "all the education that money can buy."

Birth to Death

Birth may be the result of desire for a child, of "ignorance," or of "pure carelessness." Few people are ignorant of contraception, a matter which apparently may be practiced freely, though people "do not like to speak about it." Most pregnant women are embarrassed at being seen on the street; women are criticized for appearing publicly "in that condition." There is a large and waning folklore about prenatal influence but few women are now "careful" about such hazards. A pregnant woman however should not "work real hard" right up to the last; she should not wash or iron, for example, during the last week or two of pregnancy. The mores prescribe that intercourse between the parents should stop two or three months before the child is born, but people say that it often continues until two or three days before the birth. Restraint is ordinarily phrased as for the protection of the mother, though two or three informants thought that intercourse continued too late induces abnormal sexual traits in the child. Intercourse should not be resumed until the mother is "well" again. Traditionally a woman leaves her bed on the seventh or ninth day after childbirth, but many "rest" longer nowadays. As for the proper interim between births, fifteen months were formerly thought adequate. Now two or three years are considered better.

A Plainville baby may be born in a Largetown hospital, or may be born in a hill shack without any attendance whatever. The doctor officiates at most births, which take place in the mother's home. Usually a neighbor woman or kinswoman is also present to help the doctor. Up to twenty-five years ago many births were attended only by a midwife, or "granny-woman." In those days granny-women often practiced as general "curers," and as such were sometimes called "witches." The afterbirth is simply buried or burned.

Every one denied that an older child is ever jealous of a new baby. The very idea seemed nonsensical and rather shocking. People were familiar enough with situations of jealousy between older children, especially grown children (over, for example, continued parental favoritism toward one child, or an inheritance), but "Everyone loves a baby!" All older children, they say, love a new baby and are proud of their responsibility in helping in its care.

Children are named without ceremony, ordinarily immediately after birth. Alternative names, male and female, have generally been decided on in advance. Occasionally there is a delay in selecting a name and there have been rare cases of waiting for a child to select its own name. Until a child is named, it is called, "Baby."

There have been many vogues in the selection of names. For males, biblical names (like Abraham, Isaiah, etc.) have died out with the very old. Many old men now living bear conventional names like Bob (Robert), Bill (William) and John (the favorite name); younger men have similar names or names like Alva, Oral, Merle, Delbert, Hobart, Cecil, Byron, Omer, Homer, etc.

Most people hope for a boy as a first child. This possibly reflects the fact that boys were once a great economic asset in farming. Their labor was valuable from about the age of nine until they married or reached "twenty-one." A girl as first-born is, however, welcomed with the same love a boy would have received. The ideal family today is considered to be a father, a mother and perhaps two children (a boy and a girl). The father should ideally be a year or a few years older than the mother, the son a year or two older than the daughter. Larger families (of four to six children) are also admired, "when people can take care of them." Poorer people are condemned and ridiculed for having many children: poverty, backwoodsiness, and "a pack of hounds and ignorant children" are associated together in the minds of "better-class people." An "only child" is pitied: "only children most always grow up selfish. They don't learn how to give and take."

Parents never admit favoritism toward one child over another, though many are accused of favoritism by neighbors or by a child (usually in retrospect, after growing up). Actually, favored children, when they exist, are generally youngest children, very rarely the eldest. Several factors conduce toward favoring a youngest child. First, the older children, as partial caretakers, filling an imperfectly defined role as siblings and substitute disciplinarians, have a hand in "spoiling" him; second, younger children are in general much less strictly disciplined than older children; and third, the youngest child comes to be especially cherished by parents because he generally remains at home after the older children have married. The second point is a matter of agreement and frequent comment in Plainville. "They certainly don't make him mind the way I had to. . . . People are always easiest on the younger children."

There is as much variation in routines for babies as there is in the rest of Plainville life and technology. Some babies are "raised by the book," others by old or hit-and-miss methods, others by every conceivable combination of granny-lore and modern methods of child care.

Babies are breast-fed. According to a woman informant, there had been only two or three bottle babies in the community since she moved there four years ago, except her own two, whom she was raising "scientifically" in every respect, under the guidance of a Largetown pediatrician. This was unique for Plainville; her healthy children were admired but rather pitied, for having received somewhat too little "attention." It was thought especially strange that she had no rocking chair, to "sit in and rock her babies." An interesting fact in connection with "bottle babies" is that with the bottle comes the whole complex of modern child training: the food formula, its heating to proper temperature, and regular times for feeding, play, sleep, and affection. The average baby is nursed whenever it wants food, sleeps in bed with its mother and father, and tugs at the mother's breast at will during the night. Whenever it cries it is lifted up, cuddled, and carried.

Weaning in the old days was done at almost any time from age one to age six or seven. Only the youngest or only child was generally allowed the late weaning. Sometimes a child was weaned just before starting to school, at age six, so it wouldn't "cry for its dinner" in school. Children weaned before age two or three were weaned so young to allow the mother to "dry up" a few months before its successor came. Since pregnancy often occurred quite soon after the last child's birth, most children were weaned during their second year. An older child seldom had access to the breast after a younger child was born.

Children who "nursed late" were of course ridiculed, and folkloristic anecdotes are told about them. It was told in front of one man who had been a "late weaner" that once when he was seven years old he became very hungry while visitors were in his house. He sulked and whined for awhile behind a door. Then suddenly he popped his head out, swore, and said, "Maw, I want to suck." He was asked, "Did you really say that, Willie?" He replied, "I guess I did. They say I did." It is told of an old-time and successful doctor (now dead) that when his little girl reached school age, he moved near the school, so that she might run home two or three times a day to be nursed. Such stories are told to illustrate the "ignorance of people in them old days."

The nursing period for almost all children has been shortened to between twelve and twenty-four months, despite the fact that the old pressure has largely ended for weaning one child to make way for the next one. The actual weaning ordinarily follows a gradual introduction of other foods, which begins quite early. When the child is seven or eight months old, the mother begins to offer it food from the table, where she sits holding the baby at meal times. She gives it sips of milk from a glass, tastes of gravy, potatoes and other vegetables, and sometimes meat, often pre-chewing the harder foods herself. A man said, "The first thing we used to give our'n was som'p'n soft to chew on that we knowed wouldn't hurt 'em, like a little fat hog meat." Finally the child is taken from the breast entirely. It is usually allowed to suck at night later than in the daytime because it sleeps with its parents. Sometimes, by an old and now rare practice, "sugar tits"—cloth teats filled with butter and sugar—are given to a child, but the standard use of pacifiers is to assist infants in teething. No form of bodily self-play is ever induced to quiet a child during the ordeal of weaning. Thumb-sucking by infants is sometimes not immediately discouraged, but efforts are always made to shame larger children out of the habit if it persists. They are told that the thumb won't grow, or that *they* won't grow. Other aids toward weaning an unwilling child are blackening the breast with stove soot or rubbing quinine on it, to arouse distaste. (Thumb-sucking is also often discouraged by the same means.) Bantering and shaming techniques, especially shaming, are particularly effective because weaning is often completed at an age late enough for the child to understand conversation. If a child with a smaller sibling still wants to nurse he is told that the breast is for his little sister or brother. "The baby needs that, and you can eat potatoes like mother and daddy . . . You'd be ashamed to be a little baby . . . A great big boy like you don't want to suck!"

Sphincter control is introduced, except by the most "modern" people, when the child can understand through language what is expected of it. One mother said that when each child was about two years old, she would take it to the outhouse with her, sit down on one hole herself and set the child on the other. She would grunt and induce the child to imitate her, waiting beside it until the movement took place. Then she would praise the child. "I reasoned with my children more than I ever punished them," she said.

The vocational agriculture teacher's wife decided, because eating causes peristalsis, to set her children on their pot and serve them their meals there once a day. She also by grunting induced them to grunt, urged them "to try hard," approved when they succeeded and shamed or scolded them for being "little" when they failed. Many children are severely scolded for "making a mistake" after sphincter control is initiated, and some are spanked harshly. Mothers do not seem to believe that any special problems are ordinarily encountered in teaching sphincter control to their children, full control being usually established at about the age of two or two and a half, but not before. Urethral control meets apparently with more difficulties, since a considerable number of large children and grown people are known as bed-wetters. They suffer a great deal of shame from their "failing."

The differential treatment of children according to sex begins very young. Little boys, it is thought, are "just naturally different from little girls," and the supposed and expected differences are encouraged and enhanced "in the cradle" (cradles, by the way, are no longer used). Boy babies, as "naturally stronger," are offered fingers to lift themselves up by earlier than girl babies; girl babies are admired as "pretty," oftener than boy babies. Girl babies are "dolls"; boy babies are "little men." Girl babies are often dressed "prettier" than boys; men like to see their sons dressed in blue-denim overalls as soon as they can walk. This differential treatment applies in every department of a child's life. Its purpose is to establish very early separate sets of behavior habits for boys and girls—habits which have to do with clothing, work, morality, and personality—especially with the development of aggressiveness and domination in boys, and with passivity and submissiveness in girls. Such patterns breed in boys feelings of their own superiority and of contempt for girls and women. These mores hold, with certain exceptions, for all classes. Boys and girls are treated "equally," however, in one important respect. From both is "expected" (though not always obtained) implicit obedience to the will of their parents. All children are supposed to "obey" without question, yet even here there is a difference: a boy is often spoken of as having a spirit like that of a colt, which must be broken to obedience as a colt is broken; girls are "naturally willing" to obey.

In most families siblings of opposite sex (and sometimes, in prudish families, sisters also, but never brothers) are taught not to undress in front of each other as soon as they are old enough to change their own clothes. They are not separated earlier as a matter of convenience for the mother. As they begin learning to dress themselves the mother begins to inculcate the principles of modesty by backing one child out of sight of the other behind a stove, a chair or some other piece of furniture, or off into another room. Children begin to try to undress and dress themselves at about two years of age, but they do not often become fully competent at the task before about age five. Yet with all this early stress on modesty, the mother frequently bathes children of the opposite sex together in the same tub until they are four or even five years old. Here, however, she is faced with a problem of efficiency, since water has to be carried in from the well and heated on the stove. She is more apt to bathe her children in turn, using the same water; if she follows this plan she is likely to bathe the larger children (or else the girls) first, the smaller children (or the boys) last.

Modesty is often carried to extreme ends of squeamishness. Two grown sisters living in town who share a room and the same bed were said by a neighbor woman never to undress for bed at the same time "without either turning out the light or setting up a screen between them." Many husbands and wives are said never to have seen each other undressed.

There is a great deal of variation in standards of modesty according to class. Two or three upper-class families make a "modern" point of teaching their children not to be prudish regarding nakedness, either their own or that of their parents. Certain "lower-element" families are said to be completely lacking in "modesty": "They think nothing of nakedness . . . A girl will show her brother her body and she can see his . . . The men and boys cuss right in the house and girls cuss and tell smutty stories just like boys and in front of boys." Among Holiness and other lower-class religious families, however, the taboos of modesty are intensified, like other moral taboos. It should be said regarding non-religious and even anti-religious people of any class that there is no necessary correlation between lack of religion and failure to observe and sanction the community's moral taboos. Many non-religious people are "just as moral as anybody."

Techniques of securing obedience are whipping, spanking, shaming, teasing, scolding, nagging, threats, privations, rewards, encouragements, demonstrativeness, and affection. For whipping, razor straps are sometimes used, but hickory or willow switches are more common. A "touching up" with a "peach-tree stick" is not much dreaded. A whipping is also called a "licking," a severe whipping a "larruping" or a "hiding." Spanking is with the hand, on the bottom, legs, or arms. There are also slapping, ear-boxing, ear-pulling, head-thumping with knuckles or thimble, hair-pulling, and several other formal methods of physical chastisement.

There are differences of opinion about the amount of corporal punishment children should receive, and about how and by whom it should be administered. A "reasonable amount" of whipping is recommended and practiced by most parents, especially on boys, but children "should not be whipped till the blood comes or every day like they used to be." The average boy gets perhaps a dozen or two actual "lickings" during his childhood (he is seldom whipped after the age of twelve or fourteen); the average girl gets less; some children get "one a day" or "one a week," some get none. The idea is not uncommon that a parent should not punish a child while he is angry, but this restraint is not always observed.

Teasing, kidding, and shaming, alone or in combination, are among the most effective means of molding a child to the pattern desired in the community. A child is ordinarily shamed on the grounds that it is not living up to the standard expected of its sex or its size or its age. Girls are told that they are supposed to be modest and not act like little boys. Boys are reminded that as boys they are supposed to be able to *do* things, and not act like girls or much smaller boys.

Common privations for disobedience are keeping children indoors from play, or at home from play with other children; or depriving them of a trip to town, or of some desirable food (cake, candy, or an ice-cream cone). Threats of privation, however, are much more frequent than the privations themselves. Plainville children are never "sent to bed without their supper" or "locked up in a dark closet," but many are threatened with the "bugger-man" who "lives outside in the dark" to punish or "git" bad children. Most children develop a fear of the dark.

In regard to teasing and kidding, fathers so often tease and kid children as a mere pastime, that the child sometimes becomes confused about just what is expected of it.

Some mothers are supposed to be more severe than fathers with children, but most children regard their mothers as some measure of protection against severe punishment from fathers. They do not ordinarily mistake for more than a threat the mother's frequent threat, "If you don't obey me now I'll ask your father to punish you when he comes in from the field." The majority of mothers do their own punishing, and the father his own. A father generally gets quicker obedience from a child than its mother does because—though he actually has much less role than the mother in rearing and disciplining the child—punishment from him when it occurs is more sudden, sure, and severe. He is less apt to "threaten first," and he will stand less argument or "back-talk." That many mothers will plead, cajole, nag, urge, and threaten, but not often actually punish a child above seven or eight years old, is a fact so well understood by most children that as a form of sport they often deliberately arouse the whole process "just to see how far they can go." When a mother does actually carry out her threat of reporting a child's misdeeds to the father, the latter ordinarily hears out from her (sometimes with denials or counter accusations from the child) the details of the case before executing punishment. So many variations in the disciplinary system are possible and occur in this community, that it is impossible to describe them all. Of one family with many children living in town, it is said, "Whatever either parent tells one of them childern to do, you know that the child is gonna do some other thing."

It can perhaps be said however that while the father stands in the background as a final judge and power—and for boys an ideal of male competence and superiority which they are urged to imitate—the main tutelary and executive power is the mother. Her authority is in many ways a reflection of the father's position as "lord and master." [26] In her role as an "obedient and dutiful" wife she inculcates in young children the ideals of goodness, obedience, and all good conduct. Most men will say, "I leave all this (that is, discipline and early instruction) up to my wife." The situation is altered for boys when they start "follering" the father about his work; and for both sexes when they start to school.

Not all of the whole "socialization" process, of course, is in the hands of mothers and fathers. The school, Sunday school, play groups, older children, and adults outside the family all have a hand in it.

[26] Dr. Kardiner is to be credited with part of the phrasing and meaning of this and the preceding sentence.

A listing of what children "learn" and where they learn it would fill several books. The formulation of personality, especially the personality of boys, begins very early to pass out of the hands of the mother. Fathers or older brothers teach the male agricultural techniques. From brothers, neighbor boys, and other males, including adult males in a rising series of narrow age grades—not only "welcoming" him as he rises from one to the next, but reaching downward to influence him, both directly and through the intervening age-groups—the growing boy learns gradually a great number of things that he is "supposed to know." From much of this his mother and often also his father would gladly protect him. She would spare him the teasing from older males, which begins very early to teach him combativeness and aggression. She would later spare him the rough and dangerous play and "dirty talk" of boys' gangs, and still later his "wild oats" period. If he follows her recommendations, however, and rejects those of his male companions, he will be a "sissy."

In regard to girls there is less conflict between the home (or mother) and the society. The girls' "gangs," for example, are only a weak imitation of boys' gangs. The girl, in growing up, must learn finally to pass from a situation under her mother to one resembling her mother's. All the techniques and ideals learned from her mother will apply in the new situation. She can, and often does, make the whole transition from infancy to "a home of her own," without serious inner conflict. The growing male however must learn, as a fairy tale writer phrased it, that "the world is not like what one's mother says, but what the neighbors say." In league to prevent his learning this are his mother and other women, the church, his schoolteachers, all "genteel" and "respectable" forms, stated ideals and rituals in the community, and usually the "spoken word" of his father. In league to teach him, are the older boys and men, gossip, actual observation of social behavior, and often the tacit connivance of his father. He must learn all that he is supposed to, "sow a few wild oats" without acquiring any fixed bad habits, and finally break away from the domination of his parents and settle down into a new situation, either "outside" or in his home community, where *he* is dominant in at least a matrimonial situation. To attain full adult status he must finally subscribe anew, ostensibly at least, to the fictions of "respectability" which overlie the bringing up of the next generation.

The earliest work techniques are taught by the mother; little boys and girls first learn simple chores: they fetch objects, bring in chips and cobs for kindling, and, later, carry in wood, at first a stick at a time. Children "like to help." They "want to do." They "help mother" gather in the eggs, feed and water the chickens, etc. Their play often imitates such tasks, and later ones. They also follow their father and "help him at his work," the boys more often than girls.

By age six to nine, girls can dry the dishes; a little later they can wash them. Boys also learn to dry and wash dishes, but "they don't like to." It is girls' and women's work. Girls often begin to sew at about the same age; a little later to sweep and dust, to make the beds and sometimes to cook. Many girls, however, do not learn to cook until much later. Real gardening work begins for both sexes at nine to ten.

Boys begin to milk at ten to twelve. Girls sometimes do too, though milking is "men's work." At about the same age boys learn to split and chop wood, carry in the water, assume responsibility for "barn chores" like feeding, and begin to work in the field. Few girls learn to do these men's tasks, except for carrying water into the house. Yet girls do not scorn "men's tasks" as boys scorn dishwashing, sweeping, and bed-making, nor would they be ashamed to do them. Many girls envy boys their work, their greater mobility of action, and their future roles. No boy ever says, "I wish I was a girl." Fathers and brothers are criticized who let women and girls do "heavy work."

Many girls are fully competent to take care of a home (including the mothering of smaller children) by the time they are eleven.

Many boys are fully competent to do all but the heaviest of field work at the same age. Boys learn first to drive a team, then, in turn, to harrow, plow, ride a rake, cultivate corn, ride a mower. Hay pitching and other tasks require greater strength. The order of learning is shifted somewhat on tractor-run farms, but the average boy knows from observation very early how a tractor or a car is operated and boys are often allowed to handle gasoline-run machinery as early as at age eleven. Teaching is by the father: the boy "begs" and is encouraged to learn. To learn how to handle team-operated implements, he first follows the father; he then "takes the lines" himself; he next is allowed to harrow or plow a round by himself; finally he is able to "make a full-time hand."

From now on, in the old days, he would have made a full-time hand in the fields. Any schooling he got would have been when he was not needed at home. Compulsory schooling now begins at age six, and boys and girls alike must attend school, theoretically until they are fourteen or until they have "passed the eighth grade." Most better-class children and many lower-class children now attend the high school in Plainville. Thus "the work their parents get out of them" is mostly limited to "before and after school," Saturdays, and the twenty summer weeks of school vacation. They perform many labors during these times.

The school is a new disciplinary institution. A teacher, like a parent, can "whip," despite a state law against corporal punishment. In the school, by processes bearing little resemblance to the state syllabus, most children are somehow taught the rudiments of reading, writing, and figuring. A more important aspect of schooling, however, is that the child is drawn partially away from the "mother's apron strings" and begins long periods of contact with more children than he has been accustomed to playing with before. All the children in a neighborhood are gathered into a rural school; many from a wide area into the consolidated school. In either case the children are thrown together by age, regardless of sex, for classes; outside of classes the boys play mostly with boys, the girls with girls.

The social organization of children, even in a small rural school, is extremely complex and discriminatory. One important division is of boys against girls. Girls "like to play with boys," and "want to know what boys know," but boys admit them only discretely into their games and counsels. Boys tease girls and profess disregard for them. Boys say, "Girls are a nuisance." "If a girl tags along or bothers, twist her arm and get rid of her."

But this is not the only important division or discrimination. An older boy is greatly superior to a younger one in strength, skills, and valuable knowledge. The age lines between boys are very narrowly drawn. Younger boys desire acceptance by older boys; older boys admit younger boys to their society only when they are "useful," for games, for teasing, and as an audience for the ostentation of superior knowledge. Considerable cruelty is practiced by older boys on a younger boy: they attempt to shame, tease, or torture out of him any weakness, fear, or other "babylike" quality he manifests. A boy becomes aligned most closely with the group of boys whose ages are within a year or two of his own. Such alignments, while in many ways exclusive, are also simultaneous: an eight-year-old boy who is a leader in his age-group is simultaneously often an underling among the eight to ten-year-olds. From these he collects as a tolerated spectator or as an object of condescending enlightenment, habits, attitudes, information, and misinformation, which he passes on to the awestruck members of his younger group. The main process of male socialization takes place in this fashion. The male traits and "knowledge" are passed down and inculcated, from age-group to age-group. This is one of the main social functions of the boys' gangs and age-groups.

Something similar but weaker happens among girls. Among girls however the teasing patterns are negligibly evident. Girls are "taught to be nice" to younger girls; this fits in with the doll pattern, with the ultimate roles of girls as mothers, and with the single developmental line followed by female lives.

From boys, boys learn "not to be a sissy." They learn to hammer, whittle, make pop guns and sling shots, fly a kite, shoot a gun, hunt, fish, swim, skate, and play many approved games. A country boy is also supposed to "learn the timber"—to know where all the wild foods grow, the names of snakes, birds, trees, and vines, and the habits of wild animals and birds. He is no longer, however, "really supposed" to accumulate much nature lore, though his father did.

A boy learns from other boys how to fight—to "hold his own," at least. He need not know as much about fighting as his male forebears did, because fighting, especially fighting among men but also even "real fighting" among boys, is beginning to be disapproved in the community.

From other boys he learns a great number of "dangerous" or "outlaw" traits—these are the traits his mother especially disapproves. Teasing or torturing girls or smaller boys is one of them, as is cruelty to any form of life, but he plucks the wings from horseflies and tosses them into the air to hear them buzz. He kills every snake he finds (this is approved). He climbs trees, jumps off barns, takes risks. He learns to "break things" and "destroy things" ("boys are just naturally destructive"); to have contempt for bathing and the cleanliness of girls and women. He learns to cuss and "talk dirty." He "learns about sex" from boys. He learns "how to steal watermelons from patches and fruit from trees." Prestige accrues to him among boys for learning the outlaw traits along with "useful knowledge." The outlaw traits are only feebly developed in girls' gangs.

Sex education for Plainville boys is largely left up to nature and, tacitly, to other boys. Sex is a subject which neither mothers nor fathers "feel they could discuss" with their sons. Parents teach small children no facts about childbirth. When a new baby is expected, the other children are generally bundled off to neighbors. They may be told that mother is "not feeling well." They are supposed to be greatly surprised to see a new baby when they return home. About it they are told one of the customary myths: the doctor brought it, the stork brought it, Mother found it in the grass, or Daddy found it in the orchard. Only very young children, however, subscribe to these myths. The average six-year-old child has frequently observed intercourse of animals (boys especially—it is easier to protect girls from such sights), and most of them have witnessed the births of kittens, puppies, pigs, calves, or colts. They have asked questions, first of their parents, whose hush-hush dissemblings have indicated that these are no proper subjects for adult-child discussions; later they have learned from other children a body of information in the main correct, though some garbling naturally occurs as taboo knowledge is circulated downward through the age-groups. The average seven- or eight-year-old child has integrated fairly accurately what he has seen and what he has learned from other children.

The curious thing is the total lack of realism with which fathers face the problem of instructing their boys about sex. Either they tell them nothing whatever, or they tell fifteen- or sixteen-year-old boys that masturbation will cause insanity or other sickness. A boy has probably already heard this story from other boys as a discredited myth which adults either believe or wish youngsters to believe, but it still frightens him. At about the same time the father is likely to become less guarded in front of his son; he may tell a smutty story to him or before him, or relate sexual gossip, as a form of "treating him more like a man."

Mothers (or older sisters), on the other hand, generally tell girls about menstruation before it occurs, and sometimes they tell girls "about men" before marriage. At one time, however, according to several women, "Girls were told absolutely nothing. That was considered the duty of their husbands." Menstruation is a fearfully taboo subject. Women do not like to say the word even to each other; they prefer euphemisms like "that way," "not feeling well," "indisposed," or "in that sickly way."

What all this taboo on sex actually means is difficult to say. It is undoubtedly related to the fact that sexual relations between husband and wife are said to be frequently unsatisfactory. A common complaint about marriage relations is that "the old man likes sex but the old lady don't." Many people say that the majority of women are frigid.

To return to childhood, boys are ordinarily "taught," at about age ten or twelve, by slightly older boys to perform their first "sexual" experiments. Masturbation seems sometimes to become a featured activity, in addition to hunting, swimming, fishing and "roaming the timber" together, of boys' gang life. Several men told of such, though they "had never mentioned such things to anybody else in their whole life." One man told how his "club" used to sit on a log after swimming and masturbate at the same time. The point of competition was speed. This early sex experimentation is carefully concealed from parents and all other elders; children, if caught, expect severe punishment. Grown men, however, in recalling it, seem generally to regard it as rather harmless, or as they say, "just natural." After puberty, masturbation is practiced in solitude.

Actual sex experience, when it precedes marriage, very seldom occurs at an age younger than seventeen or eighteen years. The stated ideals are the same for boys as for girls: chastity until monogamous marriage. So much restraint, however, is hardly expected from boys; what is expected is enough secrecy to avoid gossip or family scandal. A boy is tacitly expected to acquire a limited sexual experience before marriage, as he experiments with drinking and "running around." All such "outlaw traits" are associated with "sowing his wild oats." It is better if he sows his wild oats outside the community if possible, and Plainville boys sometimes pick up girls or occasionally patronize prostitutes in towns as far away as Largetown. A girl who sows any wild oats, at home or abroad, is disgraced, and her parents are disgraced. But a "disgraced" girl, even if she becomes pregnant, is accepted again into the community when she gets married, after "the talk has had time to die down."

The courtship system is only remotely connected to the data just given. Courtship grows out of the conventional and approved "dating" relationships between youths and girls, and it is directed first toward entertainment and later toward marriage, "settling down," and attaining full adult status. Sexual play in conventional courtship does not go beyond kissing or simple "necking," because courtship is between social equals. Parents are very careful of the "company" their children "keep." Class lines may not be crossed in approved dating, courtship, or marriage. Dating begins at age fourteen to seventeen; the age depends on a child's maturity and on parental consent—and, for boys, on when they are allowed use of the car. Couples used to go places together afoot and on horseback and a little later in buggies. Now no boy can hope for a date unless he has access to a car. Double-dating is popular until "a couple gets really serious"; money is scarce and it costs money for car-rides and trips "outside" to movies —the two chief pastimes for dating couples. The situation regarding dating in Plainville high school somewhat resembles that in any typical American coeducational college. The majority of both sexes (even barring very young or small children) have no dates. Fewer girls than boys have dates. The few "popular" girls are sought after by many boys; about fifty percent of the boys who are old enough to date compete for about ten percent of the girls. How both sexes finally resolve the problem of personal choice and decide to pair off and get married is a mystery, but they do. Almost no Plainvillers fail to get married. The thirty-four "surplus women" in Plainville are nearly all widows; only three or four are old maids. The situation in the country is similar. Yet a mate is considered hard to get for a woman; easy, for a man.

A further point should be made about the social organization of youth and the class system. The restriction against cross-class dating has been mentioned. If a better-class boy dated a lower-class religious girl, his family would only be greatly disturbed and fearful of a possible alliance with the girl's family; if he dated a "lower-element" girl, they would be ashamed and scandalized, because "everybody would know what he was after." For an upper-class girl to date a lower-class boy would be inconceivable. All children are obliged to learn complex rules regarding their proper relationship with socially inferior or superior children. For young boys at school together there are almost no restrictions, though their parents "teach them the difference." In later childhood boys of almost any class can play, hunt, swim, etc., together, visit each other and even "stay all night" together. A preacher's son on vacation from college spent one of his first nights at home "noodling" (illegally) for spawning catfish on the Apple River, together with two "absolutely lower-element" brothers (named Billings) from a neighboring farm. The fathers of these boys also "neighbor," exchange work or tools, chat at the line fence, or visit each other for an hour or two indoors, ostensibly as equals. The two mothers draw a sharper line. They "treat each other with respect," but they would visit only in case of serious sickness or need. The preacher's daughters were not allowed to play with the Billings girls above the age of about eight. If his oldest daughter (of dating age) meets a Billings boy in town, she greets him courteously but with constraint. The high school and the car have leveled the older important social distinctions between "town people" and "country people," but they have not lessened the distinctions between classes.

Boys generally marry at about age twenty to twenty-two, girls slightly younger. To marry, a boy should "by rights" have an established means of livelihood, but many "marry first and then figger out how to make a living." Local economic opportunities have already been described.

To suggest how a young man has attained enough knowledge of economic procedure to risk starting a new family, I must go back a number of years. At fifteen or earlier the farm boy was equipped with all the skills and techniques for making a living, except the skill of "managing." When not in school he did a man's work. In fact one of the first important blows to his self-esteem and happiness probably came about then with his discovery that through his own eagerness to learn he had been jockeyed into doing a man's work without gaining any voice in planning or helping to manage the family enterprise. His parents taught him frugality, "a proper respect for money," very early; and from other boys he learned the art of "swapping": pocket knives, marbles, anything he carried in his pockets. "Swapping" in the boys' world is an exact duplicate of sharp-trading among men. But money or property (except small spending money) like planning and managing, were very probably outside his domain. A few girls are allowed to raise a setting of eggs to sell as fryers; some boys are given a pig or a calf to raise. The proceeds usually go for clothes which they would get anyway. "Children love to own things," and most people think "they should own something." Yet few own anything. Some are allowed to "claim" a calf or pig, until it is sold or eaten, but without voice in its disposal or any share of the money it brings. Children are never paid for work they do at home. Boys, however, have the right to "work out," when not needed at home. They are paid fifty to seventy-five cents a day (in 1939)—about half men's wages, until they are, say, fifteen or sixteen ("fully grown"). Boys and girls both have a right (though no exclusive right) to any salable wild products. For girls this means that they can gather and sell wild fruits, if they can find a buyer. Boys can trap and hunt, and many a boy, in good trapping years, earns all his spending money, clothes, and sometimes school supplies, by trapping skunks, 'possums, and other small fur-bearing animals. Until 1939 he also had a sale for rabbits (shipped away as meat) at ten or fifteen cents per carcass. The upper-class contempt for "hunting and trapping" does not apply to boys. Children in general spend for necessities most of what they earn.

Before marriage, a youth therefore knows how to farm. He has earned some money and handled its expenditure. He may have some savings, or a head or two of livestock. He has been "outside" on shopping and hauling trips, visits, perhaps on "work jobs." He is anxious to break away from his father's economic domination, a situation which is "all work and being bossed" without ever being consulted about farming plans. He "has no opportunity, working with his father." He has "looked over the girl situation" and knows which girls he likes; he may be "in love" with one girl. His friends are "going away or getting married," and "there's getting to be nobody to have a good time with." He may go away too—probably to California. If he does, he may "look for somebody to marry out there"; if he stays away, he may send home for a wife or return home to marry a "home girl." If he marries away, he is almost certain to remain living away, for a girl from away "would not be likely to like it here." If he marries a home girl, his link with home is doubly strong. The chances are nearly fifty-fifty that he will decide to live near Plainville; in that case he will nearly certainly marry a girl from a neighborhood or community not far from his home town. He would once have probably married one from his own neighborhood, but nowadays the car has widened the mobility and acquaintanceship of youth.

The only indications, generally, that the community receives of a pending marriage are these: the boy and girl "seem to be going together mighty steady"—they "seem to be getting serious." The boy may also be rumored to be "looking for a location" (a job or farm to rent) or to be "saving his money." Most engagements are short (three or four months) and are nearly always kept secret until the actual marriage, which is a "surprise" to all except (usually) the two families (barring children, who "would tell") and perhaps a confidant or two of each spouse. This seems to be the one secret few confidants will reveal. The reasons for secrecy are obscure, but a couple is gratified at "putting their surprise over on people." They are also pleased at foiling, for the time being, "shivaree" plans. Another reason given for the secrecy is that engaged girls would be "embarrassed to walk up and down the street and have men look at them" if the men knew of the coming marriage.

The marriage is generally performed by a preacher, at the preacher's house, with a minimum of witnesses. When the school superintendent married a teacher he bought the license at Discovery and the couple drove directly to the Reverend B's farm. The preacher came in from the field, performed the ceremony "without even changing his clothes," and returned to his field work. The couple then drove out of the community for a short honeymoon. Better-class people like to be married by a preacher, but there is no "disgrace" to being married by a justice of the peace. Church weddings are rare and are ridiculed as ostentatious.

Most "honeymoons" are a night or two spent at the house of one of the parents concerned. Few take a longer honeymoon, and work is seldom interrupted for longer than a day or two, if at all.

The next step in life is to set up a home. This is usually done as soon as the couple's plans for a livelihood have been formulated (if these have been postponed until marriage). A house or a farm must be rented; furniture and equipment must be acquired. A farm couple often "winters" with the parents of one of them, since the rental occupancy of farms is standardized to begin on March 1. Meanwhile the groom works at a job or "helps out" with whatever is to be done on the farm where he is living.

As soon as they are fully settled into a home of their own, the young couple begin to be considered full adults. Now they are supposed to quit "running around and spending money." What few dollars they gain should buy furniture, implements, and livestock, or should pay interest of principle on debts. They should "want to start raising a family" and should "start thinking about owning a home of their own." They should "save" toward these ends.

The woman's talk should begin to center in housekeeping. She should begin to ask older women for recipes and "ask how to save."

The man should start talking of "business and politics"—a farmer's business is stock, crops, and "how to manage." It is well if they start attending church regularly.

What the life of a young couple now getting married and settling down in Plainville will be or what the lives of their children will be it is not possible to forecast. The lives of present-day married people, during the twenty or thirty years when they are full adult working members of the society, bringing up and marrying off their children, can be implied from the present chapter on the life cycle—by shifting emphasis from children to adults—as well as from all the rest of this paper.

A married couple begins to be considered old when one of the pair can no longer do his or her work. A decline in their full status and "respect" begins somewhat earlier. When their children married off they had no further reason to maintain full participation in school and Sunday school.

Old people are not now greatly respected except by other old people, but they are respected more if they have saved enough to live on than if they have to accept the Old Age Assistance. They are respected relatively more also if they have "worked hard," "lived clean, moral lives," and "raised up their children right." They get no especial credit, however, for any prowesses of their younger days, and they are laughed at and condemned if they boast of earlier physical strength or leadership. Old people are liked best who "don't meddle or advise younger people," "don't complain of their ailments," and "don't criticize too much." Old people have little contact with younger people, except their close kin.

At death people are embalmed and buried in one of the several cemeteries near Plainville. Many people come to the funeral, which is held either in church or in the home (older style). A deceased wealthy grocer, farmer, and pillar in the Methodist Church was buried in 1939. His metal casket cost $300, and the flowers (imported from florists at "X" and Largetown) must have cost nearly as much. Not all the crowd which gathered could get into the church. After the sermon those who had waited outside were allowed to pass through the church aisles and view the corpse before the crowd inside walked by the casket. Not many except kin usually follow the hearse to the cemetery for the real "burying." There is usually a great demonstration of grief at funerals. Sometimes people without any ties whatever to the deceased sob hysterically. In the older days neighbors washed and dressed the corpse, and watched by it at night before burial. A whole complex of modern funeral traits, including embalming, flower girls and bought flowers, and expensive coffins was imported into the community about fifteen years ago by the present undertaker, an excellent business man. People are very proud of modern funerals. Embalming was the single element in the trait complex to meet resistance; it is still sometimes rejected. Close kin are notified of an expected death and children are expected to return home for a parent's funeral, no matter where they are. It is considered especially desirable for them to arrive before death occurs.

CHAPTER XI

ANALYSIS OF PLAINVILLE [1]

PLAINVILLE cannot be studied in the same manner as the preceding cultures of Comanche and Alor. This community does not have an independent culture, since it is part of a nation. Moreover, Plainville as a whole has a specialized function—farming; it is a small unit in a nation which has a high degree of local function differentiation. Being a community in which only half the population remains stationary, Plainville is spared some of the tensions arising from normal population growth, though other problems are created by the dispersal of native population. These facts do not necessarily disqualify a psychological analysis along the lines indicated in our study of Comanche and Alor. Such a psychological analysis has a limited objective: to draw the main outlines of the basic personality. An analysis of this kind does not purport to explore the material for many sociological conclusions.[2]

In the two previous cultures we dealt with discrete self-contained units; the total economy was self-contained and we did not need to draw a distinction between the community under analysis and any larger entity (such as the nation). In Plainville, however, we find a specialized function for the community as a whole, of a kind that separates, in large measure, the subsistence problem from the money economy. In most urban communities subsistence and money economy are intimately fused. In Plainville, however, the prestige aspects of money economy deeply permeate the social organization, despite the minor role of money economy for the ends of subsistence. Furthermore, though its economic function is a specialized one, Plainville is joined to the nation by a complicated federative machinery which is partly formal—joint participation in county, state, and federal governments

[1] The main features of the following analysis were first presented at the seminar in Psychological Analysis of Culture, conducted by Professor Linton and myself in 1941. Since it was originally given, many changes have been made, especially in adapting to a modern community the technique heretofore used only on primitive societies. The analysis as here presented has, moreover, had the benefit of careful reading and criticism by Mr. James West. His criticisms were of enormous value and most of them are now incorporated in the text.

[2] For these implications and other facets of the material on Plainville, consult James West, *Plainville, U.S.A.* (New York, Columbia University Press, 1945).

—and partly informal—common currency, language, dress, and a large number of communication systems.

Since our objectives in this analysis are limited in scope, we cannot study all aspects of participation, the most important of psycho-social problems. We must also exclude from our analysis other significant items: a discussion of that special form of social participation which we call "democracy"; a consideration of the role of trading for profit in the psychological adaptation of modern man; a study of some of the distinctive features of modern society and the intricate social problems they create, such as the growth of organized production and distribution—monopoly and cartels on the one hand, and trade unionism on the other. These are distinctive features of our culture today and represent the multiple polarizations caused by the formation of interest groups, all of which pursue the same social goal of success and power. But the individual producers in Plainville do not belong either to cartels or to unions.

Though we shall not discuss these important aspects of contemporary society with respect to Plainville, we can advance our comparative studies by attempting to define the basic personality structure of modern man. Such an investigation enables us to understand how the Plainville personality differs from that of an Eskimo or an Alorese.

To the average student of sociology, information bearing upon personality differences between an Eskimo, an Alorese, and a Plainville citizen, is not so pertinent to the social problems of our time as would be a description of the differences between a Plainville farmer, a Wall Street broker, a factory hand, and a contemporary citizen of Switzerland or Russia. The first series of comparisons can give only in broad outlines the general characteristics of modern man, without specifying the infinite variations and emphases which this personality structure can assume under the influence of special mores and local influences. The second series of comparisons bears upon the differences engrafted on a common basic personality. However, it is part of our thesis that none of the finer variations of basic personality can be understood unless its primary potentialities are first appreciated. The religion of Alor could never have undergone such a series of changes as those that we can trace from the Book of Job to the doctrines of Calvin; for the personality structure of Alor could neither support such changes nor find them meaningful. The personality structure of modern man does not seem to differ from the one we find in Sophocles or Shakespeare. Such differences as we encounter fall within a given range; they are motivated by alterations in techniques of mastery, subsistence, and participation—all engrafted on a similar basic personality structure. Another way of stating the same proposition is to say that the religious attitudes in the Book of Job, early Christianity, Catholicism, and Calvinism do not represent variations in basic personality structure, but variations within the same kind of personality, so that many of the different types are really isometric.

General Characteristics of Plainville Culture

The use of the Plainville data for the purpose we have indicated may provoke objections on several grounds. It is quite true, for instance, that from the comparison of Plainville man with Alorese man we derive data that have little relevance to current social problems. These problems seem to be caused more by conflict of interests than by cultural differences. But we cannot understand the nature of these problems unless we first understand the personality matrix out of which they arise.

A second objection may be that comparisons with primitive man are intrinsically invalid because our society is dynamic, while primitive society is static; ours is heterogeneous, while primitive society is homogeneous.[3] These observations, as formulated by Alexander, are ambiguously stated and of dubious validity. To claim that "primitive" society is static may mean that primitive man cannot alter his adaptation in the face of strong provocations. This allegation is not borne out by our observations of Tanala or Comanche. That changes are slower in primitive society, there is no doubt; but it is equally clear that the direction of the cultural change is determined by the external provocation and the existing personality structure, just as they are in our culture.

Germane to the subject of change is the problem of cultural heterogeneity or homogeneity. There is more resemblance between Catholicism and Calvinism than between either of these and the religion of Comanche. This does not mean that Catholicism and Calvinism are not different, but the differences lie within the range of the same basic personality structure. The differences between Catholicism and Comanche, however, depend on differences in basic personality structure. Hence the heterogeneity in our culture must be explained by

---

[3] See F. Alexander, *Our Age of Unreason*, Philadelphia, Lippincott, 1943.

referring to an order of data other than dissimilarities among various cultures.

The heterogeneity of our culture becomes a troublesome question wherever we discover that within the same range of basic personality structure differences in character become involved with serious intra-social tensions and clashes of interest. These tensions and clashes of interest can cause greater difficulties than arise from differences in basic personality structure alone. It is worth noting that when clashes of interest occur among different cultural groups in contemporary society, cultural differences are magnified in importance and used as justification for the more powerful group to deny competitive rights to the less powerful. When there is no clash of interest, cultural differences are tolerated and even admired in a condescending way. For example, both attitudes, condescending tolerance and more or less controlled hostility, may coexist in the attitudes of Americans toward the Negro.

The heterogeneity of our culture in no way invalidates the attempt to establish the general characteristics of Western [4] man, irrespective of the many variations that can take place within the framework of the same personality structure. Moreover, one cannot discuss heterogeneity without attempting to show where the variations are to be found. We find multiple patterns only in peripheral institutions which are optional or gratuitous, such as religion. But variation is not tolerated in the essential institutions, such as the monogamous family. Our sex mores show some variation in different communities and countries and social strata; similarly, variations exist in the rearing of children. But all these variations take place within a certain range. Western man does not publicly sanction sexual activity in children of five, but the Comanche do. The difference between these institutions in the two cultures creates two different types of personality. In both cultures the characterological differences between parental units operate only within the framework of these basic institutions.[5]

An additional objection to our enterprise may be made on the ground that our culture is in a perpetual state of change so that one cannot catch it in any one position long enough to follow the dynam-

[4] The writer recognizes that the term "Western man" is a fictitious concept. It is here used on an assumption, still unproven, that those peoples we call "Western" have a basic personality which has many features in common.

[5] Alexander is of the opinion that the institutions do not have much to do with creation of character, but that the character of the parent does (*op. cit.*, pp. 233–40).

ics. It may be pointed out, however, that social change is selective; it takes place generally along a certain sector of adaptation. It is true that cultural change does not remain localized in its effects. The invention of the motor car brought cultural changes far beyond the limits of mere transportation. The cultural changes in our society have resulted largely from our mechanical conquests of the world, the far-reaching social consequences of which were not foreseen. But cultural changes involving family structure, sex mores, etc., have not taken place in many generations. When we speak of cultural change, therefore, its direction must be specified. Our society is just as rigid concerning certain types of cultural change as is any other. Yet, certain types of cultural change are readily accepted. In fact, our society, especially in urban centers, is eager for changes in certain modes and fashions and we have an unusual appetite for novelty.

We may now attempt a survey of the general characteristics of Plainville culture. The effectual unit is the patriarchally oriented monogamous family, with division of function between the sexes so organized as to keep mother and child in constant and close proximity. Though the mother institutes all early disciplines, the child in time comes to recognize the authority of the father. This recognition is probably coincident with growth in size, resources, and understanding of speech. Apart from the family, social organization follows three lines: common interest, common status, and common residence, in this order of importance. Since Plainville is a farming community, the degree of function differentiation is smaller than is usual in America, and this is also true with respect to personal prestige and economic claims.

Technology is of a high order. It is employed at the individual's option, and is characterized particularly by the use of manufactured tools, whose production requires a special type of urban social organization.

Although subsistence is a major concern in Plainville as elsewhere, each farmer consumes a part of what he directly produces. Thus, the pressure of the money economy is considerably reduced with respect to subsistence. Money is used for services, clothes, convenience, taxes, insurance, rent, and purchase of articles of food not locally produced. The economy is mediated by currency of fixed value and by a money system of wide ramifications and complex structure. In Plainville far more than in urban centers, therefore, subsistence economy is divorced from prestige economy. The latter has a complex organization, since it is simultaneously related to money economy, to criteria for high status, and to the *quality* or convenience of goods used.

The forms of social participation are numerous and complex. The compactness of the local group (trade area) and the completeness of the individual's work (farming) facilitate certain forms of participation; on the other hand, the size of the nation to which he belongs limits the possibility of other forms of effective participation. Most participation is optional, even voting and the related functions of citizenship. If he wishes, the citizen of Plainville can be in touch with the whole world through radio, news print, entertainment, etc.; but his preparation for participation in the greater society, by way of education and environmental influences, is scant. It is in connection with certain types of social participation that the individual is most isolated. This isolation is not peculiar to Plainville; it is true of any large community. The individual does not know directly how his needs or demands may effect such end results as the rise or fall in prices or the outcome of elections, particularly national elections. And although he has political freedom, he has no absolute security against debility or anxiety. Nevertheless, as Mr. West has observed, the individual has more guarantees against want than city people have. He is driven partly by prestige goals (success) and partly by anxieties about want. Despite political equality, a hierarchy of social-prestige values exists in the status-class-prestige complex which is so pervasive that no one can ignore it. Social mobility theoretically permits the individual to move from one "class" to another. This produces a background against which the self-esteem of the individual is always reflected. A high degree of competitiveness therefore exists about status-prestige values, though no such rivalry appears with regard to subsistence.

Because of the influences of migration, changing mores, and education, the culture is unstable. Strong tensions must therefore exist between forces of change and stability. The comparative liquidity of status-class causes the greatest instability, because the life-goals of the individual must be polarized toward the goal of success as a form of self-validation.

Our culture is generally regarded as heterogeneous because of differences in manners, value systems, religion, language, clothes, and some peripheral mores. Actually it is the exaggeration of many small and insignificant details that creates this appearance of heterogeneity. Far more significant is the polarization of our culture in many directions simultaneously. Differences in education, class, or status affiliations create different *interests* on the part of different groups within the society, all of which pull in different directions. Decisions about these interests are in the main vested in political parties which manipulate the coercive power of the state. Opportunities for actual participation are different for every individual. A man is born into a political party as into a church. Politicians are skilled in misrepresenting issues and in making Mr. John Citizen vote against his own interests. The fact that different interest groups all want the same thing—success, enjoyment, power—creates enormous tensions in our society. Though differentiation of function creates opportunities for a delicately articulated coöperation, it does not alleviate these tensions because they are all eventually transformed into a common quest for security and power. Hidden forms of aggression against the common good go undetected for long periods.

Tension does not necessarily arise when the members of a society strive for a common goal. This is clearly shown in the success of Catholicism. When the goals of living could be defined in terms of postmortem rewards, the failure to achieve material goals could not only be tolerated, it could be elevated into an additional claim for deserving rewards after death. But the invalidation of post-mortem rewards —in fact, of the whole system of values derived from projective sources —puts greater pressure on the individual to validate himself in tangible works translatable into power or enjoyment or freedom from anxiety. The presence of social mobility, or absence of fixed statuses, increases the vigor with which these tangible forms of self-validation must be pursued.

Status must therefore create two distinct problems for the individual: his security system must have a distinct structure, and the lines of coöperation and all forms of socializing must be polarized toward the centrifugal status issue. A special situation is also created for the group as a whole; the tendencies of the various interest groups become centrifugal, common interests are more difficult to define and are often obscured, and hence renunciation of self-interest for the common good becomes more difficult to envisage.

So much for the general morphology of our culture. This culture has a long history of vicissitudes, and many different factors have contributed to making it what it is. A complicated machinery implements and buttresses the organization. Our immediate concern, however, is to arrive at a method of studying it for the purpose of describing the psychological factors which operate in it. We may take the following steps:

1. We may establish the basic personality structure. Here human nature with its given biological equipment is molded in a set of conditions which are now very widespread. The human being that emerges will be different from any of those we have heretofore studied; his strength and weakness are unique, as are his values and goals. The institutions which lie at the basis of this personality structure are well defined, but they are implemented in an infinite variety of ways; hence the variations in the resulting personalities will run very high. But we cannot make the same use of basic personality structure that we have up to now; we cannot leap from it to a group of derivative institutions. Several intermediate steps must be taken.

2. We may make a general delineation of characterological types, all of which derive from similar basic situations. In our study of Alor we had our first opportunity to observe both the operational value of the concept of basic personality structure and also the large number of variations in the implementation of a given practice and the effects this had on the resulting characters of individuals. The characterological differences between individuals were considerable, notwithstanding their common features. It happened that the eight Alorese we studied at one time were of much the same status, but several others were observed who had reached a dominant social position through persistence and aggression. The really dominant individuals in the society, however, were not available for study. These variations in character types must be studied in relation not only to the position of each individual in the society, but also to the structuralization of the society itself. Such variations are likely to be much more striking in our society where status is mobile, and hence competition keener, and where there are an infinite number of opportunities for self-assertion through arts and crafts. In delineating character types it must be noted that not all character traits are socially relevant. In every society some aspects of character are "private"; but even such "private" traits have a social relevance when they can be expressed in the form of social goals compatible with the needs of a given character. In primitive cultures these characterological types have less social relevance, and therefore a smaller capacity for influencing institutions, because of the relative fixity of the reality systems.

3. Each characterological type may be interpreted in accordance with the individual's particular needs. Certain facts in the outer world will have different meanings for different individuals and we must allow for these. Of special significance is the dynamic relationship between characterological types and the status-class-prestige complex. Social mobility across class-prestige lines is possible to some degree, and institutions can be altered to the advantage of one or the other group. Characterological types, therefore, are able to influence social ideologies, whose function is to provide directives for social action. This is a striking contrast to what we found in primitive society, where internal tensions expressed themselves on a projective fantasy screen, largely by means of religious ideologies. Western society has tended to use the religious fantasy screen less and less as a factor in social stability, though it has not been discarded. This tendency has coincided with increased mastery of the external world, accompanied by decreased interest in deferred gratifications and compensations and greater desire for immediate and actual satisfactions, though the older methods of expression have never been completely wiped out. Social ideologies thus emerge as compounds of elements formerly expressed in religious systems, plus an actual effort to relieve tensions caused by the economic change resulting from inventions, industrialization, etc.

4. In the definition of social goals we find our first real evidence of heterogeneity, and by this is meant a difference in the social goals toward which various groups in society are compelled to be oriented. These goals may be examined to determine whether the differences are real, or whether the various groups desire the same ultimate goal but seek to achieve it by different methods as a result of variations in vocation and position in the status-class-prestige hierarchy.

5. Finally we may examine the way in which social goals are implemented—the machinery used for achieving them and for preserving sufficient stability in the society notwithstanding conflicts in social goals. This machinery is in part political—laws, statutes, police, etc.—which will not be discussed at length. But in part it lies in our current folklore and amusement. Though not intended for this purpose, the folklore of stories, songs, characters, etc., helps to preserve the stability of society.

Our simple scheme of formative institutions, basic personality, and expressive (secondary) institutions must thus be expanded into a much more complex scheme. The modification is due to the increasing importance of characterological types in their relation to cultural change, to the replacement of religious by social ideologies, and to the complicated mechanisms for implementing these ideologies. In this last development we see the decisive influence of empirically derived reality systems upon institutions of projective origin.

Parental Care

Owing to the division of male and female functions after marriage, the wife is obliged to take care of the house and menage, that is, to provide meals, clean, cook, and take care of the children. She therefore becomes the first and most persistent influence in the child's life and the conveyor of the earliest socializing disciplines.

By our standards maternal care is considered good.[6] The feeding, cleansing, and comforting of the child are carefully attended to. Crying is regarded as a signal of discomfort, and the convention is that the mother responds to this signal. The infant is breast-fed chiefly, supplementary foods being used only by the most "advanced." Bathing the child and changing his diapers are frequent. Care of the excreta is given special attention, and as a result the anal and genital zones are often stimulated by rubbing.

Breast-feeding is now often continued only through the first year,[7] but whether the child is fed by breast or otherwise, the constant attention by the mother fixes her in the child's mind as the reliever of his tensions. The image of the mother as a helper coming to aid in any distress is the first constellation formed.

The child's rest and sleep are also carefully guarded. The few causes of discomfort—such as unpleasant temperature, wetness, hunger—are not permitted to become the sources of tension. On the other hand, this good care, while it fortifies the child's ego in these early days, may create an inertia against moving away from this particular type of adaptation. This is one of the bad effects of good parental care; it introduces the possibility of *passive* forms of adaptation, and this passivity may show itself in a variety of particular forms.[8]

---

[6] See definition, pp. 26–28.

[7] Late weaning stories condemned and ridiculed the practice. These stories can be interpreted as meaning that formerly late weaning was more common than it is now.

[8] It may be suggested that this passive constellation in Western man fits in with his differentiation of function to some extent, because high status in a society in which mobility is free is not compatible with passivity. Passivity, however, is not disorganized; it is organized about strong parental fixation.

The character of maternal care, however, does not change with the child's growth; it is maintained on an even tenor throughout his development. And since individual parents differ, each parent may introduce unique educative factors.

The position of the infant in the home is very important: the infant is one of the main objectives in the lives of the parents. Yet it can hardly be said that the society revolves around the child. Quite the contrary. Although the child is not so important as in Comanche, the Plainville boy has the opportunity to reach maturity early, for he learns work techniques when he is still quite young. This is a striking contrast to similar conditions in urban centers. Actual induction into work, moreover, is earlier in Plainville than in urban centers, so that the life of the growing child tends more closely to approximate that of the adult. The early completion of "training" would tend to diminish parental authority. However, legally recognized participation is late, for example, citizenship, ownership of property, and so forth.

Normative influences, in the form of *affectivity* as shown by mother to child, are plentiful. The mother physically handles the child a great deal, with much emotional and affectionate play in the form of stroking and kissing, mimicry, singing, and talking. These acts of affection are generally much underestimated as an influence. They are all pressing invitations to the child to imitate and to become accustomed to receiving and giving a large variety of affective responses.

The greatest variable in maternal care is the affection given to and elicited from the child. That children need affection is commonly recognized, but the manner in which it is bestowed is bound to vary with the character of the mother. (For example, there is some concern in Plainville about "spoiling" the child, which is brought about chiefly by such parental indulgences as relaxing demands for obedience or bestowing favors in the form of sweets, money, or unusual privileges.) The chief reason why affection and approval are so important for the child is that he has no other means for deciding on his own value. Hence if he is shown no appreciation, if his affectionate impulses receive no response, the child concludes that he is not wanted, that he is of no value, etc.; and these ideas may profoundly affect the development of his self-esteem and self-confidence. It may even have a profound psychosomatic influence, preventing him from developing positive attitudes toward parts of his own body—such as the genitals. For example, a child may deduce from his mother's behavior that the bowel or stomach is the chief avenue of permissible emotional expression and that the genitals are to be ignored.

To sum up, the important features of parental care in infancy are generally close attention to the comfort of the child, feeding and cleansing, care of his body temperature, and the initial induction into affectivity. The effect of all these attentions is both to prevent the child from accumulating tensions and to build up in him a powerful constellation of the large, resourceful, and powerful parent who is always capable of relieving any tension in the event of need. As a result the child's acquaintance with his environment is facilitated, the traumatic influence of that environment is diminished, and a foundation is laid for the development or stimulation of curiosity, investigative manipulation of objects in the outer world, and some confidence in handling them. A foundation is also laid for the idealization of the parent, especially the mother and the functions associated with her, an idealization which in our culture sometimes becomes maudlin. Furthermore, it lays the basis for idealization of the supernatural and for strong superego formation.

The child is helped in his efforts at walking and climbing. The tendency is for parents to delight in these early activities and to enhance the child's feeling of value for the activities and his ability to perform them. While the parental attitude is beneficial, it carries a penalty. It builds in the child a structure of expectations from the parent, and when unfavorable influences arise, these tend to fortify the child's complex of passive adaptation. The result is twofold: inertia against accepting new adjustments, and persistence in infantile gratifications. This is the one disadvantage of good parental care.

The evidence concerning prolonged breast feeding indicates that it is not a usual practice now, though folk tales imply that it used to be rather common. (See biography of Rachel, Chapter XIII, p. 399.) However, prolonged breast feeding is not necessary to render the act of sucking a pleasurable activity in itself and apart from its nutritive function. Such a constellation can be created merely by attentive feeding during the first year of life. Prolonging the period of breast feeding serves to accentuate this constellation. In this phenomenon we see the first manifestation of a passive adaptation—to divorce the pleasure function from the utility function and thus to make the pleasure-sucking not only the vehicle for passive adaptation to feeding but also a universal symbol for all dependent attitudes. Hardships encountered in other aspects of adaptation can thus be relieved by a somatic pleasure function connected with the mouth. This set of responses is a powerful influence in the personality structure of modern man and one that is put to innumerable uses, especially in times of crisis. Other cultures have exhibited a similar tendency—not by way of the mouth but by directly stimulating the genitals—to use a pleasure organ as a distraction from other difficulties. Such masturbatic activity is strictly tabooed in Western society; it even excites horror, owing to certain traditional myths concerning the harmful effects of masturbation. This taboo is the first evidence in our culture that where a relaxer function is interfered with, the tensions which it purports to relieve end in a blocked action system.

Good parental care, therefore, is associated with a new series of adaptation possibilities, two of which must be mentioned because of their prominence: (1) passivity and (2) introversion. The first we have already discussed. Psychopathology commonly views the second as a baneful and abnormal tendency. However, viewed purely in terms of the psychic economy, introversion (which is based on the fantasy elaborations of infantile passive adaptations) makes possible new capacities for adjustment, although at the cost of restricted social participation. Furthermore, introversion has a protective function in the face of external difficulties incapable of direct resolution.

This aspect of good parental care becomes exceedingly important when we study the succeeding integrational possibilities opened up by new contacts with reality. Though it has acquired a bad reputation through the influence of psychiatry, introversion has constructive aspects that are generally ignored. These begin to show their influence when the child's growth and his parents' demands make new types of adaptation necessary.

Sphincter control, one of the earliest demands made on the child, is important only because some of the constellations that develop around it are exceedingly important. Sphincter control has different consequences, depending on when it is introduced. The child can be taught sphincter control at six months, though it is not to his advantage that this be done so early in his development. In Plainville the custom is to demand complete sphincter control at from fifteen months to two years. This is not entirely cotemporal with the child's capacity to understand the purpose of this discipline. By this time he has become accustomed to the clothed adult, but whether he yet notices the odors of excreta or has a conception of cleanliness is not known. This discipline teaches the child one of his first responsibilities and is his introduction to becoming socialized, in the sense of making a contribution of his own to the general welfare.

Sphincter control means merely the identification of certain sensations with the time and place for evacuation. The child must first signal the parent and then learn to discharge excreta in relative privacy. He can be praised for good performance and censured for delinquency, and, depending upon the character of the tie already established, this discipline will either be accepted or will be rejected with great resistance. The child can utilize either response as an ingratiation technique or as a means for continuing his period of irresponsibility. This situation may terminate in an attitude by which (a) the erotic value of the anal zone is enhanced, though at no time is this zone equipped in any way to dispose of tensions essentially sexual in nature; or (b) the activities of retention or evacuation become the vehicle for expressing suppressed aggression, whether by constipation or by diarrhea or by phobic formations about either activity—retention or evacuation.

Not to be overlooked in the basic personality structure of Western man are the special *values* attached to cleanliness and dirt and all their derivatives—values that are adventitious to the evacuating function. The evacuating function may become distorted to mean retention or expulsion and thus a psychosomatic route may be formed to carry tensions incapable of expression or release on the cortical level.

Retention may undergo a large series of elaborations, not all of which are directly related to each other. For example, it may (depending on the mother) be intimately associated with the idea of illness, which may again become a subtle method of soliciting parental aid, because it is followed by manipulations with enemas, which may in turn be associated with erotic attachments to the parent. Demand for autonomous control of this organ may thus deprive the child of a much wanted kind of attention, and resistance to its acceptance may take the form of defiance.

The parting with feces may symbolize the separation from the protecting mother and therefore a *loss*. Evacuation may thus take on the adventitious meaning of impoverishment, while constipation may acquire the meaning of a retention, adding to oneself, not parting with anything pertaining to oneself, stinginess and anxiety about loss.

Or the mere act of defiance, in connection with anal discipline, may become the starting point for an integrational system in which will-fulness—opposition to the parents' will—is expressed either in retention or in delinquencies during sleep. On the other hand, expulsion may become the starting point for quite a different integrational system. To expel something noxious may become a pattern for freeing oneself of painful stimuli or affects. The result is that an individual who has developed such a system may get a sudden urge to evacuate whenever he finds himself in a situation which demands some combativeness; this neurotic habit may manifest itself in a desire to know precisely where the toilet is, whenever he is in a strange situation. Certain *values* are generally taught in connection with feces: revulsion, disgust, valuelessness, shame, and cleanliness. These values are all new to the child and completely at variance with his earlier attitudes, for evacuation is a sign of relaxation and friendliness—a child does not relax the sphincter when he is held in the arms of those adults he fears. We must conclude from Alor that these value systems are not universal, but are unique to our culture.

Generally urethral control is less difficult for the child and more easily handled. It too can become the starting point for a large number of adventitious values. Being associated with a zone phylogenetically predetermined to be a vehicle of erotic sensations, demand for control can make it become the carrier of hidden erotic tendencies. Thus bed-wetting may be the childhood equivalent of ejaculation—or at all events of erotic stimulation of the genitals. In our society urinating the longest stream may become among boys an indicator of strength.

The problem of sexual disciplines in our society is a complicated and difficult one. All sexual activity in children is denied, and when it occasionally attracts parental notice it excites great anxiety. Sexual activity is assumed to be a "natural" function and therefore need not be fostered in any way. This is a mistaken notion. It is true that nothing needs to be done to foster it, but serious obstacles can be placed in the way of its natural development, or highly specific integrational systems can be built about it. If the sexual precocity of the human infant is phylogenetically determined, then its meaning eludes us. The so-called "normal" fluctuations, the early manifestations, the latency period, and the resurgence at puberty, may all be a result, in part, of the process of growth. How much each factor contributes to the result cannot now be determined. We may hope to solve these problems by making comparisons with such cultures as do not introduce obstacles to sexual development—as in Marquesas or Comanche.

Good maternal care fosters the attachment of the child to the parent. The particular form of this attachment may be sexual. Much evidence shows that long before the child is able to perform the sexual act, his attachment to the parent may be sexual in content. Of course, it need not involve images of actual sexual contact (though I have seen one case in which it did, in a child of five). Many instances commonly accepted as evidence that the child is sexually attached to the mother are retrospective fantasies reconstructed during puberty. But the desire to possess, to be near, to be protected by, and to be given pleasure by the mother—to the exclusion of anyone else, father or siblings— these desires may take definite form during the earliest years. Strong rivalries and hostilities may develop out of these desires, the repression of which gives rise to definite unconscious constellations. And this is the point at which our sexual disciplines, direct or implied, exert a powerful influence.

In two of the societies we have studied—Marquesan and Comanche —where ego formation was especially strong and effective, sexual disciplines of a prohibitory kind did not exist. The child was given the opportunity to exercise sex in the form he was capable of, with other children approximately his own age. In Plainville the fact that children have sexual needs and impulses is not clearly recognized. Children have the opportunity to overhear parental coitus repeatedly, especially in those small houses that have only one bedroom. Moreover, children sleep together and opportunities for clandestine play undoubtedly arise. But such sexual activity has no parental approval and is not given an established place in the life of the child. Parents generally avoid verbal references to the genitals, preferring to use euphemisms for the genital and excretory organs and their functions.

As a result, much sex knowledge among Plainville children circulates in the form of myths. In this respect, however, the Plainville child is more favorably situated than is the city child, for he has plenty of opportunities for directly observing sexual activities of farm animals. There is also much to indicate the formal mores are breached in many ways. But the outcome is left to chance. The masturbation clubs formed by some preadolescent boys is further evidence that access to the opposite sex is barred at this time. Girls seem to have no corresponding clubs, and in this community it is possible for a woman to remain relatively ignorant of sex during her entire life. On the other hand, having been seduced in childhood, she may have had a continuous sex life from then on. Some women remain frigid throughout their entire life, some do not. Some men are adequate sexually, others have varying degrees of impotence and perversions. The outcome depends on individual circumstances. However, the effect of the dominant trend of the mores in the direction of secrecy and general taboo is the most telling influence. One of the most significant data on sex morality in Plainville is the great secrecy in which engagements and marriages are held, and the anxiety of the woman lest it be known that she will be married, for on such and such a day everybody will know what will happen to her. She definitely does not want to have it known. It is clear from all this that the sexual act is in disrepute and devoid of dignity, and that it carries with it the distinct connotation of something dirty. It is associated with a none too disguised ridicule and shame.

This is evidence that relations to the sexual object and to the activity itself have been spoiled. The sexual act has become a crime and the person who submits to it is a degraded object. What has apparently happened is that the mother, whom the child has often overheard in intercourse, is denied all participation in the act and is idealized by the child into a madonna-like figure, unsullied by any sexual thought or activity. This degrading act could not have been done to her—at least not with her coöperation. On the other hand, those Plainville girls who want and permit sexual contact are "classed" almost as prostitutes, and they remain the screen on whom the whole criminal aspect of sexuality can be projected. They are the object of gossip and an enraged ridicule.

We need not repeat here what has been fully described elsewhere.[9] We need only schematize the various consequences of the sex mores in Plainville. The scheme is equally tenable, with variations, for Western society in general. At the base of the whole sex morality are the powerful ties to both parents; without these ties none of these mores would have the consequences described. Both parents in their respective provinces are established as providers, helpers, and disciplinarians. Their attributes for good or for harm can now be equally

---

[9] See Kardiner, *The Individual and His Society*, pp. 20–21.

exaggerated. They can be loved for their helpful aspects and hated for their restrictive influences.

Having described the formation of this constellation, we can now consider the sexual development with reference to relations to the sexual object, to the sexual organ, and to the sexual activity. The sexual drive is a biological datum, but on the executive side the drive can be deflected in many directions. When a drive is opposed by an obstacle we can expect:

(a) Changes in the perception of the impulse
(b) Alteration of the executive functions related to the impulse [10]
(c) Alteration of the feelings to those who impose the discipline
(d) Changes in the relations to the activity and to the objects who stimulate it
(e) The rise of new conscious attitudes about it and new behavior from the resultant constellations

We stated in an earlier paragraph that good parental care created the possibility of introversion as a mode of adaptation. This means in essence that the patterns of a previous adaptation with all the relationships involved are elaborated in fantasy, at the expense of current adaptations demanded by the current reality. The Alorese, however, have taught us that one cannot introvert with a long series of traumatic experiences—only pleasurable experiences can be used for that purpose. Hence, if maternal care is good, and the attachment to the mother is a binding one, pleasure zones and activities are likely to focus on her; that is, the child can expect, in fantasy, that these erotic stimuli will be satisfied through her. The obstacle in the form of taboos against any such activity renders these impulses incapable of satisfaction. The role of fantasy in adaptation begins here. The mother may be retained as the object of these impulses, and the father and other siblings who become claimants for her attention may be correspondingly hated. This constellation was identified by Freud as the Oedipus complex. However strong this attachment to the mother, the inability to consummate sexual activity in some form commensurate with the child's capacities, must intensify the character of the introverted fantasy, and he must seek outlets through other avenues. The

[10] It has long been recognized that the child may fail to appreciate the functions of the penis except in the light of anal and urethral functions, with the consequent destruction of the orgasmic reflex. The same applies to the vagina.

number of possibilities are very great indeed. The oral zone may be intensified in importance. The anal zone may become the vehicle through which these impulses may find vicarious expression. The object toward whom these impulses are directed may be changed; it may become the father, with the result that the entire erotic development may be deflected toward homosexuality. The executive functions themselves may become paralyzed, and the parts of the body used in these sexual activities may become blotted out of the whole scheme of awareness, resulting in frigidity or impotence. The initial sexual impulse itself may come to be regarded as a danger signal, and anxiety may develop that the executive organ (penis or vagina) will be effectively removed from the whole body scheme (castration complex).

Each of these constellations becomes the point at which further integrational systems arise. Consequently, when the individual grows up he may find that he cannot execute sexual activity in the normal way. This incapacity may take the form of neurosis or perversion. On the other hand the executive act (coitus) may not be impaired, yet the relations to the woman may become filled with anxiety. Thus we may find a woman who seemingly is well-adjusted yet is subject to constant anxiety dreams in which the man is represented as a wild beast or savage who is about to attack her. An impotent man may frequently dream that he is about to murder a woman.

These are all different forms in which the relation to the sexual act or the sexual object may become distorted. But since their significance does not remain localized in sexual activity only, sex mores are important for the society as a whole. Constellations formed in this domain do not remain localized; they spread over other activities of the individual and have an important influence in forming his life goals. Our society makes this situation easy for the individual because it offers ample opportunity for a wide choice of vocation; thus it may permit him to maintain a fixed attitude (like passivity) which may not prevent him from continuing a life adjusted to socially approved goals. Such a possibility was not realizable in Comanche, where there was no choice of either vocation or of attitude. Every man had to be a competent soldier or disappear from the society altogether.

In addition to these personality consequences, sexual mores have other secondary consequences with respect to the sexual activity itself. Much evidence in Plainville indicates that pleasurable activity associated with sex is considered wrong, if it is recognized as pleasure.[11] Secondary effects of this may be asceticism, of which there is little in Plainville, or prudery, of which there is much. The pleasure aspect may not be openly acknowledged, and for this attitude the woman is the main carrier, probably because of the idealization of the mother as a non-sexual object. From this fact comes a series of derived prohibitions against all pleasures—such as drinking, which is considered a sign of great wickedness. Drinking is regarded partly as an anodyne and partly as a reliever of tension—Plainvillers drink to get away from their wives, to forget their troubles, etc. The general hypocrisy that surrounds sexual activities in Plainville is a compromise formation between the demands of the impulse and the mores. Thus a man may have a clandestine affair provided he keeps it quiet. Should it become known, the whole situation would be altered. Boys "are supposed to" have intercourse before marriage—but with whom? With an anonymous, degraded woman. And if she is not degraded to start with, she becomes that once she is identified. There is no need to multiply examples to show that those who entirely escape sexual inhibitions seek compromises with the mores by resorting to clandestine affairs, by prudery, and hypocrisy. It is easy to see that the prudery is likely to be most intense among those who are most inhibited. It is based on the simple principle: "You should not have what I cannot have." It is on this principle that all the pent-up aggressions acquire an outlet.

We can sum up the subject of sex mores by stating that they give rise to a large number of possible changes in the act, to the objects from whom satisfaction is expected, and to the organs by which it is executed. These take the form of neurosis or perversion. In addition, there are certain secondary effects in the form of hypocrisy, prudery, and puritanism, in which pleasure connected with sex is either denied, prohibited, or concealed. The mores also create the necessity for institutionalized prostitution, which must also be concealed. The effects of sexual organization in the individual are not limited to the sexual domain, but become an integral part of the personality; they determine its mode of adaptation and contribute to the formulation of life goals.

A second consequence, socially relevant, is that if unsatisfied ten-

---

[11] This statement must be qualified. All men are expected to "like sex." Men often complain that women don't "like sex," and this difference in attitude is often the basis of marital difficulties. See biography of James X, p. 379.

sions exist in the sexual domain, other permissible forms of self-expression, such as competition for accomplishment and prestige, may become strongly reinforced. On the other hand, a character may become integrated on the pattern of a blocked-action system in which substitutive or compensatory actions become as much blocked as the original one. This is the formula for a masochistic character,[12] which serves so effectively to buttress our status-class-prestige complex. It must not be assumed, however, that sexual frustrations are the sole source of blocked-action systems and their socially relevant consequences, though they are one of the conspicuous sources.

Punishment-Reward Systems; Superego Formation

In order to evaluate the punishment-reward systems of our culture, we must again refer to the strong underlying structure of the personality created by good parental care in the early years. While the child is still very young he realizes that the parental care and affection —by now a mainstay of his adaptation—are not indiscriminately given but are contingent upon a certain behavior on his part. If he puts his finger on the hot stove and is burned, that constitutes one type of learning; if he does something wrong and is punished, that is another type of learning. We tend to acknowledge the validity of the first type of learning more readily; but the two types are equally important in building up the reality system that governs the relations of the child to the material objects in the outer world, and those which govern his relations to the human beings in his environment. The first type leads to "common sense"; the second to superego formation.

In Plainville the disciplinary system is very clear. The father outranks the mother as a verbalized source of authority and disciplines executed by the mother are often indirectly referred to him.[13] Plainville has enough social insight to know that in order to have a certain

12 The advantage of using the action system as a unit is here clearly demonstrated. Without its use we must depend upon *motivations*, without knowing how motivations become formulated. Conclusions based on the surface motivations lead to some extravagant claims, as that the individual seeks to be "free" of himself, to lose himself in another, etc. The masochist is supposed to have a strong feeling of aloneness and insignificance. But this motivation is contingent upon the executive inability in relation to specific types of organized action. When these latter fail the result may be a disorganized aggression or an ingrown aggression, i. e., masochism. It is on this basis that the motivation is built.

13 Almost all early authority is maternal and the mother is also the executor of most early disciplines. The mother's reference to the father as an ultimate authority begins after the child can fully understand language and becomes more frequent with the increase in the physical size and strength of the child.

type of human character, discipline must begin early. Moreover, the arrangement of the household is such that the child has a definite place in it, and is obliged to live within its confines. Much of the discipline concerning order and cleanliness are not given by tuition, but by a system of reproaches, scoldings, admonitions, or beatings. In Plainville (as elsewhere in Western society) beatings are done on the buttocks or legs with the bare hands, a switch, or a whip. The origin of this custom is not known, but making the buttocks the locus of punishment is probably associated with sphincter control, the earliest discipline.

Consistency is the most significant characteristic of disciplines in Plainville. The child gets to know what is expected of him, and approval and reward, disapproval and punishment, are sharply defined categories. There is little opportunity for confusion in the mind of the child. The mores within the household are generally consonant with those of the community as a whole, so that there is no need for the child to learn a different system for the world outside his home. There are some notable exceptions, pertaining to sex mores. The occasional formation of masturbation clubs by the boys is the signal for such a breakaway from the family mores, though the practice is more often solitary or in secret pairs rather than in groups. This group masturbation is, however, not anti-social. It seems to serve the function of expressing contempt for the sex mores of the household, and since it is done in gangs, the group character tends to take the brunt off the offense, to diminish the sense of guilt, and to give the boy the support of knowing openly that everyone else is doing it. This is not the only way in which the family mores may be breached by a gang of boys, who thereby establish an organization with its own authority outside the household. Other gang activities include cruelty to girls, physical dirtiness, and dirty talk.

We have already examined two systems of behavior—sphincter control and sex-organ control—which are part of the disciplinary measures constituting the socializing process. In each instance, be it in sphincter delinquencies or infantile masturbation, the instrument of discipline is complicated in structure. It involves attitudes of both parent and child, and the summation of both gives rise to the constellation known as authority. Looking at the situation from the point of view of the child, the parent can enforce authority or it can be delegated to him. A parent who frustrates the child in too many ways will never enjoy a delegated authority, though enforcement of authority may take place in either place. As far as the cohesion of the child to the family is concerned, enforced authority is of much less importance, because it rarely becomes a part of the internalized superego system. On the contrary, children who are coerced without proper rewards tend to do the very things they are told not to do, even at the cost of severe punishment, which they learn to write off as part of the gratification system based on disobedience. But a child who is aided by his parents can readily delegate authority and abide by disciplines, even at the cost of renouncing important gratifications. This is really the essence of the whole question of good parental care, so far as the cohesion of a society is concerned. Once the child is convinced of the protective role of the parent and realizes that through parental aid various gratifications and securities can be enjoyed, a powerful influence has been introduced to make him do anything in order to retain those boons already enjoyed and to acquire a great many others believed to be at the disposal of the parent. Such projection of magical powers upon the parent by the child is the natural consequence of his own lack of internal resources to combat the world by himself. Disciplines, chiefly of the restrictive kind, can therefore be imposed with excellent chances of being internalized and automatized, if the parental care is such as to guarantee the child security. Directional disciplines are imitative disciplines requiring little internalization, because tensions rarely accumulate about them. There is no superego activity in learning the multiplication table, but there is a great deal in controlling masturbation in childhood.

Yet a very sharp distinction must be made between the two kinds of learning processes: their social consequences are very far apart. Superego activity is essentially an internalization of mores. With regard to control of the sexual and aggressive impulses, internalization takes place at the cost of either suppression or conscious control, repression, or inhibition. In the event of conscious control, compensations in one form or another are effective in maintaining a balance. With respect to repression, the impulse vanishes from any conscious representation. The chief consequence of inhibition is that further growth or development of activities connected with the drive are effectively prevented, and in its place defensive activities against the original one are now subject to systematic integration. The outcome is *neurosis* or a strange character trait or both.

In Plainville, as in Western society generally, the process of suppression is adequately taken care of by two factors. The one implied compensation of all suppressive processes is parental approval, which has a great deal back of it in the form of the good parental care and the capacity of the parent to stimulate anticipation of boons to come, that is, control by anticipated rewards or promises. Children thus learn to conform for deferred rewards—and they can be deferred for a very long time indeed. No evidence exists in Plainville of any policy on the part of parents to exact conformity by means of preposterous promises that cannot be redeemed, or to cheat or fool the child. This would completely disrupt the entire superego system.

On the other hand those disciplines, direct or implied, which compel repressions pass out of conscious control, and punishment and reward systems do not apply or soon lose their relevancy. The effects of the sexual disciplines is unpredictable on a statistical basis. In a large percentage of cases the formation of distorted action systems pertaining to sex must be expected.

Two types of discipline in Plainville are conspicuous: the "kidding" of children, and the prolongation of corporal punishment by the father. The kidding purports to be a training in how to tolerate diminution in self-esteem or to withstand frustrations. It is a form of teasing, hence a form of cruelty. Its meaning is not clear, and the explanation that it is a kind of training in hardihood or in ready retaliation may be correct. If so, it follows the accepted ideal of masculinity as having the attributes of toughness, readiness to strike back, and elevation of one's self-esteem through berating the other fellow.[14] But it also includes the idea that, "You don't amount to much (in comparison with others) but you must never permit anyone else to know it." The efforts of the father to prolong arbitrary authority may be related to several other parental anxieties.

For the greater part the father has little to teach his son after the latter is ten or twelve years old, by which time he has acquired almost as much skill, though not so much strength, as his father. Parental punishment would tend forcibly to prolong this authority, which can no longer be implemented by the greater experience of the father. We may find here some relationship to the general anxiety about education, which also diminishes parental authority and tends

[14] These ideals are of course in addition to strength, competency at male skills, hard work, good fellowship, honesty, etc.

to break up the stability of the family unit, since most of the educated sons leave the community.

The "kidding" activity may also be relevant to another situation in Plainville. The father may find it necessary to institute arbitrary punishments to extend his authority because he is limited in his ability to reward his child for obedience. By the time the child is twelve, the father has already exhausted most reward possibilities. But he still controls the "big pocketbook," the desirable task, the automobile, and the access to other luxuries. The ability of the father to control these desiderata may still command much respect and obedience. However, from this time on there is increasing resentment on the part of the son toward submission. A result is the frequent pattern of leaving home during late youth. Parental cruelty at this stage would tend to enhance the value of the rewards, and their value can be maintained only by increasing the cruelty. This is, of course, an explosive situation. The obedient son finds out sooner or later that he is being cheated, and that sheer subsistence (which is all he gets) is not worth the price. The explosive aspects lie in the character constellation built in the obedient son: suppressed hatred, prudery, the need for scapegoat, etc.[15]

A final consequence of the good maternal care and subsequent conditioning to paternal authority is found in relation to sibling rivalry.[16] Sibling rivalry is motivated by anxiety that the inflated powers of the parent may no longer be at the disposal of the subject but may instead be given to someone else. Characteristic resolutions of this situation are: the wish to possess the attributes of the rival, which may lead to regressive longings; the need to set up claims on the score of incapacity or illness, which will compel the mother (or father) to be attentive; the hatred of the sibling and the wish for his death. The need to repress this hostility may backfire in the form of the subject's taking on himself the punishment he wishes his rival to suffer, to the detriment of his own self-esteem and the suppression of all aggressive attitudes or actions. The latter situation may terminate in complete submission to the rival and the idealization of the same, but always at

---

[15] The situation here described is probably the formula by which the feudal system maintained itself. However, feudalism had a strong adjunct in the theocratic state, which prevented effective action against the father or feudal lord. By increasing oppression, the value of certain minimal gratifications could be enhanced or at least maintained for a long time.

[16] See David M. Levy, *Studies in Sibling Rivalry* (New York, American Orthopsychiatric Association, 1937).

the cost of the subject's self-esteem and executive freedom in action or fantasy.

This, in brief, is a summary of the projective systems in the basic personality structure. They are the matrix out of which the character formation of the individual takes place up to late childhood. They do not include the consciously learned reality systems. It is apparent from this scheme that up to late childhood (which is the crucial period) certain situations stand out prominently. The action systems formed can be compared with those found in Comanche and Alor. The underpinning of the personality is strong, decisive, and relatively free of tension points. In this respect it resembles Comanche and is very unlike Alor. The most decisive factor is the generally good maternal care, with its effective solicitation of emotional response. This leads to the stimulation of curiosity and the beginning of positive ego feelings, and of strong affective attachment to the mother. This in turn lays the basis for strong superego formation and the idealization of the mother. At this stage the only tension points incapable of resolution are those created by the incapacity of the child to move harmoniously with growth as the result either of overprotection by the mother or of accidents like illness, which tend to create resistance to relinquishing the old adaptation. Language is a new weapon in this connection.

However, unlike Comanche, later in childhood factors are introduced—highly specific to Western man—which impede this smooth development and create tension points capable of resolution in a large variety of ways. Anal training introduces new value systems, and tension-relieving patterns arise which have a unique configuration and are adventitious to the evacuating function. They become in Western man important psychosomatic channels of expression. Most decisive in this connection are the painful factors introduced in connection with sexual disciplines. The ego receives its definite imprint from the manner in which these psychosexual constellations are formed, involving (a) psychosomatic patterns (terminating in various types of impotence), (b) the lowering of self-esteem, (c) divided feelings toward parental figures, which terminate the conflict-situation by pathological forms of self-reliance or passivity.

The situation differs from Alor in that even passivity in our culture is not deprived of executive weapons, as it is in Alor. In Alor the frustrations begin so early that effective aggression patterns cannot be formulated. We can therefore expect in our culture strong compensatory efforts to accompany any type of passivity. The number of possible characterological end-results is infinite.[17] The particular conflicts engendered by the factors in basic personality structure will depend largely on the common ideal. If the latter is directed toward salvation after death, then the conscious stimuli for compensation in a passive individual will be minimal; but if the conscious stimuli socially endorsed are toward success and achievement, all competitive factors will be greatly reinforced and the incentive to achieve these goals will create the most severe conflicts.

Adolescence

Puberty and adolescence are not marked by any formal changes; most important is the psychosomatic maturation of the sexual drive. Though no new constellations arise, one can more clearly discern those that have already been formed. In the sexual domain boys discover or are taught masturbation by others of their age, with its intense guilt-feelings and severe loss of self-esteem. The transition to heterosexual activity is impeded by an endless variety of taboos. The extent to which this situation can be successfully resolved depends upon the characterological patterns already in existence. Some of the failures are noteworthy: renunciation of sex, with the adoption of the goal of asceticism; masturbatic activity, with guilt which forms a bridge to neurosis, though it may not become manifest for ten years; or elaboration of pathological systems which terminate in psychosis—masturbation being the vehicle, not the cause, of the disturbance in personality functioning. The influence of the consequences of the conflicts engendered by masturbation may pervade every social relationship.

A second aspect of puberty and adolescence is its preparatory function for the adult role. It can be the time when the groundwork for skills is laid down; or in their absence, induction into activities in which less skill is required. In Plainville the latter is largely the

17 A case in point is the prominence of guilt, depression, and suicide in our culture, and the absence of all three in Alor. These three are end results of the capacity of the individual to introject the loved and authoritative parental object, and the formation of strong aggression patterns on that foundation. In Alor the introjection does not take place. The result is that a higher accomplishment level exists in our culture at the cost of the dangers of depression, guilt feelings, and suicide. The importance of these factors, the sources from which they originate, and the value systems derived from them cannot be overestimated. They impart to our culture a highly specific configuration.

situation. Here also there is the formation of adolescent gangs in which defiance of elders is a prominent motif. Conflicts with authority are mostly formulated at this time, and resolved in accordance with the influences laid down in childhood. The "education" of the boy is done without regard for consistency—scientific and religious systems are taught to be tolerated alongside one another. Competitive habits and games are inculcated at this time, if not long before.

Induction into labor in Plainville must tend toward strong father hatred, for the reward system breaks down. This situation is complicated by the inadequate systems of sexual-relaxor functions, for socially approved sexual activity is not possible. Overt father-hatred, deflation of religious figures, and, in Plainville, leaving home are common consequences.

The status problem enters here seriously for the first time. The decision must be made whether to continue paternal status or to utilize the opportunities for mobility. This decision is made largely by the parents.

Adulthood

It is in the assumption of the role of the adult that the action systems already formed receive their crucial test. The first test situation is the ability to compete without serious inhibitions or masochistic elaborations. Should inhibitions predominate, the individual must be satisfied with humbler status plus a large unconscious reservoir of hatred against rivals, employers, etc. The manifestations of this hatred are legion. One of the commonest and currently relevant is the "blame" psychology which finds its most convenient expression in the hatred and persecution of some scapegoat. This blame psychology also permits the individual to harbor a secret grandiose conception of himself. Such grandiosity has the formula: "I could love myself if. . . ." The self-esteem is attached to the fantasy of what one might be rather than what one is. In this regard the illusion of a life after death had a high stabilizing influence. If the individual is not inhibited and is successful in work or enterprise, the social ideals give him no rest, and he must constantly augment his margin of security economically and socially.

A second test situation is successful mating. Here more hidden constellations come to the fore. Difficulties may arise in connection with the tender relations to the mate, or with the sensual relations. In the first instance various degrees of anxiety and mistrust may pervade the relationship. In the sensual field a large number of potency disturbances may be precipitated. Other possibilities are sexual perversions and inversion (homosexuality). Related to these are the attitudes to children. This may be accompanied with more or less anxiety or hostility.

In the case of the female the sexual situation is about the same. In Plainville frigidity is likely to be the norm. Women with these disturbances of potency are likely to be firm supporters of the church, especially of those creeds which ban all pleasure outlets of man. Much of the gossip by women in Plainville is dedicated largely to the end that no one shall have any fun. The sexual disturbance of the mother conditions her reactions to the child, and so the vicious cycle is perpetuated.

Advancing age can be a crisis for either sex, economically or psychologically. With children becoming less dependable as social insurance, the inability to save enough or to continue working may create much anxiety. The psychological dangers are, however, less pressing in Plainville than in a society like Comanche. Social agencies, the church, or the government may help, but not without depressing the individual's self-esteem.

The Socially Relevant Characterological Types

In Plainville the motivational pace is set by the status-class-prestige complex, though to a lesser degree than elsewhere in the United States. The entire community has a collective inferiority feeling—characteristic anxieties of being exposed or ridiculed, and appropriate defenses, mostly of the sour grapes variety. Yet the whole community is permeated with the struggle to achieve status-prestige, whether it be in the guise of respectability or of wealth.

To achieve these ends the character formation of the individual must be attuned to the goal. Character structure, however, does not determine the degree of success exclusively; also important are (a) the status-class into which the individual is born, and (b) the opportunity to acquire skills. These factors are not of equal importance. Our ethnographer gives evidence that status-prestige acquired through birth—"family"—tends to be tenacious and can survive many slips and failures. He further tells us that the acquisition of higher technological skills, which probably spurs the boy to leave home, is not generally favored, though acquisition of basic farming skills at a young age is greatly encouraged. Moreover the acquisition of skills does not guarantee success. We must therefore conclude that the terminal result in character structure is the dominant influence which decides the extent to which the individual can achieve the accepted goals of success.

Character structure becomes involved with the status-class-prestige complex in a large variety of ways, because it conditions the various uses that can be made of social mobility. In this situation we have one constant—the goal of activity, success, security, power, etc.—and one variable, the character structure. But it must not be overlooked that we are describing various ways in which the basic personality structure emerges in the character of the individual. Character variations are therefore different modes of achieving socially defined goals. This means, in effect, that an inhibited individual has the same goal as one who is uninhibited. But the results differ.

This common goal, with varying capacities on the part of the individual to achieve it, makes for a social instability in so far as statuses cannot be inherited and because there is a constant turnover from underdog to overdog and vice versa. Another source of instability is that anxiety is mobilized on the part both of those who have status-prestige and of those who have not. Each will seek appropriate defenses for his respective position. That is, one side will seek measures to insure greater social mobility, the other, to limit it.

There is bound to be some question concerning the accuracy of the statement that basic personality structure in our society is fairly uniform and does not follow class-status lines. It can, for example, be said that sex mores are not the same in all classes. There is common agreement that the mores we described are those of the middle classes, but that the mores are laxer in the lower classes. Others will maintain that they are laxer in the upper classes. There is no evidence that basic personality structure differs for different statuses. But there are horizontal differences in character structure through all class lines, and differences in the equipment and skills that can implement self-assertive tendencies, which follow vertical lines of mobility.

The socially relevant character types can therefore be differentiated on the basis of free or blocked forms of self-assertion and the particular modalities of each. It must however be noted that the surface manifestation of a character trait gives no information concerning the nature of its composition or its genesis. For example, competitiveness must be regarded in our society as a normal manifestation of self-assertion when it is governed by the superego systems. But there are neurotic and criminal forms of self-assertion.[18] A neurotic self-assertion is an attempt to deny by force a deep feeling of inferiority or insecurity. Furthermore, in Plainville we saw some types of self-assertion that are injurious in intent, but that escape being criminal by a technicality. A good trader may misrepresent by omission but not by commission. If he misrepresents by omitting damaging details, he is merely a sharp trader and is both condemned and applauded; if he deliberately misrepresents, he is lying and is therefore only condemned. It is by this route that much concealed antisocial activity passes for normal in Plainville and in the United States generally. In the face of the acceptance of this pattern as a norm, we can expect that the average Plainviller is filled with a good deal of jealousy and envy, the intensity of which must vary with the degree of free available aggression in each individual. The evidence, if we may judge by the malignity of the gossip, points to the fact that the average individual has not much free self-assertion. The activities most condemned are cheating, stinginess, and sexual delinquencies, which indicates where the jealousy is most aroused in the inhibited individual. Cheating requires courage; and to be stingy, one must have something to be stingy with. What is really envied is the courage to make money, by fair means or foul. The sexual envy follows the customary pattern of "You shall not enjoy what I do not permit myself to enjoy."

It is quite apparent in Plainville, as it is elsewhere in America, that the person whose character formation permits him to be self-assertive and normally competitive can achieve the most highly approved goals. Only such an individual can have some degree of self-esteem. Those whose activity is blocked in the sexual and self-assertive spheres must carry a heavy load of self-condemnation, which is generally projected in the form of hatred toward those who achieve the approved goal of success. Thus social mobility increases the responsibilities of the individual and renders him much more susceptible to self-blame and self-depreciation.

In Plainville the opportunities for establishing compensations in the form of saving or hoarding money are circumscribed, because the

18 It is not altogether a certainty that criminality is related to failures in superego formation. What is more definitely known is that the factors which control inhibitions are not operating effectively.

money economy is on such a limited scale. The compensations must therefore take other forms. Several compensations are (1) to imitate and at the same time berate city folks; (2) to discipline children to take belittlement but to fight back against it; (3) not to permit city customs in the community or to let children be exposed to these influences. It is from this source that the strong feeling against progress and education must take its origin.

The imitation by Plainville of the mores of the rest of the United States is clearly shown in the way status-class lines are maintained under conditions different from those in large urban centers. This re-establishes the cycle of hatred and envy by the lower classes as against contempt and exclusion by the upper classes.

Derivatives of Projective Systems: Religion, Folklore, Social Ideologies

The religion of Plainville can be utilized only to recover the most elementary manifestations of the projective systems. We have the conventional types of Protestantism which differ from each other in minor details. The idealized deity who is permanent and all-powerful, who is looked upon as a protector, and who loves and dispenses bounty only in return for certain conditions—these are all direct transplantations of the father in the household, and of the conditions under which he loves and forgives or reinstates. These are all based on the actual experiences of the child, and hence are quite plausible. The secondary elaborations of this idea, that if I repent and suffer I will move the deity to reinstate me in his good graces, are present too.

These details are not, however, the specific features of religion in Plainville. They are present in the form of a general assumption. The weight falls in another direction, which is a remote derivation from the original Calvinistic doctrine. It is emphasized to an extraordinary degree that all sensual pleasure is sin and this includes chiefly sex, dancing, drinking, card playing. Abstemiousness is regarded as virtue and a claim not only for social regard, but for salvation after death.

It is an interesting detail that those who are "saved" are those who belong chiefly to the lower classes. This is clear evidence that social failure is regarded as a personal responsibility which can be easily rationalized as the wages of sin. For a man to accept salvation under these conditions is tantamount to the admission that his striving for success was laden with guilt, and an admission that the only recourse left is the renunciation of the goal, the submission to punishment, and the acceptance of post-mortem boons in lieu of success.

Religion in Plainville cannot be accurately evaluated without an exhaustive study of individual biographies. It is a common phenomenon in the personal histories of individuals in our society that the fate of formal religious beliefs depends largely on the outcome of the basic constellations created in the family situation. Many a child brought up in a household where religion plays a prominent role, becomes a complete agnostic as a part of the revolt against paternal authority. There is in Plainville, as elsewhere in the United States, a considerable clash between the ideals of the success goal, and those furnished by the church, which promises rewards after death. We must be guided in Plainville by the observations that irreligiosity is very widespread, but that on the other hand religion has vital meaning to members of the poorer churches. There are some conclusions that one can draw safely. The irreligiosity of Plainville is no surprise. The church moreover imposes severe restrictions upon the individual who has any self-assertive tendencies and can therefore only add to the general hostility against those who seek pleasure or relaxation. Religion buttresses the repressive side of the culture, and offers dubious rewards—that is, rewards which have a dubious currency. In a considerable measure the value of salvation is weakened by the social hierarchy of the various churches, which is in contradiction to the democratic character of salvation. Notwithstanding the fact that religion has some vitality for the poorer classes, this means that when one has few gratifications the superego becomes stronger and takes even those few away.

The statement that the socially approved goals of success and salvation do not compete on equal grounds is a practical illustration of the principle that in our culture the projective systems have lost their force as social stabilizers. The force of the projective systems depends in part on individual character, in part on education. But many individuals who have acquired a good scientific education retain religious systems learned in childhood. The two systems can apparently be kept in air-tight compartments despite serious incompatibilities.

The folklore of Plainville must be divided into the traditional and the living folklore. Much of the first relates to the idealization of pioneer days and figures. Plainville is also exposed to the living folklore which is largely urban in origin. For this living folklore we must look to the songs, movies, and successful radio characters. These are not selected by an elite, but by a popular taste. What information they give us is not specific to any locality.

Popular songs exploit a few motifs: nostalgia, loneliness, broken romance, idealization of woman, especially the mother, who is generally deserted but is looked on as a protector. The glorification of song and dance, the dionysian moods copied from Negro folk tunes—these can hardly be popular with the older folks in Plainville.

The most popular fictitious characters in America are the movie stars, many of whom represent the idealized progress from rags to riches, the common aspirations to beauty, wealth, fame, adulation. They enact in their stereotyped dramas the success story and Cinderella motif *ad nauseum;* but stop when money or love is achieved. They serve the function of fantasy gratification of needs for security, power and sexual happiness, generally denied to most.

The screen was once the commonest form of fantasy enjoyment, and some of the characters created were successful chiefly because they answered these needs most effectively. Such a character was Charlie Chaplin's bum.[19] He is Mr. Nobody and is very much aware of his own insignificance. He is always the butt of a crazy and bewildering world in which he has no place and from which he constantly runs away into a contented do-nothingness. He is free from conflict because he has abandoned the quest for security and prestige, and is resigned to the lack of any claim to virtue or distinction. He always becomes involved in the world by accident. There he encounters evil and aggression against the weak and helpless which he has no power to combat. Yet always, in spite of himself, he becomes the champion of the wronged and oppressed, not by virtue of his great organizing ability but by virtue of a streak of homely and insolent trickiness by which he seeks out the weaknesses of the wrongdoer. He always remains humble, poor, and lonely, but is contemptuous of the incomprehensible world and its values. He therefore represents the character of our time who is perplexed by the dilemma either of being crushed in the struggle to achieve the socially approved goals of success and power (he achieves it only once—in *The Gold Rush*) or of succumbing to a hopeless resig-

[19] Mr. West points out that the entire discussion here about our living folklore of nationwide vogue has little relevance to Plainvillers, but much to urbanites. Most Plainvillers apparently consider Chaplin just silly. This observation is of considerable importance. It means that the unconscious appeal of Chaplin's bum is less powerful to Plainvillers than to city folks, and that the tensions which this strange vagabond purports to ease are less intense with Plainvillers. This would mean that the Plainviller is more secure and less troubled by the pursuit of goals approved in urban centers.

nation and flight from them. Charlie's bum is a great comfort in that he gloats in his ability to outwit the pernicious forces aligned against him if he chooses to do so and affords every man the satisfaction of feeling that the ultimate flight from social goals to loneliness is an act of *choice* and not a symptom of his defeat. Mickey Mouse is a continuation of the Chaplin saga.

The radio has also made its contribution to the folk heroes: Charlie McCarthy, Bob Hope, Jack Benny, and others. All these characters exploit the failings of the "average" man. In Charlie McCarthy we again have Mr. Everyman, the wooden dummy, who is the puppet of powerful forces. Yet he constantly berates his master, calls attention to his defects—his stinginess, baldness, and failure with women. He resents disciplines and has profound disrespect for his teachers, whom he maligns mercilessly. His impudence can only be halted every now and then by calling his attention to the fact that he is nothing but a block of wood which can be sliced into a Venetian blind, or in which no one but a woodpecker could take any interest. The polarities of abasement and cruelty are epitomized in this amusing creature of fiction.

These figures of contemporary folklore are more effective in comforting the individual than is religion—though they both have the same function. The current folklore promises no rewards but it bolsters morale and self-esteem by the spectacle of man rejecting current ideals and expressing contempt for them. Movies with the moral that "wrong doesn't pay" have the same bolstering effect. For those who are lacking in enterprise such morals have an exhilarating effect and sustain hope.

This folklore does not employ the constellations of early life. It utilizes rather the end results of the battle with current ideals.

The last category of the projective systems, current social ideologies, take their origin from the same sources as our living folklore. The scope of this work does not permit an analysis of this problem, nor does Plainville afford us much opportunity to investigate its role in social life today. The social ideologies so much discussed in urban centers have no vogue in Plainville; those which are the subject of much controversy in urban centers are all looked upon with great suspicion, are ridiculed and burlesqued. There is no better indicator of this than the fact that an individual follows the political line of his family as if political conviction were inherited in the germ plasm. On the other hand, there is a general and more realistic conviction that all political ideologies are forms of misrepresentation, have the function only of enabling office seekers to obtain office, and are otherwise meaningless. The majority of the inhabitants of Plainville are Republicans, which in this particular community means they do not want anything changed. Apart from the education necessary to follow the lines of contemporary social ideologies, the little experience they have had with the New Deal has rendered them still more obdurate. The WPA has seriously upset the cash economy of the society so that the indolent and indigent live on a higher cash economy than many hard-working farmers, much of whose labor goes into subsistence with a very small cash balance.

There seem to be two main reasons why the Plainvillers have no interest in social ideologies except to be afraid of them. First, because these ideologies are for the greater part irrelevant to the issues of living as they see it. They labor hard for subsistence and are removed from the conflicts of the labor class in urban centers and they know nothing of the workings of the huge organizations to whom they in turn sell their products in excess of their private needs. They therefore behave toward "radical" social ideologies in the same way that they do toward illicit sexual relations. They feel bound to their lot; they do not see much chance of altering it, while they suffer as inferiors in the reflection of urban life. Hence they hate and despise the efforts of anyone who dares ask for more than they do. A second reason is that they identify themselves—justifiably or not—not with the labor class, but with the propertied class, in which some of them undoubtedly belong. The citizens of Plainville are not the "farm bloc"; but the arrangement is such that Plainvillers can profit somewhat by the activities of the "farm bloc" though not enough to make any substantial difference. Yet they could easily be convinced that the cause of the "farm bloc" is their cause.[20]

What is a social ideology? It is a system of ideas which seeks implementation by action to gain or preserve certain interests. Generally the part of an ideology which is unexpressed is the emotional assumptions on which it is based. The ideology is given a rational façade by a careful selection of data which support the thesis, omitting what contradicts it. It has a logical superstructure, and it usually embodies

---

[20] In recent discussions concerning price regulation the farmers have often taken violent opposition to the farm bloc in Congress.

a program of action to secure the goal. The place now occupied by social ideologies in modern life was formerly occupied by religious ideologies; but the latter have gradually been deprived, through the growth of empirically derived reality systems, of the ability to regulate certain aspects of social life. To be sure, religion never regulated social life directly, but it was able to offer compensatory and deferred gratifications for decompensations, and hence under certain conditions could contribute to social stability. The advent of science has deprived religion of its right to be considered as a tenable reality system—being derived from purely projective sources. Religious ideology from Job to Calvin was never a direct form of social critique; but one can easily follow the social conditions through the projected imagery in the religious ideology. Scientific method as applied directly to social data offered a more direct approach to social critique, and religion was left to take care of that aspect of morality not taken care of by government, police, public opinion, and custom.

Social ideologies are currently the commonest preoccupation of man. Salvation is sought through success or social well-being, and the whole system of deferred gratification has lost its standing as a social expedient. The kind of social ideology a man invents or endorses is therefore an indicator of the interaction of his status-class position and his character. The results are not always what one expects. The son of a millionaire may be a communist because it seems rational and desirable. Back of his endorsement may be an identification with the underdog. But he will present his endorsement in the form of a logical argument which has no reference to his unconscious identification with the "underprivileged."

If this is the case, then the rejection of social ideologies in Plainville may be due in part to the fact that these ideologies do not become a vital issue because there is a lack of pressure concerning subsistence. Or it may be due to the suppressed self-assertion, which finds expression in the hatred mechanism. Plainvillers are "against" forms of self-assertion, no matter what form it takes.

As supporting evidence for this we can point to the enormous amount of free hatred rampant in Plainville: the malicious and endless gossip, the general injunction against pleasure seeking, the suppression of free sexual expression, the universal feeling of inferiority, the hatred of progress, the ridicule of education, the low status of women, the paucity of aesthetic interests, the brutal kidding of children, the universality of stinginess, etc. These are all indicators that a great deal of hostility exists, though it is never of an explosive character.

The Implementation of Social Goals

This subject need not detain us long. It is a constantly changing machinery with central federal controls down to local police. This machinery is elective and its directives need public approval. The latter is always achieved without coercion, by consent, and the whole technique of government is to gain consent by compromise and by disguising the true purport of certain legislation; by intimidation; by making promises. It is beyond our purposes to discuss this aspect. The only feature pertinent to our project is the general distrust of legal mechanisms in Plainville. Part of this is a traditional hangover from pioneer days. Part of it is due to the unwillingness of the majority of Plainvillers to make any changes in anything.

Summary and Conclusions

Our analysis attempted to settle one major and one minor issue; what are the psychological features of Western man, taking Plainville as our base; and second, what are some specific features of Plainville? Unless we settle the first question we can get no perspective on the second, and we might be tempted to draw some pessimistic conclusions about Western man.[21] The general conclusions concern, first, the basic personality structure without consideration for differences in status, class, or education. We can then consider the effects of these three factors, and finally the effects of local variations in mores.

The personality gets a good start and, barring the operation of constitutional factors, receives a strong underpinning which will support the child in his initial contacts with the outer world and give him practice in eliciting expressive affects. The institutional basis for this is the division of function between male and female in which the economic load rests on both sexes. The consequence is the strong attachment to and idealization of the mother as guardian and helper in distress, an attitude easily extended to the father when the child is able to recognize his importance. Since the parental role is a dependable one, a strong incentive is laid for conscience and ideal building, and the child becomes amenable to socializing education. This

21 See Erich Fromm, *Escape from Freedom* (New York, Farrar & Rinehart, 1941).

lays a strong foundation for strong social cohesion, and for coöperation. With these many gratifications as a base, a foundation is laid for strong self-assertive expression. This is of the highest importance, because all subsequent frustrations must be evaluated with the knowledge that the personality has already acquired excellent means for self-expression. The first expression of this may be the refusal to move on to new types of adaptation forced on it by biological factors (growth) and sociological ones (expectations of elders). The first manifestation of self-assertion may thus be to oppose socializing influences. Maternal overprotection may be responsible for this, as may illness, and so on.

This favorable situation in infancy then undergoes considerable distortion under the influence of later disciplines which help the process of growth in some aspects but introduce painful factors in others, including some that are highly specific and adventitious. The painful factors are introduced chiefly in the sexual development, that is, in connection with sexual activity of childhood as a relaxor activity. The precise biological role of sexuality in infancy and childhood is not known; if it is a relaxing agency, the tension systems cannot be definitely identified. It may be a factor attending growth. No rationale can be discovered for the practice of prohibition, since the sexual activity of childhood has no relation to procreation. It does however have a definite relation to the somatic pleasure-relaxor systems of which breast pleasure-sucking is the first. The consequences of this sexual prohibition are many and complex. A blocked-action system is created which may be resolved in a large number of ways. The importance of the mother may become greatly exaggerated in the pleasure-relaxor aspects; the attachment to her may be magnified; it may be mingled with hatred. Other somatic channels may be used for this relaxor function, the mouth or anus. The hostility may be directed toward those who interfere with the child's access to her, such as the father or siblings. Such hostility may be repressed with exaggerated conscience and diligence and increased submission to parental authority as results. The blocked-action system created in this domain may spread to all activity and introduce timidity, lack of enterprise, and anxiety. This constellation was identified by Freud as the Oedipus complex and represents the consequence of an anxiety situation created by repressive mechanisms. The Oedipus complex is therefore the record of such a repressive process, not, as is commonly assumed, the cause of it.

In connection with sphincter control—a socially determined goal —we get a new series of events. It is the first training in responsibility and social acceptance under specific conditions. It lays the foundation for conscientiousness, since failure predicates the loss of the many gratifications based on parental protection. This zone has a pure evacuation function, not a "tension" relaxor function; but it may be pressed into the service of a relaxor function under certain conditions. Also in connection with this evacuating function—this is also true of urinary function—a series of social values are initiated, which have nothing to do with the evacuating function and which are the reverse of those spontaneously evolved. These values are obedience, cleanliness, orderliness, and perhaps certain aesthetic values. By this training the retentive and expulsive functions may become stressed as polarities which may subsequently be used by the individual as important psychosomatic tension points.

One of the consequences of good maternal care is the stimulation of a high degree of curiosity, which, with the aid of a free psychomotor apparatus, leads to the desire to explore, create, invent, and investigate. This aspect of adaptation need not be influenced by the blocked systems created by sexual and other disciplines. It is this freedom of curiosity and manipulative talents which is subject to much training in the form of "education." In connection with educability large variations exist because of differences in native intelligence, but even more because of the presence or lack of opportunity. The material and intellectual cultures are perpetuated through these channels. However, the opportunities for education are usually accompanied by prolonged dependency on parents, so that this aspect of personality is always developed at the cost of independence, since most "higher education" takes place between the ages of fourteen and twenty-five.

These are the constellations in basic personality structure, and it is evident that the characterological types emerging from different combinations of operative constellations are very numerous indeed. The outcome depends on how stationary the environment of the individual remains. A large number of factors influence the character structure of the individual: survival of parents; the number and sex of siblings; the patterns of sibling rivalry; the time of induction into economic activities; prolonged illness; extent of education; the special mores of status and class and the special security system of each. The crisis of puberty is usually determined by constellations laid down in childhood; so is the preparedness for marriage. The outcome of the sexual development as a rule is not apparent until adulthood. The patterns of self-assertion and aggression are also laid down in childhood, and are subject to reinforcement or modification later.

Some of the socially relevant outcomes of the basic personality structure must be stressed. Though the emerging individual has a high emotional potential, too many blocked-action systems are created. The capacity for idealization, and hence worship, of "great men" is created, as well as the foundation for a religion with an idealized deity with great power for both good and harm. On the other hand, from the blocked systems we derive (a) serious sexual disturbances, both on the affective and executive side (potency); (b) great variations in aggression patterns, with psychosomatic accompaniments; (c) marked variations in the attitude to authority, excessive submission and passivity (even to the extent of dragging in the sexual organization in the form of homosexuality, asceticism, or perversion); or excessive and premature independence (paranoid personalities).

The social relevancy of these characterological types is that they contain ferment for social instability. Status lines do not determine characterological constellations; if they did the stability of modern society would be much greater. They often work in opposing directions. Strong characters with free aggression patterns may arise in lower statuses and weaklings in higher statuses. Another contribution to the instability from the characterological side is the uniformity of the goal in all statuses. The presence of social mobility (in democracies) places greater burdens on the individual to maintain self-esteem by achieving socially approved goals of success. This leads to many paradoxical situations: for example, the essentially passive individual may compensate for defects by destructive activities. Another complicating feature is the high capacity of modern man, by virtue of strong affectivity, to combine along class or common interest lines to defend these interests, for example, cartels and unions.

The struggle for success becomes such a powerful force because it is the equivalent of self-preservation and self-esteem. Flight from these goals terminates logically in the flight from society altogether, and resignation becomes tantamount to defeat. The validation of the personality along the lines of power is facilitated by the financial system, which permits saving and investment for interest and profit. Another contributing factor is the loss of standing for deferred types of gratification offered by religion.

The removal of religion as a stabilizing influence in society—despite the persistence of dogma and ritual—was largely due to the increasing knowledge of the outer world and improvements of techniques of mastery. These have also contributed to the alteration of the social structure through the introduction of manufacture. With the increased mastery of nature, fewer anxiety situations remained that could be referred to the deity. The improvement of government (which took over the control of many types of behavior) likewise reduced the effective province of religion.

The social tensions created by the newer types of organization were not foreseen, and at present a crisis of vast dimensions has been created on that score.

The culture of Plainville shows some specific features. The culture is in a state of flux in which many values are changing. For a long time Plainville was oriented on a "feudal" plan, in which parental authority had to be augmented because of the paucity of rewards for obedience. The improvement of communication has broken down its isolation and urban values are gradually seeping in and destroying family solidarity. If "big business" farming develops on a universal scale in the good-land areas, then individual farming will disappear entirely around Plainville.

CHAPTER XII

THE PERSONALITIES OF PLAINVILLE

THE following four biographical sketches were gathered by our ethnographer, Mr. West. They were not selected on any basis other than that the subjects were willing to coöperate with the endeavor. Since our ethnographer is not a psychiatrist, he cannot be accused of picking his cases from the point of view of psychopathology. This being the case, it is amazing to see how much neurotic illness and how many serious character distortions can be found in the four individuals selected because they had the time and willingness to coöperate.

These sketches are condensations of voluminous notes; [1] only those details are included which are pertinent to our enterprise. That the telling of a true and honest biography was a new undertaking for all the subjects can be seen from their squeamishness and their desire to put the best possible face on their stories. The range of character types included in these four is very narrow. Their statuses are almost all on the same plane. But Plainville does not have a proletarian class, nor does it have a true upper class. We cannot therefore derive much information on that score. All we can expect to find is whether in this group of unselected cases we can observe some confirmation of the impressions heretofore gathered from middle-class folk in large urban centers and from individuals who have frank neurotic disturbances. Such a concept as "neurosis" is unknown in Plainville. These are all average people and the distinction between "normal" and neurotic breaks down completely here. Only one of the four can be considered relatively free of neurotic traits; the other three have, according to psychiatric standards, severe neuroses. However no quantitative or statistical conclusions can be drawn from the data; they permit only a qualitative judgment about the conjectures derived from the study of the normative influences that shape the individual. This is no dis-

---

[1] These notes were collected by Mr. West and lent to me by him for this purpose. The character analyses are my own. I was assisted in the preparation of these character sketches by two of the students: Mr. David F. Aberle and Dr. Alfred H. Stanton. The preliminary reports on James L., and Elinor were made by Mr. Aberle; those on William M. and Rachel, by Dr. Stanton.

covery; it has been known for over half a century. The biographical data can be used to establish the relation between character types and their compatibility with socially defined goals.

James L.

James L. was born at Plainville in 1897, the oldest of four brothers. He was inducted into farm labor when very young and from eleven to fifteen had to do all the hard work on the farm because his father was ill. His father ultimately recovered, and about this our subject says, "It felt as if we had all been let out of prison." It was after his father's recovery that he first went away from home to visit his grandfather. He was very uneasy during this first absence. He was anxious and feared the lightning would strike him. He says of his childhood: "People were good to me. I felt well-treated and understood. I wasn't lonely because I could always read a book or invent something." He was sent to school at six; the first incident which he remembers is being compelled by the teacher to march to the accompaniment of a little bell. He was very "scared."

His dealings with his brothers were not pleasant. He was four and a half years older than the next one, and he "bossed" them all, something he no longer regards as an accomplishment. He resented the fact that they had children come to play with them while he had to work.

He left home at fifteen, having a vague idea that what he wanted was money, not an education. He wanted adventure and to live better. Later he changed his mind and wanted an education because he thought education brought money. But he lacked the persistence to acquire an education. After he began to read books, he conceived the idea that he too wanted to be a writer.

He attempted to put this ambition into effect and at eighteen wrote a movie scenario. But he could not write grammatically. He persisted in this ambition to write until he is now fanatical about it. "It was never implanted in me to get beyond the eighth grade." This ambition was a hangover of his feeling at school. He forgot it while he was in the army, but when he lived in cities he was overcome by a feeling of inferiority. "I felt that some day I would show the local aristocracy who was superior."

It was a well-patterned idea that a boy at eighteen should go away from home, shuck corn for a year in a neighboring state, head west, and perhaps stay out there. He got enough money for this adventure from his grandmother. There, in Ohio, he saw a school building and was much impressed. But he could not follow through in his plans for an education. He therefore returned home, where he fell ill of typhoid fever. When he recovered he went off again and, accompanied by a cousin, took a helper's job on a farm. He did not want to desert his cousin, who had some "nervous trouble" and could not work. They began traveling on freight cars, but his cousin deserted and he went on alone. From this time on he had several jobs, and then "went on the bum." He fell in with the I.W.W. and joined them. He had a vague idea that he could put his adventures to some literary use, get a story out of them. He was for a time impressed with the drama of the thing. He did not admire the I.W.W.; in fact he despised them. They tried to get more pay from the farmers and would threaten to fire a farmer's house "if he didn't come across." They called the farmer a "junior capitalist" and said "they must break him because he was almost as bad as Rockefeller." During his association with the I.W.W. James was not loyal to them, wanted in fact always to play a "lone wolf" role. One day he was in a cattle car and saw some hoboes robbing harvest hands who happened to be in the car. The following day he saw some of the robbers in a cafeteria and said, "Say! Didn't I see you fellows on the train last night?" They gave him $10, and he took it, commenting nobly, "Of course it wasn't fair to take it."

In 1916 he enlisted in the army. He thought it would be an adventure, wanted to go to the Philippines or Hawaii. He also thought this would put him in line for a pension.

During the time he was "bumming" James said he behaved very well and never "bummed" a meal in his life. He once stole some oats for a bed. Once he was accused of stealing a coat and almost had to shoot the argument out. "I wasn't afraid of man or beast. But the law! I feared that. A night in jail would have disgraced me."

In 1917 while he was a soldier, he found himself on the West Coast, saw mountains and salt water for the first time, and here his first marriage occurred. He met a girl, went out with her for three weeks, had sexual relations with her, and married her. She was not a virgin, but he did not care. Shortly after, he returned home and found her in bed with another man and divorced her. His motives for marriage were, "I thought it would be nice to have someone to come home to; I'd be going to France." He had romantic visions of being seen off to France and returning eagerly to her expectant arms. "My lawyer saw me off."

. . . "My marriage was not an enriching experience. I made many innocent girls suffer over that"—but he later cut down on the number of innocent girls he victimized.

His experiences in the war were not very exciting. He never saw service overseas. He was chiefly somewhere in the East, shooting off big guns. He thinks he was a little "shell shocked." He thought he had repeated nightmares, some of which would throw him out of bed— but it is doubtful whether they were really in the nature of a traumatic neurosis. When he was discharged from the army he went back to Plainville, but soon got the idea that all people in that vicinity were hillbillies, frightfully poor and ignorant, that they knew nothing of the world and had to spend their time in silly gossip. He was dissatisfied there and went to the nearest big city.

His stay there was not long. He became sexually intimate with a girl from the West and said that for the first time in his life he was satisfied with sex. He made some attempts at song writing and had several songs printed. But he was not a success and he decided to come back to Plainville.

This time he made a better start. He began seeing people in Plainville and began to be more tolerant of their failings. He was considered a fine, friendly boy. He found his family as he had left them, with no distinction except that conferred on them by one brother's drinking. He came back to Plainville because he thought this was the only place to find a "good" girl.

His marriage was the only other important event in his life. He met his wife Elinor, wanted her to be an ideal romantic mate, promised himself that they would never quarrel and would be wonderful companions. He did not feel after short acquaintance that she was "the only girl in the world," but nevertheless "that's the way it would be!"

His marriage was a great disappointment to him, for he discovered that she was frigid. He had no idea that "it could or should be that way, because out of ten or fifteen girls I had before marriage none had been that way." He tried to "wake her up." What puzzled him was that most women he knew were "cold" in public but just the opposite when you got them alone. "But Elinor was different; she wanted me to talk to her and worship her and kiss her." Apparently this was a sensitive point with him. He thought it was due to anemia; she thought it was due to the fact that he rushed her too much. For a brief period after her second child she lost her frigidity, but relapsed shortly thereafter. At first Elinor thought all women were like that, and when another woman told her that she had "feeling" when a man kissed her, she was surprised. During nineteen years of marriage his wife has never wanted intercourse. She responds only two or three times a month. "That's what hurts so about making a woman pregnant when they do it just for the man."

Having this problem with his wife, he has been unfaithful to her twice. His wife discovered it and thenceforth would not permit him to leave for another city to work. The second time she threatened that if he did it again she would do the same. Their relations were constantly spoiled by anxiety about having too many children. He never planned children, they always came by accident. His wife wanted an operation to render her sterile.

He is now disappointed in his marriage. He wanted a companion, to go fishing and hunting with him. She doesn't like to fish or hunt. He is now also quite disillusioned about all women and would not like to make another attempt. His feeling about sex is that it had better be suppressed. His wife is very good at suppression. He often dreams of her death and is relieved to find her with him. His chief complaint about women is that he cannot find one who "caresses his organs without being asked to do so." "Too much worry about sex—fear your wife will die when she gives birth."

He feels no favoritism toward any of his children. His children all prefer their mother, but he thinks he has no jealousy on that score. His greatest difficulty with his wife is that she does not want the children to help him with farm work. She sets them against it and they refuse to coöperate. The fact is that farming is very distasteful to him. He has arranged it so that he won't ever have to work. He does not want his children to be mixed up with sex for fear that they will "get in with the wrong kind of folks." He was dismayed when his two daughters became involved with a man in some unspecified manner. He had charges brought against the man and had him locked up.

His feeling about his brother who drinks is very strong. His daughter is now engaged to a man who drinks. He wants both men sterilized. He resents his older brother, and fears his son-in-law; dreads the prospect of having to take care of his grandchildren. His attitude to his wife is one of extreme jealousy and he is extremely defensive to all potential rivals.

His chief preoccupation is with the education of his children. "He'd rather they had education than a million dollars." But his attitude to it is not undivided. He thinks college education would ruin his boy; on the other hand he thinks that this is the way the boy can become president some day. "I couldn't be a great writer, but my son will."

This brief biographical sketch gives us only the bare outlines of the outward movements of his life. He is "typical," and his personal fate is quite like that of many others in the community. He is accessible, affable, guardedly confidential and "honest" within the limits of telling as good a story as possible.

Of the formative influences in his life he recalls a good many significant episodes. He was weaned at two years. "They didn't cut my hair until I was four. I wore curls just like a girl." His earliest recollection is of sitting with his mother in the dark waiting for his father to come home. He has no definite recollections about toilet training, but he has two dreams which bear on the subject.

"I dreamed I was back at my old house sleeping on a pallet on the floor. I woke and had to go to the weeds fifty yards from the house and squatted. The phone rang. My father answered. My aunt had heart trouble. I got the impression she had died. Going back to the pallet I find that it had stretched out and the excreta were on the edge of the bed. I was dismayed. If this became known what a laugh everyone would have on me. I found some papers, mixed up part, then took a weed for the rest, but the bed was gone. Someone had taken those quilts away. I woke up looking frantically for them." There were no associations to the dream.

He remembers urination contests between boys, but otherwise remembers no incidents of a sexual nature during boyhood. The disciplinarian in the house was actually the father, but the executive end of the discipline was generally delegated to the mother. He does not remember being spanked very often. He was once punished for trying to wear out an old pair of shoes in order to get a new pair. He complained that his father was really not a pal to him; did not treat him as an equal. He had to be seen and not heard, and had to wait for his food.

The severest aspect of discipline to him was to begin work so early and so hard. He had to work with a double shovel at the age of ten, and worked from before sunrise to sundown. This was largely due to the illness of his father. It was this that made him formulate ambitions about running away and about getting an education.

The house they lived in had two rooms, and hence he frequently overheard sexual relations between parents. He thought very little of it at the time. He felt very little anxiety about the subject of sex. However some of the dreams he remembers of childhood belie his statements. He remembers dreams of being pursued by wild animals, with fear of being devoured by them. He was also scared about a house in which there had been a scandal. He thought he saw one man waiting for another with a gun.

At the age of five he was playing with a little girl in the outhouse and was caught in the act by her grandmother. The little girl was playing cow with him and was milking him into a cup. "It was reported to my mother and I was ashamed of it until ten or twelve. I was not whipped, only scolded and made to believe it was terrible." At the age of seven he began to have sex play with a girl of fifteen, his aunt, which continued four years. The girl told him that an older man tried to have relations with her, but that it hurt; she therefore wanted to play with him. This was an humiliating experience for him because he could not give her any sensation. She would have to masturbate after it. These activities were facilitated by the fact that she was his aunt, and they slept together quite openly for it passed as an innocent relationship.

His masturbation history begins at eleven or twelve, the practice being learned from an older boy. The only impression he remembers is that the ejaculation was "very little"; he expected more from what he had seen of bulls servicing cows. From fourteen to sixteen his masturbation was more frequent, once a day to once a week.

He was troubled all his life by fears that his penis was too small. He was reassured on that score by a prostitute who told him it was just right, as the big ones hurt too much. He had an opportunity for intercourse at fourteen with a cousin but did not "have the nerve." He had his first intercourse at sixteen. His preoccupation with his genitals dated from an injury to his testicles while climbing a tree. The scrotum was injured, and one of his testicles swollen to twice its normal size.

His first running away from home at sixteen was motivated to no small degree by sexual curiosity. He experimented a good deal with the girls in the family he lived with. He said that all the girls there were very loose. The oldest girl was a school teacher who "had a feller who came at noon and took her off in the corn field and the entire school would pair off." "Why didn't I get some of the girls?—But I didn't. They used to take my penis out when I lay down. I had no experience with girls because there weren't any in my family. I always felt that if I had a girl she'd be a kind of angel. I did try one of the girls and tried to hug her, but she was strong and pushed me away. I had a feeling that I didn't take with them. It would have changed my whole life if she had made up to me. But since she treated me rough, I decided to let them alone. She dated others, but not me."

Shortly after, he had his first intercourse. He had no fear of impotence. He began to have wet dreams. He was dominated through life by a strong urge to have relations with women, some of them virgins, "but after that I always had nightmares."

About his relations to the community there was one outstanding feature. He felt socially inferior. He thought he was of low caste and wanted much to prove himself, to validate himself, to be equal to others. The struggle with status began in childhood and is not settled at forty-three. It was concerned with two chief issues, money as a means to this end and education. He failed in both, as far as he is concerned, but he now has the same problem with regard to his children.

This man can be taken as an average, well-adjusted individual, with well-defined objectives in life and relatively free of incapacitating neurosis, though he has definite neurotic character. His position in the family, the oldest of four siblings, turned out to be unfortunate because of his father's incapacitating illness, as a consequence of which he had prematurely to assume responsibility for the heavy farm labor. This created envy of his younger siblings who could play while he worked. However, he seems to have managed this situation effectively, for he took a superior attitude and bossed them. This attitude he maintained into adult life and in the case of one of his siblings, actually took over a paternal role. Notwithstanding these compensatory attitudes, he retained a strong feeling of inferiority toward other children in school who "had better things," and enjoyed greater privileges. He had the tendency to regard himself as unlucky. This caused no small amount of anger against his parents; but this was safely shunted in the direction of a masochistic fantasy that "they would be miserable if he died" and would be sorry that they had not given him more. This fantasy tells an interesting story. In back of it is a story of a strong positive feeling toward the parents, a tonic superego. The fantasy gets him what he wants, parental affection and a reassurance of his worth, temporarily upset by some immediate frustration. But it is based on strong ties to the parents. The aggression he has is turned inward to himself. Its form in the unconscious is undoubtedly a death wish against his parents. Consciously he thinks his childhood was pleasant, not lonely, and there are no complaints about hunger or severe mistreatment.

His attitude toward his father shows clearly that he regarded him as the source of all disciplines, the mother being hardly held accountable for any of them, even those for which she was directly responsible, like sphincter control. There was little tendency to idealize the father, although this tendency was very strong toward his mother. It is on the pattern of this idealization that his subsequent tendency to make angels out of all women is based.

The one source of friction between him and his father was based entirely on his early induction into hard labor and his necessity to carry the responsibilities of a father without any of the advantages thereof. This led to his early departure from home at fifteen or sixteen for his "wild oats" period. It is interesting that the grandmother also was the good angel in this instance. The pattern of wandering away from home is a protest mechanism, and is undoubtedly conventionalized in this part of the country.

Of the disciplines which made a decided impression on him in childhood, the two which stand out are the anal and sexual disciplines. The dream he reports about defecating in bed, the fear of ridicule associated with it, the fear of losing something, and the death or illness of his aunt present a typical constellation found in Western man. Though the association with the death of his aunt is obscure in its meaning, it is found frequently enough to have given rise to a theory concerning an anal-sadistic stage of development. It is understandable as an induction of a discipline at a time previous to his knowledge of its significance, and represents therefore a break with the previous irresponsible period characterized by complete care of all his wants by the mother. This discipline is the first training in responsibility and is a signal to the child that its parasitic existence is coming to an end. Such a constellation therefore is really an accident which accompanies very good maternal care, sufficient to create in the child a feeling of maternal omnipotence. The cessation of this period undoubtedly brings with it much protest and a temporary hostility to the parent, which subsequently undergoes complete repression. In the case of James this seems not to have been the case, and the premature responsibilities placed on him may well have revived the wish to be free and irresponsible, with the kind, protecting parent resuming her role.

The sexual disciplines were not so explicit. He overheard parental intercourse at an early age and was not terrified by the experience. But his sex life throughout is ridden with anxiety of one kind or another; not enough anxiety to inhibit him, or to disqualify women, but enough to give him anxiety dreams when he has had intercourse with a virgin. His sexual development is marked by an early seduction at the age of seven by a girl twice his age, which made an indelible impression on him. It defined for him a life-long expectation that the woman should do all the courting and should take the active role in intercourse. He always seeks a repetition of this experience, though it left him with a deep impression of his sexual inadequacy and a preoccupation with the size of his genitals, as well as a great worry about satisfying his mate. This incident of childhood deflected his sexual goals to some extent but hardly injured him, apart from defining for him a neurotic goal of having to prove himself by his potency. It also gave him a constant feeling of his undesirability, which he had to counteract with corresponding successes.

His capacity to idealize the woman is shown clearly in his first marriage during his years of vagabondage. His romantic conception of woman overweighs his judgment, and he is disillusioned by finding his wife in bed with another man. From this point on he embarks on a pilgrimage of vengeance on the female sex, which is never very acrimonious or deeply rooted. He returns to his maternal replica in his second wife, only to find her frigid. She embodies for him his early ideals of a "nice" maternal figure, but he expects to find in her the attributes of the prostitute type to whom he is secretly grateful, because it is through them that he achieved what sexual confidence he has.

This is again a typical constellation derived from our conventions; the two-pronged tendency to idealize the woman into a maternal replica, and to degrade and abuse her for her sexual liberty, which he at the same time values and despises. His marriage is a compromise. His wife gives him no sexual gratification, but he is certain of her affection, and she gives him children. The conflict this engenders is visible, though not severe. The hostilities aroused by her are safely drained through an overconcern for her health, which he fears is being ruined by his sexual demands. His anxieties over impregnating his wife are mixed in motivation, one part of which derives from his status conflicts. On the whole he is resigned to his fate as far as his sex life is concerned, but not so resigned that he does not philander now and then when opportunity permits.

The sexual conflicts of this man, extremely mild for our culture, are resolved without the costly detour of an active neurosis. He does however continue the struggle in the sexual problems of his daughters where his guilt about sex emerges as active castrative wishes which he recommends against other men who are disqualified in his eyes.

The façade of his life is filled with his struggles to achieve status and recognition of some kind. His bad experience between ten and fifteen on the farm, with its arduous labor of which he only indirectly shared the benefits, gave him a deep distaste for hard work. There is little doubt about this having been a traumatic experience. Yet he does not run away from it until his father recovered. He is disillusioned in his father, but not to the extent of overt hostility. His ties to his mother and siblings are too strong to permit him to leave them when it is clear that he is actually the paterfamilias for the time being. But there is an undercurrent of hatred of his siblings which comes out very strongly when one brother flaunts his delinquency by indulging in irresponsible drinking. James has too much conscience to do anything like that—and it only redoubles his hatred of his brother. He fears that his brothers are taking advantage of him, and his desertion of home is partly motivated from that source.

But his career during his sixteenth to twentieth years is not very successful. Without training or education he has no claims to any work that can lead to status. His vagrancy and his joining the I.W.W. are really profoundly distasteful to him, and he ends the whole thing by joining the army. Discharge from the army leaves him where he started, and he returns home. He is however sobered by his experience. Having looked down on his home folks as old-fashioned and lowly, he tries to see their good qualities as a preparation for returning and becoming one of them. His ambitions for education and his exaggerated opinion about the high status of writers of books both suffer a decline. He must abandon these objectives and get on with living. Instead of a period of introversion, which might be expected at this point, he turns to the nearest realities and tries to exact from them not the fullest measure of gratifications but sufficient to make his existence less painful. He preserves his high opinion of education as a means to status, relegates that to a later date or to his children, and turns to the means of a livelihood. The farm is the compromise, and he accepts it with an attitude of resignation. He has never lost his distaste for it, and he fails to get his children to help him—owing to his wife's intervention—but does try to arrange so that he will not have to work too hard, and eventually not at all. From this point his status struggles are shifted to his children.

This is the story of a very successful adaptation. It is free of severe neurosis, and contains only a few neurotic trends which do not interfere seriously with his life. We must discount some of this story as a piece of favorable self-representation, but it is not seriously distorted. This personality had a good underpinning, as is shown by the strong ties that exist between him and the people about him, sufficient to build a personality that is confident except in the sexual domain. It is firm enough to support a strong superego formation. He has a conscience, is educable, systematic, pursues goals some of which are beyond his capacities, but he knows when he is beaten. He is adaptable, capable of accepting a compromise, and is willing to abandon most fictitious goals, but retains some of them in the form of an active fantasy life about literary achievements he can never realize. Another fiction that sustains him is that he has become "upper class." Excepting for minor distortions, he is capable of the role of husband and father, and does both well. He has a rich feeling for others—as shown in his relations to wife and children. He is intelligent, though not educated. His struggles for status are consummated with moderate success—at a cost of some shrewdness and planning—but without dishonesty. Unsatisfied ambitions continue to play a prominent role in his fantasy life but not at the expense of realities.

William M.

The subject is a twenty-six-year-old man who works as a janitor and lives with his father. He has a physical defect, hernia, and a sexual perversion, peeping. He is the oldest of four children, the other three being sisters. Two of his sisters died when he was nine.

His father was a man of college education, but turned from an academic career to the threshing business, which he continued until he was sixty-nine. He married late, at forty-six, a woman twenty-four years his junior. He bought a farm which he worked until four years after his wife and two daughters died. He then took the job of janitor, which he now holds with his son.

William's mother died of cancer when he was nine. She was interested in religion (his father was not) and was a much more strict disciplinarian than his father, and was inclined to be in a bad mood much of the time. William was under strict orders not to eat between meals and not to play with other children.

He became aware of his hernia early in life and between five and twelve had frequent nocturnal eneuresis. His school career was uneventful. Dreams of this period were concerned with being chased by a tiger, but he couldn't run. Also dreams of falling from great heights. He participated in the usual activities of disobeying teachers at school.

When he was twelve his father sold the farm, and William went to live with his maternal grandmother. He went to high school, where he was the only boy with four girls. Owing to his grandmother's poor health, he was moved back to Plainville, where he stayed with an aunt. There he continued school while working the farm six hours a day. He collected very little of the pay he was supposed to get for his labors. He did well at school, was president of his class and was on the debating team. He became class valedictorian; this was the most important event of his life.

His father then bought a farm which William worked until a year before the story is told. This was hard labor and spoiled all his ambitions about going to college. He says that baseball (which he could not play because of his hernia) and politics were his chief interests. There were a few episodes of minor delinquencies, but he was never severely punished for them.

Before twelve he knew nothing of sex; his father then told him how babies were born. When on another occasion his father tried to pursue the subject, he discouraged him by appearing uninterested. He picked up his information from other sources and felt guilty about his knowledge. He says that after twenty he lost interest in sex. He had some vague plans about marrying a girl, but was frightened away by her claim that "she wouldn't marry a man unless he were a millionaire." This "knocked the props from under him." Her family's being better off than his "made a difference, of course."

Some time during puberty he learned to masturbate and he in turn taught others and had parties with them in the smoke house. There was no competition and no mutual masturbation. He had a severe conflict about masturbation and tried to do other things to keep his mind busy. Reading that it caused insanity increased his anxiety, though he says he did not believe it. He made three timid attempts at sexual advances to some girl cousins, twice being rebuffed by the girls and a third time caught by his aunt, who "just raised the roof and said he ought to be horsewhipped." Several other timid sexual attempts followed (at about sixteen) with no success. One of the girls "got religion" after first encouraging him.

He once took a trip to California, but returned to Plainville to stay with his father, who now acts as housewife in the household. This is his strongest tie though he has some attachment to his sister and aunt. He is interested chiefly in politics and reading. He finds church distasteful. He has some money which he lends out at interest. He has the greatest secrecy about this money; this was "something that should be more closely guarded than anything else." His political views are against fascism and communism and for the New Deal. He professes to believe that all people are equal, but is very careful to define the status of everyone about whom he talks. He is in great awe of wealth, but in greater awe of women.

He works diligently, does not drink or smoke. The reasons why he does not smoke are: his father told him not to; it costs money; it's not good for his health; it's a nasty habit; "it takes time from some business you might want to tend to." He has a deep concern for his health, and a tacit anxiety about social upheaval. He has no attachments, hesitates to render direct opinions about anyone. He has some vague ideas about being "independent," which probably means that he fears superiors and possible criticism.

He has constant headaches which are relieved by masturbation or nocturnal discharge. He denies having any sexual desire. He has never had relations with a woman and fears prostitutes because he might "get disease," might get attached to the wrong kind of girl, and finally because he thinks he is not strong enough (one of his testes being atrophied by pressure from his hernia) and has a small penis.

He does not marry because he fears "all girls are cranky," because he has no money and no car. When he does find a girl he likes, there is always something wrong with her, "there's lots of talk against her family." His only sexual outlet is peeping in conjunction with masturbation. All forms of sexual activity are "wrong."

Some of his dreams are: "I'm out somewhere urinating and I wake up"—and discovers he has wet the bed. This persistence of eneuresis from childhood is a general indication of his sexual retardation. His parents never punished him for it, but tried to shame him out of it. Of his many disappointments he says, "If I didn't get everything I wanted, I always reasoned I was getting what was best for me and let it go at that." Another dream finds him on a porch peeping into a window where he sees three girls of his acquaintance undressing. One has nearly all her clothes off. The dream ends in an emission and he wakes up guilty and worried. Another dream of the same kind finds him meeting a married woman on a hill, with the same result as the previous dream. Several other dreams had the same content.

The integrational systems in this man are transparent. He is the only male among four children. His eneuresis points to strong sexual stimuli deflected into the permissible channel of urination. This is a masturbation equivalent and the brunt of censure falls on this activity. His capacity for competition with boys is injured by his hernia, which he uses as a pretext to avoid all manly activities. He remains an obedient child, which means repression of all sexual curiosity and activity. Under the direct tuition of other boys he learns masturbation, but this is filled with guilt. When his mother died, he transferred his allegiance to his father and remained a good boy all his life, not venturing away from his father and making no move to establish himself. He shared the vicissitudes of his father's fortunes.

This constellation of obedience in order to enjoy his father's protection prevents any emergence of real independence, sexual or otherwise. For this reason all the taboos he ever heard have the same validity for him as an adult as they did when he was a child. The protection costs him every possible contact with women. The peeping which in the normal man is a mere adjunct to sexual stimulation, remains for him the entire activity.

The use he makes of his physical handicap, the hernia, to justify his deep shyness and inhibition is typical of all his rationalizations. His sense of inadequacy is profound. He only succeeds along lines he can travel under the aegis of obedience. This is the secret of his success at school. His deep sensitivity about being found out shows itself in his extreme squeamishness in making judgments about other people. His competitive attitudes are non-existent. Naturally he has nothing to offer a woman, and probably identifies himself with women; his deep attachment to his father has an unconscious homosexual tinge.

In the previous chapter we remarked that character formation in our society plays into the status-class-prestige complex. This biographical sketch illustrates the thesis that the social position of a man is decided not necessarily by his sexual development but by the amount of free energy in the form of mobile action systems that can be used in competitive efforts to achieve socially approved goals. He is a janitor and works for a stipend. He began to acquire the implement of social advancement in the form of education. But this remained a rather peripheral achievement and owing to his deep insecurity and inferiority feelings, he could use it only in the form of being an obedient child but not as a form of enhancing his social opportunities.

What is left of his social ambitions exists in the perverted form of stinginess. He values money very highly, dreams feebly of being "independent" through saving, but not through enterprise. In his present vocation he is freed of competition, has a minimal amount of fear of criticism from superiors, and remains close to his father. But like women, real wealth is outside his reach, and he does not drive himself toward that goal. He chooses the one form of wealth compatible with his resources. He saves. But judging from his many references, he saves at the expense of pleasures generally condemned—women, drinking, and smoking. His thrift is therefore a direct function of his emotional impotence.

Elinor L.

This is a woman of thirty-six, married at eighteen to the subject of our first male biography. She has four children, the oldest of whom is eighteen and the youngest twelve. She is the oldest of eight children, four boys and four girls. Her life was externally uneventful.

Her life at home was noteworthy chiefly because of the dominant position of her mother, who had a violent temper and beat her on all occasions. This trait, our subject says, her mother acquired from her father, who used to beat all his children. Elinor's father, on the contrary, did not beat his children but delegated all discipline to the mother.

The maternal discipline apparently extended to everything the mother thought "was bad" for her. She doesn't recall anything her mother permitted, everything was forbidden. She thus recalls one occasion when she was playing with dolls with some other children, and for this she was soundly thrashed. Elinor thought that her mother suspected her of playing house and having babies and this was not "playing nice." She was hurt at her mother's injustice, because at that time Elinor says she knew nothing about babies or how they came to be.

Notwithstanding many injustices of a similar kind, Elinor had a strong attachment to her mother, mingled with occasional fantasies of revenge. Her mother often disappointed her by making promises she would not redeem. To escape her mother's anger she would lie about her activities. There were a good many kindnesses mingled with these punishments. There is a strong likelihood that her mother's irritability was due in part to heart trouble.

One of the conspicuous impressions of her childhood was that her mother claimed to be seriously hurt by Elinor's father in sexual relations. Elinor claims that she did not believe this story.

There is little evidence in her story of sibling rivalry, though she was the oldest of eight. She did not like one of her sisters and occasionally hurt her, but was very fond of a younger sister and brother. No decisive attitude about her father was elicited. The greatest pleasures of her childhood were in connection with playing with other children and later exchanging notes with boys.

Her mother never told her anything about menstruation, childbirth, and the like, and she thinks she picked things up by herself from observing animals. There is no history of masturbation, and she says she never heard about any such thing among girls. She only remembers injunctions by her mother not to let boys put their arms around her, but does not remember that this injunction applied to kissing. She was not afraid of boys, since there were so many in her own house, and being the oldest she had some advantage in this regard. She never resented being a woman or envied boys. The reason why other girls of her acquaintance wanted to be boys was that boys were not so closely watched. She had no great friendships with girls. Her ambition was to be a nurse. She was not religious and attended church only to please her mother.

She first fell in love at fourteen, with a boy of nineteen, but the affair was kept secret, being certain her mother would forbid it if she knew. This went on for two years and was broken up because the boy went to California and she was too young to be married. She had a difficult time getting over this love affair and felt she could never love anyone else. His negligence aided her in forgetting the episode. Two years later, at eighteen, she became engaged to marry her present husband.

Apparently her first reactions to marriage were unfavorable. She "didn't trust" her husband during courtship, having heard about the "mistake" of a friend who surrendered herself to a man, became pregnant, and was jilted by him. After marriage there was constant quarreling with her husband, but she was advised by his parents to "give in." Some years later she had a "nervous breakdown," though from her account it is difficult to make out precisely what its nature was. She was close to divorce several times but finally adjusted herself to the marriage.

From her own account and from her husband's, it is evident that she has no conception of active participation in the sexual act or of sexual pleasure. She thinks that the coolness of woman is natural, that when a girl makes a "mistake" it is not because she wants anything but to please her man. This sexual frigidity is a prominent source of her husband's discomfort. She says she has strong affectionate longings, but they do not include sex. Her dreams, however, are filled with phallic symbols and indirect representations of sexual activity. She has apparently much fear of sexual relations. Judging from the hostility with which phallic symbols are represented, she has an unconscious dread of being injured. The conflict about sex—a master pattern for this culture—is clearly represented by dreams of deep hatred for a woman who snubbed her. This woman is supposed to have been promiscuous before she married. Her anger is ostensibly due to social rivalry. Actually she has a great envy and fear of this woman, because she thinks her husband is fond of her.

As is customary, most of her own anxieties are extended to her children. She worries about their being home before twelve. They know more about sex than she did, a fact which augments rather than diminishes her anxiety. She also worries about the possibility of automobile accidents, etc.

Although this biographical sketch is short, it describes the main constellations of Elinor's character quite clearly. The chief feature of her life is its love-starved character, though she has met all the conventional requirements of a successful life as a woman—a good marriage and children. The main cleavage in her sexual make-up is her preparedness for strong, tender relations to a man, accompanied by inadequacy to participate in the sensual aspects of love. In its place we have a long series of anxieties, which extend themselves readily to her children. The particular difficulties in her marriage are due to her husband's special needs, for a mate who will take the initiative. This means a woman whose psychosexual make-up should be that of a prostitute—according to his experiences. Much of the discord between these mates is due to the fact that they are at cross purposes unconsciously. Each resents the other's unconscious sexual attitudes. He wants something from her that she cannot give, and her failure depresses his self-esteem. He does not get from her the reassurance which he needs about his masculinity. She is internally too terrified of sex to coöperate in any way.

There are not a sufficient number of details concerning her early development to indicate how she came by her particular neurosis. But the general features of the culture indicate the path it must have taken. Nothing else could be expected. However she tells her daughters a great deal more than she was taught, has discussed such things as masturbation and menstruation. She professes to have no feeling about her daughters' "getting into trouble" and thinks she would protect them under those conditions and not feel ashamed. One cannot say she is lying; but generally one does not know what feelings such circumstances would provoke in actuality. Several of her dreams —especially those dealing with her fear of snakes—indicate a strong necessity to conceal her own deep anxieties from her children, especially her boy.

Though she has no serious status conflicts, the deep hostility she has toward a woman whose "morals" were once freer than Elinor's indicates that her resentment is based on the fact that her rival enjoyed more than she did, and her own virtue brings no adequate rewards.

Rachel R.

This subject is an unmarried woman of sixty. She is the youngest of five children, and has three older brothers, all of whom are married. She now lives by herself, maintaining a meager livelihood from "roomers," gardening, and perhaps some small inherited funds.

The marriage of her parents was not a happy one according to her description. Her father went out West as a young man to evade military service during the Civil War and returned at about thirty-two after a career of rather shiftless roaming. He married Rachel's mother but led a restless existence for many years because he still retained a tendency to roam. She has no complaints about her father, says he took fairly good care of the family. He apparently engaged in stock trading. But it was almost exclusively her mother's duty to run the practical end of the household, which she did effectively, particularly when the boys became older. Rachel has the impression that she was discriminated against in this family made up almost exclusively of men. Both her father and mother were what she calls "stricter with me than with the rest of them." The two older boys left for California when the subject was about twelve, the only real friendship she developed with her siblings being with her next oldest brother.

She was inducted into assisting in the home when very young and by fifteen she was practically taking care of the entire household owing to her mother's illness. She went to school until sixteen but did very little work on the farm, though she did occasionally help gather corn.

The comparatively low status of country folks as against town folks evidently impressed her very early, and she has retained a lifelong feeling of inferiority on that score. This is probably the source from which she derived one of the main interests in her life, namely a taste for "nice things," particularly fine clothes. She characterizes her life by saying, "There is nothing important that ever happened to me in my life, and nothing important in the future. It's just an ordinary kind of life, I guess. I have always liked everything nice in life. I like pretty things, pretty clothes, pretty children." She compared herself with her cousins who were what she called "well-fixed," and she thinks she ought to have had the same kind of things that they did.

Another dominant complaint in her life was isolation, so that as a child and young girl she had a great many fantasies of leaving the farm, wanting to be a milliner, do office work, work in a store, etc. She said that she had very few associates on the farm. There were no young people about, and she was apparently snubbed by her more well-to-do cousins. They apparently felt that she was too tall, her feet too big, etc. She claims never to have had much feeling of inferiority on the score of good looks. She thought she was "medium-looking" and tried to compensate for defects by wearing fine clothes. She was especially proud of her long hair which, she said, reached to her toes.

Her parents had been radical in their tendencies, both religious and political. Their reputation had been such as to cause doubts as to their fitness to become guardians of the children of her older brother. She never felt ostracized on this account, particularly after she moved to town. She now lives in town and her existence there is quite secluded. She finds living in town much better and much pleasanter than living in the country, which she found much too lonesome. She had been living in town for about thirty years when interviewed.

In her relations with men she was always extremely backward. This was apparently due to the rigid discipline of her mother. She was not permitted to go out with boys until after sixteen. She timidly accepted an invitation from a boy to take her home from a party, but they were surrounded by relatives. She felt uncomfortable about this date, for she thought he was in earnest and she didn't want him. At the age of thirteen or fourteen she refused to "spark" with a young man because he had been associated with a friend of hers, and she knew he would go back to the friend. She was engaged to a neighbor but she found that he was not entirely honorable. Her father didn't like the young man, nor did her mother. Rachel was then eighteen years old. She thought she couldn't trust him but decided after a while that they were not suited to each other; thus the engagement was broken. She said that this did not cause her very much grief but there had never been another man in her life since. She thinks that she would have had better chances to meet a man had she gone away from home for only a year or two. Her mother was always protecting her against reckless men.

She has never been a member of any church, since there was no religion in the family. Her mother believed in phrenology. She also thought that it was a girl's place to learn only about the household. The decisive influence in Rachel's life seems to have been her mother's illness which began when the subject was nine years old and thereafter returned periodically. The position of nurse to her mother devolved upon her and she could never escape from her obligation.

As regards the formative influences in her life, Rachel has little to say. As the only girl in the family she was apparently subjected to more rigid discipline than the boys, which in essence meant less leisure and greater attention to household duties. She was often scolded but never whipped. Of sexual enlightenment she had none at all. At nine she asked her mother where babies came from but she got no direct answer. What she learned came from an older cousin. She read several doctors' books that were available in the house. She did not learn about menstruation from her mother.

She was weaned at the age of three, but when she was as old as seven she still would climb into her mother's lap, take her mother's breast out and suck it. On one such occasion she remembers, when about five, she wanted to nurse at the breast at a time when her mother had other things to do. Her father noticed this and threatened to call the sheriff. Rachel says she was badly frightened by this episode and crawled under the bed. She says that her brothers did not tease her about it, and her mother raised no objection to this nursing. Sphincter training began at the age of three or four. Her father showed very few affectionate attitudes toward her and from her earliest childhood she was completely under her mother's domination. To her brothers she seems always to have remained a little girl, and her position both in the household and at home was always subordinate. She lived by the grace of others, and always feared being cast off. It was always her brothers who had to take her to dances, and when dances went out of fashion she almost died of pure loneliness. The only activity she ever undertook which offered some relief to her incessant boredom was music. She learned to play the piano and kept it up until she was about thirty. Another influence which was derived from her mother was the constant tendency not to waste anything, to save things and to keep on saving them irrespective of their use—rubber bands, paper sacks, newspapers, etc.

For the past eleven years, since her mother died, she has been living alone, and for three years her health has not been good. Her mother's death apparently caused a nervous collapse of some kind. She said that taking care of her mother was very hard work, that it caused her to lose much sleep so that the only entertainment left her was eating. She ate enormous quantities of food all the time.

When asked for her earliest childhood memory she recalls an incident of the fourth year of her life. Her mother was stewing a chicken for dinner. She wanted a piece. Her mother twisted a piece of the chicken but it was too hot when she handed it to Rachel, who wrapped it in the skirt of her dress. "Somehow I felt so happy, settin' there pattin' my feet on the floor, holdin' that piece of chicken wrapped up in my dress. I can never forget that."

There seems also to have been some tendency in her childhood to imitate her older brothers. She climbed every tree in the orchard, went barefooted through rocks, didn't care to play with dolls, had a great deal of physical courage; she could shoot a bow and arrow and could shoot marbles just like a boy. But this influence apparently waned because she was disqualified from participation as the boys grew older.

The following are some samples of her dream life. She has typical recurrent dreams, of being at a dance, being well dressed, and having a gay time. However the specific record of one dream indicates that the content is not so simple. "I was at a party all dressed up in a light flowered dress of silk material. Up came a rain and my clothes got wet." She dreams frequently of her mother, seeing the latter as very young. There are also recurrent dreams of dancing about the room. These, she says, are the happiest dreams she ever had.

Another typical dream is of being in school, trying to recite a lesson and being unable to do so. In the dream she often says to herself, "Ain't I ever going to get old enough to quit going to school?" Another recurrent dream is that of an old, ugly man peering around the edge of the bed at her. She frequently dreams of having no shoes or stockings on, or of being unclothed. All these provoke anxiety, but the dreams which trouble her more than any others are those of going into a dirty toilet. "It's all smeared up and I get everything all over my clothes." The fear of dirt, extreme cleanliness and neatness seem to have dogged her all her life and are reflected in no small measure in her current behavior. "Even when I'm working I just can't stand for grease to pop out on my clothes."

The following is a current dream: "I was in a room preparing to take a bath when Mr. Ball (a man I bought wood from last winter), not knowing I was there, came to the door and started to come in to get some parts for a truck or car he was working on near by. I told him not to come in and he went away. After I got through I stepped into the toilet, which wasn't overly clean, in another room just north of this room, and not knowing I was in there he came to the door again and I told him I was there and he walked away. Pretty soon a young girl came in. She was fifteen or sixteen years old, small and neat with black, wavy hair and dark blue eyes and a fair complexion—a very pretty girl. So directly we walked out together."

In Rachel's development the one paramount influence is her mother. Her position as the only girl in the family was isolated in some respects, but favorable in others. She was singled out for attention for a while, but soon became the black sheep. This she attempted to overcome by trying to emulate her two older brothers. In this she succeeded for a time, became proficient in tree climbing, playing marbles, etc., but was disqualified as the sport of the boys became such that it excluded girls. There is little evidence that this attempt at formulating a dominant trend in her life took deep root. It seems to have been transient and never very deep.

The significant relationship to her mother continued for a lifetime. It began with late weaning at three and sucking at the breast (continued with her mother's connivance) until seven. There is little doubt that Rachel was a tractable child. Such a breast fixation, with the opportunity to have it gratified, would guarantee the obedience of any child. This is the dominant and fixed constellation in her character. She fell easy prey to her mother's anxieties that this or that would hurt her, and avoided all noxious influences—as defined by her mother. Likewise she followed along the positive indications that she was to concentrate on housework and let every other objective in life pass her by. She put up with the task of being her mother's nurse without any effort to break a path for herself and submitted in a resigned way to her fate. When her mother finally died, when Rachel was forty-nine, it created a great hiatus in her life, from which it took her some time to recover. A woman of sixty, whose most pleasant recollection in her life is being fed by her mother at the age of five, she is tied to the shallow objectives in life permitted within the range of this bond to her mother.

There is no evidence how far her sexual development proceeded. It is clear only that her interest in dress is determined partly by the sexual objective and partly has a denial motive, for she evidently had a conception of herself as extremely unattractive. Her constant dreams of being well-clad are attempts to satisfy this anxiety. But the dreams fail to carry through and end in a frustration; the rain spoils her clothes. The dream of being soiled with feces may be due in part to this anxiety. The dreams about clothes are also partly fears of exposure of her inadequacy as a female. Another way of saying it would be to say that they are exhibitionistic dreams which miscarry. It comes to the same thing.

Her preparedness for sex life was zero. From thirteen on her approaches to men were timid, full of fear for her safety, but rationalized on the basis that the man was undesirable, that she could not trust herself to him—which was really quite true. That she has vague sexual strivings is indicated clearly in her nightmares of the old, ugly man who is peeping at her. This wakes her in distress and clearly represents a childish conception of sex, which is still her only conception of it. Back of her anxiety is still the idea, "mother told me that is bad." The real reason for the anxiety is that she is totally devoid of resources to meet the sexual situations that arise. She literally knows nothing about it. She can form no conception of the sexual act itself, but must represent it by one of its associated preliminaries: looking well. She has moreover no idea of what a relationship with a man entails. The last dream recorded is probably the best representation of her sexual development.

She evidently has an interest in a man from whom she bought wood. She would like "something sexual" with him. But she represents it as his peeping on her while she is bathing. She sends him away, but he turns up again to watch her in her toilet activities. This wasn't "overly clean," which is again the fear of being soiled. What she means to say is, "I'm not attractive—to do this would be like soiling myself" (her mother was extremely insistent on cleanliness). She closes the dream in a fantasy of being a very pretty girl, small (actually she is tall). That is, she wishes she could commence all over again.

The sexual goal in life having been completely stunted, she has only two others—security and status. She began in a lowly position and was extremely sensitive about her status in relation to that of her cousins. She makes no effort to overcome this handicap, but embraces the lesser ideal of saving, which is her most effective device for insuring security. She is more secretive about her savings or wealth than she is about sex.

Notwithstanding her very difficult and lonely life, Rachel is not badly adjusted and has a good many unused resources. She never had a binding relationship except with her mother and she never made any really determined efforts to achieve any. One can say she did not need any. Judging from her dreams this is not true. But she does not know how to formulate any objectives with regard to them.

The question as to whether this biography gives us any evidence of culturally determined constellations must be answered in the affirmative. Her sexual development is not typical for our society by any means. But her ignorance of sex, the lack of preparation for it by her parents—these are typical. The end result is more extreme, and in this some accidental factors undoubtedly played a role. The typical constellations are the strong maternal fixation, and the accompanying anal complex involving concepts of order, cleanliness, and obedience. Whether associated with this or not, there is also the constellation of saving or hoarding as a form of security, a product of our money economy.

Conclusions to Biographies

From the personality studies we can confirm certain conclusions about the basic personality of Western man as well as some special features about Plainville. As compared with Comanche and Alor, Plainville man has a distinct personality structure. The two males show a strong emotional underpinning; one has plenty of self-assertion, but fails because he cannot implement his assertive tendencies in any way to win social recognition; the other succumbs to passive attitudes. Both have profound difficulties on the score of sexuality, one being adequate, but with sexual goals defined by early experiences which are at complete variance with ideals of feminine behavior. In his choice of a mate, however, it is the socially defined goals and not his sexual predilections which wield the decisive influence. The result is an unhappy marriage. The second man drags his sexuality down with his passive goals, and it never becomes socially relevant.

Both men have the same social goals, directed toward status achievement by way of money or education. Both have intense feelings of social inferiority. One perpetuates his ambitions in harmless but equally useless fantasies of accomplishment; the other, by an attitude of resignation, insisting that his status is all he can legitimately claim. Behind both attitudes lies plenty of explosiveness in the form of hatred for everyone, including themselves. The man with good potentialities for aggressive behavior is the one who was subjected to arbitrary and cruel paternal discipline without rewards. The man with poor aggression patterns was well protected, and his self-assertions are blocked in the interest of retaining paternal protection.

Both men encounter the status problem in their earliest social contacts, at school, and throughout their lives. Both regard sexual power and money as forms of self-validation; both value "independence," which from their modest social position means to do nothing, to "take it easy." Neither has any regard for work as a form of self-expression but only as a painful routine. To both "education" is a means of accomplishing status, but has no intrinsic value.

The women present a different problem. Both women fail to achieve an adult conception of sex and to neither is it a form of self-expression. They are tied to infantile conceptions of sexuality, and in both it is dominated by the obedience constellation. Both have deep longings for romantic attachments which they cannot implement in any way. To one, sex is completely unknown as an experience, to the other, it is an unpleasant routine necessary to ulterior ends of status as wife and mother. To both women sex is an exclusively masculine activity, owing to the peculiar "nature" of the male. Womanhood is a degrading status, incompatible with individual self-expression, and leads to the doom of becoming the satellite of some man. This is the highest conception of the female destiny. In Elinor, however, we find good maternal attitudes with brave attempts to correct the errors of her own parents; and judging from results she has had considerable success.

All self-assertive tendencies in both women are expressed in issues concerning status in the form of clothes or accomplishment. The unexpressed sexual cravings in both can become violent aggressions against others. In Elinor this is openly expressed in her "status" rivalries with another woman. In this regard Rachel seems more resigned.

In all four studies we find no evidence that religious ideas as such had any influence in shaping their goals. Their inhibitions are supported by no supernatural sanctions.

CHAPTER XIII

CONCLUSIONS TO PLAINVILLE

THE ANALYSIS of Plainville was the most difficult test of the technique selected for this enterprise, partly because we know more about our own culture than any other, partly because it has a long history and is even now in the throes of great changes in organization. The frame of reference must be able not only to accommodate the current picture, but to supply accurate criteria for the student who wishes to evaluate the dynamics of change.

Taking as our ground line the assumption that man is a single species with similar potentialities for reaction types to frustration, satisfaction, and so forth, and that man's psychological equipment is subject to integration, we find in Western man a special growth pattern and hence a unique organization of the personality. This organization is subject to infinite variations and emphases from one place to another. In spite of this there is more resemblance in personality organization between a Dutch fisherman and a Wall Street broker than between either of these and an Eskimo. The crucial technical question is whether this personality organization has anything to do with the conflicts and changes in our society. The answer to this question is decidedly in the affirmative.

In our study of Plainville we have introduced into our working scheme several elements not heretofore used in the primitive societies studied. The first of these is the social relevancy of characterological types. This is in marked contrast to primitive society. Judging from Alor, however, characterological types have a distinct relevancy there only in so far as they are decisive for the social fate of the individual. In Western society they are more than that; they are decisive for the society and its changing institutions. In Western society the social position of the individual is not fixed, and "classes," though their limits are not precisely defined, can by united action against each other influence or command the coercive power of the state and therefore influence the whole arrangement of institutions.

A second differential factor was the introduction of the scientific "reality system" as an integral factor in basic personality structure.

This is important for two reasons: the empirically derived reality system is a powerful implement which has greatly augmented the control of Western man over nature (manufacture, science, etc.), and, secondly, it has undermined the value of reality systems based on projection (religious systems). These two factors have set the tempo and the direction of social change in the past 600 years and have been responsible for the redefinition of social goals and of interpersonal relations. They have given man a new direction for development by suddenly increasing his power to modify and control the environment and to influence human needs. We have seen, on a minor scale, a similar phenomenon in Comanche. There the new instrument introduced was not a machine but an animal, the horse, which increased the physical mobility a hundredfold. The gun was also introduced but of the two the horse was more important. With the change in the rate of mobility came new possibilities. The changes that took place spread into almost every aspect of the culture.

If we compare this with what happened in Western society, we can say that the changes in the latter were slower and more insidious than in Comanche. The machine was created when Western social organization had a particular configuration—a feudal organization in which the governing elite were largely the landowning group and the clergy, whose status was guaranteed by their power to alleviate anxiety through their claim to be able to mediate between man and God. The machine was originally the invention of the scientist and the artisan groups. Out of this situation came the growth of manufacture in the hands of the group subsequently known as the bourgeoisie—which eventually was able to compete with and displace the landowning elite. With the displacement came the exaltation of free social mobility as a goal, which terminated in the concept now commonly known as political freedom. As long as the bourgeoisie, which had gained considerable control over the coercive power of government, could expand its activities and maintain its security through the control of the "market," there was no tendency anywhere to question the usefulness of political freedom. Once the "market," which was not inexhaustible, began to show signs of being saturated, the problem of the expediency of political freedom began to be questioned in some parts of Western society. The class which brought political freedom into the world began to try to limit it.

We cannot treat this subject in detail. It has been adequately described by Borkenau [1] and by Laski.[2] We observe coincident with these changes profound changes in the fantasy screen of man—notably in religious ideologies. The changes in this projective screen are indicators of the changes in the needs of those who created them. Religious fantasies and ideologies are tension relaxors, and if a new kind of relaxor is needed then the tension must be different. The view most commonly held on this point is the exact reverse, namely that Protestantism introduced new ideas and "freed" humanity from this and that. It is an important point to settle, for unless we do, no consistent dynamic of social change can be constructed. This we will consider in the following chapter.

This brief sketch is intended to indicate where social change strikes the individual. Adaptability is predicated by the specific influences that are exerted on the individual during growth, and his potentialities are fixed by the time growth is completed. There is little to indicate that many of the important normative influences which accompany growth in Western man have changed much in the past 2,000 years. By these influences we include parental care, impulse control, etc. On the other hand, value systems and taught reality systems have changed radically during this time. What we are following, therefore, are certain features that have remained constant for many centuries and others which are undergoing continuous change.

Western man can best be described in relation to the other cultures studied. His conditions for growth are very favorable; he is adequately aided to the full development of his capacities by being helped when he is biologically incompetent, until he can assume responsibility for himself. The feature of social organization responsible for this is a system of division of function which leaves this ego-fortifying role exclusively to the mother, while the father supplies the subsistence medium. This carries with it however the dangers of inertia, of strong parental attachments, and of the persistence of infantile goals. The gain of strong affective potentialities is a great counterbalance to the disadvantageous mishaps. The great obstacle to this excellent beginning is the introduction of taboos which prevent the exercise of biologically determined pleasure drives, the purpose of which is probably to create relaxor function for the difficult integra-

1 Franz Borkenau, *Der Übergang vom Feudalen zum bürgerlichen Weltbild* (Paris, Alcan, 1934).
2 Harold Laski, *The Rise of Liberalism* (New York, Harpers, 1936).

tive tasks of childhood. This destroys the freedom of development as we saw it in Comanche and produces many new tension points and new anxiety foci for which new relaxor systems or substitutes must be devised.

The chief consequence of the introduction of this taboo system is that it creates some doubt in the mind of the child concerning the continuation of parental care which it has now learned to appreciate, having built up an extensive pleasure and tension-relieving system by this route. The powers of the parent become inflated both for good (idealization) and evil (demonization), and the constellation of obedience becomes greatly inflated as an anxiety-relieving mechanism, at the cost however of building tension systems which have no outlet. This is clearly seen in dependent characters, where parental aid is maintained at the cost of creating one anxiety system in the field of pleasure in order to relieve another anxiety system in the field of support.

The possibilities of development are infinite, depending on the individual and the characters of his specific parents. The induction of sphincter control is universal and is hardly a differentiation point. However the punishment-reward systems do differ. More important, the value systems adventitious to evacuation become characteristic in the form of emphasizing orderliness, obedience, and varying emphases and meanings of retention and expulsion.

The taught reality systems are derived partly from projective systems (religion) and partly from empirically derived sources (science). The two are basically incompatible as regards conclusions and methods of derivation. Both of them are learned, and the incompatibilities are resolved differently by each individual. Some tolerate them alongside each other; others find it necessary to discard either one or the other. Depending on the resolution of the obedience constellation and using this resolution as a projective base, important characterological differences take place in Western man. Thomism is an ideological system with the unrecognized premise that "father is always right" or "it is right because father said so." It is the ideological system which brooks no change and no investigation; and if it does (as it did even in the case of St. Thomas), scientific investigation is used only to prove again that "father was right." Such an ideological system cannot be proven either right or wrong. Its tenure depends entirely on its ability to serve as a vehicle to express ideas not incompatible with the needs of the individual. The failure of Thomism came when this obedience principle became an obstacle and the ideologies of the Reformation sought expression for the new investigative spirit which had already validated itself in practice. The old obedience dogma was not in harmony with it.

Let us put this conception of the influence of reality systems on projective systems to a clinical test by contrasting the stabilizing factors in feudal society and in our own. Let us assume first that the basic growth pattern under feudalism was similar to our own, with certain exceptions. These exceptions were the much more despotic position and disciplines of the father in the family, which were in many ways replicas of the position of the peasant family to the landowner. Let us assume that the strong underpinning of the personality, the capacity for idealization, were the same as now, the exaggeration of the obedience constellation being a differential point in feudal society. The constellations formed in the family sufficed to supply adaptations both to the church and to the feudal lord. The whole social system, religious and secular, could be stabilized by the power of the feudal lord to withdraw protection, and of the church to impose post-mortem sanctions. Under these conditions it was possible for the feudal lord to augment greatly the value of his "protection" by increasing the hardships to which he subjected his inferiors and the church could do the same thing. Paternal authority in the household could be maintained by the inability of the sons to move away from the father's domain. Suppose we now destroy the supernatural sanctions which maintain the position of the father in the household, and of the feudal lord and the church, and the whole system will break down. If the son is given mobility to go to the cities and if the sanctions of the church are destroyed by an alteration of the dependency on supernatural aid by science, then oppression by the father or the feudal lord does not increase but diminishes the value of his "protection." And the social stability does not depend on promised rewards after death but on rewards which can be reified now and here.

This is essentially the difference between the social stability of the feudal system and our own society. In our culture post-mortem rewards carry few anxiety- or tension-relieving properties. Tensions built up in our culture can therefore be relieved only by actual and immediate gratifications in the form of success, and the social conflict to achieve it becomes all the stronger. Failure means inferiority, and though this is not the ideational equivalent of perdition after death, it is an isometric equivalent and can create the same depressive feelings and anxiety. No sooner was suffering deprived of its value as a claim for future rewards than the protest against it became manifest in direct action.

What has changed from feudal to democratic society is not only the political form, but the whole system of self-validation. The psychological burdens placed on the individual have been greatly increased and the value of power and enjoyment greatly augmented. The growth of scientific reality systems has greatly diminished the power of that aspect of the superego which conceived and endorsed supernatural sanctions. So that the only external forms of social control are vested in legally constituted coercive power, which is not exactly the expression of social conscience but rather of the coercive and immunity-granting power of the interests for whose benefit the limits of social conscience are defined.

The introduction of science into manufacture has led to the differentiation of function and to a high degree of variation in skills, each of which defines the social status, economic power, and monetary return of every individual. As the feudal caste lost its position, it was in turn, replaced by the bourgeoisie, and the differentiation of status began all over again along lines of the previous elite. But this new elite did not enjoy security of tenure; their position was only tentative; unlike a hereditary nobility, they had to continue struggling in order to maintain their position. With anxiety to maintain status at the upper end of the bourgeoisie and pressure from lower statuses to achieve some of the values of the former, we have the psychological matrix for evaluating the dominant motivations and anxieties of Western man. This discussion has been undertaken only to illustrate the value of the alterations in our operational scheme.

We noted several important emotional landmarks in Plainville. There is a great deal of anxiety and much hostility. The status of woman is relatively degraded. Religion has no such fixed position in Plainville as it did in medieval society; it is in part a social routine, in part it is completely ignored or it arouses considerable hostility. The reasons for this hostility may originate in the interference of the church with some of the relaxation or pleasure activities, such as drinking, illicit sexual relations, card playing, drinking "pop" from the bottle, wearing neckties, and several other insignificant items. On the other hand there are "believers." If experience with middle-class urbanites is a reliable guide, then the acceptance of a religious creed depends on at least two factors: (1) the religious system that is taught, and (2) whether this taught system can be harmoniously integrated with the rest of the personality. To an inhibited person the threat of hell may offer a valid rationalization for the inhibited activity; those who fail may attribute their failure to sin. Those who are successful may claim their success as evidence of divine reward for virtue. How religious belief affects individuals in Plainville could only be determined by intensive biographical studies. It would be a hasty conclusion from the widespread irreligiosity in Plainville that religion is devoid of significance as a socially cohesive force. No matter how little attention or credence is given the dogmas, the religion is the carrier of emotional patterns which exist in believers and disbelievers alike. This is clearly demonstrated in acculturation studies on Ojibwa Indians. The religion altered the entire emotional economy in the acculturated natives, because it was the vehicle through which new patterns of interpersonal relations were conveyed.

The skepticism of Plainville is not limited to the church; it extends also to government. Paradoxical attitudes coexist; on the one hand voting is a social routine, for one votes according to family convictions and one is born either a Republican or a Democrat. On the other hand the routines of mutual slander by contending candidates are tolerated as part of a show, with no really hard feelings on either side, and on the part of the voters there is a widespread conviction that the candidates are all "crooks."

Where does all the deep intrasocial hostility come from? Partly from blocked pleasure avenues. There is not only a fear that the other fellow will get more money and economic power (note the subjects of gossip: stinginess, illicit sexuality, dishonesty) but more *pleasure of any kind*. So that the strongest social cohesive force comes from the unification of the many against the few who dare to get more power or pleasure through illicit channels. This cannot be considered a powerful cohesive force.

All four of the personalities studied had a profound feeling of inferiority, three with major sexual defects. The frustrated drives for social recognition and sexual release are therefore mutually reinforcing, and result in general hostility to everyone else. The socially approved goal of success is made the vehicle of compensation for all other shortcomings in pleasure and relaxor functions. As long as the individual can pretend to some goal of success or security, he can claim some self-esteem. Failing in these, he left with only salvation.

The individual is not isolated here because he is a cog in a wheel or because he lives in a great, bewildering world of which he is an insignificant part, but because he is prevented from building friendly relationships because of mutual hostility, and he is barred from the opportunity to work with others toward a common goal of which he is the beneficiary. Thus "rugged individualism" exacts a heavy toll in the security of the individual by compelling him to maintain defensive hostilities to all around him outside the family unit and even within it. Modern man feels this isolation keenly, for in his make-up there is a strong need for emotional ties. If his personality were laid on the plan of the Alorese, his suffering would not be so keen—but neither would his accomplishments be as great.

The personality of modern man has not caught up with him yet. The tide of events has taken him beyond his depths. The growth pattern of modern man is better suited to the feudal system than it is to our own. Too many obsolete patterns still persist in our growth system, and there is too much insecurity in the social order. As long as both of these persist, we must expect the continuation of all those defenses which mutual hostility and envy create, the most destructive of which is our "class" system in which everyone is obliged to safeguard his self-esteem by having social relations only with those who can act as mirrors to his effective self. This seems to be the motive for exclusiveness, snobbishness, cliques, clubs, neighborhoods, race hatreds, and the like. It is a fear of contamination, a fear of having one's precious self-esteem injured by an unfavorable mirror reflection. This is all negative evidence of a strong need for emotional ties which are prevented expression in any other way. In the structure of the personality of modern man are very explosive elements which can lead to mutual destruction. The effects of this destructiveness we are feeling today.

This book did not undertake to study Western man and his long, complicated history; it undertook only to map out a working scheme. Up to this point we have limited ourselves exclusively to the examination of material brought to us by direct observation. In order to test out the value of the operating scheme on the problem of social stability and change we employ in the next chapter some data derived from history.

CHAPTER XIV

BASIC PERSONALITY AND HISTORY [1]

THIS book was planned as a testing ground for a technique. In the application of this technique we were obliged to use source material which did not in all instances satisfy the ideal requirements. Those cultures which had more complete data served as a check on the cultures in which, for lack of adequate data, we had to guess. We may not in the future be obliged to study each culture with the thoroughness that we did Alor. The conclusions there reached will stand; but they will hold only for such cultures as present a façade similar to Alor. Otherwise we have learned that each culture has a unique psychological fabric, and that there are no two alike.

There is one technical problem with which we have not been able to come to grips—the problem of following a wide historical arc with the aid of the working principles here laid down. We have not attempted this—except in a fragmentary way in Tanala and Comanche—for two reasons. First, because it was a part of the plan not to venture on the historical problems prematurely, before our operating principles were sufficiently clear. Second, because we had no culture apart from our own which offered the opportunity. It is therefore very likely that if we approach this problem after we have studied many simpler cultures, our conclusions will differ from those drawn by students who approach our culture without the preliminary efforts here recorded. Such a historical enterprise would require a long book in itself; we can therefore here only discuss a plan of operation. [2]

We have already encountered the historical problem in several forms. In one form the problem reduced itself to one of social origins, which we avoided on grounds that they were fruitless speculations. But the more important form is the one we find in Western culture, where a large body of historical facts are known, stretching over some four thousand years or more. We know that this "history" has been

[1] This chapter is a condensation of another book, now in preparation, which deals with the application of the technique in this book to the main currents in Western civilization. The deeper analysis of many psychosocial constellations are not presented here, but are reserved for the later publication.
[2] For an attempt to survey some facets of Western history, see Erich Fromm, *Escape from Freedom* (New York, Farrar & Rinehart, 1941).

rewritten many times, a clear indication that this so-called history is susceptible to many interpretations, depending on the point of view. Since the turn of the century at least four disciplines have contributed new points of departure for editing this history: the theory of evolution; the social theories of Marx; anthropology, which invented the culture concept; and lastly, psychodynamics.

That the concept of culture with the aid of psychodynamics can become a powerful weapon of interpretation we surmise from what it can do to give us a cross section at any given moment in the time trajectory—as in Alor. In the latter case the concept of basic personality could be used with confidence. We did not need to answer the question whether basic personality remained the same over long periods of time, or whether it changed, in what specific directions it changed, and in response to what specific stimuli. Since in the study of history we are always beginning somewhere in a continuum, we can assume that from the particular point which we take as our beginning, the history that follows will in some measure be determined by the basic personality at that point. We can assume with complete confidence that the history of the Alorese would be different from the Comanche even if both were subjected to the same external vicissitudes, because each culture is characterized by different life goals and values. The lines of intrasocial tension would be different in each case, and hence the capacity for coöperation would differ.

If this is the case, with what assumptions about basic personality can we approach Western society? That basic personality remained the same throughout its history and that nothing changed except social organization and types of coöperation compatible with a unitary basic personality? Or shall we assume that the basic personality is likewise subject to continual change, along with other purely external vicissitudes? The answer depends on what we are willing to include within the ambit of the concept basic personality. If we include the methods of dealing with the external environment, then basic personality has changed much within four thousand years. We can operate on the assumption that some features of basic personality have remained constant; some have changed; and that most adjustments of an intrasocial character, for organization and coöperation, have at least in part been determined by those features in basic personality which have remained constant. If nothing in our basic institutions has remained constant but the patriarchally oriented monogamous family unit with good parental care and a series of disciplines imposed on the child, then it is a safe enough assumption that certain features of basic personality have remained constant. These features alone would be enough to render the history of Western society distinctive, as compared with Alor or Comanche.

No matter in what form and with what qualifications we use the concept of basic personality as a weapon of historical interpretation, we do away permanently with a uniform and constant "human nature" which can be counted upon to behave in a uniform manner under all conditions. This assumption has been in use for a long time. The use of basic personality introduces a relativistic factor into the conception of history which can best be described in contrast to other operating assumptions. The idiosyncratic elements in the culture traits of a given society were often attributed to intrinsic racial differences which could not be qualified definitely except in anatomical terms. Between the anatomical features and the psychological ones there was an unbridgeable gap that could not be filled with the concept *constitutional*. The latter was merely a verbal subterfuge to escape more precise definition of the idiosyncratic factors in culture. In lieu of this obscurantist procedure, we can employ a large field of psychological factors before resorting to vague idiosyncratic factors that are supposed to originate in constitutional factors, which in turn rest on anatomical features. The concept of racial idiosyncracy cannot be used operationally, because we are dealing with a series of unknowns.

Once we tie the concept of history to a psychological base, we also destroy an age-old assumption that society can be treated as if it were an organism or a machine with many parts. This assumption leads to the use of a concept like *nation* anthropomorphically, that is, as an entity that behaves as an organic unit. This is permissible only in a metaphoric sense. The meaning of this point, that society is not an organism, is that there is no automatic regulation of the relation of individual parts to each other. There is no such thing as a *social homeostasis*—to use Cannon's physiological term, a society being made up of individuals who are all potentially alike.[8] Human society has no resemblance to that of arthropods, where differentiation of function is based on underlying anatomical differences. The point of this is that

---

[8] We are omitting discussion of the influence on society of the differences between masculine and feminine needs.

the harmonious or inharmonious relations of members of society to each other depends on the voluntary coöperation or resistance of each human unit in the society.

If this is the case, then the adjustment of tensions between individuals in a society can be affected either by some alteration within the individual—control, suppression, repression, hysteria—or by forcibly altering the relation of the individuals to each other, by flight, combat, coercion, or submission. It is self-evident that a society in which intrasocial tensions are relieved by alterations within the individual has greater chances of survival and stability; those with forcible alterations, fewer chances of either. The difference between the two techniques can best be illustrated by the respective roles played by the church and police force. The church operates on the basis of internalized controls, of which church dogma and practice are the projected forms. Hence the supernatural always has greater controls over repressed impulses. Control by police is largely over impulses that have undergone no repression, but have to be managed by suppressive measures. A society controlled predominantly by suppressive techniques is bound to be anxiety ridden and filled with mutual hostility and distrust.

The presence or absence of these internal controls in a society is already an indicator of the existing basic personality in a given external setting. The existence of these internal controls not only makes a difference to the viability or stability of a society, but also defines in a specific manner the precise problems of adaptation for each individual within the group. We have learned from our comparative studies that we cannot count upon a natural and spontaneous development of a stereotyped "human nature" to supply the controls which are necessary to keep a society going. But as we vary the growth pattern, we vary the potentialities and patterns with which the individual can handle the vicissitudes to which his needs compel adaptation within the social setting. We may therefore safely conclude that the kind of controls established for intrasocial tensions will determine the potentialities of the society for certain types of coöperation, and this in turn will determine some aspects of the history of this society.

From Alor we learn to appreciate a group of factors which heretofore we were inclined to regard as a part of human nature—the capacity for idealization of the parent, the capacity to introject the parent and thus lay a firm basis for superego formation, so essential to the stability of a culture. Alor teaches us that these essential features in the development of the personality can be strangulated in infancy. But if these features are absent in all Alorese, then the result is not a private matter for each individual, but a different kind of society. The needs and expectations of the individual in Alor are calibrated differently from those in our society. The projective systems are different in both; that is, we cannot expect a religion like Judaism or Christianity to be formulated in Alor. We cannot expect in Alor the kind of problems that arise in our society in connection with social justice. The patterns of mental disorder and the psychosomatic patterns will be different in both cultures. Can we conceive that the history of Western society could have run its course without the role played by depression, feelings of guilt, masochistic phenomena?

If the basic personality in different societies is a variable, then the character of the relations between the units that compose the society will differ in a manner that will influence the cohesiveness of the society to withstand strains due to external sources like warfare or earthquakes, as well as those due to factors operating within the society. The differences in solidarity, cohesiveness, the presence or absence of great amounts of anxiety, will influence the stability or instability of any culture. The stability or instability of a culture cannot be gauged by any value judgments concerning the desirability of a certain type of social organization. Democracy, which we value so highly, is a very unstable form of organization—under some conditions like a contracting economy, whereas during an expanding economy (like the frontier stage) the tensions are readily absorbed. Feudalism, to us a most undesirable type of organization, had a much higher degree of stability than democracy—while it was supported by a hidden theocracy, and while social well-being was not considered a goal to be pursued by everyone, and while status lines were fixed and not questioned.

In other words, among the factors which promote the stability of a society are those which govern the creation of a given type of personality conducive to higher degrees of coöperation, the diminution of mutual hostility, suspicion, and mistrust. Some societies, like Tanala, are able to achieve such stability under conditions like an unchanging subsistence economy. Once the latter is destroyed, as was actually the case, the personality, which was geared for coöperation under the old conditions, is completely unsuited for the new conditions. The society is therefore thrown into a disequilibrium which may last for centuries. The causative factors in this kind of disequilibrium are not to be found in the cultural lag, or in any abstract principle of inertia, but in the fact that types of interpersonal adaptation cannot keep pace with the new conditions. One cannot have a stable society if the growth pattern is conducive to a personality whose chief instruments are submissiveness and ingratiation, while the demands of the economy are for independence, initiative, and free use of aggression.

In the case of Alor, the relation of the growth pattern to the economy is the most confusing we have thus far encountered in a primitive society. Here the growth pattern interferes with the development of all those features in personality which insure both freedom from anxiety and higher degrees of coöperation. How this came about we do not know. Apparently the problem of intrasocial tension was solved there by making the woman the chief carrier of the means of subsistence, and this in turn led to the neglect of the children. However the particular growth pattern of a society comes into being, in it we find a factor which decides in a large measure certain basic traits in the personality, and hence creates a factor which is decisive for the potentialities for institutional development. The weakness of this argument lies in deciding whether the growth pattern is an arbitrary or capricious choice, or whether it is intimately related to the main problems of adaptation, such as subsistence economy. We are obliged to accept this latter as a working assumption. Tanala and Comanche both offer important data on the relation of growth pattern to the dynamic equilibrium in a society.

Growth Pattern and Dynamic Equilibrium

In Tanala [4] we see a society which under one set of conditions had strong stability and through the change of subsistence economy became extremely unstable by virtue of the enormous amount of mutual hostility unleashed by the new economy. The stable and unstable forms are worth examining from the point of view of psychodynamics.

In the stable form the economy was based on communal land ownership. The land was worked by the younger sons of family groups belonging to a single lineage. There was no incentive to either hoarding

---

[4] Fully described by Ralph Linton in: Kardiner, *The Individual and His Society*, pp. 251–90.

or raising more than was needed, for produce could not be sold. The crop, chiefly rice, was stored and prorated to each member of the group according to needs. There was no important division of function, except for blacksmiths, warriors, and medicine men. This did not mean that there was no private ownership of property; there was—in the form of cattle, which were not used as food or dray animals. They had a pure prestige value. Wealth was also concealed.

The social organization was a patriarchal hierarchy, with the oldest son, successor to the father, being in a privileged position of immunity from labor and mediator with the ancestral spirits, a priestly function. Otherwise gradations in wealth and status were not marked by difference in living standards or ostentation. The power of the father and oldest son were perpetuated by their ability to retain the largest share of material wealth and give or lend it to the younger brothers or sons. There were institutionalized outlets for aberrant characters, warrior or medicine man for the enterprising, and homosexuality for the passive ones. Competitive activities were between lineage heads, but not within the lineage itself. Magic was forbidden within the lineage. The religion was a projection of strict disciplines of childhood and was in every way harmonious with the social structure.

We have here a model of perfect stability, not because it is an ideal arrangement, but because for each tension point created in the individual there is an adequate discharge permitted, whether it be regressive or progressive. This allows for variations in character structure of individuals. We must also note that all forms of hostility which might be engendered are anticipated and prevented from exerting a disrupting influence on the society. This is notably the case with forms of ostentation and discrimination. The self-esteem of the individual is not permitted to rise or fall despite rigid gradations in rank. There is no social mobility from the status determined at birth, except that expressed in medicine man or warrior. The latter can if they wish set up a lineage for themselves. Therefore a kind of social mobility is available only for the most enterprising.

This culture, which we called one of remarkable stability, would in our values have to be classified as a despotic one. The despotism is not to be evaluated from the form alone. As a matter of fact, the individual is not shut off from any satisfactions. He is conditioned to obedience from earliest infancy, and is set into a social environment where habits of obedience bring impulse satisfaction. If there is any accidental mishap in his character formation he can live it with public approval, be it homosexual or warrior. The stability comes from the fact that the personality after it is set is permitted to function according to those reaction patterns which, once learned, never lose their expediency throughout the life cycle of the individual. It does not matter how many tension points are raised in the development of the individual, provided proper outlets are permitted. The sexual disciplines in Tanala are a case in point. Premarital chastity is expected of both sexes, but likewise the male is expected to have his adventures with older women, widows, or by way of adultery. Since this is commonly accepted, the adolescence is not as painful as it otherwise might be, because an important psychosomatic tension release is afforded through these channels which need not be used to compound guilt and obedience constellations.

This psychological balance could, however, be maintained only while the economic basis for subsistence was based on communal land ownership. No sooner did the subsistence economy and the social organization for it change than the whole psychological structure collapsed. The dry method of rice production became obsolete through depletion of land suited for this purpose. For the wet method there were only a few available valleys, and those who "possessed" them—for this was a new concept in Tanala—held on to them, and there followed a mad scramble for valleys. This broke up the old family lineage organization; the villages had to be defended against marauders by powerful forces; slaves who were of no economic importance in the old set-up now became an economic asset, not alone as workers but as sources of revenue by ransom; the tribal democracy disappeared, and a king with absolute power and a feudal hierarchy whose tenure of land was in perpetuity were instituted; wealth became valued, for now in an atmosphere of insecurity it became the custom to hoard it; land could now be inherited. Among the psychological changes were a rigid system of class lines difficult to move into and general all-round hostility, as shown by great increase in hysterical illnesses and in magic practices and choice of sorcery as a vocation. The individual was confronted with a long series of new anxieties which he could in no way handle. The old method of ingratiation with the father was of little value because the father had little to give away. The anxieties confronted both those who had property and those who did not. Those who had property had to defend their title by a group of awe-inspiring ostentations in the form of dress and manners; children were taught gradations in deference. The property owners also had control of the weapons of coercion. Two new anxieties hitherto unknown made their appearance, fear of poverty and fear of oppression; and the general increase in crime and homosexuality were witness to this anxiety. Even religious concepts were changed and concepts denoting "evil spirits" were invented.

Social changes therefore do not take place in isolated and detached items. The human mind is integrative, and hence systems of ideas and attitudes become involved, not separate items. Thus when a change is introduced in one place we cannot expect its influence to remain localized. This principle has been traced in the analysis of Alor, where the whole integrational system is interfered with by the group ignorance of the conditions of growth. The effects of this interference are not limited to infants; they spread and ramify and pervade the entire culture.

Judging from Tanala, social stability does not therefore depend so much on an intrinsic rightness about living practices as it does upon recognizing the anxieties and discomforts any system is bound to create and introducing appropriate balances. This precaution was exercised in Tanala by the prevention of strong hostilities. Differences of rank could be tolerated as long as these could not be implemented by artificial ego-enhancing attributes, such as better food, clothing, and claims to deference, nor could they be maintained against popular will by the use of some arbitrary coercive power created by the community. In fact, there was no necessity for police as long as the people in inferior position could make their disapproval felt.

A second factor in the stability of the old Tanala is that the individual did not have to alter his set of adaptive tools during his entire lifetime. This makes for great economy of energy. Human beings show little capacity to alter adaptive modes once they are established.

In Comanche we see another form of social stability and social change. The transition from the Plateau to the Plains culture is a striking lesson in social change, especially as regards those features of the Plateau which remained unchanged and those which were modified or discarded altogether (see page 84).

The taking-off point of the Comanche culture was the introduction into a given Plateau culture of the horse and the gun, the former multiplying mobility a hundredfold and the gun increasing the capacity for action at a distance. These alone could not account for the change. A factor of enterprise and daring was necessary to furnish these implements with a dynamic power. The whole of the Plateau culture did not become Comanche; only a part of it did. The new way of life was more daring and dangerous and could not be started by timid and inhibited men. There must have been operating a bit of natural selection; those who lacked the ability, adaptability, or skill were either killed off or left behind, and the culture of Comanche was therefore the perpetuation of those most suited to withstand the risks involved in the new life.

We find that once this was initiated the cultural ideological changes did not take place in isolated items but in closely interwoven systems. The organizing principle is the known constellations built around anxiety points, and the fewer anxiety points encountered during growth and in the interpersonal relations, the fewer the necessities for correctives. In Comanche we see another type of almost frictionless society, owing to the fact that the rules governing the growth of the child are strictly, though spontaneously, observed. No foci of anxiety due to repression are built up in the growing individual. Contrast this with Alor, where nothing but anxiety foci are furnished the child. In Comanche the basic personality is free of the necessity of circumventing painful tensions, biological necessities are recognized, and permitted free outlet; the individual is permitted a high self-esteem. This is true largely for the males.

These features do not preclude competition. It is a widely held view that the factor which makes for such great instability in our society is the presence of competition. This is an inaccurate conclusion. In Comanche the competition is of the very keenest; but the competition does not involve security in the form of subsistence or social regard. With security of subsistence guaranteed and the freedom to display and develop abilities unobstructed, competition is accepted and the best man becomes leader. Moreover he has tenure on his leadership only as long as he can validate the claim. This is very democratic and can easily be accepted. The rivalry is not, however, permitted to obstruct the common good. In Comanche the participation of the individual is direct, not through representatives; the results of participation are immediately felt. The coöperation is not on the basis of division of function, but on the principle of many doing more effectively what one alone could do. It is an additive, not a compounded, co-operation.

The stake in the rivalry for leadership is pure prestige with a few additional tangible rewards not damaging to the common good. Moreover this common good is tangible and is readily perceived by everyone. Self-confidence is at a high level and mutual regard is high. No neurotic anxiety is permitted to accumulate except in the case of a few aberrants. Hence we find that their religion is direct, free of ingratiating attitudes and complicated guilt reactions toward the deity. There is not even the fear of death which is so commonly regarded as a real and not a neurotic anxiety. The only anxiety known in this society is that contingent upon the decline of natural powers. Advancing age is a state not anticipated with any eagerness in Comanche.

The stability of this culture is maintained largely by the fact that the individuals are not blocked in development, and the individual can contribute to the common good and participate in it according to his talents. It is a true democracy. There are no impediments to free competition in the form of hereditary rights, privileges, or titles. No position can be maintained unless validated. The only hardships are for those who are constitutionally unfitted for the role. There is no avenue of expression for aberrants. These are eliminated. There are no drones in this society, except the aged, against whom there are no hard feelings, since as parents to the child they contracted no animosities. The factors in the stability of Comanche are therefore: absence of difficulties in the growth pattern which block development of capacities; an assured place for each individual to participate fully in the society; and an elimination of the post-mature male either in his persistent participation after his powers have waned or in the ability to give his status to his offspring in the form of status or wealth.

As regards the emergence of such a society from the old Plateau culture, one can say that it had the proper *Anlage* for the culture which took its place.

From these two cultures we may attempt to abstract some principles concerning stability and change: A stable culture can be defined (in psychological terms) as one in which the integrational systems of the individual are consistent with the role that he must subsequently play in the society. The stability has nothing to do with any value judgments about the merits of the society. A stable society can be based on a human unit which is integrated on an obedience principle as well as on a free acting principle. If the systems become twisted—a training for submission in a society which demands freedom and initiative, or vice versa—a powerful element of instability is introduced. No society we have studied yet is either one or the other; all are mixtures. Tanala was stable as long as obedience was expedient in satisfying elementary biological needs and a social security; it was unstable when this technique failed as an adaptive expedient. A Comanche would make a poor constituent of a modern community with high degree of function differentiation. He is not attuned to that type of coöperation.

A society which interferes with effective integrational systems during growth cannot have any stability. But here it is a matter of degree and of which action systems are interfered with. No ideal formula can be given on how to foster growth of all action systems without knowing what the social role of the individual is to be. For Tanala, their system is excellent. For our society, our system falls far short of the mark.

The instability that characterizes Alor cannot be taken as a prototype of all social instability. The action systems of the individual render him unfit for any kind of coöperation on a sexual or social plane. Too many blocked action systems and the defenses made necessary by them impede the individual at every point. The low emotional tone of social relationships precludes the possibility of much in the way of elaborate forms of coöperation.

In societies where the individual is integrated to accommodate himself to obedience, he can do so provided his security is not impaired and his self-esteem is not injured by comparison with others. Status differentiation alone seems not to be a source of instability unless the gradations in status destroy security for one group as against another. In this case both those who enjoy status and those who do not must each devise appropriate defenses against each other. This, not the status differentiation itself, is the real tension point.

The role of differentiation of function presents a problem not very different from the one concerning status. Differentiation of function makes possible a high degree of finely articulated interaction. If there is a common goal in which all can participate, division of function promotes stability. However, where function differentiation is treated as a status differentiation and the common good is lost sight of, then differentiation of function can promote instability. One of the most important types of function differentiation is that between males and females. This is important because of the significant role the mother has in insuring favorable conditions for growth. If her functional role demands that she provide food as well as prepare it and care for children, the growth of the latter will suffer. This particular disturbance in growth starts a vicious cycle which seeps into every aspect of the culture.

If now we consider tension points created in the growth cycle of the individual (such as sexual taboos in childhood or adolescence or both) we will see that the social result will differ depending on whether adequate channeling along compensatory lines is furnished. There is no substitute for sexual gratification, and other zones pressed into pleasure-release function cannot perform this role. Compensations can be only in the form of deferred gratifications or rewards. Meanwhile, if the exercise of sexuality falls under the influence of parental authority, all obedience constellations are reinforced, the parents' value for good or evil becomes exaggerated, and guilt about sexual activity leads to anticipation of punishment and the fear of success. The social relevancy of this constellation lies in the fact that in a society where the need for self-validation is strong, the pull and tug between the need for accomplishment and the fear of being successful creates a great deal of anxiety for the individual, and the value of the social goal of success becomes exaggerated. Thus impairment of the growth of the individual in one domain like sex can augment social tensions that have no direct relation to the sexual impulse.

The discussion concerning failures in growth must include a discussion of those factors in growth which influence forces which hold society together. This is entirely a psychological problem, for it does not include any of the external sanctions or forces such as government and police. These forces are the only ones which seem automatic regulators; actually they are not automatic but are integrated during growth. We are referring to the superego mechanisms, which are the internalization of disciplines externally imposed on the child. They include all conscience and ego ideal constellations.

In the creation of conscience mechanisms it is not parental authority that is the most important factor but those forces which create parental authority. These are entirely protective functions. A case in point is the contrast between conscience in our society and that in

Alor. In the latter there is nothing in the behavior of the parent which can establish parental authority except coercion. The superego is based on affection, not hatred; on delegated and not enforced authority. The strongest factor in its establishment is good parental care, the relief and not the creation of painful tensions. This acts as an incentive to accept discipline in order to perpetuate the boons of the past. The fear of loss of them is the greatest threat to the security of the child. Hence the child is able to renounce important gratifications in order to preserve the magical powers of the parent. It is this constellation which is projected on the deity and is the cornerstone of all religions.[5]

This leads us to one of the most difficult problems in social dynamics, the role of the projective systems in social stability. We have in this work used religion and folklore as the chief social manifestations of common projective systems as part of the basic personality structure in any society. It would therefore follow that religion would have a very stabilizing effect on any culture. Though it is projective in origin, that is, an externalization of internal processes, it is treated as an *external reality*. The deity is conceived as a real object—generally with human understanding, sympathy, and emotions—possessed of extraordinary coercive power by virtue of being able to inflict pain now or in the future by means completely out of the power of the individual to combat or flee. But since every religion furnishes the individual means of winning the protection of the deity, usually by maintaining the practices and mores in the society, there is in religion a strong factor which makes for stability of the practices which characterize it.

The situation is not, however, so simple. Religion can maintain stability up to a point. The vigor of any projective system can be maintained only so long as it represents a true projection of the basic practices in a society. When these practices change and the human relations are redefined, the projective system also changes—but much later. Changes in religion therefore may represent changes in social relationships that have already taken place, which are in the process of taking place, or for which there is a need. Without this key the changes in religious ideology, dogma, and ritual which occurred from the Book of Job to Calvin cannot be understood. For there is no incentive to alter a security device like religion if it continues to be harmonious with the other practices of living. That is, the incentive

---

[5] See Kardiner, *op. cit.*, pp. 63–77.

to change is not ideological nor does it spring from the necessities of some abstract and universally applicable "morality." However, like every projective system, religion has always been treated as a piece of external reality, and often in the history of Western society the preoccupation has been chiefly with the projective systems and not with the social realities of which these projective systems were only the shadows. Thus, by writing a history of the change in religious ideologies from Job to Calvin we are studying the projective screen only, leaving the social realities of which they are the expression unaccounted for.

This very fact, that the projective system was mistaken for the reality, has in itself accounted for no inconsiderable portion of the phenomena of history. A case in point is the change in religion from the cult of Re to the cult of Osiris in the V dynasty in ancient Egypt. This change is the record of an aborted social revolution with illusory gratifications substituted for changes in the social order. But it does not come down to us as a social revolution but rather as a change in religious dogma. The essential issue concerned itself with the democratization of post-mortem boons hitherto only the prerogative of the ruling feudal class. The cult of Osiris democratized these post-mortem boons and placed them within reach of every man, Osiris being the popular god of death. Thus a social revolution terminated with an *illusory gratification,* as there is little evidence to indicate that any social changes in the feudal system of Egypt took place coincident with this change in religion.

This particular illustration seems to contradict our argument that changes in religious ideology are changes in social relationships that have already taken place. The force of the illustration is not lost; the tensions which gave rise to the need for alteration in religion were indeed present. These needs were not, however, met by changes in real gratifications; they were met by changes in anticipated post-mortem rewards, and hence could preserve the social conditions which made change of some kind imperative. Illusory gratifications can be used to preserve social stability. This was surely not a ruse on the part of the ruling classes of Egypt and was decidedly a concession and a loss of prestige. What gave such an illusory gratification the force of a real social gain is that status in Egypt was considered a fixed and settled issue, as it was in Western society in the Middle Ages. Some of the attributes of the ruling class were thus acquired by the lower classes. We have no evidence that the change in religion was accompanied by any social changes. But the cult of Osiris persisted down to the Roman conquest and resisted the efforts of Ikhnaton to introduce monotheism.

We can summarize the argument to this point and then take up the factors which make for stability and change in our own society. Society has no automatic controls; all stability and change take place only with coöperation of the constituents of a society. Hence factors which make for stability are those which promote a high degree of harmony in interpersonal relationships and a minimum of discord. Among the factors conducing to harmony are absence during growth of restrictions which create blocks to development of expression of inborn tendencies, so that the individual can emerge from growth to adulthood with free command of resources in affectivity and executive functions. Once these blocks to growth are introduced, the harmonious relations between parents and children, the sexes, and groups for coöperation can be maintained only by an adequate system of compensations and means of discharge. The most common form of compensation for disturbances in the growth pattern and other intrasocial tensions is the effort to preserve stability by means of the projective systems as employed in religion. The fewer the tensions in the growth pattern the less elaborate the religion (Comanche, in contrast to Christianity). Up to a measure this can preserve stability; when tensions get too high, the religion is altered. A society which is relatively free of discordant factors introduced during growth is Comanche. A society which abounds in discordant factors is Alor. A society which has many discordant factors but with adequate checks, compensations, and outlets is Tanala and our society. But the balance in Tanala was easily thrown completely out of joint by the introduction of private land ownership; then the whole system of checks and balances could no longer be maintained, and the discordant factors in the original plan of growth came to roost in the form of organized or disorganized forms of aggression. These took the form of neurosis and crime, and the latter could be held in check only by augmenting police measures and punitive systems. The latter do not resolve the tensions; they only suppress the tensions temporarily. Meanwhile the original plan which is followed in the Tanala growth pattern, with its emphasis on obedience, is restored and the tensions caused by the inequality of opportunities for expression gave rise to mutual anxiety; the higher status must protect itself against the lower, and vice versa. Tanala merely represents a stable society thrown into decompensation by the introduction of scarcity in an item essential to life. This turns the society into an anarchy, in which everyone wants to take the scarce commodity by force and to hold it against all comers. The instability is really a constant fight between the haves and the have-nots. The haves try to consolidate their gains by the introduction of awe into the status of being a "have" by external tokens of distinction, manners, dress, snobbishness, all of which are merely overdressed forms of anxiety against the have-nots; by the use of coercive power; by the continued activity of the post-mature male; and by handing the gains to direct offspring.

In short, one cannot evaluate stability or change in a society without reference to the growth pattern followed by it and the basic personality it produces, because changes are predicated by the needs created in the basic personality. Hence all extraneous sources of change (discoveries, destruction, necessity for new types of subsistence techniques, etc.) must be evaluated from the point of view of the basic personality structure.

But no matter what the growth pattern of any society may be, each society creates its own characteristic projective system one of whose forms—religion—has a high stabilizing function. If we contrast the religion of Comanche with that of Alor and Tanala, we get some important points of reference. Comanche is poor in religious ideology, and the technique for solicitation of aid from the deity is devoid of the concepts of sin, forgiveness, retribution, expiation, etc. This is due merely to the fact that the growth pattern of Comanche does not precipitate these issues; the individual during growth encounters fewer anxieties. But, notwithstanding, the idea of a supernatural power is present. In Alor it is also present; but the individual acts toward the deity only under the coercive threat of punishment and hence behaves toward the deity as if he were an insistent creditor whom he would rather not pay off. In Tanala the attitude to the deity resembles that of a child toward a strict but just parent, who only punishes for a real delinquency but protects for obedience.

This particular manifestation of the projective screen in religion, whose origin is in the growth pattern, tends therefore to perpetuate the institutions from which it arises. The reason for this is that the whole religious system is treated as a bit of external reality, and alterations in this projective screen are often used as substitutes for real tension release. The rise of the cult of Osiris and of Christianity amply illustrate this principle.

Dynamic Equilibrium in Western Society

The application to the history of Western society of the principles outlined in this book presents numerous difficulties. Some of these are concerned with deciding from the vast detail, where the essentials lie. But more germane to the enterprise is whether the concept basic personality has any usefulness at all. As long as it was considered that Western man represented "human nature," the issue was irrelevant to the enterprise. As soon as we operate on the assumption that "Western man" is a unique creature, different in his mental and emotional equipment from an Alorese or a Comanche, this issue must be decided.

We can for this purpose deploy evidence from about five different sources:

1. Direct observation of those features in the growth pattern which have remained constant
2. The evidence of changes in the projective systems
3. The character of the neuroses and psychoses in Western society
4. The changes in economy, and the organization necessary to make them effective
5. The influence of scientific reality systems

Taking Plainville as our base line and allowing for variations all along the line, we have a picture of basic personality with the following features: capacity for strong attachment to parent, capacity to idealize parent, to exaggerate capacities for good and harm. This combination, derived from good maternal care, lays a firm base for strong superego formation, which in its projected forms takes on the configurations of the religion of the Hebrews or Christianity. Good maternal care also permits development of curiosity and executive capacities. The constellation of sibling rivalry then takes on a specific character. The features which enter into it are strong attachment to the mother and well-formed aggression patterns. The introjection of the loved object, conducive to strong superego, makes social discipline easy but creates the problem for the child of the disposition of strong aggressions. These must be repressed, with, as a result, typical constellations like Oedipus complex and a large variety of masochistic variations. A new factor is introduced with impulse control related to the sexual drive. Repression plays a decisive role as evidenced by strong superego and introjection mechanisms. Regression to earlier erotic or supplementary erotic zones (oral and anal) may help tide over the gap in childhood but may prevent full development of capacity for tender and sensual relations to the opposite sex. Constellations formed in the sexual sphere influence others and vice versa, the chronological sequence being subject to much variation. The character configurations are capable of depressive reactions and strong feelings of inferiority created by discrepancies between the real and the ideal self. The basic personality therefore contains elements conducive to a high degree of coöperation, but also of high-tension hostilities.

What is the evidence of psychopathology? This question cannot be answered unequivocally. Psychiatry is a very recent accomplishment of man, and none can say whether the clinical syndromes which we see today—apart from the endogenous psychoses like manic depressive psychosis and schizophrenia, of which only the content is likely to be influenced by basic personality—were in existence in the same form two centuries ago. But taking the prominent neurotic disturbances of today as evidence, we would say that hysteria is one of the outcomes of this particular basic personality that involves chiefly the consequences of sexual repressions. The writer holds no brief for the exclusive etiology of hysteria from specific sexual repressions; but they do play a prominent part whether as primary or secondary factors. In the obsessional neurosis we have the same problem as in hysteria, with the emphasis falling in a particular direction—that concerned with the management of aggressive or destructive trends falling under repressive influence. But in both syndromes the operation of strong superego, plus potentially strong emotional attachments, shows up with great clarity. The psychosomatic patterns of Western man have not been studied exhaustively enough to make us certain of their relation to basic personality. But a few syndromes are clearly related—gastric ulcer (Alexander, French), asthma (the same authors), hypertension (Dunbar, Binger, and Ackerman). Even in the endogenous psychoses (manic depressive and schizophrenia—some equivalents of which are probably universal) the content shows up basic personality. The narcissistic exaltation of the ego in schizophrenia and the persecutory trends are both reflections of the original but now distorted capacity to love the object. In the reactive depression and the strong feelings of inferiority so common in our society we have a reflection of the operation of the powerful ego ideal, one of the forms of love toward the ideal and the wish to approximate it.

Have we any evidence that this basic personality of Western man has changed very much within the span of some three thousand years? The characters in the Old Testament, in the dramas of Sophocles and Shakespeare, and in the novels of James Joyce are all cast in the same mold. None of these characters has any resemblance to Lomani (see page 206).

In evaluating history therefore we have to know what kind of human being it is whose vicissitudes we are describing. Certain value systems, judging from Alor, derive from basic personality directly; others are precipitated by this basic personality in a given organization of the human environment. What are the features of our social organization (using modern urban organization as ground line) against which this personality is pitted, what specific values thereby become accentuated and what specific life goals emerge? This question needs a historical background for a complete answer.

In the light of the criteria established in the three cultures just discussed, our society of today is a scarcity culture (like Tanala-Betsileo) not because we cannot produce enough, but because of the unique economic structure. There is no pattern for the disposition of the post-mature male, whose influence continues because he has the greatest experience (though he has also the least elasticity) and whose influence is perpetuated by the ability to hand down his wealth. The scarcity in our culture is due to the fact that the individual has no assured participation, partly because of the complicity of the social machinery, partly because of the differentiation of function which carries with it a high degree of differences in claim for social recognition, and partly because labor or skill is treated as a commodity, like potatoes. The defined social goal is success, which means that the individual designated as successful has acquired a skill for which there is a demand, has acquired money and therefore some power to command the service and also the regard of others. The individual enjoys political "freedom" without any economic guarantees; but in actual practice the political freedom is not implemented by direct participation in the policies or direction of the coercive power of the national state, but in the choice of general directives given to representatives, who are not necessarily bound to these directives. His political freedom however guarantees him security of life, against unjust persecution or exploitation, and also gives him a degree of social mobility whereby through effort or chance he can alter his status or that of his children. Today the projective religious systems play only a formal role and can in no way be said to exercise any influence on social stability. The reality systems of modern man are sophisticated as compared with primitive society, a fact which gives him remarkable control over nature. The application of rationality to the difficulties of modern life have generally failed. The social stability (or instability) is maintained by a differentiation of "classes" with conflicting social goals and is settled from time to time by force, but most of the time by mutual concessions. Among the factors which modern man has to deal with, however indirectly, is the relation of his own national state to other states—the international scene.

We have therefore in Western society many more factors to deal with than are encountered in any primitive society. Moreover our society (and those from which we derived many cultural configurations) has a long history, and its present status is the product of this long development. We cannot here study this long history, but we can pick out certain critical situations which give us some notion of the dynamics of how we got where we are. In general we can say that "human nature" as we find it in Western man has not changed much in so far as his character structure, or rather the range of characters, is concerned. This means in effect that the family structure, the basic disciplines and normative influences, have not changed in configuration; but they have changed much in content. This means also that the basic personality has not changed much as regards the character of the projective systems derived from basic life experiences. But the reality systems have changed a great deal, and though these latter have not altered the projective systems, the reality systems have robbed the projective systems of their influence (in religion, for example) on social stability. This is the most important distinction between modern man and the early Christians or ancient Hebrews. For our illustrations of social change we can select certain phases of Hebrew history, the rise of Christianity, the Reformation, the rise of the bourgeoisie, and finally the growth of science.

Some pages back we described the powerful role that the projective system (as found in religion) exercised on social stability. In religion we have a system for explaining some of the vicissitudes of society.

So long as the Hebrews were a theocracy and no serious threat to their integrity as a nation arose, no challenge to the religious doctrine took place. Such a challenge did however arise during the first Babylonian captivity (700–600 B. C.). This was after a kingdom had replaced the theocracy, largely through the necessity for strong military leadership and the consequent failure and conquest of the Hebrews. The Book of Job (written during the Babylonian captivity) expresses a passionate skepticism concerning the value of a very ancient dogma —that virtue is rewarded and that suffering is the punishment for sin and wrongdoing. How does it happen that the virtuous and law abiding become victims of a divine wrath which permits their enemies to conquer them? By this skepticism the whole structure of the religion was endangered, and to this skepticism several courses of action were open: either to overthrow the whole ethical system and abandon oneself to hedonism and, by implication, antisocial activity; or to submit to suffering and interpret it as part of the chastisement for guilt from hidden sources, and await reinstatement into the graces of God. Most individuals in any society are too timid to take the first course, though the Bible is full of references to such delinquencies on a large scale; the second course—to wait for reinstatement—is the more common and requires much less daring and is less disruptive to the society.

What actually happened after the Book of Job was very interesting. The concept of the deity or the conditions for being reinstated were not changed. But a new idea was added—some 400 years later—in the Book of Daniel. This idea was that aid from the deity would take the form of a special emissary, a Messiah, who would be a divinely inspired military leader. This concept of the Messiah then underwent a series of changes until, in the first century B. C., it came to mean a direct representative of God who would either put down the forces of evil or render the people more susceptible of divine grace. It follows that if the meaning of the Messiah changed from a military leader to one who would cleanse the people of guilt; it meant that the people had lost the power of military effectiveness and that continued frustration had had the effect of greatly augmenting the sense of guilt, and finally that all aggressions now took on a masochistic character.

Moreover these newer beliefs or hopes were no longer the common faith of all the Hebrews, but only of a group of them. The bulk of the Hebrews accommodated themselves to the submission to Rome. The

Messianic beliefs were the credo of the disaffected and socially outcast; they could appeal to none other. The actual form in which these beliefs were consummated was in the mission and crucifixion of Christ, who was recognized as having redeemed the world through his own sufferings and death. From this point an entirely new group of possibilities for elaboration was opened up, dealing with the relations of Christ to God, to His Mother Mary, etc. These changes and elaborations were consonant with new conditions in social life which created new stresses and therefore new types of projection phenomena. One phenomenon deserves special notice in the development of Christian dogma and ritual practice, the phenomenon of mediation. Christ first appears as a mediator between man and God, who recedes in importance because of his inaccessibility. Later, Christ recedes because of inaccessibility and Mary appears as a mediator. Jesus eventually became a severe Judge, not the saviour, of fierce countenance and carrying a flaming sword in His hand. This prevented direct access to Jesus. Only the Virgin Mary could now be approached directly. Eventually, in the fifteenth century, the idea grew up that the Virgin herself had to be interceded with through her mother, St. Anne.[6] The church was in itself nothing but an organized intercessor, and the frequency of change of intercessors is not only a commentary on the formal structure of the church, but also attests to the fact that its role as intercessor became more and more defective.[7]

These illustrations of changes in the projective screen indicate not only the important role the projective systems play in social stability, but that they served to distract attention from the actual realities from which they arose. The shadow was mistaken for the substance. The real issues in the Roman world were concerned with subsistence, distribution of wealth, status, etc. These issues cannot be seen as long as one is occupied with debating whether this or that form of baptism leads to the desired result. Preoccupation with the projective screen is nevertheless a type of accommodation to conditions that were deemed unalterable or not recognized as the source of the social difficulty.

Another factor emerges from these considerations. We have no right to assume that any fundamental changes in the social organiza-

---

[6] *Cambridge Modern History*, II, 107.

[7] For a fuller discussion of this problem, see K. Kautsky, *Foundations of Christianity*, 13th ed. (New York, International Publishers Co., 1926). Also, Erich Fromm, *Entwicklung des Christusdogmas* (Imago, 1930).

tion of the Hebrews took place between 700 B. C. and 33 B. C. All these variations in the fantasy screen are therefore compatible with the same basic personality structure. They therefore reflect the changes in the alteration of the fantasy screen in response to certain social conditions, but without alteration of family structure or basic disciplines. From the numerous accommodations in the projective fantasy screen, one can conclude that the greatest pull in any society is toward stability.

What stands out in this story of the rise of Christianity is that it was in every respect the fantasy equivalent of a social revolution, much like that which accompanied the rise of the cult of Osiris and with similar content. It was a democratization of deferred gratifications, meanwhile leaving completely alone the whole reality system on which the discomforts of society were based. Nevertheless the Romans regarded Christianity as a revolutionary movement. The fact that Christianity left the social system intact gave rise later to the distinction between spiritual and temporal power, the boundaries between which were never quite definitely settled, and encroachments of spiritual on temporal affairs were continually taking place. By this division the church gave its tacit support to the feudal system, which went unmolested until the beginning of the fifteenth century. Christian dogma played into the hands of the feudal system and perpetuated it not by any active support, but by affirming that man was born with a burden of guilt and suffering was therefore his natural lot. A lifetime spent in obliterating the effects of this congenital sin leaves little time or interest for studying social ills or even for questioning them.

Christianity did bring with it an important idea, though it limited the scope of its operation. This idea was that man was responsible for his own personal fate as defined within the limits of salvation. The definition of this responsibility was largely in the form of impulse control, and not in the form of perfecting his resources for dealing with the outer world. This was not in the domain of the church and hence was outside the range of the most effective incentives. Exploitation of the environment had not begun to be an objective during the Renaissance; it was an objective of the Egyptians, Greeks, and Romans. It was temporarily smothered in the so-called Dark Ages.

The instrument which gave this tendency new life was the beginnings of modern science. Its beginnings were purely investigative and not utilitarian; in fact it took several centuries for investigative techniques to become hitched to utilitarian purposes. The important thing about this technique of investigation and later of exploitation is that it led to a new definition of man to himself, and, of necessity, to a redefining of his relations to God. It is well known that the church recognized this threat to its authority and waged a futile battle against the encroachment on its established domain. This battle was the same in content as any other battle to preserve a vested interest.

Another factor, independent of science, made its importance felt, though this importance was only an emphasis and not a new creation, having been in existence from the earliest times. That factor was organized mercantilism with the aid of the systematized use of money or capital. The story of the rise of influence and the growing prestige of the city is an exciting one. The separation of peasant class, burgher, and noble and their struggles for growth and power and influence, as well as the separation of communities into states, is a part of this social change.

From all this milling about there arose a movement which decided the fate of the projective systems in Western man and removed them permanently as the battleground on which social issues were to be waged. That movement was the Reformation in its many forms. This movement has been fully studied by Max Weber [8] and retold many times. There is considerable reason to question the validity of the analysis of Weber and of those who follow a similar argument.[9] The first point is a purely methodological one. If Christianity was originally the fantasy escape by a group of oppressed people, how is it that the process is reversed in the Reformation and that in the latter it is ideologies which give rise to certain practices. There is much evidence to support the interpretation that the practices and social situations which made for the Reformation existed long before Luther. His immediate attack was against the Papacy, and the defiance of papal authority was a catalytic agent which set off a movement which at the time had no ideological framework. This came later. The fact that the church could not deal with the defiance of Luther and that excommunication failed was due to the fact that the mere defiance of the Pope drew enormous support from nobles, burghers, and peasant classes alike. As the Reformation spread, each group that supported it had its own particular advantages to gain from so doing, and these advantages were by no means alike. The ideologies which crystallized

[8] *The Protestant Ethic and the Spirit of Capitalism* (New York, Scribner, 1930).
[9] See Erich Fromm, *Escape from Freedom* (New York, Farrar and Rinehart, 1941), pp. 40–102, whose interpretation differs from Weber.

cannot be said to have been created by the Reformation, unless we include in this caption all social, ethical, scientific, and economic innovations which occurred in the sixteenth century. And to do this would confuse the entire issue.

The Reformation was not a movement of the oppressed lower classes; Luther did not lend his support to the Peasant Revolution in Germany. The group which supported the defiance of the Papacy and had most to gain from it was the new burgher class; the feudal class interests were only partly involved and partly threatened. Nor can it be said that this relatively new burgher class was seeking fantasy expression in some form through the church reformation. It assuredly did not seek any redefinition of gratifications after death. It wanted ecclesiastical sanction for a whole series of values already in practice, rapidly gaining vogue, but under heavy censure of the church. The church could implement its veto with spiritual threats and actual economic power. The church was international; and the new entity that was struggling to be born was the secular state, which sought for itself the role of becoming the guardian of social efficacy and well-being.[10] For this purpose the bourgeois class became the spearhead and the group which most urgently felt the need of a redefinition of social goals.

This statement of the problem indicates that new values had already supplanted those defined by the church, and it became the task of Luther and many others, notably Calvin, to reconcile these divergent goals of human activity. The corruption in the church was the spark which set off the explosion, but it did not create the powder. The Reformation was no flight into fantasy but away from it into realities translatable into objectives like free economic activity and the accumulation of wealth. These objectives had to be reconciled with those defined by the church. This reconciliation was gratuitous and not of the essence of the social change.

The values toward which Western society was now polarized were concerned directly with human relations as defined by economic activity, and not through the indirect channel of the projective screen which characterized the cult of Osiris and Christianity, both of which left the direct social relationships alone. While some reconciliation with the fantasy screen was necessary, an important factor in the sta-

10 Harold Laski, *The Rise of Liberalism* (New York, Harper, 1936), p. 57.

bility of society effected through the fantasy screen was thus destroyed in part. The adjustment was no longer made exclusively on a fantasy plane, and man came to grips with the ordering of the social fabric directly. This does not mean that the projective screen had completely lost its function, for it had to take up the disposition of the enormous tensions created by direct hostilities arising in the new society as it emerged.

The answers which Luther and Calvin gave in the form of dogma did not confer an unequivocal new liberty on man. The new freedom could only be used in new directions found by the burgher class. As far as impulse control was concerned, the Reformation made the psychological task more difficult. Man had to become his own judge, for with the break with the church went the opportunity to keep the conscience externalized. The internalization of conscience had an equivocal effect on social stability, because it did not operate on those hidden forms of aggression concealed in commercial practice. It could only operate on those impulses which fell under disciplinary ban in childhood—chiefly the pleasure drives. Calvin, more than Luther, became the mouthpiece for the claims of the rising bourgeois class. He opposed many secular controls on the basis that submission to them was a kind of idolatry. In this sense Calvinism was an avowal of middle-class revolutionism. It demanded an active and not a submissive discipline. In practice Calvinism worked out so that repression of the pleasure drives acquired a reward in the new liberties, which became filled with new opportunities for self-assertion and aggression. On the basis of the success of these new assertive efforts, the Calvinist could claim that he was one of the "saved"—for essentially the concept of salvation always referred to the renunciation of the pleasure drives. Thus the Calvinist was quite consistent in his claims that he was saved because he had renounced pleasure. In the angry God of Calvin we recognize the old angry Hebrew God, with all his cruelty but without his sense of fair play, and completely lacking the mercy and forgiveness of Jesus. So there is not much use trying to achieve salvation; the best one can do is to prove by one's works that he is saved. Success in worldly life is one of the ways of establishing the fact that one is saved, hence industry is exalted to a high position, operating now with the sanction of the new church and in harmony with new social goals. The adoption of this new Calvinist plan of life—

essentially the definition of the bourgeois goals—by the lower classes led to a unique practice called Puritanism with its emphasis on industry and thrift.

The Calvinistic break with the church did not relieve man's psychological burdens; it increased them. The old church, to be sure, maintained that man was born tainted with original sin but from baptism onward was offered continuous opportunity for the achievement of salvation. This task the church facilitated by reproducing the parent-child relationship, thus externalizing the superego (or conscience) mechanisms and by prorating pain as advance payment on suffering in the future world, or substituting a small for a greater punishment. There was tyranny in this, but there was also love, on the pattern of parental love for obedience. The Calvinist dogma destroyed the externalized conscience and placed it where it could wield far more despotic power than was ever done by the church. The Reformation internalized conscience in return for a freedom from externalized tyranny which shackled self-expression along lines which had become imperative. From the idea that success is a proof of virtue to a contempt for the poor and unsuccessful is only one step. However, the most startling thing about the Reformation is that, whereas it internalized conscience, this conscience still operated on the same factors which were emphasized by the old church, chiefly the pleasure drives the repression of which were fundamental in the family disciplines. The doctrine exerted no restricting influence on the social and mercantile practices of the middle class; if it had, in all probability the support of that group would have been withdrawn.

When one asks from what sources Luther and Calvin constructed their conception of the deity and the definition of human relations to the deity, the answer must be, from the same sources that the Hebrew patriarchs constructed him, or that any contemporary compulsion neurotic does—that is, out of the fabric of relations to the father in the family and by submission to the same disciplines that have been continuous in our culture from those ancient times until today. The most direct attack is on sensuality which is much more effectively banned by an internalized conscience than by any externalized power. Judging from the consistency of man's relations to God when traced for five thousand years, the basic personality structure of Western man has not changed. The changes from the Pentateuch to Calvin are not changed in essence; they all fall within the range of the same personality structure subjected to different strains. The more the arrangement in the projective screen seemed to change, the more it was the same.

However the change to an internalized conscience is one not to be underestimated. From this point such a conscience or superego could follow several fates: it could create an individual like the Puritan, who acquires virtue by renouncing all pleasure devices that fell under parental ban in childhood and bases his value and self-confidence on the completeness with which he performs this self-discipline. Such a conscience could deteriorate and become subject purely to secular conditions; it could be chained to the demands of reason and social well-being. In the latter case there were two alternatives to the eventual separation of conscience from supernatural threats: they might be replaced by hypochondriacal anxieties [11] or by social anxieties. In place of the anxiety of salvation we now have the anxiety as judged by self-esteem. This alteration of the locus of conscience brought greater responsibility for one's own welfare, and was an inevitable consequence of the growth of science, even though the latter was not yet made subservient to practical needs.

The old church could not redefine human goals in terms of the new values, and the new freedom to investigate and explore was not accompanied by any plan on which social relations could be confidently charted. There were no precedents to go by. The medieval world was stable because it was a world state whose secular subdivisions rested on no competitive production economy. The values which later became dominant in the secular state were not newly created. Money, exchange, banking, mercantilism were as old as civilization itself, but were never before made into overt instrumentalities of social well-being.

It must be noted that the new tool of science acted on Western man much as the advent of the horse and gun did upon the old Plateau tribes, and like these, were responsible for the redefining of the ob jectives of living. But this redefinition had to utilize the secular organization existing at the time. That there was a relation between the

---

[11] It is interesting in this connection that the popular treatises on the evils of masturbation during the 17th, 18th and 19th centuries do not invoke supernatural sanctions but excite hypochondriacal fears. It was a change from fear of punishment to fear of illness, both isomeres of the same basic idea, with different conscious representations. These views were widely held in both Catholic and Protestant communities. One can safely say that such hypochondriacal notions could not be held by the ancient Hebrews. The conscience was too externalized.

new goal of social well-being (in place of salvation) and the secular state was at first not suspected. This became clear only when one difficulty after another was precipitated out in the workings of the secular state. The conflicts (personal and social) were not unlike those which followed the introduction into Tanala of private land ownership. There was a great increase in anxiety. Social history from the sixteenth century on is the history of this effort to define the secular state and all the minutiae of interpersonal relations in terms of the goal of personal well-being. In this effort only temporary plateaux of relative stability were achieved, and we are still milling about the same problem today.

How the change of values took place which so radically redefined the goals of life and of which the religious Reformation was one of many simultaneous manifestations cannot be precisely recovered from history. From a psychological point of view the prime mover was not the economic factors but the growth and development of that method of dealing with phenomena of nature which we call scientific. This instrument altered the whole reality system of man, and it rapidly became a means of subjecting nature to its power. The changes in social organization were secondary to these. This instrument of science would automatically reduce the number of anxiety situations for which divine intervention was necessary. It altered the technique for handling certain types of anxieties arising from the outer world but had no effect on those anxieties arising from intrasocial sources which were now augmented by the new method of self-validation by social well-being. It was this reality system which eventually meant the dissolution of the projective screen as a major factor in social stability and allocated the personal character of the individual as the only place where this projective system could now operate. The projective system could now express itself in personal character, which became more and more important as the means of achieving social well-being was less limited by inherited status. This projective screen could now operate on definitions of social well-being in interpersonal relations or in the definition of the relations of the individual to the state—that is, in social ideologies.

We have not discussed many of the way stations on the long trajectory described. It is needless to emphasize that the social validity of the projective screen (in religion) did not ever disappear altogether and is even today a factor to reckon with. Interest in religion is still a function of personal character, early training, education, but it is more or less a social routine without influence on goals of living. Nor have we described the various political way stations, the gradual transition from the feudal to the democratic state, the brief but stormy history of the vicissitudes of the democratic state and the crisis through which it is now passing to whatever may follow. But there is one phase that deserves closest scrutiny, the union of science with the objectives of social well-being.

This subject has been studied by many authors; the latest study by Franz Borkenau [12] is most stimulating. Although the change of handicrafts by manufacturing techniques had begun in the sixteenth century, the natural sciences did not do much in the way of techniques of production even in the seventeenth century. But the knowledge of mechanics did lead to an attitude of seeing in all natural phenomena analogies to the processes of manufacture. Animals, for example, were conceived as soulless mechanisms. Laski puts it this way: "The new outlook codified in the Principia of Newton emerged from a nexus of problems presented to science by business men." [13] Borkenau holds that eventually man himself became mechanized and the social relations of man conceived on the analogy with mechanical processes.[14]

To evaluate the importance of this alteration of the viewpoint of natural phenomena we can contrast it with the crudest manifestation of projection—animism, which attributed to the inanimate world the motivations and reactions of man. Or contrast it with the Augustinian conception that the "laws" of nature are not in the things themselves, but are foisted on them by divine command, just as the moral law is the direct command of God. No matter in how many different ways this idea was formulated by Thomas Aquinas, or the reconciliation of this concept with human capacity to reason and the existence of drives, it always remains the same anthropomorphic conception. This divine law naturally applied to the social organization of man according to medieval theology. This theology was vigorously contested by Calvin, who did not deny the existence of moral law but saw little evidence of it in worldly life. Hence it had to be imposed by God. The Reformation, through the denial of natural law in human affairs, founded a

---

[12] *Der Übergang vom feudalen zum bürgerlichen Weltbild* (Paris, Alcan, 1934), Chapter I.
[13] *Op. cit.*, p. 77.   [14] *Op. cit.*, p. 14.

positive law, or at least sought a new definition of it. In Luther and Calvin we see, therefore, the operation of a new conception of the social order.

We stated above that the psychological task of adaptation to the new conception of the personality and its relations to the outer world had to be evaluated from the social organization existing at the time it began. Just as the church perpetuated the mental habits acquired in the family, so the feudal system did much the same thing. The feudal lord and his tenants were a replica of the peasant family, where the son worked for the father and the son's independence was deferred and difficult without his father's aid. Paternal authority was severe, but was kept in place by the relative immobility of the son. The social organization of the city was of necessity different, and it was these city dwellers (burghers) who promoted both mercantilism and scientific investigation.

The question is whether the personality structure of Western man was attuned to the new possibilities opened up. We pointed out that the personality derived from the growth pattern in Western man is not consistent; it fosters strong potentialities for investigation and utilization of the outer world; strong foundations for parental idealization, strong superego formation. But it also introduces by its sexual disciplines great obstacles to development, which not only affect the specific action systems concerned with sexual activity but all other action systems as well. The pleasure mechanisms of man have a relaxor function, and we have seen by a series of cultural contrasts that when this pleasure mechanism is blocked, since it is a biologically determined drive, the effects of their suppression are not lost. They turn up again in some form of destructiveness, either against oneself or against others. The personality structure of Western man was attuned to the requirements of the feudal system, and the aggressions accidental to discipline were kept in check by the system of rewards after death for obedience. When this reward system gradually lost vogue and currency, the basic personality structure was not altered, and the aggressions turned either into channels of self-abnegation (the Puritan) or into competition for the new opportunities for self-validation. Heightened self-esteem took the place of salvation, and these two ideas are not exactly isometric; they lead to entirely different social consequences. Heightened self-esteem could only be validated by prosperity, and the goal of prosperity had become a religion.

The application of the techniques of science to the concrete details of economic practice ended in failure, because its chief objective was to define the terms of the social contract and to stop arbitrary power. And, as Laski pointed out, every attempt to define social relations in terms of reason only turned out, in the long run, to be nothing but new nostrums for bigger and better prosperity.

The new goal demanded a new social milieu, and this was finally achieved in democracy. This movement encountered different obstacles in different places, but in the long run the bourgeoisie conquered, first religion, then culture, and finally the state (Laski). It is in the culture defined by this group that we now live. It is a highly unstable culture owing to the enormous anxieties under which each individual lives. And it is to these anxieties that we must direct our attention.

No evaluation of these anxieties can be made without bearing in mind that the social goals of success and prosperity are subject to no rational criticism or choice and that they are the product of a trend in history which is five centuries old, that there is no vocation immune from their influence and that to these objectives are now harnessed all the resources of man's power over nature. The anxieties of Western man are therefore concerned with success as a form of self-realization in the same way that salvation was in the Middle Ages. But in comparison with the individual who merely sought salvation, the psychological task for modern man is much more arduous. It is a responsibility, and failure brings with it less social censure and contempt than it does self-contempt, a feeling of inferiority and hopelessness. Success is a goal without satiation point, and the desire for it, instead of abating, increases with achievement. The use made of success is largely power over others, since the advantages in the form of luxurious types of subsistence, "conspicuous waste," are easily exhausted. Those who have power or wealth set the fashion for all others to imitate, and social mobility is interpreted largely as the achievement of more success, to improve the standard of living, to ape the manners of those who are rich, and to have the gratification of having some "power" too.

Let us examine the growth pattern to see whether there are factors there which create anxiety. The growth pattern does not conduce to the creation of a secure individual. It begins by laying a strong foundation for the personality by good maternal care, which includes not only purely executive functions but lively training in responsive affectivity. The disciplinary factor which does most of the damage pertains to the sexual taboos, which ignore the biological function of the pleasure drive and the apparently useful role it plays in growth. The damage is done by the taboos and not by the pleasure drive. These disciplines introduce into a pleasure drive a pain element which augments guilt, and obedience constellations that are incompatible with social goals. Hence they become the focus of conflicts, destroy self-confidence, foster self-contempt and hatred to the parent. If this sexual drive were not subject to integrational development, then these disciplines would make no difference and we could, without damage to the individual, arbitrarily set the time for approved sexual relations. But these sexual disciplines continue through adolescence, and the fact is that the sexual effectiveness of modern man, but especially woman, is impaired in adult life as a consequence. Moreover the effects of these disciplines are not confined to the sexual function. Beginning early in life, these disciplines have an influence in defining the action patterns of the individual for life. One of the effects is that they dislocate the operation of the conscience (superego) mechanism into the government of forces not injurious to society. A second effect is that frustrations from this source have an explosive force in the form of (a) neurosis, psychosomatic disorders, and many masochistic adaptation types; (b) the degradation of the sexual impulse of man, of which degradation the female is the chief victim; (c) or it sets into motion the need for compensatory forms of validation or self-assertion. It is perhaps no accident that wealth and sexual vigor are equated in our society.

The effect of these disciplines is therefore to spoil the relation of child to parents and of the sexes to each other. In view of the fact that the personality gets such a good start, with lively affectivity patterns, the anxiety generated by these sexual disciplines is enormous, and the destructive social effects very great.

The inconsistencies in the growth pattern make it therefore a matter of chance whether the individual develops potentialities for accomplishing the social goal. Some do and some do not. To be sure, the possibility of compensatory activity always exists, and many a "success" is achieved by this compensatory route, or even by "sublimation," though the latter is a dubious working concept.

The capacity to participate in society is determined not only by this characterological equipment, but by the acquisition of skills. In his training the individual is continuously beset by competitions and comparisons. More anxiety about validation results. In connection with traning one cannot omit the confusing character of our taught systems, some of which are based on scientific empiricism, some on religious systems.

The opportunity for acquiring skill is defined by parental status largely. In any of these skills the same competition without security persists. Failures or frustrations can always be expressed in compensatory fantasies. Rarely are religious values invoked to explain failure; failure is rarely interpreted as punishment for sin; most commonly it is interpreted as inferiority, which is never accepted as a just desert but as an additional incentive for more effort, or more hatred of those who surpass.

Among the working classes rational compensations exist in the form of the new institution of trade unions, which increase bargaining power. This has in some instances a relation to subsistence; in others to prestige. Among the merchant or production entrepreneurs the augmentation of power is achieved by diminution of competition within the group (monopoly or cartel) and by getting better conditions for getting more power or profit or by maneuvering to get the coercive power of the national state on its side. Thus the high value of fine function differentiation is lost by internecine fights for power on the one hand against exploitation on the other.

These are the external socio-economic configurations which exist today and within which no individual can find security. This is no less true for the powerful. But one psychological factor in this class warfare must not be overlooked. The upper classes have training in the ready use of aggressions of crude or refined forms; the working classes do not have this ready aggression, until it becomes explosive.

In all this system we must note the absence of "social conscience," which from the origin of Christianity escaped serious religious sanctions. It is one of the signal failures of the Reformation that it also failed to introduce religious sanctions into the hidden forms of aggression.

Our society can no longer hope to acquire stability through the use of illusory gratifications after death. The chances of a social balance maintained by force are very dubious. The chances even of pure political freedom unsupported by economic security are just as poor, interpreting this security only in so far as subsistence is concerned. But even if the latter were achieved, there would still remain the anxiety created by our inconsistent growth pattern—and these anxieties can only be removed by a tedious process of education which has to penetrate many layers of defenses made up of outworn superstitions and of many customs which are unsupported by any rationale.

Summary and Conclusions

The concept of culture becomes an operational tool when implemented by the psychological insight into the knowledge that different practices of living are created by different problems of adaptation, and that these practices have specific influences on the individual if integrated during the process of growth. This does away with the pseudo-problem of biological as against sociological influence. For when we speak of specific influences on the individual during growth we take for granted and assume the existence of uniform biological drives. We only qualify the integrated control of these drives and the influence which these controls have upon the completed personality. In this book and its predecessor we have studied five cultures, with the result that each society was found to have a distinctive psychological profile which we designated basic personality. This concept was used upon data of varying degrees of completeness. In each case, however, the basic personality gave us an inventory of the differences in the mental and emotional equipment for adaptation that each group had at its disposal, notwithstanding an identical biological makeup. The particular equipment that we found in any group gave us no time perspective; that is, we could not tell in what way the basic personality changed when the society encountered new problems in adaptation.

We therefore attempted to solve this problem by studying a culture with a long history, in a hasty and sketchy manner. The results of this preliminary survey yielded the following conclusions. Cultural changes do not involve all institutions simultaneously; some basic institutions—notably those pertaining to family organization, the patterns for raising children, early discipline—have a tenacity that other institutions pertaining to organization of the economically active individuals for coöperation do not possess. Hence when we follow cultural changes over a long time we note that certain essential determinants of personality configuration remain constant while others can undergo numerous modifications. However, if the factors which are decisive for basic personality remain fundamentally unchanged, all other cultural changes are, in part at least, contingent upon the psychological effects of those features which remain constant or which vary within a narrow range.

We have, therefore, in this formula a scheme for appraising the differences between cultures, which will specify why the life goals and value systems differed in each. This procedure does away with the so-called idiosyncratic factor which used to be attributed to racial differences. Our conclusion is supported by recent advances in psychosomatic patterns which are now shown to be not racial idiosyncrasies but caused by specific patterns in the handling of emotional tensions and anxieties. There is perhaps a residue, after all these factors have been taken into account, which can then be called constitutional. At all events, no refuge should be taken in the concept of "constitutional," which can only at present be defined in terms of unknowables and conjectures.

A second conclusion in following a wide arc of a historical trajectory is that basic personality limits the types of adaptation which we follow in the history of a people. A society whose cohesiveness is determined by a strong superego will have a very different history from one whose cohesion depends on the application of external force. In other words, the nature of the intrasocial tensions in a society will determine how it meets external vicissitudes like hunger, external enemies, earth-quakes, discoveries, etc.

In the history of Western society we examined evidence of several varieties. The chief of these was the examination of the projective systems found in religion from Job to Calvin, in correlation with the growth pattern, changes in social organization, and the growth of empirically derived systems of knowledge. In Western history we find therefore a continuous series where the basic constellations are similar but whose projective manifestations change with the necessity to express or relieve tensions created by new problems in adaptation. The religion under a theocracy, an oppressed lower class, or a rising middle class took on different dogmatic form. In each case, however, the function of the religion was to exercise a stabilizing influence by externalizing the basic disciplines which prevailed in the community. However advantageous this was in preserving stability, a price was paid in that a new source of inertia was introduced because the projective manifestations were mistaken for the reality of interpersonal relations. In the old Hebrew theocracy equilibrium was possible when the love of the deity was assured by an emphasis on equal protection for all during the frontier period of the ancient Hebrews. This equilibrium broke down when the vicissitudes of the Hebrews under a kingdom raised doubts about the validity of the ancient dogma that obedience brought security. The solution, mainly through the influence of the disaffected, took the form of Christian redemption, in which the old dogma could be retained only at the cost of the devaluation of all worldly goals. That is, the solution was by way of a fantasy reward collectible after death. With Calvinism the influence of the external realities of class differentiation, of social well-being, contributed more to the dogmas of the new religion than was the case with early Christianity. With Calvinism the projective system was intact in so far as the government of pleasure drives was concerned. The new types of interpersonal relation had come into being when mercantilism became an instrumentality of social well-being completely outside religious control. In fact, no end of cruelties were sanctioned on the justification that the renunciation of pleasure ensured salvation. In Calvinism the successful middle class staked out a claim of being the chosen people. The externalized conscience of the old church was dislocated, and an internalized conscience took its place. Delinquencies in the form of pleasure drives, instead of giving rise to fears of post-mortem punishment, now sponsored hypochondriacal fears, as attested by the masturbation literature of the seventeenth and eighteenth centuries. The fear of failure replaced the fears of post-mortem pain, and the goal of success and social well-being became heir to all the emotions that were once attached to the concept of salvation. The state, however, unlike the Hebrew theocracy, found itself unable to take over the responsibilities that were once loaded on the deity, because it was the coercive power of the state and not its benevolence and forgiveness that was the chief instrumentality of social balance. In this way social conflicts centered about the possession by dissident factions of the coercive powers of the state. When the state was obliged to take over the function of adjudicating disputes, it could only do so within the limits of the definition of the social contract, which was governed not by superego or internalized mechanisms but by external force.

This situation could only lead to greater and greater intrasocial friction as the ability to stabilize society on the basis of rewards collectible after death was destroyed. The explosive pressures within society then had to be exerted by one secular state in relation with other secular states or between the stratifications within the same society. For a long time the first method was in vogue and by now seems to be exhausted. We are now living in the phase in which the greatest strain is falling on the stratifications within society.

The crucial problem in connection with this study is how much light it can cast on the contemporary scene. Here the diagnostic problem is to evaluate the effect on the basic personality of the current socio-economic order and what the lines of tension are likely to be.

The good parental care leads to strong parental attachment and idealization. The disciplines make this care contingent upon certain controls of impulse. In its projected form it is this which forms the basis of religious systems from the Pentateuch to Calvin. This good care forms the basis of two other systems, the superego systems and the self-esteem systems. The superego systems rest on the capacity to introject the protecting and disciplining parent with the consequences of depression, guilt, and feelings of inferiority—various forms of registering discrepancies between the socially approved or disapproved ego. The good parental care also leaves free the development of all aggression patterns, "giving scope to" strong investigative, constructive, and artistic capacities. The other side of this picture shows the pathological consequences of strong parental attachments—too great dependency on the parent with resulting retardation of development; to the strong aggressive components must now be added the possibilities of masochistic elaborations—under the influence of the superego system. In other words sado-masochism is not a biologically determined polarity; it is contingent on strong emotional attachments and well-organized aggression patterns in the foundations of the personality. To this basic series must now be added the consequences of sexual repression, with all its influences on character formation, hysteria, and obsessional neurosis. From all this it is clear that the sado-masochistic complex is not nuclear but is the outcome of other interacting constellations. Sado-masochism can be called the currency of all disorganized aggression patterns, whether temporary or incorporated into the character structure, and under the governing control of a tonic superego.

As regards the socio-economic setup, what concerns us about it here are the emotional values created by it for the individual. The fluidity of class lines—social mobility—and the high degree of function differentiation with varying status values attached all conduce to a highly emotional pursuit of the goal of social well-being as defined in terms of standard of living, prestige, power over others, etc. Some of the expedients of social stability by way of religious ideologies are now for the greater part closed off. Their value lay in the relief of intra-social tensions by the promise of deferred gratifications. Their weakness showed itself as soon as the goal of social well-being displaced that of salvation. It is not only that a deferred gratification cannot compete equally with a current goal or that there is no fantasy equivalent of social well-being. It is also due to the difference in superego influence on the formulation of these two goals. The superego systems in our basic training govern the sexual impulse and certain crass forms of aggression. Social well-being is governed by the coercive power of the state, and the state defines aggression according to the rules made by those who control this coercive power.

The strains and tensions to which the basic personality of Western man was subjected are best illustrated in the distortions and compromises in Calvinist doctrine. The basic training of the individual demanded control of pleasure and aggressive impulses in return for the future support and affection of the parents. The definition of social well-being demanded the abandonment of control over certain types of aggression that did not fall under superego control. The Calvinists solved this problem by giving free rein to those forms of aggression that were compatible with the new goals of social well-being and at the same time retained the strictest control over the pleasure drives. It was not perceived by the Calvinists that this inordinate control of pleasure drives was unconsciously interpreted as a form of cruelty, which in turn had to lead to either masochistic or externalized forms of cruelty. The result was that the achievement of the social goal of success and the repression of pleasure drives became at once the formula for social regard and the evidence of salvation, and gave new opportunity for the expression of pent-up aggressions. If one can interpret success in the achievement of social well-being as a part of the reward system, then by the same token failure in the achievement of these goals could be interpreted as punishment. The Calvinist doctrine does allow for this latter possibility. There is another possibility which seems more frequently to have prevailed. If the individual interprets his failure as an evidence of inadequacy or of not being loved, then he may feel himself absolved of the necessity for all impulse control. If there is no hope of being loved for obedience control or discipline, then the internalized conscience fails and the social control passes from the internalized disciplines to dominance-submission polarities waged on a plane of coercion, forcible elimination of competition, or even annihilation.

It is interesting to speculate on what happens to the previous manifestations of the superego. They do not disappear; they take on new forms. The former expectation of love may become a certainty of hatred, and against this hatred strong militant measures of a defensive nature must be instituted. The resultant self-contempt must be counteracted with claims of superiority and the real hatred passed on to some convenient and preferably helpless scapegoat, who now becomes the carrier of this projected self-contempt. To maintain the integrity of this system, all allegiance to rationality must be abandoned to facilitate the release of controls on all pleasure and destructive drives. Thus in the most abandoned destructiveness that we see exemplified in some of our contemporary societies, we can still see the operation of the old superego mechanisms, torn from their normal moorings, bolstered by a tenuous system of rationalizations, but still consistent with the need for self-validation and social approval.

In whom does such a disorganization take place? In any individual or group which is cut off from the achievement of the approved social goals. Many new problems are created by the banding together of many people with the same objectives, whose combined efforts can forcibly alter the structure of the social order—but only temporarily; for it is hard to see how any new social order can eventually be polarized in any direction other than the one it destroys so long as the basic disciplines remain stationary.

The explosive force of the combination of factors described above for the stability of our contemporary society should not be underestimated. But in the attempt to decide what steps are necessary to achieve a social balance, all these factors discussed must exercise full weight. Illusory systems no longer work, and it is a certainty that no segment of the world community will indefinitely accept a position of acknowledged inferiority; compromises such as Calvinism are an enduring lesson in the harm done by training superego systems on the control of impulses which are not injurious to the common good while at the same time giving free rein to the most destructive forces along other lines. In fact, Calvinism is in itself an illustration of how a dominant interest can deflect superego systems in the direction of an approved or desired social goal and justify this by a system of flimsy rationalizations.

Though the value of basic personality in describing differences between different cultures may be conceded, some question can be raised about its value in studying the long history of the same culture. The sketch in this chapter does not exhaust the possibilities, because we only undertook to indicate the direction for study. The actual psycho-social constellations derived from the impact of a given basic personality with changes in social organization and the influence of empirically derived reality systems have not been touched here in any systematic way. This task must be deferred. Such research must concern itself chiefly with the sources of changing ideals, social goals and value systems. But whatever the conclusions, they must be established on the base line of those features of basic personality which have remained relatively constant. Basic personality does not determine all the vicissitudes of a culture; but it supplies direction and defines the manner in which the vicissitudes of adaptation are handled.

Whether such a study will yield definite social directives or not is now problematical. Such directives could exercise influence only if the conclusions of this research could be demonstrated experimentally, or by some equivalent of experiment. The study of western history can be effectively used to describe how we got where we are today. After this a study of the individual subcultures which make up western society is indicated. In this latter study we are likely to deal with fine variations of basic personality, which though narrow at the base, may make for great differences in national temperament. Such a body of evidence might furnish the basis for a critique and offer directives which might compete effectively with the cruder methods in use today for dealing with the social discomforts of our time.

INDEX

Aberle, David F., 378*n*

Abortion, among the Alorese, 160

Acculturation, changes and conflicts in Western society and relation of personality organization to them, xii, 339, 405 ff.; changing conditions in the life of a society, ix; cultural heterogeneity or homogeneity, 338 f.; historical data as test of the operating scheme on problem of social stability and change, 412, 413-54; principles, 423 ff., 429; social change does not take place in isolated and detached items, 421; Tanala as example, 418 ff., 424, 428

—— Alorese an old culture: reasons for its continuance, 253, 256

—— Comanche: alterations in culture after retirement under government protection, 96; factors that facilitated change, and preparedness for their use, 94, 406; shift from old to later culture, 82 ff. *passim*, 94, 421 ff.

—— Plainville: attitudes toward progress and modernity, 290, 291, 300, 307, 315; changes caused by automobile, 281*n*, 332; changes relating to birth and baby training, 316, 318 f.; child work now limited by compulsory schooling, 326; from country to consolidated school, 265, 281 f., 326; functioning of kinship weakened, 276; growing equation of rural-urban classes, 300; modern funerals and undertaking techniques, 334 f.; shift from lodges to newer kinds of clubs and cliques, 282

Achievement Day, 305

Action systems, xvii; assumption of the role of adult, their crucial test, 363; Comanche, 94-96; elements in composition of, 21; formation in Western culture, 361, 376; interference with relaxer function resulting in blocking, 348; prevention of effective, by tensions, 169; sexual frustrations a conspicuous source of blocking, 356, 361, 374

Adaptation, 4, 6 f.; adaptive purpose of character trait, 219; aspects described by psychoanalysis, 10 ff.; in Comanche, 47, 81; influence of basic personality upon types of, 448, 449; failure as cause of disequilibrium, 418; good parental care associated with new series of possibilities, 348, 353; relation between projective techniques and, 44, 45; relation to stability, 421; successful example of, 389

Adoption and infanticide, 49, 83, 96

Aesthetic interests, Plainville, 307

Affectivity, 229, 245; induction of, 26; strangulation, 170; why and how important for the child, 346, 361; *see also* Emotion

Affects and motivations, 21

Afterbirth, 71, 130, 316

Aged, *see* Old people

Age of Reason, 44

Aggression, Alorese, 137, 146, 155, 159, 165 f., 170, 247; defined by those in control, 452; Comanche, 166; masochism a disorganized or ingrown, 356*n*; not purely a form of reaction to frustration, 165; patterns in our culture and Alorese, 230; Plainville, 264, 304, 320, 342, 403, 404; results of control of, 358; use by upper and working classes, 447

Agriculture, *see* Farming

Aid for dependent children, 266

Alexander, Franz, base of character derivation, 219; *Our Age of Unreason*, 338, 339*n*

Alor, island: location, size, climate, population, villages, 102 ff.

Alorese culture, xix, 24, 26*n*, 34, 35, 36, 42, 336, 338, 343, 353, 361, 362*n*, 405, 412-18 *passim*, 421, 424, 426, 432; abandoning, or running away from, a situation, 156, 157, 207, 210; action systems ineffective, 169; adornment, 104, 139; adulthood analyzed, 162-66; aggression, 137, 146, 155, 159, 165 f., 170, 230, 247; anxiety, 146, 158, 164, 170, 226, 240, 422; appearance, 103, 139, 142; arresting feature of the culture, 253; attitude toward ethnographer, 171, 172, 184, 189, 191, 197, 208, 212, 216, 222; basic personality analyses (*q.v.*), xi, 146-61, 169 f., 171, 228-34; blocked action systems, 152, 163, 206, 211, 231, 247; ceremonies, 116, 119, 136; children (*see under* Children; Parents); cleanliness, 105, 141; clothing, 104; cooperative techniques absent, 146; death, ceremonies and financial transactions following, 111-14, 115 f., 118-24, 165,